HOUGHTON MIFFLIN
Reading
A Legacy of Literacy

Expeditions

Senior Authors
J. David Cooper
John J. Pikulski

Authors
Patricia A. Ackerman
Kathryn H. Au
David J. Chard
Gilbert G. Garcia
Claude N. Goldenberg
Marjorie Y. Lipson
Susan E. Page
Shane Templeton
Sheila W. Valencia
MaryEllen Vogt

Consultants
Linda H. Butler
Linnea C. Ehri
Carla B. Ford

 HOUGHTON MIFFLIN

BOSTON • MORRIS PLAINS, NJ

California • Colorado • Georgia • Illinois • New Jersey • Texas

Cover and title page photography by Michelle Joyce.

Cover illustration by Gary Aagaard.

Acknowledgments begin on page 689.

Printed in the U.S.A.

ISBN: 0-618-01236-2

3456789-VH-06 05 04 03 02 01 00

Expeditions

Nature's Fury

4

Reader's Library

- **Riding Out the Storm**
- **White Dragon: Anna Allen in the Face of Danger**
- **Floods**

Theme Paperbacks

If You Lived at the Time of the Great San Francisco Earthquake
by Ellen Levine
  ALA Recommended Book for Reluctant Young Adult Readers

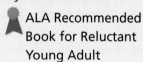

Drylongso
by Virginia Hamilton
  American Bookseller Pick of the Lists

Hurricanes: Earth's Mightiest Storms
by Patricia Lauber
  Outstanding Science Trade Book for Children

Focus on

Tall Tales

Contents
Theme 2

Give It All You've Got

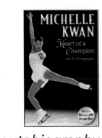

Taking Tests **Filling in the Blank** 230

Reader's Library

- **Meet Yo-Yo Ma**
- **Victor Sews**
- **Falling Off a Log**
- **Buck Leonard: Baseball's Greatest Gentleman**

Theme Paperbacks

Supergrandpa
by David Schwartz

Off and Running
by Gary Soto

 Virginia State Reading Association Young Readers Program

Island of the Blue Dolphins
by Scott O'Dell

 Newbery Medal, Horn Book Fanfare, Nene Award

8

Focus on

Poetry

Contents
Theme 3

Voices
of the
Revolution

10

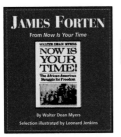

Reader's Library

- **Bunker's Cove**
- **The Drummer Boy**
- **Deborah Sampson: Soldier of the Revolution**

Theme Paperbacks

Daughter of Liberty
by Robert Quackenbush

Phoebe the Spy
by Judith Berry Griffin

Guns for General Washington
by Seymour Reit

Contents
Theme 4

Person to Person

Reader's Library

Person to Person

- **Something for Everyone**
- **Pretty Cool, for a Cat**
- **Trevor from Trinidad**
- **Upstate Autumn**

Theme Paperbacks

The Junior Thunder Lord
by Laurence Yep

Frindle
by Andrew Clements

 William Allen White Children's Book Award, Young Reader's Choice Book Award Pacific Northwest Library Association

Where the Flame Trees Bloom
by Alma Flor Ada

Focus on

PLAYS

Contents
Theme 5

One Land, Many Trails

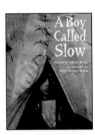

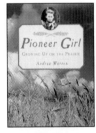

historical fiction

Taking Tests **Writing an Answer to**

Reader's Library

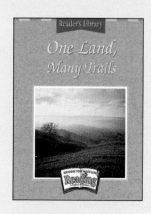

- **Shell-Flower**
- **Journey to a Free Town**
- **Zachary's Ride**
- **America: A Dream**

Theme Paperbacks

Meet the Wards on the Oregon Trail

    by John J. Loper

Children of the Wild West

    by Russell Freedman

    ALA Notable, Booklist Editors' Choice, Horn Book Fanfare, IRA Teacher's Choice

High Elk's Treasure

    by Virginia Driving Hawk Sneve

Focus on

Autobiography

Animal
Encounters

realistic fiction

Reader's Library

- **The Hyrax of Top-Knot Island**
- **Saving Sea Turtles**
- **Kat the Curious**

Theme Paperbacks

Dolphin Adventure
by Wayne Grover

The Tarantula in My Purse: and 172 Other Wild Pets
by Jean Craighead George

To the Top of the World
by Jim Brandenburg

    ALA Best Book for Young Adults, NCTE Orbis Pictus Honor, Children's Book Bulletin Blue Ribbons

....

Nature's Fury

Now the house of wind is thundering.

Now the house of wind is thundering.

As I go roaring over the land,

the land is covered in thunder.

—from "Wind Song" (Pima)

Nature's Fury

Contents

Reader's Library

- **Riding Out the Storm**
- **White Dragon: Anna Allen in the Face of Danger**
- **Floods**

Theme Paperbacks

If You Lived at the Time of the Great San Francisco Earthquake

by Ellen Levine

Drylongso

by Virginia Hamilton

Hurricanes: Earth's Mightiest Storms

by Patricia Lauber

Book Links

If you like . . .

Earthquake Terror

by Peg Kehret

If you like . . .

Eye of the Storm: Chasing Storms with Warren Faidley

by Stephen Kramer

Then try . . .

Then try . . .

The Volcano Disaster

by Peg Kehret (Minstrel)
Warren and Betsy get more than they expect when they research Mount St. Helens.

Earthquake! A Story of Old San Francisco

by Kathleen Kudlinski (Puffin)
Philip must save his horses during the San Francisco earthquake.

Rain Player

by David Wisniewski (Clarion)
Pik hopes to save the people of his Mayan village from a drought by challenging the rain god to a match of *pok-a-tok* on the ball court.

Night of the Twisters

by Ivy Ruckman (Harper)
A boy and his family struggle to survive a series of devastating tornadoes.

If you like . . .

Volcanoes
by Seymour Simon

Then try . . .

Tornadoes

by Seymour Simon (Morrow)
Simon explains how tornadoes are formed and what we can do to protect ourselves from them.

El Niño

by Caroline Arnold (Clarion)
Learn more about the wild weather phenomenon that's making headlines around the world.

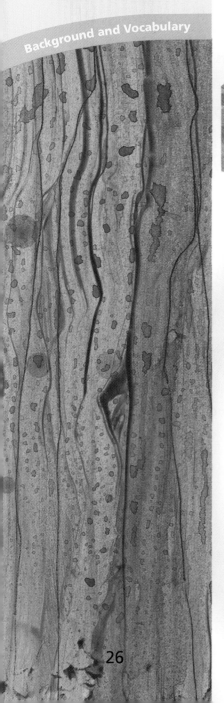

BUILDUP TO A SHAKEUP

What forces cause the earthquake in *Earthquake Terror*? The answer lies deep underground.

Pressure Builds

Pressure has been building along a deep crack in the earth's crust, the San Andreas Fault in California. The rock on one side of the fault is pushing against the rock on the other side, until . . .

Earthquake!

Too much pressure! The rock on each side of the fault slips with a jolt. All that released energy causes the ground to go undulating for miles. The upheaval may cause terrible devastation to anything standing.

The San Andreas Fault runs from southern California to just north of San Francisco. The author puts Magpie Island, the fictional setting of *Earthquake Terror*, in its path.

A road in California's Santa Cruz Mountains, south of San Francisco, shows extensive damage from the "World Series Earthquake" that struck part of the San Andreas Fault in October, 1989.

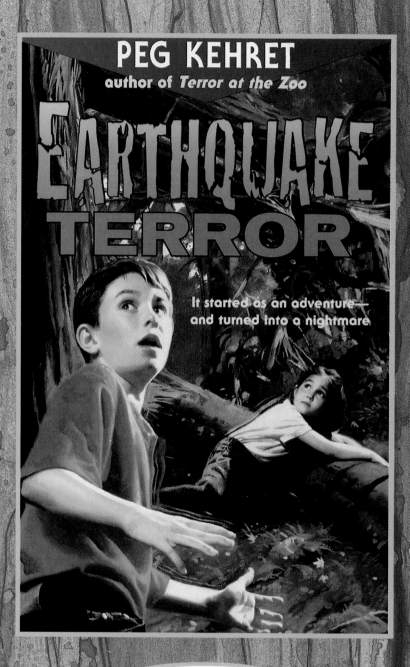

PEG KEHRET
author of *Terror at the Zoo*

EARTHQUAKE
TERROR

It started as an adventure—
and turned into a nightmare

Strategy Focus

Think about the selection, title and cover illustration.
What do you **predict** Jonathan will do to protect
himself and his younger sister when a powerful
earthquake strikes?

A family vacation begins peacefully in the woods of Magpie Island. Then Jonathan and Abby's mom breaks her ankle, and their dad has to rush her to the hospital. He promises to return in three hours, leaving Jonathan, age twelve, in charge of his six-year-old sister, whose legs are partially paralyzed. Moose, the family's dog, is with them. But Jonathan is uneasy.

In his mind, Jonathan could see his father unhitching the small camping trailer. He pictured the car going along the narrow, winding road that meandered from the campground through the woods. He saw the high bridge that crossed the river, connecting the island campground to the mainland.

He imagined his father driving across the bridge, faster than usual, with Mom lying down in the back seat. Or maybe she wouldn't lie down. Maybe, even with a broken ankle, she would wear her seat belt. She always did, and she insisted that Jonathan and Abby wear theirs.

Moose cocked his head, as if listening to something. Then he ran toward the trail, sniffing the ground.

"Moose," Jonathan called. "Come back."

Moose paused, looked at Jonathan, and barked.

"Come!"

Moose returned but he continued to smell the ground and pace back and forth.

"Moose wants Mommy," Abby said.

Moose suddenly stood still, his legs stiff and his tail up. He barked again.

"Silly old dog," Abby said.

He knows something is wrong, Jonathan thought. Dogs sense things. He knows I'm worried about Mom. Jonathan patted Moose's head. "It's all right, Moose. Good dog."

Moose barked again.

"I'm hot," Abby said. "It's too hot to eat."

"Let's start back. It'll be cooler in the shade and we can finish our lunch in the camper."

Maybe he could relax in the camper. Here he felt jumpy. He didn't like being totally out of communication with the rest of the world. Whenever he stayed alone at home, or took care of Abby, there was always a telephone at his fingertips or a neighbor just down the street. If he had a problem, he could call his parents or Mrs. Smith next door or even nine-one-one.

Here he was isolated. I wouldn't do well as a forest ranger, Jonathan thought. How do they stand being alone in the woods all the time?

He rewrapped the uneaten food, buckled the backpack over his shoulders, and put the leash on Moose. The goofy way Moose was acting, he might bolt down the trail and not come back.

Jonathan helped Abby stand up and placed her walker in position. Slowly, they began the journey across the sand and into the woods, to follow the trail through the trees.

Jonathan wished he had worn a watch. It seemed as if his parents had been gone long enough to get partway to town, but it was hard to be sure. Time had a way of evaporating instantly when he was engrossed in an interesting project, such as cataloging his baseball cards, or reading a good mystery. But time dragged unbearably when he was in the dentist's office or waiting for a ride. It was hard to estimate how much time had passed since his parents waved good-bye and walked away. Forty minutes? An hour?

Abby walked in front of him. That way he could see her and know if she needed help, and it kept him from going too fast. When he was in the lead, he usually got too far ahead, even when he tried to walk slowly.

While they walked Jonathan planned what he would do when they got back to the camper. As soon as he got Abby settled on her bed, he would turn on the radio and listen to the ball game. That would give him something to think about. The San Francisco Giants were his favorite baseball team and he hoped they would win the World Series.

Jonathan noticed again how quiet it was. No magpies cawed, no leaves rustled overhead. The air was stifling, with no hint of breeze.

Moose barked. Jonathan jumped at the sudden noise. It was Moose's warning bark, the one he used when a stranger knocked on the door. He stood beside Jonathan and barked again. The dog's eyes had a frantic look. He was shaking, the way he always did during a thunderstorm.

"What's wrong, boy?" Jonathan asked. He reached out to pet Moose but the dog tugged toward Abby and barked at her.

"Hush, Moose," Abby said.

Jonathan looked in all directions. He saw nothing unusual. There were still no people and no animals that would startle Moose and set him off. Jonathan listened hard, wondering if Moose had heard something that Jonathan couldn't hear.

Abby stopped walking. "What was that?" she said.

"What was what?"

Jonathan listened. He heard a deep rumbling sound in the distance.

Thunder? He looked up. The sky was bright and cloudless. The noise came closer; it was too sharp to be thunder. It was more like several rifles being fired at the same time.

Hunters! he thought. There are hunters in the woods and they heard us move and they've mistaken us for deer or pheasant. Moose must have seen them or heard them or possibly smelled them.

"Don't shoot!" he cried.

As he yelled, Jonathan felt a jolt. He stumbled forward, thrusting an arm out to brace himself against a tree. Another loud noise exploded as Jonathan lurched sideways.

He dropped the leash.

Abby screamed.

A bomb? Jonathan thought. Who would bomb a deserted campground?

The noise continued, and the earth moved beneath his feet. As he felt himself lifted, he knew that the sound was not hunters with guns. It was not a bomb, either.

Earthquake! The word flashed across his brain as if he had seen it blazing on a neon sign.

He felt as if he were on a surfboard, catching a giant wave, rising, cresting, and sliding back down again. Except he was standing on dry land.

"Jonathan!" Abby's scream was lost in the thunderous noise. He saw her fall, her walker flying off to one side as she went down. Jonathan lunged forward, arms outstretched, trying to catch Abby before she hit the ground. He couldn't get there fast enough.

The ground dropped away beneath his feet as if a trapdoor had opened. His legs buckled and he sank to his knees. He reached for a tree trunk, to steady himself, but before his hand touched it, the tree moved.

Jonathan's stomach rose into his throat, the way it sometimes did on a fast elevator.

Ever since first grade, when the Palmers moved to California, Jonathan had practiced earthquake drills in school each year. He knew that most earthquakes occur along the shores of the Pacific Ocean. He knew that the San Andreas fault runs north and south for hundreds of miles in California, making that land particularly susceptible to earthquakes. He knew that if an earthquake hit while he was in school, he was supposed to crawl under his desk or under a table because injury was most likely to be caused by the roof caving in on him.

That was school. This was Magpie Island. How should he protect himself in the woods? Where could he hide?

He struggled to his feet again. Ahead of him, Abby lay whimpering on the ground. Moose stood beside her, his head low.

"Put your hands over your head," Jonathan called.

The ground shook again, and Jonathan struggled to remain on his feet.

"I'm coming," he shouted. "Stay where you are. I'm coming!"

But he did not go to her. He couldn't.

He staggered sideways, unable to keep his balance. He felt as if he were riding a roller coaster standing up, except the ground rocked back and forth at the same time that it rolled up and down.

A clump of small birch trees swayed like dancers and then fell.

The rumbling noise continued, surrounding him, coming from every direction at once. It was like standing in the center of a huge orchestra, with kettle drums pounding on all sides.

Abby's screams and Moose's barking blended with the noise.

Although there was no roof to cave in on him, Jonathan put his arms over his head as he fell. The school's earthquake drills had taught him to protect his head and he did it the only way he could.

Earthquake.

He had never felt an earthquake before and he had always wondered how it would feel. He had questioned his teacher, that first year. "How will I know it's an earthquake?" he asked. "If it's a big one," the teacher said, "you'll know."

His teacher had been right. Jonathan knew. He knew with a certainty that made the hair rise on the back of his neck. He was in the middle of an earthquake now. A big one.

The ground heaved, pitching Jonathan into the air.

Jonathan hit the ground hard, jarring every bone in his body. Immediately, the earth below him moved, tossing him into the air again.

As he dropped back down, he saw the trunk of a giant redwood tree tremble. The huge tree swayed back and forth for a few moments and then tilted toward Jonathan.

Frantically, he crawled to his left, rushing to get out of the tree's path.

The roots ripped loose slowly, as if not wanting to relinquish their century-long hold on the dirt.

As Jonathan scrambled across the unsteady ground, he clenched his teeth, bracing himself for the impact.

The tree fell. Air whizzed across Jonathan as the tree trunk dropped past, and branches brushed his shoulder, scratching his arms. The redwood crashed beside him, missing him by only a few feet. It thudded down, landing at an angle on another fallen tree. Dirt and dry leaves whooshed into the air, and then settled slowly back down.

The earth shuddered, but Jonathan didn't know if it was from the impact of the tree or another jolt from the earthquake.

With his heart in his throat, Jonathan crept away from the redwood tree, toward Abby. Beneath him, the ground swelled and retreated, like ocean waves. Twice he sprawled facedown in the dirt, unable to keep his balance. The second time, he lay still, with his eyes closed. How much longer would this go on? Maybe he should just lie there and wait until this earthquake was over.

"Mommy!" Abby's shrill cry rose above the thundering noise.

Jonathan struggled toward her again, his heart racing. When he finally reached her, he lay beside her and wrapped his arms around her. She clung to him, sobbing.

"We'll be okay," he said. "It's only an earthquake."

Only an earthquake. He remembered magazine pictures of terrible devastation from earthquakes: homes toppled, highways buckled, cars tossed upside down, and people crushed in debris. Only an earthquake.

"We have to get under shelter," he said. "Try to crawl with me." Keeping one arm around Abby's waist, he got to his hands and knees and began crawling forward on the undulating ground.

"I can't!" Abby cried. "I'm scared. The ground is moving."

Jonathan tightened his grip, dragging her across the ground. A small tree crashed beside them. Dust rose, filling their noses.

"I want Mommy!" Abby shrieked.

He pulled her to the trunk of the huge redwood tree that had uprooted.

"Get under the tree," he said, as he pushed her into the angle of space that was created because the center of the redwood's trunk rested on the other tree.

When Abby was completely under the tree, Jonathan lay on his stomach beside her, with his right arm tucked beneath his stomach and his left arm thrown across Abby. He pulled himself in as close as he could so that both he and Abby were wedged in the space under the big tree.

"What's happening?" Abby sobbed. Her fingernails dug into Jonathan's bare arm.

"It's an earthquake."

"I want to go home." Abby tried to push Jonathan away.

"Lie still," Jonathan said. "The tree will protect us."

The dry forest floor scratched his cheek as he inhaled the pungent scent of dead leaves. He felt dwarfed by the enormous redwood and tried not to imagine what would have happened if it had landed on him.

"Moose!" he called. "Come, Moose."

Beneath him, the ground trembled again. Jonathan tightened his grip on Abby and pushed his face close to hers. A sharp crack rang out beside them as another tree hit the ground. Jonathan turned his head enough to peer out; he saw the redwood branches quivering from the impact.

What if the earthquake caused the redwood to move again? What if it slipped off the tree it rested on and crushed them beneath it? Anxiety tied a tight knot in Jonathan's stomach.

The earth shuddered once more. Abby buried her face in Jonathan's shoulder. His shirt grew wet from her tears. The jolt did not seem as severe this time, but Jonathan thought that might be because he was lying down.

Moose, panting with fear, huddled beside Jonathan, pawing at Jonathan's shoulder. Relieved that the dog had not been injured, Jonathan put his right arm around Moose and held him close.

As suddenly as it had begun, the upheaval stopped. Jonathan was unsure how long it had lasted. Five minutes? Ten? While it was happening, time seemed suspended and Jonathan had thought the shaking might go on for days.

The woods were quiet.

He lay motionless, one arm around Abby and the other around Moose, waiting to see if it was really over. The air was completely still. After the roar of the earthquake, the silence seemed both comforting and ominous.

Earlier, even though there were no other people in the area, he'd heard the magpies cawing, and a squirrel had complained when Jonathan tossed a rock.

Now he heard nothing. No birds. No squirrels. Not even wind in the leaves.

He wondered if his parents had felt the quake. Sometimes, he knew, earthquakes were confined to fairly small areas.

Once Grandma Whitney had called them from Iowa. She had seen news reports of a violent California earthquake less than one hundred miles from where the Palmers lived.

"Are you all right?" Grandma cried, when Mrs. Palmer answered the phone. "Was anyone hurt?"

Grandma had been astonished when none of the Palmers knew anything about an earthquake.

After several minutes of quiet, Jonathan eased out from under the tree. He sat up and looked around. Moose, still trembling, licked his hand.

Jonathan put his cheek on the dog's neck and rubbed his ears. He had chosen Moose at the animal shelter, more than six years ago. The Palmers had planned to get a small dog but the moment Jonathan saw the big golden retriever, who was then one year old, he knew which dog he wanted.

Mrs. Palmer had said, "He's too big to be a house dog."

Mr. Palmer said, "I think he's half moose."

Jonathan laughed and said, "That's what I'll name him. Moose."

His parents tried unsuccessfully to interest Jonathan in one of the other, smaller dogs, before they gave in and brought Moose home.

Despite his size, Moose was a house dog from the start, and he slept beside Jonathan's bed every night. They played fetch, and their own version of tag, and Jonathan took Moose for long walks in the county park. In the summer, they swam whenever they had a chance.

When Abby had her accident and Jonathan's parents focused so much of their attention on her, Moose was Jonathan's comfort and companion.

Now, in the devastation of the earthquake, Jonathan again found comfort in the dog's presence. He let go of Moose and looked around. "Wow!" he said, trying to keep his voice steady. "That was some earthquake."

"Is it over?" Abby's voice was thin and high.

"I think so."

He grasped Abby's hand and pulled her out from under the tree. She sat up, apparently uninjured, and began picking leaves out of her hair.

"Are you okay?" he asked.

"My knee is cut." She touched one knee and her voice rose. "It's bleeding," she said, her lip trembling. "You pushed me under the tree too hard."

Jonathan examined her knee. It was a minor cut. He knew that if he made a fuss over it, Abby would cry. He had seen it happen before; if his mother showed concern about a small injury, Abby got practically hysterical, but if Mom acted like it was no big deal, Abby relaxed, too. It was as if she didn't know whether she hurt or not until she saw how her parents reacted.

"It's all right," he said. "If that tiny little scrape is all you got, you are lucky, and so am I. We could have been killed."

"We could?" Abby's eyes grew round.

Quickly Jonathan said, "But we weren't, and the earthquake is over now."

Meet the Author
Peg Kehret

Favorite outfit: Jeans and sweatshirt

Favorite dish: Spaghetti

When not writing: Reads, plays her player piano, bakes bread, volunteers at The Humane Society

Home: An eighty-year-old house in the state of Washington with apple and pear trees, blueberry and blackberry bushes, and a big vegetable garden

Popularity: Kehret has won children's choice awards in fifteen states. Twice a year she and her husband travel across the country in their motor home so that she can speak in schools and meet her readers.

More Kehret books: *Volcano Disaster, Blizzard Disaster, Nightmare Mountain, The Richest Kids in Town, Shelter Dogs: Amazing Stories of Adopted Strays*

Meet the Illustrator
Phil Boatwright

Lone Star boyhood: Boatwright grew up in Mesquite, Texas, a suburb of Dallas.

Favorite children's book: *Treasure Island,* by Robert Louis Stevenson

Favorite illustrators: Gennady Spirin, Jerry Pinkney, John Collier, and N. C. Wyeth

Tips for success: "You have to love to draw, take all the art classes possible, read all the art books available, and study the artists you admire."

Internet

For more information about Peg Kehret and Phil Boatwright, visit Education Place. **www.eduplace.com/kids**

Think About the Selection

1. How does the author create suspense before the earthquake hits? Find examples from the story.

2. Summarize what Jonathan does to protect himself and Abby from the earthquake.

3. Sometimes the author interrupts the action with events that happened earlier. Do you think this adds to the story? Why or why not?

4. What did you learn about the fault that runs through the island?

5. How would you describe Jonathan's relationship with his sister? Give examples from the selection that show how they feel about each other.

6. Jonathan thinks about how time goes fast when he's excited or interested, and slowly when he's not. Give examples of that from your own life.

7. **Connecting/Comparing** Do you think *Earthquake Terror* is a good way to begin a theme called *Nature's Fury*? Why or why not?

Narrating

Write an Adventure Story

Use what you learned about Jonathan and Abby in *Earthquake Terror* to write an adventure story with them as characters. Your story can tell how they escape from another natural disaster, such as a fire, a flood, or a storm.

Tips

- **Begin by thinking about the problem the characters face and write down details.**
- **Show how the characters feel.**
- **Include details of the setting.**

Demonstrate Earthquake Safety

On pages 35 and 36 of the selection, Jonathan remembers what he learned in school about earthquake safety. Use that information to demonstrate for classmates what to do in case an earthquake strikes.

Deliver a Newscast

With a partner, present a newscast about the earthquake on Magpie Island. You might wish to take on the roles of a television anchorperson and an on-the-scene reporter. Use information from the selection to give details.

Tips
- **Plan the order in which you will present your information.**
- **Write notes on cards or slips of paper.**
- **Use exact details.**

Internet

Post a Review

Write a review of *Earthquake Terror.* Tell others what you liked or didn't like about it. Visit Education Place. **www.eduplace.com/kids**

Skill: How to Read a Science Article

Before you read . . .

❶ Look at the title, captions, and illustrations.

❷ Identify the **topic** and ask yourself what you already know about it.

❸ Predict what you will learn in the article.

While you read . . .

❶ Identify the **main idea** and **supporting details** in each paragraph.

❷ When you don't understand something, ask yourself questions and then reread.

El Niño

by Fred Pearce

In the winter of 1998, heavy rains caused mudslides in California that washed houses off cliffs. Ice storms on the eastern seaboard from Maine to Quebec downed so many power lines that thousands of people had to live in the dark and cold for weeks. Indonesia's rain forests got no rain, and the months of dry weather turned the forests into the world's largest pile of firewood. At the same time, the worst drought in a hundred years hit neighboring New Guinea, killing crops and leaving some of the most isolated people on Earth starving. On the other side of the globe, lack of rain left the water level in the Panama Canal so low that large ships couldn't make it through.

Mudslides in California

48

Early 1998 also saw intense storms in places not used to them. Kenya suffered the worst floods in 40 years — in the middle of the *dry* season. Neighboring Uganda was cut off for several days, when both road and rail links were washed away. In South America, floods made half a million Peruvians homeless along a coastline that often has no rain for years at a time. Neighboring Ecuador said it would take 10 years to repair the damage. And in northern Tibet, the worst snow in 50 years starved or froze to death hundreds of Mongol tribesmen.

Was it just bad luck that there was so much bad weather in so many parts of the world at around the same time? Fifty years ago, most people would have said yes.

Flash floods in Ecuador, South America

Floods in Kenya, East Africa

Forest fires in Indonesia, Southeast Asia

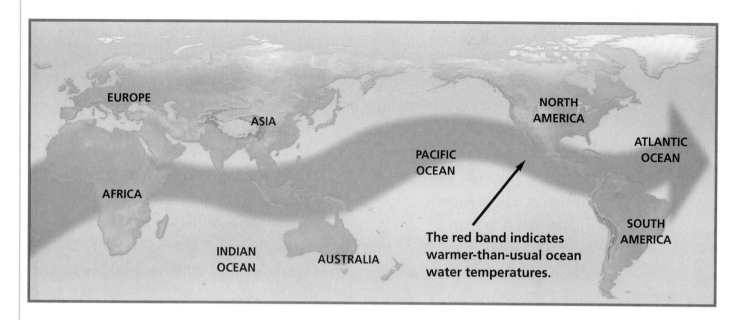

The red band indicates warmer-than-usual ocean water temperatures.

But today, meteorologists (scientists who study weather) blame most of 1998's weather disasters on a giant blip in the weather system called *El Niño*. Many years ago, Spanish-speaking Peruvian fishermen noticed that the fish suddenly disappeared whenever warm waters flowed in from the west. They called the warming El Niño (Spanish for "the child") because it usually happened around Christmas. El Niño is caused by a sudden shift in the winds and ocean currents in the Pacific Ocean that pushes a layer of warm water across the ocean, taking weather systems with it.

El Niño is rather like a wave in your bathtub, only the tub is huge and the wave takes months to go from one end to the other. The huge bathtub in this case is the Pacific, the world's largest ocean.

Most of the time, winds and ocean currents at the equator move from east to west across the Pacific — from the Americas to Asia. The winds and currents push the ocean's water toward Asia. After a few years of this, the sea level around the islands of Indonesia is actually over a foot higher than on the American side. This can't go on forever. And it doesn't. Eventually, like a wave reaching the far end of your bathtub, the water bounces back, moving toward the Americas. Scientists have clocked this wave moving about 125 miles a day.

The water around Indonesia is the hottest in the world — usually warmer than 80° F, which is as warm as many swimming pools. As the wave moves toward the Americas, it spreads a layer of the warm Indonesian water across the ocean. And because ocean currents and winds are connected, the Indonesian weather follows, too. This means that the heavy rains that normally hit Indonesia for most of the year get moved thousands of miles east, soaking the Pacific Islands and normally dry coastlands from Peru to California. Meanwhile, normally wet Indonesia and its surrounding areas suffer drought.

No one is really sure how long El Niño has been around. Dan Sandweiss of the University of Maine has found telltale signs of sudden El Niño-style floods in old *sediments* in Peru. (Sediments are the solid stuff that settles out of water at places like the mouth of a river.) When it doesn't rain, few plants grow, and there isn't much pollen in the sediments. But when El Niño occurs in these normally dry regions, more plants grow and more pollen shows up. From the amount of pollen in the sediments, Sandweiss can tell that "El Niño has been around for at least 5000 years. Before that there seems to have been a gap."

El Niño isn't just about some rainstorm in California in 1998; it's about wild weather around the world through recorded history.

Episode Two: La Niña Strikes Back!

El Niño typically lasts some 18 months, and usually returns every three to seven years, probably when enough warm water has built up again in the western Pacific. But when El Niño's warm water retreats, it's sometimes followed by a *cool* water wave. Scientists call this cooling of the Pacific *La Niña.* La Niña's effect on the weather is harder to predict than El Niño's. But during La Niña years, the normal weather in some regions becomes *exaggerated*: it gets extra wet in wet Indonesia, extra dry in dry Peru. That's also when we get big droughts in the American Midwest. The great Dust Bowl drought of 1930s America is thought to have been caused by a decade of La Niña-like conditions.

Photo by Arthur Rothstein,
Dust Storm, Cimarron County, 1936.

51

A Description

A description is a picture in words that helps the reader share the writer's experience. Use this student's writing as a model when you write a description of your own.

By the Sea

The **beginning** tells what the description is about.

My grandfather has an apartment that we visit every summer for a few days. My favorite place is a beach where my family goes to play and walk along the shore.

Imagery lets readers visualize how something looks, sounds, smells, tastes, and feels.

When the weather is nice, the sky is blue and the clouds are pure white. The ocean is greenish blue and when the waves crash, the foam is white. Along the water's edge, there are clam shells, crabs, baby shrimp, and once my brother found a starfish! The seagulls walk around like scavengers, looking for clams and crabs to eat. Sometimes I feel like a seagull, because we are both walking around trying to find something special. The seaweed washes up along the shore. It's green and long, and when it wraps around your leg it is ticklish. When we play in the water, we are always careful of the jellyfish.

Similes give the reader a clear mental picture.

Some are red and some are clear, but they all sting.

52

When the weather is cloudy and stormy, the skies are gray and the waves crash along the shore. It sounds like thunder or like a roaring lion. We don't walk along the shore during a storm, but we can watch from the boardwalk.

The prettiest part of the day is when the sun sets over the bay. It seems as if every time we look up, the colors in the sky change. At first, there is pink, blue, and some green. Then the colors darken to red, orange, blue-gray, and purple. Finally the sky goes dark blue and the sun sets.

I love my grandfather's beach house!

> A good description puts **details** in time order, in spatial order, or in order of importance.

> A good **ending** wraps up the description.

Meet the Author

Dena S.

Grade: five
State: New York
Hobbies: ice skating, singing, and basketball
What she'd like to be when she grows up: a singer

Eye of the Storm: Chasing Storms with Warren Faidley

Photographing
Wild
Weather

Eye of the Storm tells about Warren Faidley, professional weather photographer and storm chaser. Here's a look at where he goes and the dangers he faces on the job.

The Risks

Lightning Danger

▶ Lightning heats the air around it to a sizzling 50,000 degrees Fahrenheit.

▶ Each bolt carries hundreds of millions of volts of electricity.

▶ Lightning kills an average of 100 people each year in the United States.

The Route

Every spring, Warren brings his cameras to "Tornado Alley" in the central United States, where warm and cool air collide to form funnel clouds that might become tornadoes. For the summer, Warren returns to his home state of Arizona to photograph lightning storms.

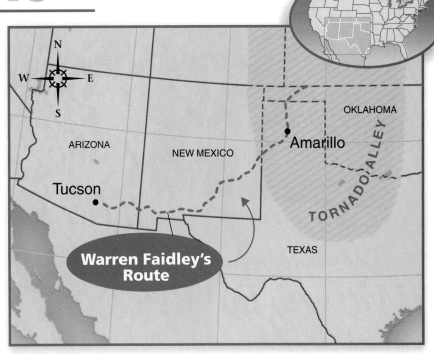

Warren Faidley's Route

Tornado Danger

▶ The winds inside a killer tornado may rotate at jet speed — spinning up to 300 miles per hour.

▶ Tornadoes kill an average of 80 people per year in the United States.

Meet the Author
Stephen Kramer

Stephen Kramer teaches at an elementary school near Vancouver, Washington. He has written several other books on nature topics, such as *Avalanche, Caves, Tornado,* and *Lightning. Lightning* features the photographs of Warren Faidley.

Meet the Photographer
Warren Faidley

Warren Faidley's dramatic weather photographs appear not only in books, but in movies, videos, calendars, magazines, and museums. Faidley also served as a consultant and cinematographer for the movie *Twister.* He and his cat, Megamouth, live in Tucson, Arizona.

For more information about Stephen Kramer and Warren Faidley, visit Education Place. **www.eduplace.com/kids**

56

Eye of the Storm

CHASING STORMS WITH WARREN FAIDLEY

STEPHEN KRAMER

PHOTOGRAPHS BY
WARREN FAIDLEY

Warren Faidley's job takes him all over the country, getting close-up shots of dangerous storms. As you read the selection, think of **questions** about his job to discuss with your classmates.

Storm Chasing

In the evening shadows, a dusty black truck rolls along a dirt road. A rattlesnake feels the vibrations, lifts its head, and crawls off into the rocks. Giant saguaros sprout from the hillsides, arms held high. Somewhere in the distance, a cactus wren calls. But Warren Faidley isn't looking for rattlesnakes, saguaros, or cactus wrens.

He stares through the windshield, eyes glued to a cauliflower-shaped cloud. Behind the cloud, the setting sun turns the sky the color of a ripe peach. Warren has been watching this cloud, and hoping, for almost thirty minutes. The truck heads toward a hill with a clear view of the sky.

Suddenly, a jagged bolt of lightning shoots from the cloud.

"That's it," says Warren.

The truck speeds to the top of the hill and Warren jumps out, arms full of photographic equipment. His fingers fly as he unfolds tripods, mounts his cameras, and points them toward the cloud. Before the road dust has settled, the cameras are clicking.

For twenty minutes, lightning erupts from the cloud. Warren moves back and forth between the cameras — peering through viewfinders, changing film, switching lenses. Tomorrow, when the film is developed, Warren will know whether he had a successful night. In the meantime, he stands and watches, hoping his cameras are capturing the spectacular lights and colors of the evening thunderstorm.

Watching the Sky

From earliest times, people have watched the sky. Astrologers used the positions of the stars to predict the future. Storytellers used rainbows, winds, the sun and moon to weave tales about the past. Farmers, shepherds, and sailors have all watched the clouds, wondering what tomorrow's weather will be like.

The spectacular storms that sometimes appear in the sky have helped to make weather one of the most mysterious of all natural forces. Myths and legends from around the world describe the fear and awe people felt as they watched lightning explode from a cloud or a tornado appear on the horizon, or listened to the howling winds of a hurricane.

For some people, storms have an irresistible call. These storm chasers head for the mountains, prairies, or seacoasts whenever weather conditions are right.

People chase storms for many reasons. Some storm chasers are scientists, who use video cameras, Doppler radar, and other instruments to learn about what happens in a tornado or a thunderstorm. Photographers follow storms to try to capture the beauty of wind and sky on film. Still other people chase storms in order to catch a brief glimpse of the awesome power of nature.

Warren Faidley: Storm Chaser

Warren Faidley lives in Tucson, Arizona, with a one-toothed cat named Megamouth. He has been interested in storms for almost as long as he can remember.

Warren still remembers the tremendous thunderstorms he saw as a boy in Tucson. Tucked safely in bed, he watched the lightning and listened to the thunder. After the storms had passed, he fell asleep to the smell of wet creosote bushes outside his window.

Warren also had his first encounter with windstorms when he was a boy. Dust whirlwinds — spinning columns of wind that look like small tornadoes — often formed in the dusty vacant lots of his

neighborhood. One day Warren decided to put on safety goggles and a heavy jacket, and ride his bike into the center of a dust whirlwind. He'll never forget the excitement he felt when he rode through the wall of swirling winds:

"The inside was still and almost dust free. The light was orange, filtered, I guess, by the wall of dirt that was spinning around me. This rotating wall was filled with all kinds of debris, including tumbleweeds and newspaper pages. Looking up, I could see the very blue sky."

Becoming a Storm Chaser

Warren hadn't always planned to be a storm chaser. He enjoyed studying science in school, and he loved being outside. But he didn't really become interested in taking pictures of the sky until he was working as a photographer for a newspaper.

Warren began by trying to take pictures of lightning from the balcony of his apartment. Although the pictures didn't turn out very well, he soon found himself spending more and more time taking pictures of lightning on summer evenings. Warren read everything he could about weather, and he began to dream about making a living as a weather photographer.

The storm that started Warren's career arrived in Tucson long after the end of the summer thunderstorm season. On that October afternoon, Warren glanced out the back window of his apartment and saw the sharp edges of the storm cloud. He grabbed his equipment, loaded his car, and drove toward a highway underpass on the east side of town.

When Warren reached the underpass, lightning was flashing just a few miles from it. Snatching up his equipment, he scrambled up the steep bank toward a dry ledge where he could set up his cameras. As he set up his tripods, a huge lightning bolt leaped from a cloud about a mile away, striking the ground next to an air traffic control tower.

But the storm was moving quickly. Suddenly, the air was filled with wind and rain, cutting off the view of any lightning to the east. Warren looked overhead and saw small lightning bolts leaping between the clouds. He knew there was about to be another large bolt — and he was pretty sure that the next big flash would be to the west, on the other side of the underpass.

Warren knew he had to get to the other side of the underpass right away. There wasn't enough room between the ledge and the top of the underpass to walk upright, so he scooted along on his knees. He grabbed hold of overhead rain gutters to keep his balance in the darkness.

Suddenly, Warren stuck his hand into a tangle of thick cobwebs. He quickly pulled his hand back. Then he pointed

his penlight toward the ledge and gutters. The whole walkway was lined with webs, and rainwater washing through cracks in the concrete overhead was driving out hundreds of angry black widow spiders!

Ka-boom! A huge bolt of lightning flashed overhead. Warren knew the next bolt would strike somewhere on the west side of the underpass, and he knew he had one chance to capture it. Pushing ahead in the darkness, he used the legs of his tripod as a broom, sweeping aside the cobwebs and trying to brush off any spiders that landed on his clothes.

Near the end of the underpass, and clear of the spider webs, he decided to set up his cameras. The air was sizzling, and Warren could feel that something was about to happen. He slid a few feet down the rough concrete embankment, using his hands and the soles of his shoes as brakes. When the cameras were set up, Warren quickly wiped the raindrops off the lenses. Then he moved back up the slope to a safer place to wait.

Seconds later, he heard a loud crackling, and at the same time he saw a blinding flash of pure, white light. It sounded as if the sky were being torn apart. Next came the boom of a thunderclap roaring through the underpass. It had the energy of a bomb blast, and it lifted Warren's body right off the ground.

Warren lost his hold on the slope and began sliding downhill toward his cameras. He knew that he had to close the shutters on them without bumping the tripods — or the film with the lightning would blur and be ruined. Using his hands and feet and the seat of his pants as brakes on the concrete, Warren slid to a stop just above his tripods. Carefully, he reached up and closed the shutters on the cameras. Then he looked down at his palms and saw that they were covered with blood.

Warren stayed under the underpass long after the storm had passed, thinking about what had just happened. He knew the lightning strike had been close, because when he closed his eyes he could still see its jagged outline.

The next morning, when Warren had his film developed, he was astonished by what he saw. In the center of one of the rolls was an incredible image of a lightning bolt hitting a light pole in front of some metal storage tanks. The picture had been taken from less than four hundred feet. Warren knew that he was holding the closest good picture ever taken of a lightning bolt hitting an object.

The lightning picture changed Warren's life. It was analyzed and written about by Dr. E. Philip Krider, a lightning scientist at the University of

Arizona. *Life* magazine printed the picture, calling Warren a storm chaser. *National Geographic* called, wanting to film a special program about his work. The *National Enquirer* ran an article about Warren, calling him a "fearless spider-fighting photog." He even got a call from a Japanese game show that wanted to feature him on a TV program in which contestants try to guess a mystery guest's occupation. Warren began making enough money from selling his pictures that he could think about being a full-time storm chaser.

What Happens to Warren's Photos After He Takes Them?

You've probably seen some of Warren's photographs. His pictures of lightning, tornadoes, and hurricanes have appeared in books, magazines, newspapers, advertisements, and scientific films. One of his lightning pictures was even used on stage passes for rock concerts by singer Paul McCartney.

Warren's business is called a stock photo agency. It's like a library of sky and storm photographs. People pay him for the use of his photos.

Suppose, for example, that you are a magazine editor. If you need a lightning photo for an article, you could go out and try to take a picture of lightning yourself. But you might have to wait a very long time for the right kind of storm, and unless you have lots of practice your lightning photograph probably won't be very good.

An easier way of getting a good lightning photo is to write to Warren. He'll send you samples, and you can select the one you like. Then, after sending Warren a fee, you can use the photo in your magazine.

When Warren began selling his lightning photos, he found that people were also asking for pictures of tornadoes and hurricanes. He didn't have photographs of these kinds of storms, so he read everything he could find about tornadoes and hurricanes —

and he made plans to photograph them as well.

Storm Seasons and Chasing

Storms are caused by certain kinds of weather patterns. The same patterns are found in the same areas year after year. For example, every spring, large areas of cool, dry air and warm, moist air collide over the central United States. If the winds are right, tornado-producing thunderstorms appear. That's why tornadoes in the south central United States are most likely to happen in spring. During July and August, shifting winds push moisture from the south up into the Arizona desert. When the cool, moist air is heated by the hot desert, storm clouds form. That's why Tucson has summer thunderstorms. In the late

| April | May | June | July | August | September | October |

summer and early fall, when oceans in the northern Atlantic are warmest, tropical storms form off the west coast of Africa. A few of these turn into the hurricanes that sometimes batter the east and gulf coasts of North America.

Because Warren is a storm chaser, his life also follows these weather patterns. Each spring, Warren goes on the road, traveling through parts of the United States likely to be hit by tornadoes. During the summer, he stays near Tucson so he can photograph the thunderstorms that develop over the desert. In the late summer and fall, he keeps an eye on weather activity in the Atlantic Ocean, ready to fly to the east coast if a hurricane appears.

Chasing Tornadoes

One of Warren's favorite tornado photos is a picture he took near Miami, Texas. Most of the sky is filled by the lower end of a huge storm cloud. A tornado hangs from the cloud, kicking up dust from the empty prairie, while the blue and yellow sky seems to go on forever.

In some ways, this wasn't a difficult picture for Warren to take. He's an experienced photographer. But before he could shoot this picture, he had to be in the right place at the right time — and that's what makes photographing tornadoes such hard work.

On a spring day, dozens of thunderstorms may develop over thousands of square miles in Texas, Oklahoma, and Kansas, but usually only a few will produce tornadoes. Since many tornadoes are on the ground only a few minutes, they will disappear before Warren can photograph them unless he is nearby. Other times, he will follow a promising storm, only to have it head off into an area where there are no roads. Tornadoes may be hidden by falling rain, making it impossible to take a picture of them. Still other storms may produce tornadoes at night, when it's too dark for Warren to take pictures and too dangerous for him to be out chasing because he can't see what's happening.

A successful tornado photographer needs patience, a good understanding of

weather, up-to-the-minute forecasts, and lots of experience watching the sky. Even so, days, weeks, or even whole years can go by without a chance to see a tornado.

Every spring, Warren makes a trip to an area called Tornado Alley. This area stretches from northern Texas up into Oklahoma, Kansas, and Missouri. Warren and his tornado chase partner, Tom Willett, spend about six weeks tracking down giant storms and searching for tornadoes.

Getting ready to go tornado chasing takes lots of time and work. Warren checks all his cameras and buys plenty of film. He makes sure he has up-to-date copies of road maps for all the states he'll be traveling through. He arranges for friends to take care of Megamouth.

Finally, toward the end of April, Warren and Tom stow all their equipment in Shadow Chaser, Warren's black four-wheel-drive vehicle. Warren designed Shadow Chaser to help him find tornadoes and chase them safely. It is packed with electronic equipment, including radios, radio scanners, and a weather center that can take many different kinds of measurements. Shadow Chaser has emergency flashing lights, a long-range cellular phone, and special cabinets for storing equipment. It even has a front-mounted video camera that can make videotapes through the windshield.

As Warren and Tom drive toward Tornado Alley, their hopes are high. They know that they'll cover thousands of miles before returning to Tucson. They know they'll chase storms that never produce tornadoes and they'll probably hear about nearby tornadoes they can't get to in time. But with hard work, careful study of weather data, and a little luck, sometimes they'll have a day like the one they had on May 5, 1993.

Tornado Chase Diary: May 5, 1993

Warren keeps a diary, in which he writes about his storm chases. Here are some of the things that happened on May 5, 1993, a remarkable day.

Amarillo, Texas — Morning

I awaken in a motel in Tornado Alley. As I walk to the window to peek out the drapes, I remember that last night's weather forecast showed that this might be a good chase day. Tom climbs out of bed and turns on The Weather Channel.

Later in the morning, Tom and I get the Shadow Chaser ready for the day. I test the radios, check under the hood, make sure the tires are inflated and the lights and wipers are working. We clean, pack, and return each piece of equipment to its usual place. During a chase, there isn't time to look around for a roll of film or lens for a camera.

Finally, we check out of the motel and head for a nearby restaurant for breakfast. Then we drive into town to fill the gas tank and get a few supplies.

National Weather Service Office — Early Afternoon

We arrive at the Amarillo office of the National Weather Service. Here I get an update on local weather conditions, as well as a chance to see a satellite picture

of the area. I use current weather information to draw a map of where today's thunderstorms are likely to form. The reports are saying that there is a moderate chance of severe weather in our area, and some of the thunderstorms will probably produce tornadoes. Since the storms aren't expected to develop until later in the afternoon, we take some time off and drive to a nearby garage to have the oil changed in Shadow Chaser.

A couple hours later, we're back at the National Weather Service office to make our final chase decisions. It's beginning to look like the area north of town is our best bet. We pull out the highway maps and start looking at possible routes.

As we leave town, I call a friend and fellow chaser who gives weather reports for a local TV station. He confirms that severe storm clouds are building right where we're headed. He also says that a news team from his station is already headed there.

Near Panhandle, Texas — Late Afternoon

The sky is hazy, but in the distance we can see the tops of anvil-shaped storm clouds. We stop the truck to pick up the TV report. My forecaster friend is on. He's pointing to an area on his map about fifty miles north of our location. "It looks like we're going to have some severe storms in this area!" he says. We get back into the truck and drive north.

Near Gruver, Texas — Early Evening

The overcast skies clear enough to show a giant thunderstorm just ahead. Then our radio scanner locks onto a message from the TV crew's chase unit. "There's a large funnel cloud coming from this storm," says the message. While the crew describes its location, I look at the map. "They're only eight miles from here," I tell Tom. "Let's go and find it!"

As we approach Gruver, we see the red TV van parked on the side of the road. A cameraman is pointing his camera at a huge, gray-white funnel cloud hanging from the base of a dark cloud. As Tom parks the truck, I use the radio to call in a weather report to the National Weather Service station in Amarillo. The funnel cloud pulls back up into the storm.

We head north, following the storm. As we drive, watching the back of the storm, we can see the clouds darkening and beginning to rotate. The white clouds at the top of the storm take on the shape of a giant mushroom. I'm excited, but I'm worried too. I know that anyone in the path of this storm is in terrible danger.

We follow the storm down the highway. Gradually, it turns and heads back toward the road. We pull over and wait for the storm to cross. While we're waiting, a large semi truck pulls up beside us. The driver opens his window and leans out.

"Hey, are you guys tornado chasers? Is that a tornado forming? Is it safe for me to drive under it?"

"We're not sure if it's going to turn into a tornado, but I'd wait here and let it pass," I answer.

We all watch as the swirling mass crosses the highway. A small funnel cloud reaches down from the storm cloud — and then quickly disappears. I reach for the microphone and call Amarillo:

"This is Warren. I'm about eight miles north of Gruver, just west of Highway 207. Tom and I are looking at a large cloud mass that is organizing and rotating."

"Roger, Warren," replies the spotter coordinator. "We're watching the same area on radar. Thanks."

Now we begin to worry about losing the storm. There aren't very many roads in this area, and most of them run north–south or east–west. Since most storms don't continue for long in these directions, following a storm is a little like playing a huge game of chess. Tom loads his cameras back into the truck while I check the road map.

We make our way along a tangle of unmarked farm roads a few miles from the Oklahoma border. Since the storm is on our west side, and it's moving northeast, we can safely stay quite close to the updraft without getting in the direct path of a tornado.

Near the Oklahoma/Texas Border — Evening

We keep an eye on the swirling clouds as we drive along. Suddenly, from the center of the clouds, a large white funnel appears.

"Look, Tom! Another tornado!" I exclaim. "That thing is less than a mile away!"

I reach for the microphone and call in another report. The funnel cloud begins to stretch. Soon it looks like the trunk of a huge elephant, wiggling over the green fields below. Then it touches down, officially becoming a tornado. When the funnel touches the ground, wispy little vortices appear around the main cloud of wind. As these mini-tornadoes spin, they kick up dust of their

own. I grab the microphone and send another message to the spotter coordinator:

"We're about three or four miles south of the Texas/Oklahoma state line," I explain. "And we're looking at a large, multivortex tornado on the ground."

Just inside the Oklahoma state line, the road turns slightly toward the northwest. The tornado begins to cross the road a little ahead of us. We stop to try and get some pictures, but the light isn't good. It's hard to see the tornado clearly against the background of the cloud. The air is hazy, and another storm to the west is blocking the sunlight.

"We've got a great tornado here," I say to Tom, "but the light is terrible." We load our gear back into the truck and roll down a bumpy dirt road, looking for better light, while the tornado swirls along beside us.

As Tom drives, he keeps glancing at the tornado. Suddenly he yells, "Warren! There's another tornado forming!" I peer through the window and see a debris cloud forming, sucking up soil from a field.

"Wow," Tom says. "Look what it's doing to that fence!" We watch as it rips a section of barbed-wire fence out of the ground and scatters it across the field. The small area of spinning wind, with no

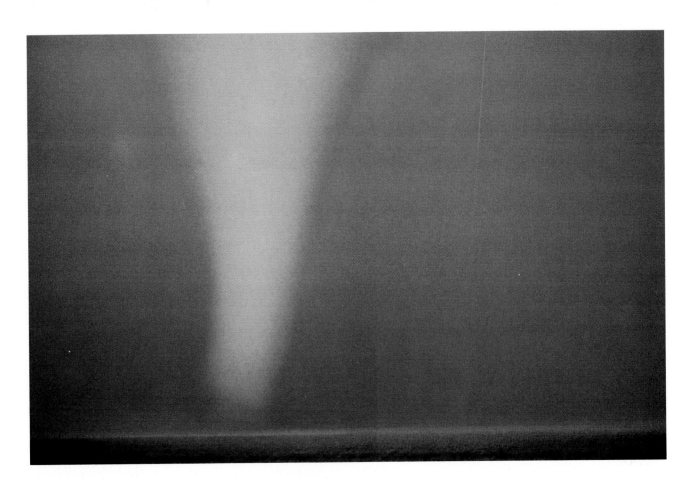

visible funnel cloud above, tears across the fields.

"Slow down, Tom," I say. "I can't see the funnel cloud connected to that thing — and we sure don't want to get hit by it." A few seconds later, the debris cloud disappears.

We follow a maze of unmarked dirt roads until we reach a dead end. As we turn around and drive back toward the highway, we watch as the edges of the storm cloud wrap around the tornado, hiding it from sight. Many sightings of "our" tornado, as well as others in the area, are being reported over the radio. I'm happy to hear that so far the tornadoes haven't hit any populated areas.

East of Guymon, Oklahoma — Evening

It's about 7:30 p.m. when we pull back onto the highway. As we head east, we see a long, thin tornado crossing the road a few miles ahead.

"I bet that's our tornado," I tell Tom. "It looks like it's weakening. We've got to shoot it now!" When Tom stops, I jump out the door, set my camera on the hood to steady it, and go through another roll of film. As we watch, the funnel pulls back up into the dark clouds.

West of Hooker, Oklahoma — Evening

Traveling along the highway, we're joined again by the crew from the TV

station. Down the road, I see a huge wedge-shaped tornado on the ground.

"Stop!" I yell to Tom. Tom hits the brakes and we stare through the windshield. The tornado looks like it's about seven or eight miles from us, moving away, although the fading light makes it hard to be sure. As we watch, the funnel slows down, and then it disappears. We continue on and I spot another tornado. This one looks like a long stovepipe.

"This is incredible," I say to Tom. "We've got two large thunderstorms here, and they're dropping tornadoes everywhere!"

The stovepipe tornado swirls into the clouds before we can get close enough for pictures. As we watch it disappear, I realize that it's getting too dark for any more photos. I know the storms are still active, and I'm worried that the fading light could hide any newly forming tornadoes. Chasing any more tornadoes today would be too dangerous.

Near the Oklahoma/Kansas Border — Evening

As the last of the light disappears, we see two more tornadoes in the distance. One is headed north, rolling into Kansas. As we drive back to Amarillo, we listen to news reports on the radio. "With as many tornadoes as we have had on the ground tonight," says a reporter, "it's a miracle that none of them have hit a town. We do have at least one report of a farm being destroyed, with no injuries so far. But beyond that, we have been extremely fortunate."

Amarillo, Texas — Night

It's 11:00 p.m. by the time we finally pull back into the motel parking lot. As Tom and I unload Shadow Chaser, we're still shaking our heads about what we've seen. The tornadoes we saw caused some damage, but there have been no reports of any deaths or injuries. That makes it easier to celebrate our seven-tornado day.

Responding

Think About the Selection

1. Think about Warren Faidley's decision to ride his bike into a whirlwind. What does this action tell you about about him?

2. Do you think Warren would face any danger in order to get a spectacular storm shot? Use facts from the selection to support your answer.

3. How did the section headings of *Eye of the Storm* help you understand the selection? How did the calendar on page 65 help you understand Warren's job?

4. On page 62, the author writes, "The air was sizzling" before Warren took his famous underpass photograph. What do you think he means?

5. Would you want to accompany Warren on a storm chase? Why or why not? If so, which kind of storm would you want to see up close, and why?

6. Warren's interest in storms led to his career as a weather photographer. What interests do you have that might lead to a career?

7. **Connecting/Comparing** Compare Warren's risk from tornadoes and lightning with Jonathan's risk in *Earthquake Terror*. How are their situations alike and different?

Describing

Write a Job Description

Think about what a storm chaser does. Then write a job description for a storm chaser. Include the character traits and skills a storm chaser should have. Note any special equipment a storm chaser should be able to use.

Tips
- List the job requirements in two categories: traits and skills.
- In the skills category, include special equipment.

Math

Estimate Mileage

Estimate the number of miles Warren Faidley drove from his home to where he began his tornado chase diary for May 5, 1993. Use the map on page 55, a ruler, and this scale — one inch equals 300 miles.

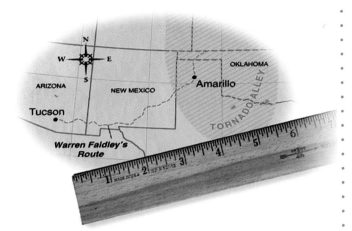

Viewing

Compare Photographs

Choose two photographs from the selection and write a caption that compares and contrasts them. Choose two lightning photographs, two tornado photographs, or one of each kind. Tell about both the details and the mood of each photograph.

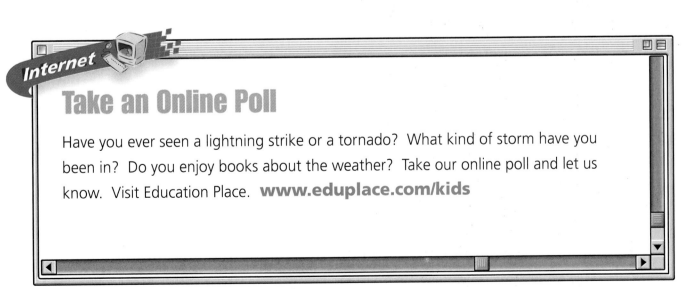

Internet

Take an Online Poll

Have you ever seen a lightning strike or a tornado? What kind of storm have you been in? Do you enjoy books about the weather? Take our online poll and let us know. Visit Education Place. **www.eduplace.com/kids**

Skill: How to Read a Sequence Chart

Skill: How to Read a Sequence Chart

❶ Read the **title** of the sequence chart. It tells what **process** is being shown.

❷ Read the **steps** in the process by following the **arrows** from top to bottom or left to right.

❸ Look for **order words**, such as *next, then, resulting,* and *now*.

STORM WARNING

When TV viewers of 7 News in Boston tune in to Mishelle Michaels's weekend weather forecast, they're seeing the end of a long day of data collection and weather analysis — the complex job of the meteorologist.

Mishelle's New England telecast relies on information collected at thousands of points around the world. These "eyes" and "ears" that scout the weather include radar, satellites, surface observing sites, and weather balloons.

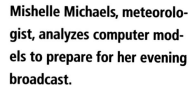

Mishelle Michaels, meteorologist, analyzes computer models to prepare for her evening broadcast.

Collecting the Data

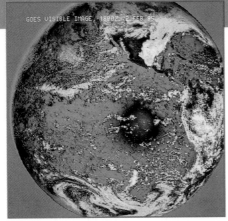

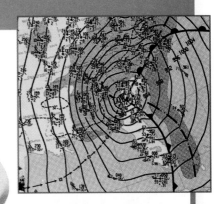

Surface observing sites report the current weather conditions every hour of every day of every year.

Weather satellites 22,000 miles up take photographs of clouds to show the movement of weather systems.

Through a network of NEXRAD (Next Generation Radar) stations, radar images display the motion and intensity of rain or snow.

Weather balloons take measurements of the atmosphere from ground level to thousands of feet above the earth.

The National Weather Service's supercomputer then processes this information, making sixteen billion calculations per second.

The resulting charts and weather images are made available to Mishelle and other meteorologists around the United States to help them create their forecasts.

Analyzing the Weather

Reviewing Conditions

To begin her forecast, Mishelle checks the current conditions — temperatures, winds, and weather patterns — for the city of Boston, its surrounding communities, and much of New England.

Observing Radar Images

Enhanced Doppler radar provides Mishelle with images of thunderstorms moving toward Boston from the west. Next Generation Radar can detect dangerous shifts in wind direction that may result in tornadoes.

Mishelle analyzes hundreds of the charts and images that the National Weather Service provides. But that is only part of the studying and interpreting she has to do before she can create a forecast. The data gathered from the radar and satellites requires the explaining abilities of the meteorologist so that it makes sense to the rest of us.

Hearing from Weather Watchers

Local volunteers of all ages phone Mishelle daily with detailed weather reports from their communities. These observations are often invaluable in helping Mishelle put together the pieces of the forecasting puzzle.

Analyzing Computer Models

By analyzing weather charts and maps created by the National Weather Service from computer models, Mishelle develops a four- to five-day forecast for Greater Boston and New England. She relies on her education and experience to accurately predict how the atmosphere will change.

Career File

Meteorologist

Are you interested in following the weather professionally? You'll need a four-year college degree in Meteorology or Atmospheric Science. It also helps if you enjoy . . .

- Watching clouds and chasing storms (from a safe distance)
- The challenge of problem-solving
- Communicating your knowledge with others

Meanwhile, contact your local television station about becoming a volunteer weather observer.

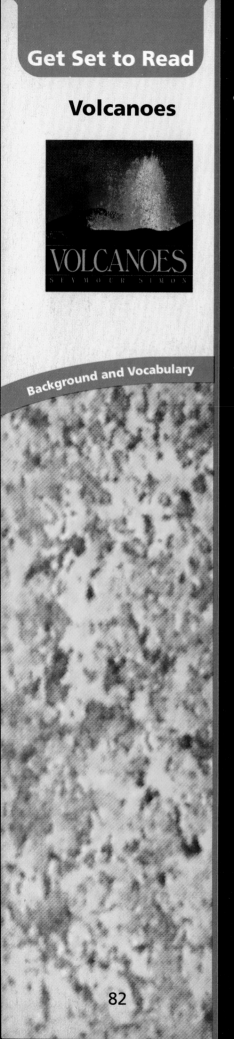

VOLCANOES
SEYMOUR SIMON

The World of Volcanoes

From Hawaii to the Pacific Northwest, from Guatemala to Iceland, Seymour Simon's *Volcanoes* will take you on a world tour. You'll see more than mountain peaks. The heart of the story is about the part of the earth that's deep underground, where the heat turns the earth's crust into molten rock.

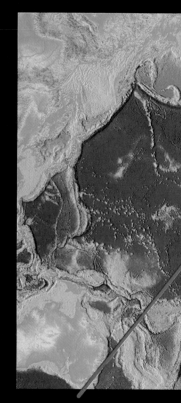

Mauna Loa
Molten rock erupts as flowing lava from Hawaii's Mauna Loa.

Mount St. Helens
One of many volcanoes in the Pacific Northwest, Mount St. Helens cooled down to form a hard lava dome in its **crater**.

Surtsey
An undersea volcano near Iceland created a new island, Surtsey.

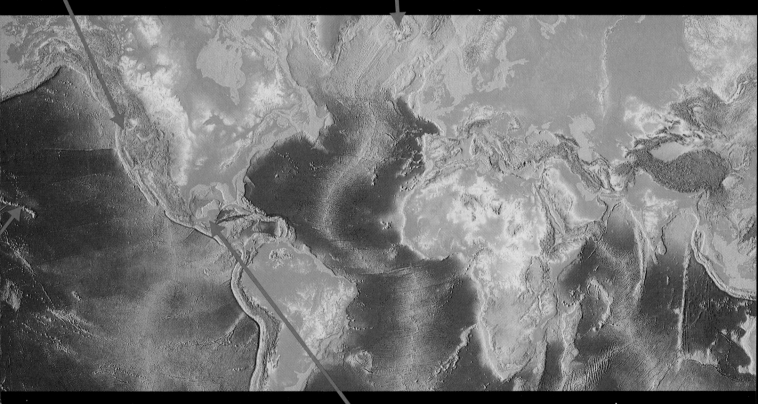

Fuego and Acatenango
These volcanoes in Guatemala are built of **cinders** and ash.

VOLCANOES

S E Y M O U R   S I M O N

Throughout history, people have told stories about volcanoes. The early Romans believed in Vulcan, their god of fire. They thought that Vulcan worked at a hot forge, striking sparks as he made swords and armor for the other gods. It is from the Roman god Vulcan that we get the word *volcano*.

The early Hawaiians told legends of the wanderings of Pele, their goddess of fire. Pele was chased from her homes by her sister Namaka, goddess of the sea. Pele moved constantly from one Hawaiian island to another. Finally, Pele settled in a mountain called Kilauea, on the big island of Hawaii. Even though the islanders tried to please Pele, she burst forth every few years. Kilauea is still an active volcano.

In early times, no one knew how volcanoes formed or why they spouted fire. In modern times, scientists began to study volcanoes. They still don't know all the answers, but they know much about how a volcano works.

Our planet is made up of many layers of rock. The top layers of solid rock are called the crust. Deep beneath the crust, it is so hot that some rock melts. The melted, or molten, rock is called magma.

Volcanoes are formed by cracks or holes that poke through the earth's crust. Magma pushes its way up through the cracks. This is called a volcanic eruption. When magma pours forth on the surface it is called lava. In the above photograph of an eruption, you can see great fountains of boiling lava forming fiery rivers and lakes. As lava cools, it hardens to form rock.

A volcano can be two things: a hole in the ground that lava comes through, or a hill or mountain formed by the lava. Mount Rainier in the state of Washington is a volcano even though it has not erupted since 1882.

Not far from Mount Rainier (top, right) is Mount St. Helens (bottom, left). Native Americans and early settlers in the Northwest had seen Mount St. Helens puff out some ashes, steam, and lava in the mid-1800s. Yet for more than a century, the mountain seemed quiet and peaceful.

In March 1980 Mount St. Helens awakened from its long sleep. First there were a few small earthquakes that shook the mountain. Then on March 27 Mount St. Helens began to spout ashes and steam. Each day brought further quakes, until by mid-May more than ten thousand small quakes had been recorded. The mountain began to swell up and crack.

Sunday May 18 dawned bright and clear. The mountain seemed much the same as it had been for the past month. Suddenly, at 8:32 A.M., Mount St. Helens erupted with incredible force. The energy released in the eruption was equal to ten million tons of dynamite.

The eruption of Mount St. Helens was the most destructive in the history of the United States. Sixty people lost their lives as hot gases, rocks, and ashes covered an area of two hundred thirty square miles. Hundreds of houses and cabins were destroyed, leaving many people homeless. Miles of highways, roads, and railways were badly damaged. The force of the eruption was so great that entire forests were blown down like rows of matchsticks.

Compare the way Mount St. Helens looked before and after the eruption. The entire top of the mountain was blown away. In its place is a huge volcanic crater. In 1982 the mountain and the area around it were dedicated as the Mount St. Helens National Volcanic Monument. Visitor centers allow people to view the volcano's astonishing power.

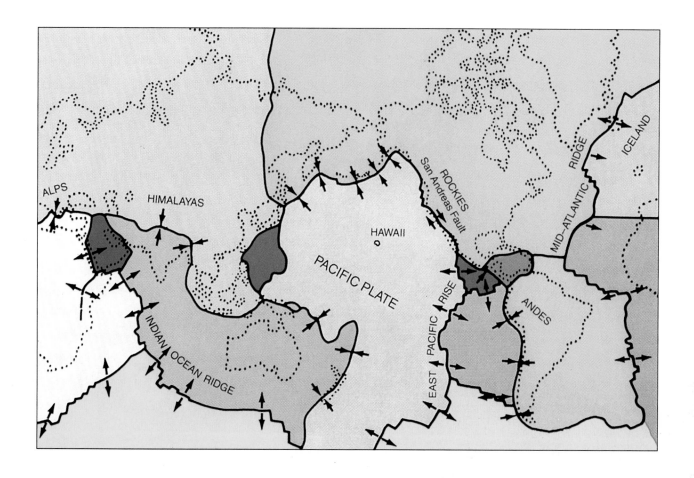

ALPS

HIMALAYAS

ROCKIES

San Andreas Fault

MID-ATLANTIC RIDGE

ICELAND

HAWAII

PACIFIC PLATE

INDIAN OCEAN RIDGE

EAST PACIFIC RISE

ANDES

Volcanoes don't just happen anyplace. The earth's crust is broken into huge sections like a giant cracked eggshell. The pieces of the crust are called plates. The United States, Canada, and Mexico and part of the North Atlantic Ocean are all on the North American plate. Almost all the volcanoes in the world erupt in places where two plates meet.

Down the middle of the North Atlantic Ocean, two plates are slowly moving apart. Hot magma pushes up between them. A chain of underwater volcanoes runs along the line where the two plates meet. Some of the underwater volcanoes have grown so high that they stick up from the ocean floor to make islands.

Iceland is a volcanic island in the North Atlantic. In 1963, an area of the sea near Iceland began to smoke. An undersea volcano was exploding and a new island was being formed. The island was named Surtsey, after the ancient Norse god of fire.

Ten years after the explosion that formed Surtsey, another volcano erupted near Iceland. It was off the south coast of Iceland on the island of Heimaey. Within six hours of the eruption, more than 5,000 people were taken off the island to safety. After two months, hundreds of buildings had burned down and dozens more had been buried in the advancing lava. Then the volcano stopped erupting. After a year's time, the people of Heimaey came back to reclaim their island with its new 735-foot volcano.

ost volcanoes and earthquakes are along the edges of the large Pacific plate. There are so many that the shoreline of the Pacific Ocean is called the "Ring of Fire." But a few volcanoes are not on the edge of a plate. The volcanoes in the Hawaiian Islands are in the middle of the Pacific plate.

A million years ago, magma pushed up through cracks in the Pacific plate. Over the years, eruption followed eruption. Little by little, thin layers of lava hardened, one atop another. Thousands of eruptions were needed to build mountains high enough to reach from the deep sea bottom and appear as islands.

The largest Hawaiian volcano is Mauna Loa. It is seventy miles long and rises thirty thousand feet from the ocean floor. It is still growing. Every few years, Mauna Loa erupts again.

Hawaiian volcano lava usually bubbles out quietly to form rivers or lakes, or spouts a few hundred feet in the air in a fiery fountain. Hawaiian volcanoes erupt much more gently than did Surtsey or Mount St. Helens. Only rarely does a Hawaiian volcano throw out rock and high clouds of ash.

Steam clouds billow as a flow of hot lava enters the sea. Hawaii is constantly changing as eruptions add hundreds of acres of new land to the islands. In other parts of the shoreline, old lava flows are quickly weathered by the waves into rocks and black sand.

Hawaiian lava is thin and flows quickly. In some lava rivers, speeds as high as thirty-five miles per hour have been measured. In an eruption in 1986, a number of houses were threatened by the quick-moving lava. Fire fighters sprayed water on the lava to slow down its advance.

When lava cools and hardens, it forms volcanic rocks. The kinds of rocks formed are clues to the kind of eruption. The two main kinds have Hawaiian names. Thick, slow-moving lava called *aa* (AH-ah) hardens into a rough tangle of sharp rocks. Thin, hot, quick-moving lava called *pahoehoe* (pah-HO-ee-ho-ee) forms a smooth, billowy surface.

Earth scientists have divided volcanoes into four groups. Shield volcanoes, such as Mauna Loa and Kilauea, have broad, gentle slopes shaped like an ancient warrior's shield.

Cinder cone volcanoes look like upside-down ice cream cones. They erupt explosively, blowing out burning ashes and cinders. The ashes and cinders build up to form the cone shape. The cinder cone volcano to the near left erupted in Guatemala, Central America, in 1984. The cinder cone volcanoes in the background are still smoking from earlier eruptions.

Most of the volcanoes in the world are composite or strato-volcanoes. Strato-volcanoes are formed by the lava, cinders, and ashes of an eruption. During an eruption, ashes and cinders fall to the ground. The eruption quiets down and lava slowly flows out, covering the layer of ashes and cinders. Further eruptions add more layers of ashes and cinders, followed by more layers of lava. Mount Shasta (above) in California and Mount Hood in Oregon are strato-volcanoes. They are still active even though they have not erupted for many years.

The fourth kind of volcano is called a dome volcano. Dome volcanoes have thick, slow-moving lava that forms a steep-sided dome shape. After an eruption, the volcano may be plugged with hardened lava. The plug prevents the gases from escaping, like a cork in a bottle of soda water. As the pressure builds up, the volcano blows its top, as Mount St. Helens did. Lassen Peak in California is a dome volcano that erupted violently in 1915. You can see the huge chunks of volcanic rock near the summit.

Around the world there are many very old volcanoes that no longer erupt. These dead volcanoes are called extinct. Crater Lake in Oregon is an extinct volcano. Almost seven thousand years ago, Mount Mazama in Oregon erupted, sending out a thick blanket of ashes that covered the ground for miles around. Then the entire top of the volcano collapsed. A huge crater, called a caldera, formed and was later filled with water. Crater Lake reaches a depth of two thousand feet, the deepest lake in North America.

After a volcano erupts, everything is buried under lava or ashes. Plants and animals are nowhere to be found. But in a few short months, life renews itself. Plants grow in the cracks between the rocks. Insects and other animals return. Volcanoes do not just destroy. They bring new mountains, new islands, and new soil to the land. Many good things can come from the fiery explosions of volcanoes.

Meet the AUTHOR

Seymour Simon

"**M**any of the books I write are really in the nature of guidebooks to unknown territories. Each territory has to be discovered again by children venturing into it for the first time."

"**I**'m always working on several books at the same time. I may be writing a book and researching another book and writing for information about a third book and thinking about plans for still a fourth book."

FACT FILE

- Graduated from the Bronx High School of Science
- President of the Junior Astronomy Club at New York's Museum of Natural History
- Taught science and creative writing in New York City public schools, 1955–1979
- First published work: a magazine article about the moon
- Author of more than two hundred books in thirty years

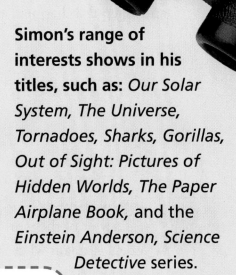

Simon's range of interests shows in his titles, such as: *Our Solar System, The Universe, Tornadoes, Sharks, Gorillas, Out of Sight: Pictures of Hidden Worlds, The Paper Airplane Book,* and the *Einstein Anderson, Science Detective* series.

 Internet

For more information about Seymour Simon, visit Education Place.

www.eduplace.com/kids

Think About the Selection

1. Why do you think people have used folktales to explain volcanoes?

2. Find examples in the selection of both the helpful and harmful things that volcanoes do.

3. Why do you think earthquakes often happen just before volcanoes?

4. Of the different volcanoes mentioned in the selection, which one impressed you the most? Why?

5. Which word best describes a volcano for you: *beautiful, scary, exciting, ugly,* or some other word? Explain why.

6. What do you think would be the best and worst things about studying volcanoes for a living?

7. **Connecting/Comparing** Compare the conditions that cause a volcanic eruption with those that cause a tornado. Think about how, where, and when they happen, and how much warning people have.

Explaining

Write a Travel Brochure

Use information from the selection to create a travel brochure for a tour of the world's volcanoes. Explain where the tour will go and what volcanoes you will see.

> **Tips**
> - Fold a sheet of paper into three panels.
> - Describe the tour on the inside panels and illustrate the outside panels.
> - Check your spelling and capitalize all proper nouns.

Science

Create a Poster

Use information from Seymour Simon's *Volcanoes* to make a poster. You might show how magma rises to erupt as lava, or show the four different kinds of volcanoes.

Social Studies

Create a Fact File

With classmates, create a volcano fact file. Using the information in *Volcanoes*, each person chooses a country or state, such as Iceland or Hawaii, and lists the volcanoes for that place, along with a brief description of the volcanoes and a small map.

Bonus: Find information about the volcanoes of a country not mentioned in the selection, such as Italy or Japan. Add a fact file about that place.

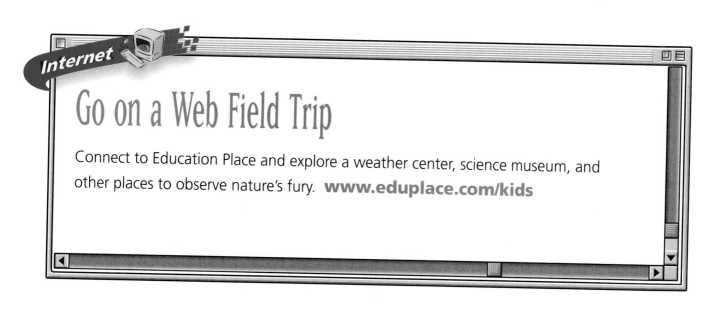

Internet

Go on a Web Field Trip

Connect to Education Place and explore a weather center, science museum, and other places to observe nature's fury. **www.eduplace.com/kids**

ktale Link

Skill: How to Read a Folktale

1. Notice that the **characters** are simple — good or bad, wise or foolish.
2. Notice that the **action** moves quickly, in brief episodes.
3. Look for information about the **country** the folktale comes from.

THE PRINCESS AND

A Mexican Folktale

Not far from Mexico City, two mountains, only five miles apart, rise more than 17,000 feet into the sky. One is an inactive volcano, Ixtaccihuatl (ees-tah-SEE-wah-tul). Its outline is said to resemble that of a sleeping woman. The other is Popocatépetl (poh-puh-CAT-uh-pet-ul), an active volcano that regularly sends up clouds of smoke and ash. This ancient Mexican folktale tells the story of how the two companion volcanoes came to be.

Many centuries ago, there was an Aztec emperor who had a good and beautiful daughter named Ixtaccihuatl.

One day the emperor received word that his enemies were preparing to attack his lands. He called his brave young warriors to the

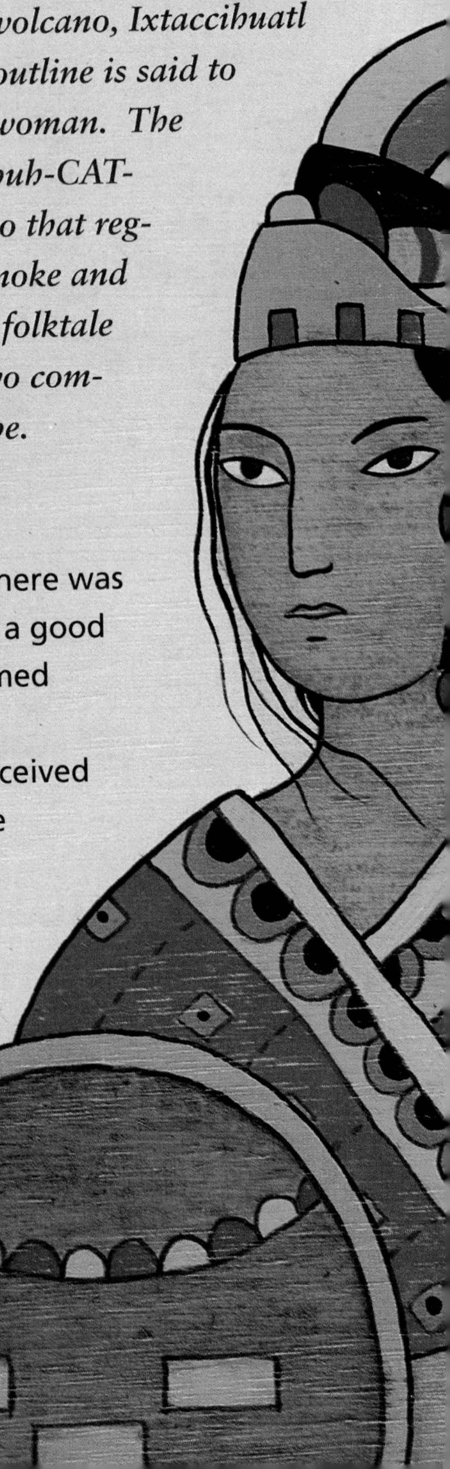

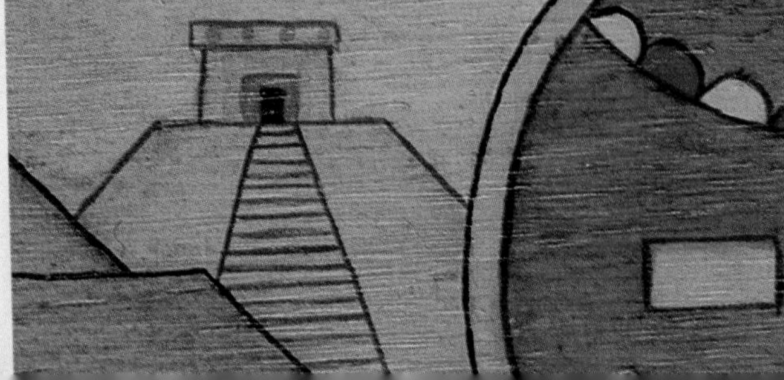

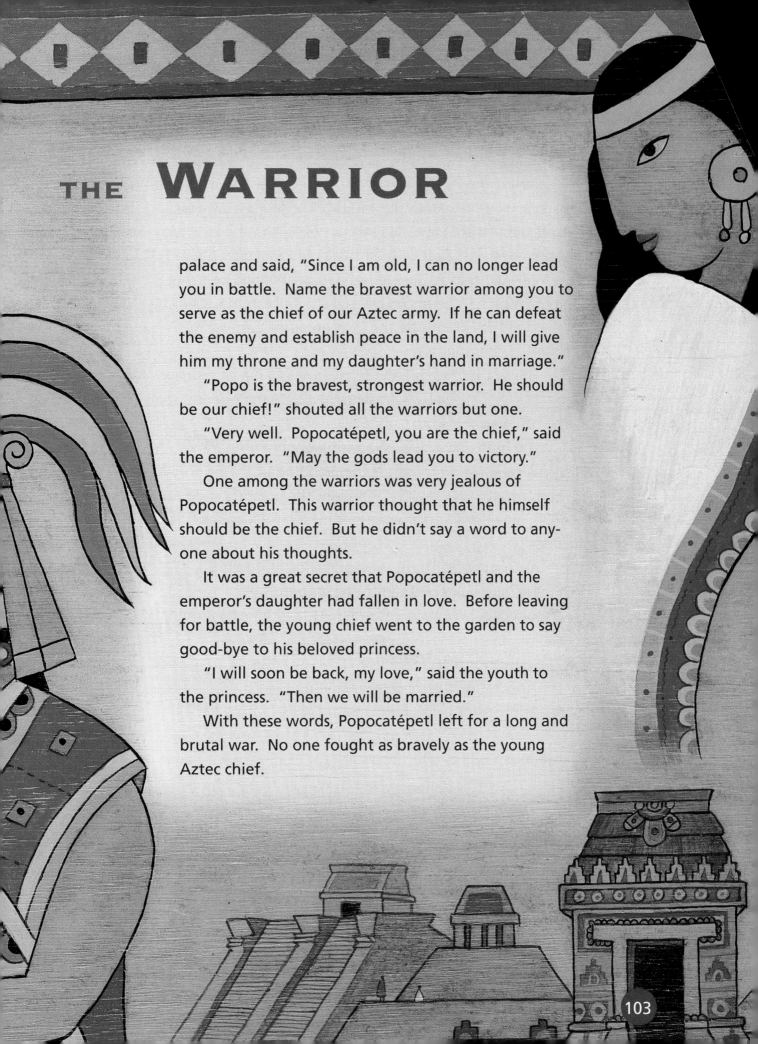

THE **WARRIOR**

palace and said, "Since I am old, I can no longer lead you in battle. Name the bravest warrior among you to serve as the chief of our Aztec army. If he can defeat the enemy and establish peace in the land, I will give him my throne and my daughter's hand in marriage."

"Popo is the bravest, strongest warrior. He should be our chief!" shouted all the warriors but one.

"Very well. Popocatépetl, you are the chief," said the emperor. "May the gods lead you to victory."

One among the warriors was very jealous of Popocatépetl. This warrior thought that he himself should be the chief. But he didn't say a word to anyone about his thoughts.

It was a great secret that Popocatépetl and the emperor's daughter had fallen in love. Before leaving for battle, the young chief went to the garden to say good-bye to his beloved princess.

"I will soon be back, my love," said the youth to the princess. "Then we will be married."

With these words, Popocatépetl left for a long and brutal war. No one fought as bravely as the young Aztec chief.

At last the Aztec warriors defeated their enemies and prepared to return to the capital. The jealous warrior was the first to leave. He ran so swiftly that he reached home two days before the others. Immediately he announced that Popocatépetl had been killed and that he himself had been the hero of the final battle. Thus he claimed the right to be the next emperor and the husband of the princess.

The poor princess! She felt she would die of sadness.

The emperor, too, was saddened by Popo's death, for he believed the warrior's story.

The next day at the palace, the people prepared a great celebration to honor the wedding of the princess and the jealous warrior. Suddenly, the princess cried out, "Oh, my poor Popocatépetl!" And she fell dead to the floor.

At that moment, the Aztec warriors entered the palace. Popocatépetl ran to the emperor and announced, "We have returned. Now the princess and I can get married."

There was a great silence. Everyone turned to look at the princess.

At the sight of his beloved, the youth ran to her side and began to cry. He took her in his arms, saying, "My precious, I will be with you until the end of time."

Then the brave chief carried her body to the highest mountains. He laid her gently in a bed of beautiful flowers and sat down beside her.

Days passed. Finally, one of the good gods transformed the warrior and the princess into two volcanoes. Ixy remains quiet. But from time to time, Popo trembles and tears of fire flow from his heart. Then all of Mexico knows that Popo is crying for his beloved princess.

✔ Choosing the Best Answer

Many tests have multiple-choice items, or items with a question and three to five answer choices. How do you choose the best answer? Look at this sample test item for *Eye of the Storm: Chasing Storms with Warren Faidley*. The correct answer is shown. Use the tips to help you answer this kind of test question.

Tips

- Read the directions carefully to make sure you know how to mark your answer.
- Read the question and all the answer choices.
- Look back at the selection if you need help.
- Go back and check all your answers if you have time.

Read the question. Choose the best answer and fill in the circle in the answer row.

1   What does the calendar on page 67 of *Eye of the Storm* explain?

   A   It explains where storms take place.

   B   It explains how storms form.

   C   It explains what time of year storms take place.

   D   It explains how often storms take place.

ANSWER ROW 1

Now see how one student figured out the best answer.

I am looking for the answer that best describes the calendar in *Eye of the Storm.* I look back at the calendar. It shows three kinds of storms under different months of the year.

I reread the answer choices. I see that **A** and **B** aren't correct because they aren't about time. The choice for **D** comes close, but **C** is more exact. Now I see why **C** is the best answer.

Tall Tales

A tall tale starts out like a regular story, but it tends to stretch the facts a little.

Well, actually, it stretches the facts a lot.

Where was the first tall tale told? Probably around a campfire. Out on the frontier of the 1800s, American settlers liked to exaggerate. They created heroes and heroines who were larger than life, capable of amazing deeds. In a big land with wild weather and wild animals, the stories had to be just as big and just as wild.

Tall tales are still being told today. In fact, after you read these examples, you're invited to add to the tradition and write your own!

Contents

> *As loggers changed the landscape of America in the 1800s, they told tales about a giant lumberjack of incredible strength. Paul Bunyan quickly became a folk legend from Maine to the Pacific Northwest.*

Paul Bunyan, the Mightiest Logger of Them All

Retold by Mary Pope Osborne
Illustrated by Chris Van Allsburg

It seems an amazing baby was born in the state of Maine. When he was only two weeks old, he weighed more than a hundred pounds, and for breakfast every morning he ate five dozen eggs, ten sacks of potatoes, and a half barrel of mush made from a whole sack of cornmeal. But the baby's strangest feature was his big, curly black beard. It was so big and bushy that every morning his mother had to comb it with a pine tree.

Except for that black beard, the big baby wasn't much trouble to anybody until he was about nine months old. That was when he first started to crawl, and since he weighed over five hundred pounds, he caused an earthquake that shook the whole town.

The baby's parents tried putting him in a giant floating cradle off the coast of Maine; but every time he rolled over, huge waves drowned all the villages along the coast.

So his parents hauled the giant toddler to a cave in the Maine woods far away from civilization and said good-bye. His father gave him a fishing pole, a knife, some flint rocks, and an axe. "We'll think of you often, honey," his mother said, weeping. "But you can't come back home — you're just too big."

That's the story of how Paul Bunyan came to take care of himself in the Maine woods. And even though he lived alone for the next twenty years, he got along quite well.

In those times, huge sections of America were filled with dark green forests. It would be nice if those trees could have stayed tall and thick forever. But the pioneers needed them to build houses, churches, ships, wagons, bridges, and barns. So one day Paul Bunyan took a good look at those trees and decided to invent logging.

"Tim-ber!" he yelled, and he swung the bright steel axe his father had given him in a wide circle. There was a terrible crash, and when Paul looked around, he saw he'd felled ten white pines with a single swing.

After that Paul traveled plenty fast through the untamed North Woods. He cut pine, spruce, and red willow in Minnesota, Michigan, and Wisconsin. He cleared cottonwoods out of Kansas so farmers could plant wheat and oaks out of Iowa so farmers could plant corn.

When next heard of, Paul was headed to Arizona. He dragged his pickaxe behind him on the trip, not realizing he was leaving a big ditch in his tracks. Today that ditch is called the Grand Canyon.

When Paul got back from the West, he decided to start a logging camp. Word spread fast. Since all the woodsmen had heard of Paul Bunyan, thousands of them hurried to Paul's headquarters at Big Onion on the Big Onion River in Minnesota to be part of his crew.

"There's only two requirements," Paul announced to the men who'd gathered to apply for the job. "All my loggers have to be over ten feet tall and be able to pop six buttons off their shirts with one breath."

Well, about a thousand of the lumberjacks met those requirements, and Paul hired them all. Then he built a gigantic logging camp with

bunkhouses a mile long and bunks ten beds high. The camp's chow table was so long that it took a week to pass the salt and pepper from one end to the other. Paul dug a few ponds to provide drinking water for everyone. Today we call those ponds the Great Lakes.

Things went pretty well at the Big Onion Lumber Company until the Year of the Hard Winter. One day Shot Gunderson, the crew boss, complained to Paul, "Boss, it's so cold that the flames for all the lanterns are freezing. And, Boss, when I give orders to the woods crew, all my words freeze in the air and hang there stiff as icicles."

"Well, haul away your frozen words and store them somewhere next to the lantern flames," Paul advised. "They'll both thaw out in the spring."

Sure enough, they did. The only problem was that, come spring, the melting lantern flames started some mean little brush fires. And when Shot's frozen words thawed, old cries of "Timber!" and "Chow time!" started to echo throughout the woods, causing all sorts of confusion. But other than that, things ran pretty smoothly.

Well, there's stories and stories about Paul Bunyan. For many years, old loggers sat around potbellied stoves and told about the good old times with Paul. Those loggers are all gone now, but many of their stories still hang frozen in the cold forest air of the North Woods, waiting to be told. Come spring, when they start to thaw, some of them might just start telling themselves. It's been known to happen.

Stories and songs about John Henry have been around since the 1870s. He became famous as the steel driver who hammered faster than a machine. Did John Henry exist? No one knows for sure. But like Paul Bunyan, he stands for the deeds of many others.

John Henry Races the Steam Drill

Retold by Paul Robert Walker

The Big Bend Tunnel was the longest tunnel in America — a mile and a quarter through the heart of the West Virginia mountains. The C & O Railroad started building it back around 1870. There was plenty of hard work for everyone, but the steel-driving men worked the hardest. And the hardest-working steel-driving man of them all was John Henry.

Now, John Henry was a powerful man — six feet tall and two hundred pounds of rippling muscle. He swung his nine-pound hammer from sunup to sundown, driving a steel drill into solid rock. Little Bill, the shaker, turned John Henry's drill between hammer blows and pulled it out when the hole was done. When there were enough holes, the demolition boys filled them with nitroglycerine and blew the rock to kingdom come. Then John Henry drove more steel — day after day in the heat and darkness and stale air of the tunnel.

114

John Henry always sang while he drove the steel — and at the end of every line he brought that nine-pound hammer down like a crash of thunder.

This old hammer (Bam!)
Rings like silver (Bam!)
Shines like gold, boys, (Bam!)
Shines like gold. (Bam!)

Ain't no hammer (Bam!)
In these mountains (Bam!)
Rings like mine, boys, (Bam!)
Rings like mine. (Bam!)

One day, Captain Tommy interrupted John Henry in the middle of his song. "John Henry," he said, "the company wants to test one of those new steam drills. They say a steam drill can do the work of three or four men. But I say a good man can beat the steam. And I say you are the best man I have."

John Henry rested his nine-pound hammer on his broad, muscular shoulder. "Captain Tommy," he said, "a man ain't nothin' but a man. Before I let that steam drill beat me down, I'll die with my hammer in my hand."

"Son," offered Captain Tommy, "if you beat that steam drill, I'll give you one hundred dollars and a new suit of clothes."

"That's mighty generous," said John Henry, "but don't you worry about that. Just go to town and buy me a twenty-pound hammer. This nine-pound maul is feeling light."

The news of the contest spread through the camp like a strong wind whipping down the mountain. The company men said John Henry was a poor working fool who didn't stand a chance against that mighty steam drill. Some of the working men thought the same. But the steel-driving men knew John Henry — and they believed in the power of a mighty man.

That night, John Henry told his wife, Polly Ann, about the contest. "Don't you strain yourself, honey," said Polly Ann. "'Course we could use that hundred dollars — and you need a new suit of clothes."

John Henry smiled and kissed Polly Ann. "I ain't worried about money or clothes," he said. "Don't y' see sugar — a man ain't nothin' but a man, and a man's got to beat the steam."

The next morning, the steel drivers crowded into the Big Bend Tunnel. It was hot and dusty, and the air was so foul that a man could hardly breathe. The only light was the flickering of lamps burning lard oil and blackstrap molasses.

The company man wheeled the steam drill into the tunnel and set it up against the rock. It was nothing but a machine — all shiny and modern and strange. Then John Henry walked in and stood beside it. He was nothing but a man — all black and fine and natural.

Captain Tommy handed John Henry a brand-new twenty-pound hammer. "There ain't another like it in West Virginia," he said. "Good luck, son."

John Henry held the hammer in his hand and felt its fine natural weight. In the flickering light of the tunnel, the head of that hammer shone like gold. "Gonna call this hammer Polly Ann," he said.

Little Bill sat on the rock, holding the six-foot drill in his hands. John Henry towered above the steel, just waiting to begin. It was so quiet in that tunnel, you could hear the soft breathing of the steel-driving men.

Captain Tommy blew his whistle. The company man turned on the steam drill. John Henry swung his twenty-pound hammer back and brought it down with a crash like thunder. As he swung it back again, he began to sing:

> *This old hammer* (Bam!)
> *Rings like silver* (Bam!)
> *Shines like gold, boys,* (Bam!)
> *Shines like gold.* (Bam!)

John Henry kept driving steel and the steam drill kept drilling. Pretty soon the whole mountain was rumbling and shaking. John Henry's muscles bulged and strained like they never bulged and strained before. Sweat cascaded down his powerful chest, and veins protruded from the sides of his handsome face.

"Are you all right, John Henry?" asked Captain Tommy.

"Don't you worry," said John Henry. "A man ain't nothin' but a man —
and a man's got to beat the steam." Then he went on singing:

> *Ain't no hammer* (Bam!)
> *In these mountains* (Bam!)
> *Rings like mine, boys,* (Bam!)
> *Rings like mine.* (Bam!)

When they hit the end of the six-foot drill, Little Bill pulled it out and
shoved in a longer drill — and then a longer one and a longer one still.
John Henry swung his twenty-pound hammer and drove that steel. He
swung and drove faster and harder, and faster and harder, until that Polly
Ann hammer caught fire. The whole Big Bend Tunnel glowed with the blue
flame of John Henry's hammer.

"Time!" shouted Captain Tommy.

"Time!" cried the company man, shutting off the steam drill.

"Time," gasped John Henry, leaning on his hammer. "I need a cool
drink of water."

While John Henry drank his water, Captain Tommy and the company
man measured the holes. The steam drill had done nine feet; John Henry
had drilled fourteen.

"John Henry!" shouted the steel drivers. "John Henry beat the steam!"

"Congratulations, son," said Captain Tommy, slapping him on the back.
"I don't care what you say — I'm gonna give you a hundred dollars and a
new suit of clothes."

John Henry leaned heavily on his hammer and sucked in the stale air
of the tunnel. "That's mighty generous, Captain Tommy. But you give that
hundred dollars to Polly Ann. And you bury me in that suit of clothes."
Then he slumped to the ground, clutching his hammer in his hand. "I beat
the steam," he gasped, "but I broke inside."

As his eyes closed, John Henry lay back against the black earth and
whispered, "A man ain't nothin' but a man."

The Tennessee frontiersman, Davy Crockett, was the real-life subject of many a tall tale. But there is no truth to the story that he had a wife named Sally Ann Thunder Ann Whirlwind. Good thing for Davy, because in her he would have met his match!

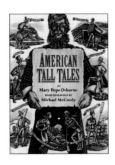

Sally Ann Thunder Ann Whirlwind

Retold by Mary Pope Osborne

One early spring day, when the leaves of the white oaks were about as big as a mouse's ear, Davy Crockett set out alone through the forest to do some bear hunting. Suddenly it started raining real hard, and he felt obliged to stop for shelter under a tree. As he shook the rain out of his coonskin cap, he got sleepy, so he laid back into the crotch of the tree, and pretty soon he was snoring.

Davy slept so hard, he didn't wake up until nearly sundown. And when he did, he discovered that somehow or another in all that sleeping his head had gotten stuck in the crotch of the tree, and he couldn't get it out.

Well, Davy roared loud enough to make the tree lose all its little mouse-ear leaves. He twisted and turned and carried on for over an hour, but still that tree wouldn't let go. Just as he

119

was about to give himself up for a goner, he heard a girl say, "What's the matter, stranger?"

Even from his awkward position, he could see that she was extraordinary — tall as a hickory sapling, with arms as big as a keelboat tiller's.

"My head's stuck, *sweetie*," he said. "And if you help me get it free, I'll give you a pretty little comb."

"Don't call me sweetie," she said. "And don't worry about giving me any pretty little comb, either. I'll free your old coconut, but just because I want to."

Then this extraordinary girl did something that made Davy's hair stand on end. She reached in a bag and took out a bunch of rattlesnakes. She tied all the wriggly critters together to make a long rope, and as she tied, she kept talking. "I'm not a shy little colt," she said. "And I'm not a little singing nightingale, either. I can tote a steamboat on my back, outscream a panther, and jump over my own shadow. I can double up crocodiles any day, and I like to wear a hornets' nest for my Sunday bonnet."

As the girl looped the ends of her snake rope to the top of the branch that was trapping Davy, she kept bragging: "I'm a streak of lightning set up edgeways and buttered with quicksilver. I can outgrin, outsnort, outrun, outlift, outsneeze, outsleep, outlie any varmint from Maine to Louisiana. Furthermore, sweetie, I can blow out the moonlight and sing a wolf to sleep." Then she pulled on the other end of the snake rope so hard, it seemed as if she might tear the world apart.

The right-hand fork of that big tree bent just about double. Then Davy slid his head out as easy as you please. For a minute he was so dizzy, he couldn't tell up from down. But when he got everything going straight again, he took a good look at that girl. "What's your name, ma'am?"

"Sally Ann Thunder Ann Whirlwind," she said. "But if you mind your manners, you can call me Sally."

From then on Davy Crockett was crazy in love with Sally Ann Thunder Ann Whirlwind. He asked everyone he knew about her, and everything he heard caused another one of Cupid's arrows to jab him in the gizzard.

"Oh, I know Sally!" the preacher said. "She can dance a rock to pieces and ride a panther bareback!"

"Sally's a good ole friend of mine," the blacksmith said. "Once I saw her crack a walnut with her front teeth."

"Sally's so very special," said the schoolmarm. "She likes to whip across the Salt River, using her apron for a sail and her left leg for a rudder!"

Sally Ann Thunder Ann Whirlwind had a reputation for being funny, too. Her best friend, Lucy, told Davy, "Sally can laugh the bark off a pine tree. She likes to whistle out one side of her mouth while she eats with the other side and grins with the middle!"

According to her friends, Sally could tame about anything in the world, too. They all told Davy about the time she was churning butter and heard something scratching outside. Suddenly the door swung open, and in walked the Great King Bear of the Mud Forest. He'd come to steal one of her smoked hams. Well, before the King Bear could say boo, Sally grabbed a warm dumpling from the pot and stuffed it in his mouth.

The dumpling tasted so good, the King Bear's eyes winked with tears. But then he started to think that Sally might taste pretty good, too. So opening and closing his big old mouth, he backed her right into a corner.

Sally was plenty scared, with her knees a-knocking and her heart a-hammering. But just as the King Bear blew his hot breath in her face, she gathered the courage to say, "Would you like to dance?"

As everybody knows, no bear can resist an invitation to a square dance, so of course the old fellow forgot all about eating Sally and said, "Love to."

Then he bowed real pretty, and the two got to kicking and whooping and swinging each other through the air, as Sally sang:

We are on our way to Baltimore,
With two behind, and two before:
Around, around, around we go,
Where oats, peas, beans, and barley grow!

And while she was singing, Sally tied a string from the bear's ankle to her butter churn, so that all the time the old feller was kicking up his legs and dancing around the room, he was also churning her butter!

And folks loved to tell the story about Sally's encounter with another stinky varmint — only this one was a *human* varmint. It seems that Mike Fink, the riverboat man, decided to scare the toenails off Sally because he was sick and tired of hearing Davy Crockett talk about how great she was.

One evening Mike crept into an old alligator skin and met Sally just as she was taking off to forage in the woods for berries. He spread open his gigantic mouth and made such a howl that he nearly scared himself to

death. But Sally paid no more attention to that fool than she would have to a barking puppy dog.

However, when Mike put out his claws to embrace her, her anger rose higher than a Mississippi flood. She threw a flash of eye lightning at him, turning the dark to daylight. Then she pulled out a little toothpick and with a single swing sent the alligator head flying fifty feet! And then to finish him off good, she rolled up her sleeves and knocked Mike Fink clear across the woods and into a muddy swamp.

When the fool came to, Davy Crockett was standing over him. "What in the world happened to you, Mikey?" he asked.

"Well, I — I think I must-a been hit by some kind of wild alligator!" Mike stammered, rubbing his sore head.

Davy smiled, knowing full well it was Sally Ann Thunder Ann Whirlwind just finished giving Mike Fink the only punishment he'd ever known.

That incident caused Cupid's final arrow to jab Davy's gizzard. "Sally's the whole steamboat," he said, meaning she was something great. The next day he put on his best raccoon hat and sallied forth to see her.

When he got within three miles of her cabin, he began to holler her name. His voice was so loud, it whirled through the woods like a hurricane.

Sally looked out and saw the wind a-blowing and the trees a-bending. She heard her name a-thundering through the woods, and her heart began to thump. By now she'd begun to feel that Davy Crockett was the whole steamboat, too. So she put on her best hat — an eagle's nest with a wild-cat's tail for a feather — and ran outside.

Just as she stepped out the door, Davy Crockett burst from the woods and jumped onto her porch as fast as a frog. "Sally, darlin'!" he cried. "I think my heart is bustin'! Want to be my wife?"

"Oh, my stars and possum dogs, why not?" she said.

From that day on, Davy Crockett had a hard time acting tough around Sally Ann Thunder Ann Whirlwind. His fightin' and hollerin' had no more effect on her than dropping feathers on a barn floor. At least that's what *she'd* tell you. *He* might say something else.

Sid Fleischman has created his own tall tale characters in his stories about farmer Josh McBroom. In this tale, the McBroom family has to cope with unpredictable weather and, as usual, neighbor Heck Jones.

February

by Sid Fleischman

Illustrated by Walter Lorraine

It's not generally known, but I invented air conditioning. I read in the paper the idea has already spread to the big cities.

But, shucks, everyone is welcome to it. Folks around here call it McBroom's Natural Winter Extract & Relief for the Summer Dismals. You can make your own, same as us.

February is about the last month you can lay in a supply of prime Winter Extract.

Wait for an infernal cold day. When the mercury in the thermometer drops to the bottom — you're getting close. But the weather's still a mite too warm.

When the mercury busts the glass bulb and rolls over to the fireplace to get warm — that's Extract weather.

"Will*jill*hester*chester*peter*polly*tim*tom*mary*larry*andlittle*clarinda!*" I shouted to our young'uns. "Bulb's shattered. Fetch the ripsaws, the crosscut saws, and let's get to work!"

Cold? Mercy, it was so cold outside *the wind had frozen solid*.

Didn't we get busy! We began sawing up chunks of frozen wind.

Now, you got to do the thing right. Wind's got a grain, just like wood. So be positive to use the crosscut saw against the grain, and the ripsaw along with it.

It fell dark before we finished harvesting and hauling that Winter Extract to our icehouse. And there stood our neighbor Heck Jones. That skinflint is so mean and miserly he brands the horseflies over at his place for fear someone will rustle 'em.

"Are you hidin' my left sock, McBroom?" he asked.

"Of course not," I said.

"Someone stole it off the clothesline. My best black sock, too! It only had three holes in it. If I catch the thief, I'll have him in a court of law!"

He loped away, grumbling and snarling.

We finished packing sawdust around the chunks of wind to keep them frozen. "Good work, my lambs," I said. "We're all set for the Summer Dismals."

Well, Heck Jones walked around in one sock the rest of winter, and summer, too.

As soon as the days turned sizzle-hot, we'd set a chunk of Winter Extract in the parlor. In a second or three it would begin to thaw — just a cool breeze at first. But when that February wind really got whistling, it would lift the curtains!

One hot night I fetched in a nice chunk of frozen wind without bothering to scrape off the sawdust. A few minutes later I saw a black thing shoot across the room. Something had got frozen in our Winter Extract.

"Heck Jones's sock!" I declared. "I can smell his feet!"

He was sure to think we'd stolen it. He'd have us in a court of law! I made a grab for it, but the February wind was kicking up such a blow it shot the sock past the curtains and far out the window.

I could see Heck Jones asleep in his hammock, one sock on, the other foot bare. The left sock hoisted its tail like a kite in the air and started down.

I declare, if I didn't see it with my own eyes, I'd think I was scrambly-witted. That holey black sock had the instinct of a homing pigeon. It returned right to Heck Jones's left foot and pulled itself on. I think it navigated by scent.

What Heck Jones thought when he awoke and looked at both feet — I can't reckon.

Narrating

Write Your Own Tall Tale

Now that you've read a few tall tales, write one of your own.
Think of a heroic main character with amazing abilities.
Think of a problem that the character has to solve. Then write
a tall tale about how the character solves the problem. The
postcard images on this page might give you some ideas for
your tall tale.

Tips

- Exaggerate qualities or features of your character, such as size or strength.
- Exaggerate features of the setting, such as the weather, landscape, or animals.
- Have your character change something in nature — for example, end a heat wave or create a river.

More Tall Tales to Read

Swamp Angel

by Anne Isaacs (Dutton)
A brave woodswoman in Tennessee saves the community from the dangerous bear, Thundering Tarnation.

The Gullywasher

by Joyce Rossi (Northland)
Leticia's grandfather tells her how a gigantic gullywasher changed him from a daring young vaquero to the old man he is now.

Pecos Bill

by Steven Kellogg (Morrow)
The most famous cowboy in Texas grew up among the coyotes, invented many useful things such as the lasso, and married the equally famous Slewfoot Sue.

The Bunyans

by Audrey Wood (Scholastic)
Meet Paul Bunyan's giant wife, Carrie, and their enormous children Little Jean and Tiny, who helped Paul create many famous American sites.

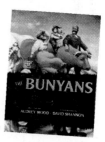

Cut From the Same Cloth

by Robert San Souci (Philomel)
This collection features tall tales about legendary women from all corners and populations of America.

Give It All You've Got

"You never fail until you stop trying."

—**Florence Griffith Joyner**

Give It All You've Got

Contents

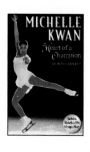

Reader's Library

- **Meet Yo-Yo Ma**
- **Victor Sews**
- **Falling Off a Log**
- **Buck Leonard: Baseball's Greatest Gentleman**

Theme Paperbacks

Supergrandpa
by David Schwartz

Off and Running
by Gary Soto

Island of the Blue Dolphins
by Scott O'Dell

Book Links

If you like . . .

Michelle Kwan: Heart of a Champion

by Michelle Kwan

Then try . . .

Play Like a Girl

by Sue Macy and Jane Gottesman (Holt)

Women and girls are playing and breaking records in almost every sport.

On the Course with Tiger Woods

by Matt Christopher (Little)

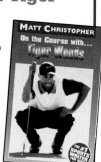

Golf's newest sensation has played the game since age two.

If you like . . .

La Bamba

by Gary Soto

Then try . . .

The Big Bike Race

by Lucy Jane Bledsoe (Holiday)

Ernie thinks he must have a new sleek bicycle in order to enter the big bike race.

Ice Story: Shackleton's Lost Expedition

by Elizabeth Kimmel (Clarion)

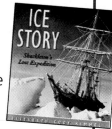

When his ship *Endurance* is crushed by ice in the Antarctic, Shackleton must do all he can to save the lives of his men.

If you like . . .

The Fear Place
by Phyllis Reynolds Naylor

Then try . . .

Top of the World: Climbing Mount Everest

by Steve Jenkins (Houghton)

Experience what it is like to climb the summit of the highest point on earth.

White Water

by P. J. Petersen (Yearling)

When his father is bitten by a rattlesnake, Greg must overcome his fear of the rapids to save his father's life.

If you like . . .

Mae Jemison
by Gail Sakurai

Then try . . .

True Heart

by Marissa Moss (Harcourt)
Bee, who has always loved the railroad, finally gets a chance to drive a train.

Iditarod Dream

by Ted Wood (Walker)
Fifteen-year-old Dusty prepares for the grueling 158-mile Junior Iditarod in Alaska.

Internet

For more great books, visit **www.eduplace.com/kids** and **www. bookadventure.org**.

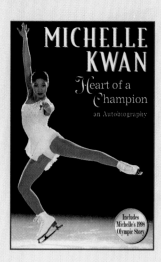

Figure Skating

In *Michelle Kwan: Heart of a Champion*, Michelle explains why figure skating isn't as simple as it looks. Senior ice skaters are under **intense pressure** to perform well, not only for themselves, but for the audience and the **judges**.

Skaters work long hours to practice their **presentations**. While skating, they need to balance both the **artistic** and **technical** sides of their performance. In other words, the feeling they bring to the music is as important as the number of spins they can turn in the air. ▶

◀ Competitive skaters are expected to perform a **required** number of **elements**, or skills, in their **programs**. A panel of judges evaluates the skaters on their jumps, spins, and footwork.

After the judges fill out worksheets, they put their marks on scorecards and hand them to the referee. The scores are then put into a computer and flashed on the scoreboard. The highest score an **amateur** skater can receive is 6.0. ▼

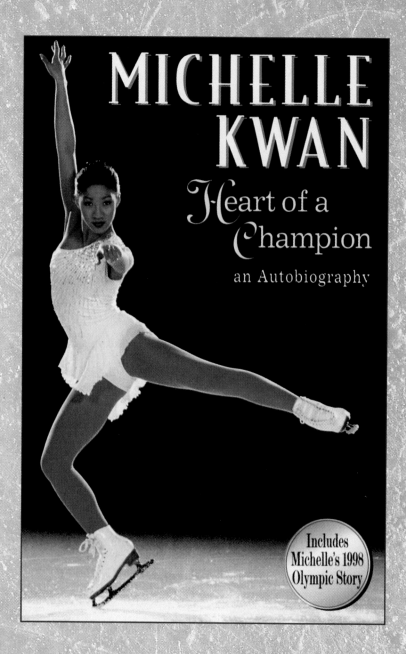

MICHELLE KWAN

Heart of a Champion

an Autobiography

Includes Michelle's 1998 Olympic Story

Strategy Focus

This autobiographical selection is told by Michelle Kwan. As you read, **evaluate** how well you get to know her through her own words.

The year was 1992. Twelve-year-old Michelle Kwan was feeling confident about her ice skating. She and her sister, Karen, had been practicing at Ice Castles, a private skating rink, with their new coach, Frank Carroll. Michelle thought she was ready to compete at the Junior Nationals that year. Anticipating perfection, she skated disastrously. After the Nationals, Michelle was determined to prove to herself, her coach, and the rest of the world how much better she could skate.

Okay, so I learned a lot from my experience in Junior Nationals. But even after bombing there, I still believed in myself. *I* knew I was a much better skater than that. Not just a better Junior skater — I thought I was ready to become a Senior skater, at the age of twelve.

As usual, I was impatiently thinking ahead. It was nice that Karen and I were skating at the same level, but if I didn't take the test now so that I could qualify my way into the 1993 Senior Nationals, I'd never make it to the 1994 Olympics. Karen was working hard as a Junior and didn't feel ready to move up to the highest level yet. But I really did feel ready — even if I had to move up without her.

I had this burning desire to compete in the big time. To be out there with Lu Chen and Surya Bonaly and Nancy Kerrigan. To compete with Tonya Harding, the only American woman who could do a triple Axel. I knew myself, and I knew my skating. I didn't see why I couldn't do it.

Others did. Frank, for one. He said the thing to do was to wait. If we worked hard all year, I'd have a good chance of winning the Junior Nationals in 1993. Frank said the judges like to get to know a skater before they give them high scores at Seniors competitions. They like to know you've paid your dues.

Frank went off to a coaches' conference in Canada for a week. And I did something that I don't usually do: I ignored the wisdom of somone who was older and wiser than me and I took the Senior test. This is a good example of what I mean when I say I'm impatient. I do have a mind of my own, and at that moment I felt like I knew me and my abilities better than anyone else.

Anyway, we went to Los Angeles to take the test. All I had to do was skate my program for a panel of judges. If I could do all the skills the USFSA required for Senior skaters in competitions, they move me on up. Easy as pie. I'd get my little pin, and go home as a *Lady* skater. After that, I couldn't skate at the lower levels anymore.

I passed, no problem, like I expected. But then came the hard part. I had to tell Frank.

Frank is one of the greatest coaches in the world. I already had a huge amount of respect for him. At the same time, I couldn't resist a challenge. When he came home, I explained to him that the challenge of becoming a top-level skater and maybe getting into the 1994 Olympics was irresistible to me. I hoped he'd understand.

All the same, he flipped his lid. He was furious. For a few days he wouldn't talk to me. He didn't think I was ready for the big leagues. He thought I'd skate onto the ice in my first Senior competition, and the judges would say, "Who is this *kid?*"

Michelle Kwan (right) at the Olympic Training Center and (below) performing at the 1992 Nationals.

Things were bad between us for a while. I apologized and apologized, and hoped he would calm down.

When he finally did, he sat me down and said, "Young lady, you have no idea what it means to be a Senior skater. You know next to nothing about the artistic side of skating. You need to understand how to *hear* the music. You are going to have to *transform* your skating."

I took it all in. Frank was right, of course. I was a good jumper, but my skating wasn't elegant or beautiful. And I hadn't thought that much about really *listening* to the music. I just got out there and jumped around.

Frank said I would have to be a perfectionist in every aspect of my presentation. My costumes, my hair, my face. My spirals, my edges, my footwork. He asked if I had any idea of the work I had ahead of me. I told him that *now* I did, and that I would do whatever I had to do . . . whatever he told me to do.

Kwan spends hours on the ice practicing with her coach, Frank Carroll (above), and her choreographer, Lori Nichol (left).

Kwan's father (left), mother, and sister (below) help her balance hard work and fun.

My parents listened to what Frank said, too. My mom was worried that I wasn't ready for this next big step. My dad reminded me of the thin line between discipline and pressure. Although they both wanted me to have discipline, they were afraid I was too young for the kind of pressure I'd face.

But my parents said that if I wanted it with all my heart, and if I was ready for the hard work ahead, they'd back me up like they always had. And they'd keep an eye on me to make sure I was still having fun and being myself.

I did want it, and I did feel ready. The judges gave me a pin that said I was a Senior skater. But I wouldn't really be one until I could make myself one. So that's what I set out to do. Like I said, I *love* a challenge.

Now that I'd made the leap to the Senior level, it wasn't enough anymore to be a talented kid. All of a sudden I would be compared to the best skaters in the world. I had to study them and think about the ones who came before me, like Peggy Fleming and Dorothy Hamill, Janet Lynn and Linda Fratianne.

I would need to take parts from all of them. Peggy Fleming's grace and artistry. Brian Boitano's heart. Dorothy Hamill's elegance.

Every skater has qualities that make him or her special. When I was little, my jumping made me stand out. I had good "spring," which means I could get up high in the air without seeming to make much effort. At a very young age I was able to do the triple jumps that most skaters don't get till they're older.

But my programs were simple. I was young and I looked it. I had a lot of work ahead of me to bring my programs up to the level of the elite skaters. In a great program, every movement should flow naturally into the next one. The music and skating should seem like they were meant for each other. The music should seem to *fill* the skater, just like it fills the arena.

Each skater has two programs for competitions. There's the "technical" or "short program," which is two minutes and thirty seconds long. And there's the "freeskate" or "long program," which is four minutes long for women (four and a half for men). The long program is by far the more important of the two. That's where "artistry" counts most.

The judges look for many required elements in a program. If the skater leaves any out, they deduct points from the score. You have to make sure the judges see those ele-

Dorothy Hamill (left), Brian Boitano (below, right), and Peggy Fleming (below, left), have all inspired Kwan.

ments, but you can't interrupt the flow of the program to point at yourself and say, *"Look at this!"*

Spirals and spread eagles, which are harder to do well than you might think, show off edges, balance, flexibility, and speed. But they have to seem effortless and smooth.

Spins can be more tiring than jumps. You have to use all your muscles to hold your body tight in order to get the most revolution and speed that you can while staying centered on one spot. You have to be able to step out of a spin and into the next part of your program as if it's the easiest thing in the world.

Kwan needs to stay focused both before and during a competition.

As with spins, the most difficult and athletic jumps take great strength. You have to have speed going into your jump and speed coming out of it. You need power in your legs to push yourself high into the air.

But a skater's mind has to be strong, too, and focused. It shouldn't look to the judges like this triple Lutz is any more difficult than anything else you've done. With combination jumps, the second one has to follow the first one smoothly.

Look at three-time world champion Elvis Stojko. He does quadruple/triple combinations. That's *seven revolutions,* total! It's amazingly difficult, but he makes it look simple.

When I started as a Senior, my programs were bumpy. The jumps and the steps and the spins weren't connected. I didn't let the music help me flow from one move to another. I didn't understand about *interpreting* the music. I rarely even smiled when I skated back then. To get to the level of great artists like Peggy, Dorothy, and Brian, you have to be *both* an athlete and an artist.

Most elite skaters have three forty-five-minute long practice sessions on the ice every day, usually with their coaches. They spend at least another hour in a gym making their muscles stronger and more flexible. On top of that, they work "on the floor" with their coaches, practicing jumps without the momentum and speed the ice gives them. They spend hours and hours with their choreographers developing new programs.

At the end of a day like this your body aches everywhere. Your back hurts from doing layback spins. Your bottom hurts from falling. Your shoulders, your legs — you just hurt all over. But there's still more to do.

Every month there's at least one major competition, plus exhibitions. The most important competitions come in the late winter and early spring. Nationals are in January or February and Worlds are in March. And in an Olympic year, the Olympics take place between Nationals and Worlds. So you can see, there's hardly any time between the competitions to take a breath!

There are costumes to be fitted and fixed — costumes are my mother's specialty (she works together with a designer on mine). But aside from practice clothes and gloves, the only piece of equipment a skater needs is her skates. (A warning about gloves: Skaters use them to wipe their noses, which run like crazy on an ice rink. Never borrow a skater's gloves!)

Most skaters use just one pair of skates all year long. They usually get a new pair at the beginning of the season, and it takes weeks and weeks to break them in. Sometimes it takes all season to get them just right. When I first start using new skates, it's agony. Most skaters have really ugly feet. You should see how swollen and gnarled my toes are when I take off my skates. On second thought, you don't want to!

I'd always worn used skates and didn't get an actual brand-new pair of skates until 1995 (they're expensive!). A skater has to pick out the right boot and then put the blade on with screws.

My father is good with skates. For years he cut the heels of my boots lower for me so that my weight wouldn't go too far forward. And he always has to fiddle with the blade, making sure it's placed properly.

Sometimes everything feels different in new skates. Your weight is distributed differently. Your balance feels strange. A jump that was no problem at all last year is suddenly impossible — until you figure out how to adjust yourself to new skates.

Adjustment is something young skaters have to deal with just about every day. Our bodies are always changing. Not only do we get taller all the time, but as we get older we find a pound or two in places we never even noticed before. Luckily the changes don't usually happen overnight. When we're on the ice every day, we can adjust to them gradually.

I *love* moving across the ice. So I didn't mind when I started to get a little bigger and stronger because I could put some real weight into my edges and increase my speed. I was able to really *cover* the surface of the ice. That's when I feel most like I'm flying.

Another change that happened when I became a Senior skater was that I had the chance to be noticed by the millions of people who watch skating on TV.

If you're an amateur and eligible to compete in all the major competitions, like the Olympics, that doesn't mean you can't do *any* professional work. There are professional competitions and exhibitions throughout the year that the USFSA allows eligible skaters to do, and some of them pay very well.

Kwan's love of skating shows in this spectacular leap.

Money wasn't in the picture for *me* yet, though. If anything, the cost of training went up then — by a lot. The scholarships that Karen and I received paid for our living expenses and ice-time at Ice Castle. The USFSA gave us some support, too. But we had to pay Frank and buy skates. We also each had to have three costumes a year. Plus it was expensive to travel to the competitions — which, now that I was a Senior, were all over the world!

The life of a top-level skater is intense. A lot of skaters get so overwhelmed by it that they can't even think about their schoolwork. Many drop out of school. But I'd never want to do that, and my parents would never let me.

While all of this new activity was going on, I also had to study. I went to a regular school until the eighth grade when I became a Senior skater and my schedule got crazy. Since then I've had a tutor, who comes to my house. But that doesn't mean I have it easy. I still have to take tests and do homework (lots of it!), just like everybody else.

One of the most difficult and important challenges of being a full-time skater at such a young age is remembering that skating isn't everything. You have to work hard to remember that you're just at the very *beginning* of your life. People may call you a "Lady" or a "woman skater" or a "Senior," but you can't forget that you're really still a kid. And you can never forget how important school is.

That's why I've always tried to carry two images of myself in my mind. There's the picture of the skater I dream of being. But skating is only a sport, after all, and you should only do it if you really love it. The bigger picture I keep in mind is of the *person* I want to be and the life I want to live. That's the real challenge.

Meet the Author

MICHELLE KWAN

FACT FILE

Born: July 7, 1980

Birthplace: Torrance, California

Hometown: Lake Arrowhead, California

Family: Michelle Kwan is the youngest of three children. She has a brother, Ron, and a sister, Karen.

First skating experience: She first stepped onto the ice at age five, after watching her older brother play hockey.

Early success: Kwan won her first skating competition at the age of seven.

Continued success: She was named the 1996 Female Athlete of the Year by the United States Olympic Committee.

Records: Kwan is the only multiple winner of the Skater of the Year Award from the U.S. Figure Skating Association. At the U.S. Nationals she received fifteen 6.0s (out of eighteen) for artistry, more than any other U.S. skater in history.

Hobbies: When she's not skating, Kwan enjoys swimming, bowling, bicycling, and spending time with friends.

Skating philosophy: "Work hard, be yourself, and have fun."

Second book: Kwan is also the author of *The Winning Attitude: What It Takes To Be a Champion.*

Internet

If you would like to learn more about Michelle Kwan, visit Education Place. **www.eduplace.com/kids**

151

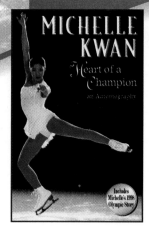

Think About the Selection

1. Do you think Michelle's decision to become a Senior skater is a good one? Why or why not?

2. Would you rather be the best member of a less-skilled group, or, like Michelle, a newcomer in a very talented group? Explain.

3. How do Michelle's parents support her desire to become a great skater? Give examples from the selection to support your answer.

4. Would you enjoy the challenges and hard work of a skater's life? Why or why not?

5. How does Michelle's opinion of herself change during the time period of the selection? What events help cause this change?

6. Michelle says she has two images of herself: as a great skater and as a good person. Why do you think these two images are important to her?

7. **Connecting/Comparing** Compare Michelle Kwan's determination with Warren Faidley's in *Eye of the Storm.* How are they alike? How are they different?

Write About a Performance

Write a newspaper article that describes a skating performance. Tell whether the skater performed well or not and why. What qualities or skills made the skater stand out?

Tips

- Use active verbs and colorful, specific, descriptive words.
- Order the details in a way that makes sense. Consider chronological order or order of importance.

Calculate Elapsed Time

Six skaters, two women and four men, each present a "long program" (described on page 144). There is a ten-minute break between skaters. How long will the performance for all skaters last? How much of the total time will be skating time, and how much will be waiting time?

BONUS **Make up your own math "riddle of the rink." Give it to a friend to answer.**

Give a Pep Talk

A skating coach might give a pep talk to encourage a skater before a performance. Draft a pep talk Frank might give to Michelle just before she goes onto the ice at a big competition. Then, with a partner playing the role of Michelle, give your pep talk in front of the class.

Tips

- **Use cheerful, encouraging language.**
- **Include a few last-minute pointers about the performance.**

Internet

Complete a Web Crossword Puzzle

You've learned a lot about ice skating and Michelle Kwan. Test what you know by completing a crossword puzzle that can be printed from Education Place.

www.eduplace.com/kids

The Eleven Cities Tour

Hundreds of miles of canals criss-cross the Netherlands, a flat, low-lying country on the western edge of Europe. For much of the year, boats use these canals to travel between Dutch towns and cities. But when the weather gets cold enough, the traffic on the canals changes as Dutch skaters by the millions hit the ice. Those long, straight stretches of frozen canals allow the Dutch to give full rein to their national passion: speed skating. ·······························

If figure skating is a little like dancing, speed skating is like running. And because the Netherlands is one of the few countries in the world where you can run from town to town on skates, the skating **tour** has become especially popular. In a tour, skaters follow a route that visits a certain number of cities. Tours may be skated as races, or just for the fun and challenge of completing them.

The Eleven Cities Tour, or *Elfstedentocht*, is probably the most famous of these tours. The idea behind it goes back to the 1700s, when individuals attempted to skate between all eleven towns of Friesland, a northern province of the Netherlands. Those who made it were considered to be very skilled skaters.

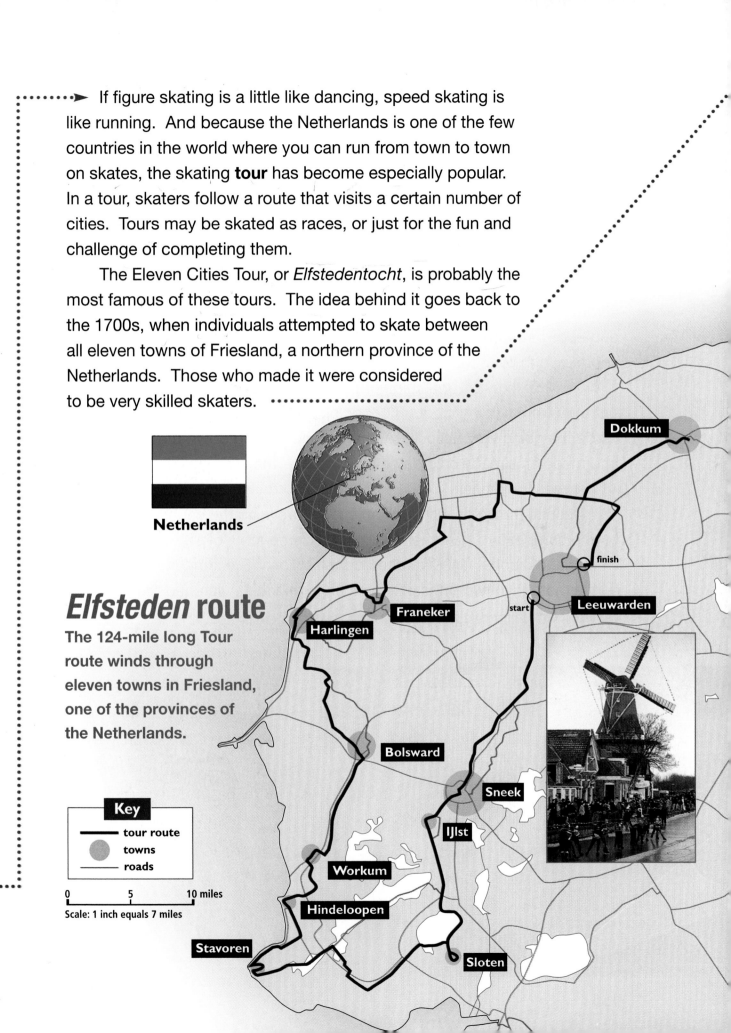

Netherlands

Elfsteden route

The 124-mile long Tour route winds through eleven towns in Friesland, one of the provinces of the Netherlands.

Dokkum

finish

Franeker

start

Leeuwarden

Harlingen

Bolsward

Sneek

Key

—— tour route

● towns

— roads

IJlst

0   5   10 miles

Scale: 1 inch equals 7 miles

Workum

Hindeloopen

Stavoren

Sloten

The first official Eleven Cities Tour race took place in 1909, but it has been held only fourteen times since then. In order for the Tour to take place, the ice must be frozen at least six inches thick all along the race route. Winters in the Netherlands don't usually get that cold, so many years may go by between one race and the next. There was no Eleven Cities Tour between 1963 and 1985, a gap of twenty-two years!

The winter of 1997 was an especially cold one, though, and on January 2, the board in charge of the Tour made an announcement: the race — the first since 1986 — would be held in two days. Skaters scrambled to make it to Leeuwarden, the city where the race begins and ends. Finally, at 5:30 in the morning on January 4, the starting gun sounded and over 16,000 racers were off and skating.

Competitors had until midnight to complete the 124-mile race, but they were skating in tough conditions. Bumps and holes in the ice made the going very difficult. A strong wind slowed down the racers and made an already cold day even colder — the wind-chill factor was –4 degrees Fahrenheit.

Despite the cold, half a million spectators lined the canals to cheer on the competitors. Another nine million, three-fifths of the Netherlands' population, watched on television. (By comparison, only a little more than two-fifths of American households watched the 1997 Super Bowl.)

The first racers crossed the finish line a little after noon. Other skaters continued to come in throughout the afternoon. By midnight, many were begging spectators to push them across the finish line so they could receive a medal for completing the race. Over 6,000 competitors weren't able to finish, dropping out because of exhaustion, frostbite, or other injuries.

Obstacles were nothing new for the Eleven Cities Tour. The winner of the 1929 race lost a toe to frostbite. And the 1963 race took place in a blizzard so severe that only 126 of the 9,862 participants were able to make it to the finish line.

Although there were several Olympic skaters in the field, the winner of the 1997 Tour was Henk Angenent, a Dutch Brussels-sprout farmer who completed the course in 6 hours, 49 minutes. The winner of the women's division, Klasina Seinstra, had a time of 7:49. Their prizes? No cash — just a medal and the honor of having their names placed on the winners' list of the Netherlands' greatest race.

Klasina Seinstra and Henk Angenent join the list of Tour champions.

A Personal Essay

A personal essay explains the writer's opinion on a topic and gives reasons to support the opinion. Use this student's writing as a model when you write a personal essay of your own.

Becoming an Actor

My name is Johnny, and I am currently a fifth grader in California. There are many things I like to do such as drawing, swimming, or playing with my friends Colby, Matt, and Benji. When I grow up, I want to become an actor. My goal is to follow my dream and give it all I've got to become a professional stage and film actor.

I really think that if you want to be a well-rounded actor, it is important to learn how to be a great dancer. Right now I am taking a musical theater class in San Diego. Some people my age think that dancing is just for girls. In my opinion, jazz, ballet, and tap are fun to learn. Some of the greatest football players have learned ballet to help them with their form. I am taking dancing classes because I have always liked dancing, and I know in the long run it will help me with my acting.

A **beginning** often states a goal.

A personal essay states an **opinion** near the beginning.

Acting classes are getting me ready to become an actor. My dad drives me up to Los Angeles every Saturday for acting classes. I am learning how to read scripts, and I am also learning how to pull out emotions on the spot. It's not as easy as it looks to be on the stage or on television. I am learning that becoming an actor is a lot of hard work but a lot of fun at the same time.

My advice to anyone wanting to become an actor would be not to give up hope. There are so many people who want to become actors and so many good actors who work very hard, but many of them give up too fast and too soon. It is very easy to get discouraged if you are rejected at auditions.

I feel lucky to be starting so young. I know that if I learn from the best and I am dedicated to becoming a well-rounded actor, I will someday reach my goal of acting on the stage, television, or film.

> It's important to stay with the **focus**.

> Using **details** makes an essay come alive.

> A good **ending** ties the essay together.

Meet the Author

Johnny U.
Grade: five
State: California
Hobbies: acting, drawing, and swimming
What he wants to be when he grows up: an actor

La Bamba

Baseball in April

AND OTHER STORIES
GARY SOTO

Talent

Have you ever been to a talent show? Most talent shows include several different kinds of acts. For example, the main character in "La Bamba" pantomimes, or acts out, the words to a forty-five record.

Show!

Whether the talent show is competitive or just for fun, being on stage in front of an audience can be a little scary. But, if you really like being in the limelight, you'll forget all about your fears once you hear the applause!

Everyone has a talent. Yours might be playing an instrument, reciting a poem, acting in a skit, or telling jokes. What would you perform in a talent show?

Meet the Author GARY SOTO

Gary Soto grew up in a Mexican American neighborhood in Fresno, California. Memories from his childhood inspire many of his short stories. His idea for "La Bamba" comes from a classmate who forgot the words to the song "Sugar Shack" during the school talent show.

Besides writing, Soto enjoys reading, Aztec dancing, traveling, and practicing karate. In 1999, he was honored with the Literature Award of the Hispanic Heritage Foundation. Soto's other books for young readers include *Boys at Work*, *The Pool Party*, *Off and Running*, *Local News*, and *Crazy Weekend*.

Meet the Illustrator JOSÉ ORTEGA

Born in Guayaquil, Ecuador, José Ortega moved to the United States when he was five years old. He tells young people that "the most important thing is what gets you excited about working on something for hours. In the end, you are discovering yourself."

To find out more about Gary Soto and José Ortega, visit Education Place.

www.eduplace.com/kids

162

La Bamba

From **Baseball in April**

By **Gary Soto**

Selection Illustrated by **José Ortega**

Strategy Focus

What will happen when Manuel enters his school's talent show? As you read the selection, **summarize** the problem and the events in your own words.

163

Manuel was the fourth of seven children and looked like a lot of kids in his neighborhood: black hair, brown face, and skinny legs scuffed from summer play. But summer was giving way to fall: the trees were turning red, the lawns brown, and the pomegranate trees were heavy with fruit. Manuel walked to school in the frosty morning, kicking leaves and thinking of tomorrow's talent show. He was still amazed that he had volunteered. He was going to pretend to sing Ritchie Valens's "La Bamba" before the entire school.

Why did I raise my hand? he asked himself, but in his heart he knew the answer. He yearned for the limelight. He wanted applause as loud as a thunderstorm, and to hear his friends say, "Man, that was bad!" And he wanted to impress the girls, especially Petra Lopez, the second-prettiest girl in his class. The prettiest was already taken by his friend Ernie. Manuel knew he should be reasonable, since he himself was not great-looking, just average.

Manuel kicked through the fresh-fallen leaves. When he got to school he realized he had forgotten his math workbook. If his teacher found out, he would have to stay after school and miss practice for the talent show. But fortunately for him, they did drills that morning.

During lunch Manuel hung around with Benny, who was also in the talent show. Benny was going to play the trumpet in spite of the fat lip he had gotten playing football.

"How do I look?" Manuel asked. He cleared his throat and started moving his lips in pantomime. No words came out, just a hiss that sounded like a snake. Manuel tried to look emotional, flailing his arms on the high notes and opening his eyes and mouth as wide as he could when he came to *"Para bailar la baaaaammmba."*

After Manuel finished, Benny said it looked all right, but suggested Manuel dance while he sang. Manuel thought for a moment and decided it was a good idea.

"Yeah, just think you're like some rock star," Benny suggested. "But don't get carried away."

During rehearsal, Mr. Roybal, nervous about his debut as the school's talent coordinator, muttered under his breath when the lever that controlled the speed on the record player jammed.

"Darn," he growled, trying to force the lever. "What's wrong with you?"

"Is it broken?" Manuel asked, bending over for a closer look. It looked all right to him.

Mr. Roybal assured Manuel that he would have a good record player at the talent show, even if it meant bringing his own stereo from home.

Manuel sat in a folding chair, twirling his record on his thumb. He watched a skit about personal hygiene, a mother-and-daughter violin duo, five first-grade girls jumping rope, a karate kid breaking boards, and a skit about the pilgrims. If the record player hadn't been broken, he would have gone after the karate kid, an easy act to follow, he told himself.

As he twirled his forty-five record, Manuel thought they had a great talent show. The entire school would be amazed. His mother and father would be proud, and his brothers and sisters would be jealous and pout. It would be a night to remember.

Benny walked onto the stage, raised his trumpet to his mouth, and waited for his cue. Mr. Roybal raised his hand like a symphony conductor and let it fall dramatically. Benny inhaled and blew so loud that Manuel dropped his record, which rolled across the cafeteria floor until it hit a wall. Manuel raced after it, picked it up, and wiped it clean.

"Boy, I'm glad it didn't break," he said with a sigh.

That night Manuel had to do the dishes and a lot of homework, so he could only practice in the shower. In bed he prayed that he wouldn't mess up. He prayed that it wouldn't be like when he was a first-grader. For Science Week he had wired together a C battery and a bulb, and told everyone he had discovered how a flashlight worked. He was so pleased with himself that he practiced for hours pressing the wire to the battery, making the bulb wink a dim, orangish light. He showed it to so many kids in his neighborhood that when it was time to show his class how a flashlight worked, the battery was dead. He pressed the wire to the battery, but the bulb didn't respond. He pressed until his thumb hurt and some kids in the back started snickering.

But Manuel fell asleep confident that nothing would go wrong this time.

The next morning his father and mother beamed at him. They were proud that he was going to be in the talent show.

"I wish you would tell us what you're doing," his mother said. His father, a pharmacist who wore a blue smock with his name on a plastic rectangle, looked up from the newspaper and sided with his wife. "Yes, what are you doing in the talent show?"

"You'll see," Manuel said with his mouth full of cereal.

The day whizzed by, and so did his afternoon chores and dinner. Suddenly he was dressed in his best clothes and standing next to Benny backstage, listening to the commotion as the cafeteria filled with school kids and parents. The lights dimmed, and Mr. Roybal, sweaty in a tight suit and a necktie with a large knot, wet his lips and parted the stage curtains.

"Good evening, everyone," the kids behind the curtain heard him say. "Good evening to you," some of the smart-alecky kids said back to him.

"Tonight we bring you the best John Burroughs Elementary has to offer, and I'm sure that you'll be both pleased and amazed that our little school houses so much talent. And now, without further ado, let's get on with the show." He turned and, with a swish of his hand, commanded, "Part the curtain." The curtains parted in jerks. A girl dressed as a toothbrush and a boy dressed as a dirty gray tooth walked onto the stage and sang:

Brush, brush, brush
Floss, floss, floss
Gargle the germs away — hey! hey! hey!

After they finished singing, they turned to Mr. Roybal, who dropped his hand. The toothbrush dashed around the stage after the dirty tooth, which was laughing and having a great time until it slipped and nearly rolled off the stage.

Mr. Roybal jumped out and caught it just in time. "Are you OK?"

The dirty tooth answered, "Ask my dentist," which drew laughter and applause from the audience.

The violin duo played next, and except for one time when the girl got lost, they sounded fine. People applauded, and some even stood up. Then the first-grade girls maneuvered onto the stage while jumping rope. They were all smiles and bouncing ponytails as a hundred cameras flashed at once. Mothers "awhed" and fathers sat up proudly.

The karate kid was next. He did a few kicks, yells, and chops, and finally, when his father held up a board, punched it in two. The audience clapped and looked at each other, wide-eyed with respect. The boy bowed to the audience, and father and son ran off the stage.

Manuel remained behind the stage shivering with fear. He mouthed the words to "La Bamba" and swayed from left to right. Why did he raise his hand and volunteer? Why couldn't he have just sat there like the rest of the kids and not said anything? While the karate kid was on stage, Mr. Roybal, more sweaty than before, took Manuel's forty-five record and placed it on a new record player.

"You ready?" Mr. Roybal asked.

"Yeah . . ."

171

Mr. Roybal walked back on stage and announced that Manuel Gomez, a fifth-grader in Mrs. Knight's class, was going to pantomime Ritchie Valens's classic hit "La Bamba."

The cafeteria roared with applause. Manuel was nervous but loved the noisy crowd. He pictured his mother and father applauding loudly and his brothers and sisters also clapping, though not as energetically.

Manuel walked on stage and the song started immediately. Glassy-eyed from the shock of being in front of so many people, Manuel moved his lips and swayed in a made-up dance step. He couldn't see his parents, but he could see his brother Mario, who was a year younger, thumb-wrestling with a friend. Mario was wearing Manuel's favorite shirt; he would deal with Mario later. He saw some other kids get up and head for the drinking fountain, and a baby sitting in the middle of an aisle sucking her thumb and watching him intently.

What am I doing here? thought Manuel. This is no fun at all. Everyone was just sitting there. Some people were moving to the beat, but most were just watching him, like they would a monkey at the zoo.

But when Manuel did a fancy dance step, there was a burst of applause and some girls screamed. Manuel tried another dance step. He heard more applause and screams and started getting into the groove as he shivered and snaked around the stage. But the record got stuck, and he had to sing

Para bailar la bamba
Para bailar la bamba
Para bailar la bamba
Para bailar la bamba

again and again.

Manuel couldn't believe his bad luck. The audience began to laugh and stand up in their chairs. Manuel remembered how the forty-five record had dropped from his hand and rolled across the

172

cafeteria floor. It probably got scratched, he thought, and now it was stuck, and he was stuck dancing and moving his lips to the same words over and over. He had never been so embarrassed. He would have to ask his parents to move the family out of town.

After Mr. Roybal ripped the needle across the record, Manuel slowed his dance steps to a halt. He didn't know what to do except bow to the audience, which applauded wildly, and scoot off the stage, on the verge of tears. This was worse than the homemade flashlight. At least no one laughed then, they just snickered.

Manuel stood alone, trying hard to hold back the tears as Benny, center stage, played his trumpet. Manuel was jealous because he sounded great, then mad as he recalled that it was Benny's loud trumpet playing that made the forty-five record fly out of his hands. But when the entire cast lined up for a curtain call, Manuel received a burst of applause that was so loud it shook the walls of the cafeteria. Later, as he mingled with the kids and parents, everyone patted him on the shoulder and told him, "Way to go. You were really funny."

Funny? Manuel thought. Did he do something funny?

Funny. Crazy. Hilarious. These were the words people said to him. He was confused, but beyond caring. All he knew was that people were paying attention to him, and his brothers and sisters looked at him with a mixture of jealousy and awe. He was going to pull Mario aside and punch him in the arm for wearing his shirt, but he cooled it. He was enjoying the limelight. A teacher brought him cookies and punch, and the popular kids who had never before given him the time of day now clustered around him. Ricardo, the editor of the school bulletin, asked him how he made the needle stick.

"It just happened," Manuel said, crunching on a star-shaped cookie.

At home that night his father, eager to undo the buttons on his shirt and ease into his recliner, asked Manuel the same thing, how he managed to make the song stick on the words *"Para bailar la bamba."*

Manuel thought quickly and reached for scientific jargon he had read in magazines. "Easy, Dad. I used laser tracking with high optics and low functional decibels per channel." His proud but confused father told him to be quiet and go to bed.

"Ah, *que niños tan truchas*," he said as he walked to the kitchen for a glass of milk. "I don't know how you kids nowadays get so smart."

Manuel, feeling happy, went to his bedroom, undressed, and slipped into his pajamas. He looked in the mirror and began to pantomime "La Bamba," but stopped because he was tired of the song. He crawled into bed. The sheets were as cold as the moon that stood over the peach tree in their backyard.

He was relieved that the day was over. Next year, when they asked for volunteers for the talent show, he wouldn't raise his hand. Probably.

Think About the Selection

1. Describe the different emotions Manuel feels at the beginning of the story. How would you have felt in his position?

2. How well do you think Manuel handles the unpleasant surprise of the scratched record? What else could he have done when the record started to skip?

3. Compare Manuel's experience with the flashlight and his experience with the record. Which one do you think was worse? Why?

4. What do you think Manuel learns about himself as a result of the talent show?

5. Think about the different talents of the students who perform in "La Bamba." If you could perform in a talent show, what would you do?

6. Why do you think the author ends the story with the word *Probably*?

7. Connecting/Comparing What advice about performing might Michelle Kwan give Manuel? What advice might he give to her?

Write a Sequel

Suppose that Manuel *does* volunteer for the next school talent show. What kind of act might he perform? Write a follow-up story about what Manuel does to get into the limelight once again.

- List five words that describe Manuel.
- Keep these qualities in mind as you write your sequel.
- Be sure to include a problem and a solution.

List Sounds in a Sequence

Frequency is the number of sound waves made per second. A low sound, like a rumble, has a low frequency. A high sound, like a squeak, has a high frequency. List all of the sounds of the talent show in "La Bamba," including applause. Order them according to what you think their frequencies are, from lowest to highest.

Bonus **Create a similar chart for the sound frequencies of your classroom.**

Make a Poster

Create a poster that advertises the talent show in "La Bamba," including the acts. Make the poster colorful and exciting so that people will want to come and see the show. You can cut out pictures from magazines or draw your own.

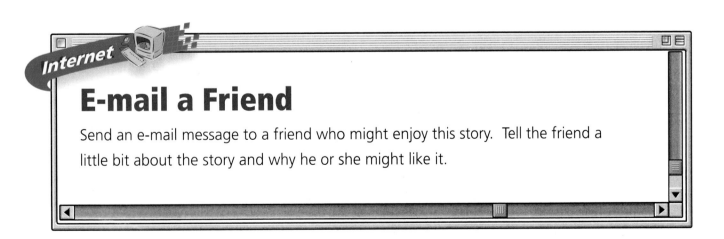

Internet

E-mail a Friend

Send an e-mail message to a friend who might enjoy this story. Tell the friend a little bit about the story and why he or she might like it.

Skill: How to Read a Timeline

❶ Read the title to find out what events the timeline shows.

❷ Locate the **first** and **last dates** to find out what time period is being shown.

❸ Read the **events** from left to right, or from earliest to latest event, depending on how the timeline is arranged.

History of Recorded Sound

If you were to pantomime in a talent show, as Manuel did, you would probably play a cassette tape or a CD, not a vinyl record. The timeline below shows how recording and listening to music has changed in just a few generations.

1870   1880

1877

Thomas Edison invents a phonograph with a tinfoil cylinder, making the first recording of a human voice ("Mary Had a Little Lamb").

1887

Emile Berliner patents the Gramophone, a new type of phonograph, by using a disc made of durable shellac.

1927

The electric "juke box" is invented to replace pianos that play when coins are inserted.

1906

The Victrola, a phonograph in an enclosed cabinet, is introduced.

1890   **1900**   **1910**   **1920**

1898

Valdemar Poulsen patents the first magnetic recorder, called the Telegraphone, using steel wire.

1915

The "record player" is invented; it allows records to be played at 78 revolutions per minute (rpm).

1960s

Music is recorded on plastic tape — either on 8-tracks, which are about the size of a standard paperback book, or on cassettes.

1949

The first extended play 45 rpm vinyl record is introduced.

1935

The Magnetophone, the first true magnetic tape recorder, is invented.

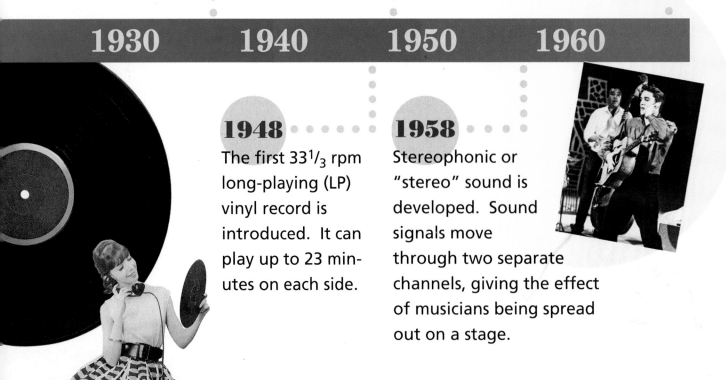

1930	1940	1950	1960

1948

The first 33$\frac{1}{3}$ rpm long-playing (LP) vinyl record is introduced. It can play up to 23 minutes on each side.

1958

Stereophonic or "stereo" sound is developed. Sound signals move through two separate channels, giving the effect of musicians being spread out on a stage.

Twenty-First Century:
Enhanced CDs, recordable mini-discs (MDs), and Digital Compact Cassettes (DCCs) will become more widely available.

1983

Compact discs (CDs) and players, which use laser technology, are available for the first time in the U.S. Unlike vinyl records, CDs cannot be worn down.

1970s

Music is recorded digitally using laser beams.

1970   1980   1990   2000   2010

1988

CDs outsell record albums for the first time.

1979

The first portable audio cassette player with head-phones is introduced.

Facing Fear!

Everyone is afraid of *something*. The main character in *The Fear Place* is **terrified** of being on a high mountain ledge. Do you have a fear place?

It's a mystery why people are **frightened** by some things, but not other things. You might be scared of spiders, while your friend keeps one as a pet. Your friend might dislike roller coasters, while you get a feeling of **excitement** or **adventure** from them.

There are many ways to deal with fear. You could try to avoid the thing that scares you. Or, little by little, you could get used to something until one day it doesn't seem as scary as it did before. Sometime you may find yourself forced to face your fear. You just might surprise yourself by having more courage than you thought possible.

Meet the Author **Phyllis Reynolds Naylor**

Early writing: In elementary school, Naylor began writing her own stories. She made booklets by stapling scrap paper together. After writing the story and drawing the pictures, she would glue an envelope to the inside cover. Placing an index card inside it made it look like a library book that her friends could check out. "I was the author, illustrator, printer, binder, and librarian, all in one."

Favorite part of her job: She says that "the best part about writing is the moment a character comes alive on paper, or when a place that existed only in my head becomes real."

Accomplishments: Naylor published her first story at age sixteen and since then has written over 100 books for children and adults, including the Newbery Award-winner *Shiloh*. She is also the author of *Saving Shiloh*, *Shiloh Season*, *The Grand Escape*, *The Healing of Texas Jake*, and *The Boys Start the War*.

Meet the Illustrator **Paul Lee**

Hobby: "I yo-yo. Wherever I go, I always have at least one yo-yo on me, usually in a holster on my belt. It comes in handy when I have to wait in line for something."

Career choice: "I realized that I would not be happy unless I had a future in which I could draw all the time."

Advice to artists: "Practice. Practice. Practice."

Internet

For more about Phyllis Reynolds Naylor and Paul Lee, visit Education Place.

www.eduplace.com/kids

T·H·E Fear PLACE

PHYLLIS REYNOLDS NAYLOR

Strategy Focus

Look at the title, introduction, and illustrations before you read the selection. What can you **infer** about Doug? What do you **predict** will happen?

185

On vacation in Colorado, Doug Grillo is alone. His parents have left on an emergency. His brother Gordie has gone off by himself after a fight with Doug. (Their mom and *her* brother fought, too.) Doug has kept busy studying mammals for his Scout merit badge, even befriending a cougar he calls Charlie. But now he has set off to find Gordie. To reach him, Doug must find the same courage his dad found when he fled Cuba. Doug must get past his Fear Place: a narrow ledge six hundred feet above a canyon, which he had vowed never to face again.

What path there was led over scattered pitches of bedrock, across ramps of boggy tundra, then climbed some more, becoming a narrow, zigzagging passageway. Doug followed the steep-slanting boilerplate rock, ledged with wildflowers, catching glimpses now and then of a distant snowfield. At one point he could see a ridge far above where he could just make out an elk cow leading her calf.

At times the journey seemed futile, for Doug would climb, scrabbling and panting, up the rock face, around steep boulders, then make his way, feet sliding, down another gully, losing all the altitude he'd worked so hard to gain.

He was dismayed that he was thirsty again. At this rate, there would be little left for Gordie, so he took the cap off his canteen and drank only a swallow.

Every time he stopped, the fear inside him grew larger, however. At times it seemed to be the climb that frightened him most; other times it was worry about his brother. And then, as though that weren't worry enough, his parents. He plowed on, keeping his mind on other things, trying to remember the wildlife he'd seen so far. Elks — he could use those in his report; a snowshoe rabbit — he'd use that one, too. And a marten. He'd also seen two Steller's jays and a gray jay. Too bad he wasn't working on a merit badge in Bird Study while he was here.

Doug was nearing the first ridge. At nine thousand feet, he'd read, oxygen was about half of what it was at sea level. He had no idea how high he was. Stormy Peaks, to his left, was over twelve thousand feet. With each ascending step, the air seemed to change. A mountain has its own weather, Dad had told him. At high altitudes, a hiker could encounter sunshine, rain, sleet, ice pellets, wind, and snow, all in one afternoon, sometimes even in the space of an hour. The weather changed minute by minute, valley by valley, range by range.

It helped to keep his mind busy.

"This isn't so bad," he said aloud, wanting to hear a human voice, even his own. "You've climbed a lot worse than this."

Walking along the ridge crest, he followed a route through a long granite fin that stretched like a roofless tunnel before him. He remembered this tunnel from the first time he was up here, and was reassured he was on the right path. If only it went on like this all the way to where Gordon was camped, he'd have no problem. He had strength; stamina. A climb like this, no matter how rocky, he could do forever, as long as there were sides to enclose him.

When he came out again into open space, the winds buffeted him. A hawk he had startled from a nearby rock flew directly past, so close that Doug could hear the steady flap of its wings. He held tightly to a rock, not wanting to look down, but did. It didn't frighten him particularly, because there was plenty of room between him and the edge. Over the rocky hogbacks slabbed with quartz and sprinkled with muscovite, he could see a tongue of aspen crowding the narrow gorge below. It looked like the set for a model railroad.

It occurred to him that if he were more like the other members of his family, he would actually enjoy a hike like this. He would have set out that morning with a feeling of excitement. Then he thought of Gordon and how this wasn't the time for adventure. What would he find when he got up there? All the possibilities . . .

That was another word to remember, possibilities. Almost anything was possible, Mom had told him once. But not everything was probable. Which was more likely, that he'd find Gordon okay up there on the ridge, or that something awful had happened? That he'd find Gordon okay, he guessed.

Which was more likely, that he would get around the ledge just fine, or that his foot would slip and he'd fall six hundred feet to his death? He shakily sucked in his breath. That everyone else would be able to get around the ledge without trouble he had no doubt. That he, Doug Grillo, could do it, was a different story.

So he tried to think of the climb as something ordinary. When he stopped at the next level place on the trail, not even winded, he took time

190

to look out between the trees. He could just make out Longs Peak from here — "old granitehead," they called it.

Weird, he was thinking now, that there were probably a hundred climbers on it right this minute, and Doug couldn't see any of them. Looking into the distance at Longs Peak, in the quiet of morning, it looked peaceful and unthreatening.

It didn't fool him for a minute. He knew the stories of the people who had died. He knew about the guy who . . . Doug pushed the thought out of his mind. Don't! he told himself as he set off again. Concentrate on rocks.

Okay. Rocks. Precambrian rock, his dad had told him. The rock that formed Longs Peak was here before there was anything else on the planet. Heat and pressure changed sediments to harder and harder rock, until sediments became schist and gneiss, quartz and feldspar. Mica. Layers of rock. Layers that had their beginnings in some huge disturbance inside the earth. He'd done a paper on it once for science.

Doug didn't know why, but he felt a vague sense of discomfort, like some unpleasant memory tapping at the side of his head. No, he thought fiercely. He was doing too well. No unpleasant thoughts now, thank you.

The muscles in Doug's legs carried him easily with each stride. He forced himself to think positively, concentrating on his strength. He didn't even bother to rest at the next place the ground leveled out, but moved on around the curve of the mountain, inching down steep, rocky troughs chiseled out by water, then making his way through a long maze of rocky outcrops.

Layers. It came back to him now. That was the word that seemed so unpleasant. Layers of rock, he'd been thinking, that had their beginnings in some huge . . . Layers of feelings, of grudges. Wasn't that how Mom had described it, with her and Uncle Lloyd? One thing piled on top of another, she had said. So many layers we never did get to the bottom of it.

Would Mom have climbed this mountain to rescue Lloyd? Well, Doug was doing it for Gordon, wasn't he? So no, what happened between her and Lloyd was not the same as him and Gordie at all. She was right.

There was a noise behind him and he stopped. It was like a rock falling, tumbling — rolling behind him down the trail, too far back for him to have caused it. He turned and waited, seeing nothing, hearing nothing more, then moved on again.

At this point there was a vertical face of rock on one side of him, boulders and scrub trees on the other. With each upward step he took, the small trees retreated from the landscape, but the wide expanse of boulders remained. He liked that — liked a wide span between him and the gorge below, a monstrous guardrail. If ever the fear that terrified him in high places convinced him to simply fling himself over the edge and get it over with, the boulders would be there to say no.

Suddenly he felt that familiar thump against his thigh.

"Man, Charlie!" he gasped, leaning against the rock wall. "You scared me half to death!"

The cougar came up around him, looked at Doug a moment, then moved on, checking once to see if he was coming.

"Hold your horses," he said, unsure of whether he wanted her with him or not.

Was it conceivable, he wondered, that the cougar had a den up here? That she spent most of the day among the rocks, coming home each morning, then going out to hunt around dusk?

That was another thing to think about now, one more thing to occupy his mind. But thinking about Charlie led to thinking about Gordon, and Doug decided it would have been better if the cat hadn't come.

The rocky path far up ahead suddenly fell into shadow, and Doug glanced at the sky. The clouds overhead were hard to read. Dark around the edges, with the sun gleaming behind them, and the wind trying to push them, unwanted, from this part of the sky.

The farther Doug climbed, the narrower the stretch of safety on his left. When he first started out, there was nothing at all but trees and meadow, then trees and rocks, then mostly boulders and a few scrubby trees. Each time he stepped, however, the span on his left grew smaller.

Now the low, twisted trees gave way to rock entirely, and the span had narrowed to the point that Doug could see the gorge below almost continuously. The hillside seemed to be receding, the edge coming closer to the trail. There were a few places, Doug was sure, where, if he were to lie down crosswise on the path, his feet against the cliff, his arms stretched above his head, his fingers would touch the drop-off.

He tried to redirect his thoughts.

"How you doin' up there, Charlie?" he called shakily to the cougar, who seemed to be waiting for him at the next rise. The cat stretched out her head toward the sun and panted, the closest thing yet to a smile.

But there was a drumbeat starting now in Doug's chest; he could feel it. Seemed almost to hear it. Like a foghorn out over a bay; the far-off whistle of a train. . . .

He thought of various guys in his troop — how they would be enjoying the trail about now, exclaiming every time there was a new view of the canyon below. He tried to imagine himself in their bodies, becoming Frank Jameson, for example, or Teddy Heinz. They were always the first ones to the top of any climb.

But it didn't work. He *wasn't* Teddy or Frank, he was Doug Grillo, who had come up this way with his family two years ago and had not been able to make it back without help. Now he was Doug Grillo here alone.

About two hundred yards more, he guessed, and he'd be at the spot. Snow-splattered ridges gleamed in the distance. He felt he could remember every rock, every root of the ledge. Should he stop awhile and get his nerve up? Catch his breath?

He kept going, making his way around the next bend. The wind was soundless, sweeping the sun-filled sky. And suddenly, there it was, sooner than he had thought. The span of safety on his left gave way entirely, and he was face-to-face with the Fear Place.

Even the cougar stopped, lifted her head, and sniffed the air. She looked down over the edge, then back, as if to see if Doug were coming.

I can't! A swell of fear engulfed him, and for a moment the trees far below seemed to come up to meet him. Clinging tightly to a scrubby bush growing out of the face of the rock, Doug stared without blinking at the ledge stretching before him, even narrower than he remembered. Was this possible? Could it have eroded to twenty inches in places?

There was nothing separating him from the edge of the cliff and a plunge downward. There were even places that the ledge tipped slightly toward the yawning gap, places where loose rocks and stones lay ready to trip him, make him skid.

He could smell the difference in the air here above the canyon, sharp and moist. It beckoned him downward, and each breeze seemed to punch him in the stomach, shoot upward, socking him again beneath the chin.

Far below him, the rocky floor of the canyon waited. He could see the tops of the trees, a meandering stream, boulders. He wondered how long it would take his body to reach the bottom. How it would feel to . . . *no!*

194

Immobile, Doug swallowed and tried to get a grip on his fear. His mouth felt as though it were lined with dust. He attempted to measure the length of the ledge with his eyes — the length of the place where his heart stopped pumping and his legs wouldn't move. *That* place. About nine yards to the curve, and a few yards more after that, if he remembered right. It didn't seem so long when he thought about it, but looking out there now, it seemed impossible.

Maybe there were times it paid to be cautious. Maybe there were places that only fools would tread. Hadn't his mother said something like that once, or was it "Where angels fear to tread?" If there was such a place, this was it.

Would he ever make Eagle Scout if he couldn't try something like this? Would he even *live* to make Eagle Scout if he did? One slip of the foot and . . .

Stop it. His other self. As though he never took any other kinds of risks — riding his bike at top speed around corners, for example.

Look at the ledge, he told himself, and see if you could make it without falling off if it was drawn on the sidewalk with chalk.

Sure, no problem.

Could he do it if it were only half as wide, drawn with chalk on the sidewalk?

Of course. A fourth as wide, even. Give him a path on the sidewalk five inches wide, marked with chalk, and he could go for a mile, never stepping outside the boundaries once.

Okay, then. He had twenty inches, minimum. Do it, he told himself.
It was the cougar who showed him how.

The cat simply walked out on the ledge, hugging the side of the
mountain, but not too closely. Not leaning inward, as Doug tended to
do. As he followed, and as he thought about it, Doug realized that were
his body at an angle and he slipped, his feet would be pointing toward the
edge of the cliff. He needed to keep upright. He would remember that
chalk line on the sidewalk.

It wasn't so bad at first. The ledge varied in width between three
and three and a half feet.

Three feet is a yardstick, he told himself. Three feet is the width of
a kitchen table, the width of a cot. Probably wider here than his sleeping
bag. Yet he lay on top of it on hot summer nights and never rolled off,
not even in his sleep. He could do this. Piece of cake. He swallowed.

Ahead, the cougar's left hind foot seemed to displace a small stone at
the side of the path, and it rolled over the edge. Doug heard it hit a rock
below, then another. The cougar glanced toward the gorge and kept
going, ears up.

The path was narrowing now, and somewhere ahead was the curve where it was narrowest of all, where he couldn't see what he was getting to. Somewhere, right on the bend, was the place he had flattened himself against the rock. *I can't.* The words seemed to be building up already in his throat.

He felt the needle pricks in the palms of his hands again, and in the soles of his feet. Felt the tightening of his body, the rigidity of his chest, as though, if he tensed himself enough, he might be too stiff or too hard or too impenetrable to topple.

Ahead, the cougar's body swayed with every motion, limbs sleek and relaxed. She took the curves as easily as a tire rolling along on its own momentum. She didn't walk carelessly, but in a deliberate, rhythmical manner, joints loose, paws secure.

As he approached the curve, Doug took a deep, shaky breath and let it out. Then another. He looked down at his feet and blew upward, to fan his face.

His right bootlace was untied, the ends dangling.

He would not try to tie it here. Bend over here and he might lose his balance altogether. He would have to go around the bend dragging that lace.

Hollow-eyed with terror, his mouth dry, he began to maneuver himself around the narrow curve, watching each step to see where his foot would go next, scanning the wall of rock to see what his hand could clutch.

He would not allow himself to look down at the canyon. Would not let himself even glance at the large birds that were circling, soaring, just off in the huge space to his left. The cougar had gone on, probably so far ahead Doug would find it sitting beside Gordie's tent.

"Remember Dad on the raft," he said aloud, his voice trembling. He tried to remember the day Dad had told him about, when he was sure the sun would kill them all, broil them there in the open sea. They had seen a rowboat and paddled toward it, and when they got there it had four men in it, all refugees like themselves, and all of them dead. Was this as bad as that?

Then, answering his own question, he said aloud, "No."

He lied. It was worse.

He was still moving forward. Had decided not to face the wall and walk sideways for fear his repositioning himself might be more dangerous than walking straight. But just as he rounded the narrowest spot on the ledge, he came face-to-face with the cougar.

His strength almost gave way.

Was this it, then? He had come all this way to face a cougar who wanted to turn around and go back? Who would nudge him backward, step over step, possibly pushing between him and the cliff wall, sending him over the edge?

Their eyes were on each other — fixed solidly on each other for the first time.

"Ch-Charlie," Doug said. "I can't get by. You've got to move."

The cat came on, so close her muzzle was almost against Doug's hipbone. Nudged him. And then the animal backed off. It seemed to Doug that her long body must be moving backward in sections, like a caterpillar. He couldn't see the rest of her, only that tawny head, the amber eyes, moving slowly away from him, leading still. She had not wanted to go back, perhaps; only wanted to see how Doug was doing.

Any minute Doug expected to hear the clawing, scratching sounds of a cougar falling over the edge. Things happened, even to the most expert of animals. And then Charlie disappeared silently from view. But when Doug took the last few steps along the ledge, he saw the cougar's tail ahead of him, Charlie having turned herself around again.

The path was widening here — on ahead, wider still. And finally there were scrub bushes to the left, making a safety rail between him and the canyon below.

He'd made it. Done it.

Think About the Selection

1. Of all the obstacles Doug faces, which one is the most difficult for him to overcome? How do you know this?

2. What does Doug do to keep his mind off the danger he is in? Do you think his strategy works?

3. What do you think happened before at Doug's "fear place"? Find clues in the story that suggest what might have occurred.

4. Doug says that his scout troop would have enjoyed the hike. Would you enjoy it? Explain why or why not.

5. Do you think Doug would have succeeded if the cougar hadn't been there? Give reasons for your answer.

6. What do you think will happen next in this story? Why?

7. **Connecting/Comparing** Compare Doug's act of courage in *The Fear Place* with Manuel's act of courage in "La Bamba." How are the boys' actions alike? How are they different?

Narrating

Write About an Experience

Write a few paragraphs about a time when you had to overcome an obstacle to reach an important goal.

> **Tips**
> - First, list the most important details of the experience.
> - Check your verbs to be sure they are all in the right tense.

Social Studies

Study the Geography of a Region

Find details in the story that give information about the terrain where Doug is hiking. These may include details about rock types, landforms, and wildlife. Use this information to write an entry for a guide book about the Rocky Mountains.

Bonus **Read more about the geography and wildlife of the Rocky Mountains. Then write a description of the region.**

Viewing

Describe an Illustration

Choose an illustration from the selection that you think best represents the "fear place." Then write a paragraph that tells why you chose that illustration.

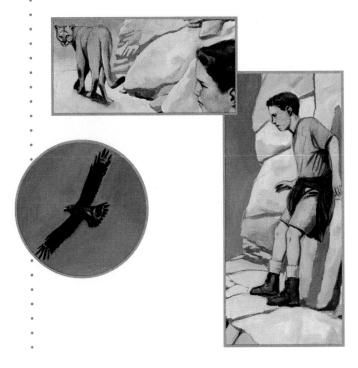

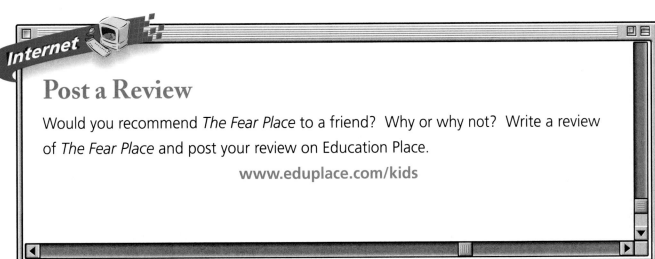

Post a Review

Would you recommend *The Fear Place* to a friend? Why or why not? Write a review of *The Fear Place* and post your review on Education Place.

www.eduplace.com/kids

Blind to Limitations

By Brent H. Weber

With the wind howling at their backs, the five climbers cautiously made their way up the unforgiving stretch of mountain. The icy trail was only two feet wide, with a drop of 9,000 feet on one side and 2,000 feet on the other.

And Erik Weihenmayer could not see a thing.

"I was just so tired and dizzy, my head was spinning," says Weihenmayer, who is blind. "I took this giant step up, and the guy in front of me said, 'Congratulations, you're on top of North America.'"

Erik Weihenmayer climbed North America's highest peak despite being unable to see.

From left, Jeff Evans, Erik Weihenmayer, and Sam Epstein display the American Foundation for the Blind flag at the top of Mount McKinley.

With that giant step, Erik had reached the top of Alaska's Mount McKinley, the highest peak in North America.

Erik is a modern-day adventurer. The fifth-grade teacher has quite a list of accomplishments for someone who lost his sight at age thirteen because of an eye disease. He hiked the Inca Trail in Peru, trekked the Boltera Glacier in Pakistan, and crossed jungles in New Guinea. He has been scuba-diving and skydiving.

Erik knew that a blind woman named Joni Phelps had climbed the 20,320-foot Mount McKinley in 1993. He decided to try to become the first blind man to do it. He knew it would be his most ambitious adventure yet. He hoped the climb would help raise money for the American Foundation for the Blind.

But Erik was not completely prepared for what he would face. Even in midsummer, with its daylong sunshine, temperatures on Mount McKinley can drop to forty degrees below zero. Huge crevasses, unexpected snowstorms, and even an occasional avalanche can present perilous conditions for any climber.

After they were about a third of the way up the mountain, one of the other climbers said to Erik, "I want you to point to the summit."

"I was standing at seven thousand feet," Erik recalls. "I pointed up to where I thought the summit would be. He said, 'Nope.' And I kept pointing higher and higher until I pointed where I honestly thought the sun would be. He said, 'There it is.' I was just blown away, and thought, 'Am I going to be able to do this?'"

Sighted people often wonder if Erik's experiences are incomplete because he is not able to see.

"I use my other senses to gain pleasure from what I do, so even though I can't see what's around me, I experience it in a different way," he says. "I have the sense of feeling the snow and hearing the wind, and I even have a sense of space around me."

Erik's family have supported his many adventures. They even rented a small plane and flew over Erik as he neared the top of Mount McKinley.

"We heard this buzz coming through the air; they had timed it perfectly," Erik says. "We all waved our ski poles. It was just an incredible feeling. That was probably my proudest moment, to know that my whole family was up there watching me."

Two days later, Erik had another surprise as the climbers made their way back down the mountain toward their base camp.

"We were near the bottom of Heartbreak Hill, and I heard 'Hip-hip-hooray!' It was my family. They had flown to our base camp and were standing in a big chorus, cheering us on." Erik's brothers ran to him as he approached. "One brother grabbed one side of my pack, the other grabbed the other side, and I was kind of floating over the last half of that hill."

"When I got to the base camp, my girlfriend, Ellen Reeve, was waiting with chocolate milk and Oreo cookies."

Erik is looking forward to his next challenge.

"People can do extraordinary things," he says. "Although mountain climbing has nothing to do with blindness, I told myself that it would be an awful tragedy if blindness had to change and limit the enjoyment I get out of life. I can get to the top of most of the things I set my mind to. I just have to get there differently."

"If you ask the kids in my class if there is anything that holds them back, almost everyone will say something," Erik says, referring to his students at Phoenix Country Day School in Arizona. "So, in a way, the climb up Mount McKinley was to say that whatever your obstacles in life, you can get around them."

"I can get to the top of most of the things I set my mind to. I just have to get there differently."

Erik does some rock climbing in Arizona.

MAE JEMISON
Space Scientist

By Gail Sakurai

Exploring Space

When the Soviet Union launched the first artificial **satellite** in the 1950s, the space race between the Russians and the Americans began. Since then, there have been many historic space events, including the first mission to have an African American female astronaut aboard, described in *Mae Jemison: Space Scientist.*

1957
The Soviet Union launches the first artificial satellite, *Sputnik 1*.

1961
The first human in space is Russian cosmonaut Yuri Gagarin aboard *Vostok 1*. The first American in space is Alan Shepard (left) aboard *Freedom 7*.

1962
John Glenn aboard *Friendship 7* is the first American to **orbit** the Earth.

1963
Russian Valentina Tereshkova is the first woman in space.

1999
Eileen Collins is the first female commander of a shuttle mission.

1995
Cosmonaut Valery Polyakov completes a record 488 days in space aboard the Russian space station *Mir*.

1992
Mission specialist Mae Jemison (left) is the first African American woman in space.

1983
Sally Ride is the first American woman in space.

1981
The first **reusable spacecraft**, the space shuttle *Columbia*, is launched.

1969
Americans Neil Armstrong and Edwin "Buzz" Aldrin (right) walk on the moon during the *Apollo 11* mission.

209

MAE JEMISON
Space Scientist

By Gail Sakurai

As you read about space missions in this selection, **monitor** your understanding. If you do not understand something, reread or read ahead to **clarify**.

THREE . . .

TWO . . .

One . . .

Liftoff!

The space shuttle *Endeavour* thundered into the morning sky above Kennedy Space Center. Higher and higher it soared over the Atlantic Ocean. A few minutes later, *Endeavour* was in orbit around Earth.

Aboard the spacecraft, astronaut Mae Jemison could feel her heart pounding with excitement. A wide, happy grin split her face. She had just made history. She was the first African-American woman in space. The date was September 12, 1992.

But Mae wasn't thinking about dates in history books. Her thoughts were of the wonder and adventure of space travel. "I'm closer to the stars — somewhere I've always dreamed to be," Mae said during a live television broadcast from space.

Mae Jemison and the other Endeavour *astronauts pose for a picture during their mission (above). Jemison's dream of becoming an astronaut came true in 1987 (right).*

Mae's dream didn't come true overnight. It happened only after many long years of hard work, training, and preparation. Her success story began nearly thirty-six years earlier, in a small town in Alabama.

Mae Carol Jemison was born on October 17, 1956, in Decatur, Alabama. While she was still a toddler, Mae and her family moved to the big city of Chicago, Illinois. Mae considers Chicago her hometown because she grew up there.

Mae was the youngest child in her family. She had an older brother, Charles, and an older sister, Ada. Her parents, Charlie and Dorothy Jemison, were helpful and supportive of all of Mae's interests. "They put up with all kinds of stuff, like science projects, dance classes, and art lessons," Mae said. "They encouraged me to do it, and they would find the money, time, and energy to help me be involved."

Other adults were not as encouraging as Mae's parents. When Mae told her kindergarten teacher that she wanted to be a scientist, the teacher said, "Don't you mean a nurse?" In those days, very few African-Americans or women were scientists. Many people, like Mae's teacher, couldn't imagine a little black girl growing up to become a scientist. But Mae refused to let other people's limited imaginations stop her from following her dreams.

Mae loved to work on school science projects. She spent many hours at the public library, reading books about science and space. On summer nights, she liked to lie outside, look up at the stars, and dream of traveling in space. Mae was fascinated by the real-life space flights and moon landings that she watched on television. Mae Jemison knew that she wanted to be an astronaut. Although all the astronauts at that time were white and male, Mae wasn't discouraged.

Science and space were not young Mae's only interests. She also loved to dance. Mae started taking lessons in jazz and African dance at the age of nine. By the time she was in high school, Mae was an accomplished dancer, and she frequently performed on stage. She was also skilled at choreography, the art of creating a dance.

In 1973, Mae graduated from Chicago's Morgan Park High School, where she was an honor-roll student and excelled in science and math. That fall, Mae entered Stanford University in California. At Stanford, she specialized in African and Afro-American studies, and chemical engineering. Mae continued her dancing and choreography. She also became involved with student organizations, and she was elected president of the Black Student Union.

After receiving her Bachelor of Science degree from Stanford, Mae enrolled at Cornell University Medical College in New York. She had decided to become a doctor. Medical school was demanding, but Mae still found time to participate in student organizations. She served as president of both the Cornell Medical Student Executive Council and the Cornell chapter of the National Student Medical Association.

Mae traveled to several countries as part of her medical training. She studied medicine in Cuba. She helped provide basic medical care for people in rural Kenya and at a Cambodian refugee camp in Thailand.

Mae received her Doctor of Medicine degree from Cornell University in 1981. Like all new doctors, she served an internship, a period of practicing under experienced doctors. Mae completed her internship at the Los Angeles County/University of Southern California Medical Center. Then she started working as a doctor in Los Angeles.

Although she had settled into a career as a doctor, Mae wasn't finished traveling yet. She remembered the trips she had taken during medical school, and she still wanted to help people in other parts of the world. Mae decided to join the Peace Corps, an organization of volunteers who work to improve conditions in developing nations.

Before NASA chose Jemison for the space program, she was working as a doctor in Los Angeles.

Mae spent more than two years in West Africa. She was the Area Peace Corps Medical Officer for Sierra Leone and Liberia. She was in charge of health care for all Peace Corps volunteers and U.S. embassy employees in those two countries. It was an important responsibility for someone who was only twenty-six years old.

"I learned a lot from that experience," Mae said. "I was one of the youngest doctors over there, and I had to learn to deal with how people reacted to my age, while asserting myself as a physician."

When her tour of duty in the Peace Corps was over, Mae returned to Los Angeles and resumed her medical practice. She also started taking advanced engineering classes.

Jemison learns wilderness and water survival skills as part of her NASA training sessions.

Mae had not forgotten her dream of traveling in space. Now that she had the necessary education and experience, Mae decided to try and become an astronaut. She applied to the National Aeronautics and Space Administration (NASA), which is responsible for U.S. space exploration. After undergoing background checks, physical exams, medical tests, and interviews, Dr. Mae Jemison was accepted into the astronaut program in June, 1987. She was one of only fifteen people chosen from nearly two thousand qualified applicants!

Mae didn't let success go to her head. "I'm very aware of the fact that I'm not the first African-American woman who had the skills, the talent, the desire to be an astronaut," she said. "I happen to be the first one that NASA selected."

Mae moved to Houston, Texas, where she began a year of intensive training at NASA's Johnson Space Center. She studied space shuttle equipment and operations. To learn how to handle emergencies and deal with difficult situations, Mae practiced wilderness and water survival skills. Survival training also helps teach cooperation and teamwork. These are important abilities for astronauts who must live and work together for long periods in a cramped space shuttle.

Mae took lessons on how to move her body and operate tools in a weightless environment. On Earth, the force of gravity keeps us from floating off the ground. But in space, there is less gravity, so people and objects drift about. Since there is no "up" or "down" in space, astronauts don't need to lie down to sleep. They can sleep in any position. To keep from drifting while asleep, they zip themselves into special sleeping bags attached to the shuttle's walls.

During training, Mae got a preview of weightlessness. She flew in a special training jet that simulates zero gravity. The jet climbs nearly straight up, then loops into a steep dive. This is similar to the loop-the-loops on many roller coasters. For thirty seconds at the top of the loop, trainees feel weightless. Their feet leave the floor and they can fly around inside the padded cabin.

At the end of her training year, Mae officially became a mission specialist astronaut. "We're the ones people often call the scientist astronauts," Mae explained. "Our responsibilities are to be familiar with the shuttle and how it operates, to do the experiments once you get into orbit, to help launch the payloads or satellites, and also do extravehicular activities, which are the space walks."

Jemison and astronaut Jan Davis experience weightlessness in NASA's zero-gravity training jet.

In the 1970s, NASA designed the space shuttle as the first reusable spacecraft. A shuttle launches like a rocket, but it returns to Earth and lands on a runway like an airplane. A space shuttle has many uses. It carries both equipment and people into space. Astronauts aboard a shuttle can capture, repair, and launch satellites. Shuttles are often used as orbiting laboratories, where space scientists conduct experiments in a zero-gravity environment. In the future, space shuttles might transport supplies and workers for building space stations.

Although Mae was a full-fledged astronaut, she still had to wait four more years before she went into space. While she waited, Mae worked with the scientists who were developing experiments for her mission. She also trained with her fellow crew members. In her spare time, Mae liked to read, travel, ski, garden, dance, and exercise. She also enjoyed taking care of Sneeze, her white, gray, and silver African wildcat.

On September 12, 1992, the long wait was over. Space shuttle *Endeavour* perched on the launch pad like a great white bird waiting to take flight. Everything was ready for the liftoff.

Mae awoke early to shower and dress. She ate breakfast with the other astronauts. Then, Mae and the crew put on their orange space suits and boarded a van for the short drive to the launch pad. For two-and-a-half hours until liftoff, they lay on their backs, strapped into their seats, as the countdown progressed. At 10:23 A.M., precisely on time, *Endeavour* lifted off on its historic space journey.

Dr. Mae Jemison earned her place in the history books as the first African-American woman in space. Mae said, "My participation in the space shuttle mission helps to say that all peoples of the world have astronomers, physicists, and explorers."

Endeavour's mission was devoted to scientific research. Mae was responsible for several key experiments. She had

The crew of the Endeavour *heads toward the launch pad (left). The illustration (below) shows the space shuttle in flight. Spacelab, the laboratory where the experiments are conducted, is located near the front of the shuttle.*

helped design an experiment to study the loss of bone cells in space. Astronauts lose bone cells in weightlessness, and the longer they stay in space, the more they lose. If too many cells are lost, bones become weak and can break easily. Scientists hope to find a way to prevent this loss. Mae explained, "The real issue is how to keep people healthy while they're in space."

Mae investigated a new way of controlling space motion sickness. Half of all astronauts experience space sickness during their first few days in space. They often feel dizzy and nauseated. Astronauts can take medicine to control space sickness, but the medicine can make them tired.

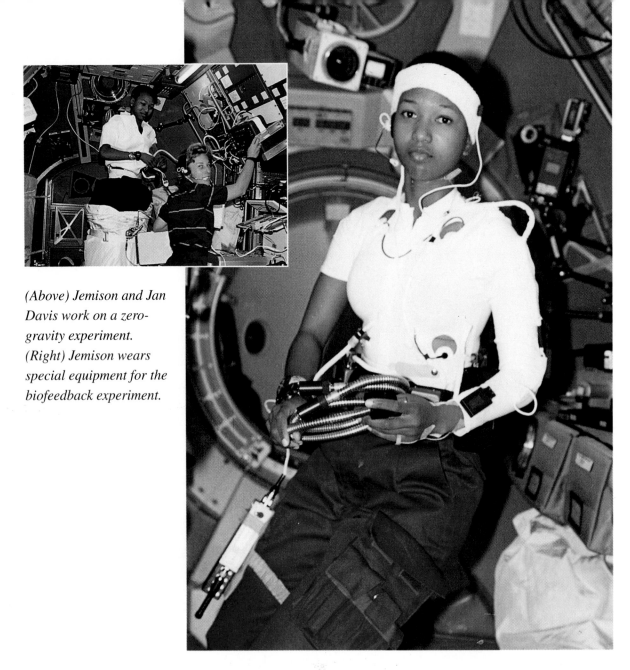

(Above) Jemison and Jan Davis work on a zero-gravity experiment. (Right) Jemison wears special equipment for the biofeedback experiment.

To carry out the space-sickness experiment, Mae had been trained in the use of "biofeedback" techniques. Biofeedback uses meditation and relaxation to control the body's functions. Mae wore special monitoring equipment to record her heart rate, breathing, temperature, and other body functions. If she started to feel ill, she would meditate. She concentrated intensely on bringing her body back to normal. The purpose of the experiment was to see if Mae could avoid space sickness without taking medication. The results of the experiment were not conclusive, but space researchers still hope to use biofeed-back in the future.

Mae was also in charge of the frog experiment. Early in the flight, she fertilized eggs from female South African frogs. A few days later, tadpoles hatched. She then watched the tadpoles carefully. Her goal was to find out if the tadpoles would develop normally in the near-zero gravity of space. "What we've seen is that the eggs were fertilized and the tadpoles looked pretty good," said Mae. "It was exciting because that's a question that we didn't have any information on before."

On September 20, 1992, at 8:53 A.M., *Endeavour* landed at Kennedy Space Center. The crew had spent more than 190 hours (almost eight days) in space. They had traveled 3.3 million miles and had completed 127 orbits of Earth!

After her space mission, Mae returned home to Chicago. Her hometown welcomed her with six days of parades, speeches, and celebrations. Then she went to Hollywood to accept the American Black Achievement Awards' Trailblazer Award for being the first African-American woman in space. In 1993, Mae was inducted into the National Women's Hall of Fame in Seneca Falls, New York.

Mae Jemison had made her childhood dream come true. She was ready for new challenges. A few months after her space flight, Mae took a leave of absence from NASA to teach and to do research at Dartmouth College in New Hampshire. Then, on March 8, 1993, she permanently resigned from the astronaut corps.

The Endeavour *touches down at the Kennedy Space Center.*

Jemison congratulates Jill Giovanelli, age thirteen, winner of the International Peace Poster Contest.

Mae formed her own company called The Jemison Group, Inc. The Jemison Group's goal is to develop ways of using science and technology to improve the quality of life. Mae's company makes a special effort to improve conditions in poor and developing countries.

The company's first project used satellite communications to provide better health care for people in West Africa. Mae also established an international summer science camp for young people.

Besides her work with The Jemison Group, Mae spends much of her time traveling around the country, giving speeches, and encouraging young people to follow their dreams. Mae Jemison believes in the motto:

"Don't be limited by others' limited imaginations."

Meet the Author

Gail Sakurai first decided to become a writer as a child. She had hoped to have her first book published by the time she was a teenager, but her plan did not quite work out. Sakurai says, "My childhood dream came true with the publication of my first book in 1994 — only twenty-nine years later than originally planned."

Her first book, *Peach Boy: A Japanese Legend*, is a retelling of a Japanese folktale that her husband used to tell to their sons at bedtime. She has continued to write nonfiction books and retellings of folktales.

She says that the two most difficult parts of her job are having enough time to write and starting. Once she does begin, she writes quickly because she has already planned the words in her mind.

Sakurai has written several other books for young people, including *The Liberty Bell*, *Stephen Hawking*, *Paul Revere's Ride*, and *The Jamestown Colony*.

If you would like to read more about Gail Sakurai, visit Education Place. **www.eduplace.com/kids**

Responding

MAE JEMISON
Space Scientist

By Gail Sakurai

Think About the Selection

1. What obstacles did Mae Jemison have to overcome to achieve success in her life?

2. How did Mae show that she had many talents even before she graduated from high school? Use examples from the selection to support your answer.

3. What do Mae's career changes tell you about her?

4. Think about the Jemison Group's goals. In what way do these goals represent a mix of Mae's talents and lifelong interests?

5. Since childhood Mae dreamed of traveling in space. What are some of your dreams for the future?

6. Which one of Mae's accomplishments impressed you most? Why?

7. Connecting/Comparing Why do you think the stories of Mae Jemison, Michelle Kwan, Doug Grillo, and Manuel Gomez all belong in a theme titled *Give It All You've Got*? What qualities do they share?

Informing

Write an Interview Script

Write the script that you would use if you could interview Mae Jemison. What questions might you ask her about her life and work?

Tips

- **Brainstorm what you're most interested in finding out about Mae Jemison.**
- **Use the correct end marks for statements and questions.**

Science

Create a Fact Sheet

With a partner, create a fact sheet about what it is like to travel in the space shuttle. Include information about how to train for a space mission. Use information from the selection and from other sources. You might use the fact sheet to give an oral presentation.

Space Travel
I. Getting Ready

Listening and Speaking

Present a TV Broadcast

Mae Jemison made a live TV broadcast from *Endeavour*. Present your own version of this broadcast. Tell viewers all about *Endeavour*'s mission.

Tips

- **Write a broadcast script, or note your important points on index cards. Put the cards in order.**
- **Speak slowly and clearly.**

Internet

Complete a Web Word Find

You've learned a lot of vocabulary related to space missions in this selection. Try finding those words in a puzzle that can be printed from Education Place.

www.eduplace.com/kids

Into the Deep

Explorers in new underwater vehicles hope to unlock the secrets of the oceans' depths.

Sea explorer Graham Hawkes is ready to take a historic plunge. In the next few months, he will venture deep into the Pacific Ocean in an awesome new vessel. Most ocean-exploring vehicles drop straight down through the water. Some creep slowly along the ocean floor gathering samples and information. But *Deep Flight I,* which Hawkes helped design, zips around like a fighter plane.

Steering with joysticks, Hawkes can make the vessel roll, turn, dive and shoot for the surface. He'll get a close-up view of the wondrous life and landscape of the dark, silent world under the sea. "These vehicles are so small and light, you can send them anywhere," says Hawkes.

For years people have said the last unexplored frontier is outer space. But we really don't have to leave our planet to boldly go where no one has gone before. About 75 percent of the earth's surface is covered by the sea, and we haven't come close to seeing it all. "We know more about Mars than we do about the ocean," says Sylvia Earle, a marine biologist who helped create *Deep Flight I.*

What's Down There?

With *Deep Flight I* and a fleet of other new vessels and robot craft, explorers hope to discover all sorts of riches in the sea. Among these riches are unusual living creatures. Some may prove useful as sources of medicine, food and chemicals.

The deep ocean is home to some of earth's oddest creatures. The anglerfish, the gulper eel and other deep dwellers have crushproof bodies that allow them to survive the ocean pressures 5,000 feet down. Some have body parts that can glow in the dark to attract prey.

At even greater depths, researchers have found bizarre eight-inch-long tube worms, and clams that are the size of dinner plates. They live in the boiling-hot waters near ocean vents. The vents are cracks where seawater seeps into the earth's crust and then shoots back up like a geyser. With temperatures reaching 750°F, it's amazing that anything lives nearby!

The vents constantly spew out valuable minerals like iron, copper, nickel, cobalt and manganese. The material hardens into chimneys known as "black smokers." (One of the biggest is nicknamed Godzilla.) Parts of the Pacific sea floor are littered with potato-size nuggets of these minerals. Mining companies are eager to scoop them up.

The Very, Very Bottom

The ocean floor is not flat. Valleys, canyons, mountains and even volcanoes shape the underwater world. The deepest known point is the Mariana Trench near the Pacific island of Guam. In 1960 two scientists in a research vessel traveled 35,800 feet down — about seven miles — to explore it. A Japanese vessel went nearly that deep again last year.

Japan has a good reason to explore the ocean bottom. Southern Japan sits on a shaky part of the sea floor where three pieces of the earth's crust meet. Those pieces, called tectonic plates, shift slightly each year. The shifting can trigger earthquakes like the one that killed 5,500 people in Kobe, Japan, in 1995. Scientists say studying the plates may help them predict earthquakes.

A Costly Quest

It costs millions of dollars to explore the deep sea. Not everyone agrees on how to do it. Some explorers say we should focus on the part of the ocean that is 20,000 feet deep or less. That's about 97 percent of the ocean. Exploring the deepest 3 percent requires more expensive equipment and is more dangerous.

But other scientists say exploring the very deepest part of the ocean will be worth the risk and cost. Greg Stone, a marine biologist in Boston, Massachusetts, says we can count on finding new animals and other discoveries we can't even imagine. "We won't know what it holds until we've been there," he says.

Creatures of the Deep

1 **Hatchet Fish**
1,000 ft.–5,000 ft.
Up to 5 in. long

2 **Snipe Eel**
2,000 ft.– 6,600 ft.
Up to 5 ft. long

3 **Deep-sea Shrimp**
6,600 ft. –9,900 ft.
Up to 6 in. long

4 **Fangtooth**
2,600 ft.–5,000 ft.
Up to 10 in. long

5 **Cranchid Squid**
1,600 ft.–6,600 ft.
8 in. long

6 **Gulper Eel**
2,000 ft.–6,600 ft.
Up to 5 ft. long

Filling in the Blank

Some test items ask you to complete a sentence. You do this by selecting the best answer from three to five answer choices. How do you choose the best answer? Look at this sample test item for *Mae Jemison: Space Scientist*. The correct answer is shown. Use the tips to help you answer this kind of test question.

Read the sentence. Fill in the circle in the answer row for the answer that best completes the sentence.

1   The main idea in the first three paragraphs of the selection is —

   A   Mae Jemison felt happy and excited to be in space.

   B   The space shuttle *Endeavour* was launched into space and soon was orbiting Earth.

   C   Mae Jemison made history as the first African American woman in space.

   D   The date was September 12, 1992.

ANSWER ROW 1   Ⓐ Ⓑ ● Ⓓ

Now see how one student figured out the best answer.

I turn back to the first page of the selection. I look for important ideas. I decide that the most important idea is that Mae Jemison was the first African American woman in space.

I read the answer choices again. **A** and **D** don't work because they are details rather than the main idea. **B** is an important idea, but **C** is the most important idea in all the paragraphs. So **C** is the best answer.

Poetry

"If there were a recipe for a poem, these would be the ingredients: word sounds, rhythms, description, feeling, memory, rhyme and imagination. They can be put together a thousand different ways, a thousand, thousand . . . more."

—Karla Kuskin

A poem can be about almost anything. It can start with whatever is right in front of you: a spider, a pair of sneakers, even your nose. The poem grows with color, sound, rhythm, each word carefully chosen to build an image or tell a story. As the poem grows, familiar things may change and begin to look less familiar. Poems often end in a very different place from where they began.

After you've read these poems, you can discover how a poem grows by writing a poem of your own.

233

Contents

Places and Seasons

Árbol de limón

Si te subes a un árbol de limón
siente la corteza
con tus rodillas y pies,
huele sus flores blancas,
talla las hojas
entre tus manos.
Recuerda,
el árbol es mayor que tú
y tal vez encuentres cuentos
entre sus ramas.

— *Jennifer Clement*

Lemon Tree

If you climb a lemon tree
feel the bark
under your knees and feet,
smell the white flowers,
rub the leaves
in your hands.
Remember,
the tree is older than you are
and you might find stories
in its branches.

— *Jennifer Clement*

Translated by
Consuelo de Aerenlund

235

Travel

The railroad track is miles away,
    And the day is loud with voices speaking,
Yet there isn't a train goes by all day
    But I hear its whistle shrieking.

All night there isn't a train goes by,
    Though the night is still for sleep and dreaming,
But I see its cinders red on the sky,
    And hear its engine steaming.

My heart is warm with the friends I make,
    And better friends I'll not be knowing;
Yet there isn't a train I wouldn't take,
    No matter where it's going.

— *Edna St. Vincent Millay*

knoxville, tennessee

I always like summer
best
you can eat fresh corn
from daddy's garden
and okra
and greens
and cabbage
and lots of
barbecue
and buttermilk
and homemade ice-cream
at the church picnic
and listen to
gospel music
outside
at the church
homecoming
and go to the mountains with
your grandmother
and go barefooted
and be warm
all the time
not only when you go to bed
and sleep
— *nikki giovanni*

237

A Patch of Old Snow

There's a patch of old snow in a corner
    That I should have guessed
Was a blow-away paper the rain
    Had brought to rest.

It is speckled with grime as if
    Small print overspread it,
The news of a day I've forgotten —
    If I ever read it.

                        — *Robert Frost*

Early Spring

In the early spring, the snowfall is light
upon the mesa.
It does not stick to the ground very long.
I walk through this patchwork of snow and earth,
watching the ground for early signs.
Signs of growth. Signs of rebirth.

Larkspur and wild onions are still
within the warmth of the earth.
I hear cries of crows off in the distance.
A rabbit bounds off into the sagebrush flat.
A shadow of a hawk disturbs the landscape momentarily.
It sees food and life abundant below that I cannot see.
The cycle of life continues.

Even as I stand here shivering in the afternoon chill,
just below me, young seedlings start
their upward journey.
Insects begin to stir.
Rodents and snakes are comfortable in their burrows.
Maybe to them we also disappear with the cold.
Not to be seen until spring.

For this generation, and many more to come,
this land is beautiful and filled with mysteries.
They reveal themselves and their stories —
if you look very carefully, and listen . . .

— *Shonto Begay*

Civilization

I've stood here lately, looking at the path
Where deer once came to watch the sun go down,
Standing with their ears pricked for the sound
Of cars along the street.

I've longed to hear coyotes call again
Across the valley, howling from the hill,
Baying when the night stands black and still
Where sky and mountain meet.

I've watched for the raccoons, who crept
Along the rocks and over fallen wood,
Begging near our windows for some food,
Staring with black-ringed eyes.

Lizards, rabbits, snakes and moles. They came,
Chewing the poppies, digging up the lawn,
Burrowing homes and holes. But they have gone.
The mournful owls remember. So do I.

— *Myra Cohn Livingston*

Animals

Dinner Together

Sitting by the barbecue
waiting for sausages and hot dogs
blue-gray smoke the same color
of the sky
I see a tiny spider
walking down from the sky with tiny six-
footed steps
down
down
in a perfectly straight
line
all the way
down
to the floor
then back up
the same line
rising from one cloud
up to another,
a silver speck
glistening
at its mouth,
climbing the invisible ladder.

— *Diana Rivera*

Whirligig Beetles

We're whirligig beetles	
we're swimming in circles,	
black backs by the hundred.	We're whirligig beetles
	we're swimming in circles,
	black backs by the hundred.
	We're spinning and swerving
We're spinning and swerving	as if we were on a
as if we were on a	mad merry-go-round.
mad merry-go-round.	
We never get dizzy	
from whirling and weaving	We never get dizzy
and wheeling and swirling.	from whirling and weaving
	and wheeling and swirling.
	The same goes for turning,
	revolving and curving,
The same goes for turning,	gyrating and twirling.
revolving and curving,	
gyrating and twirling.	
The crows fly directly,	
but we prefer spirals,	The crows fly directly,
arcs, ovals, and loops.	but we prefer spirals,
	arcs, ovals, and loops.
	We're fond of the phrase
"As the whirligig swims"	"As the whirligig swims"
	meaning traveling by
	the most circular

circular
roundabout
backtracking
indirect
serpentine
tortuous
twisty,
best possible
route.

roundabout
backtracking
indirect
serpentine
tortuous
twisty and
turny,
best possible
route.

— *Paul Fleischman*

The Shark

My sweet, let me tell you about the shark.
Though his eyes are bright, his thought is dark.
He's quiet — that speaks well of him.
So does the fact that he can swim.
But though he swims without a sound,
Wherever he swims he looks around
With those two bright eyes and that one
    dark thought.
He has only one, but he thinks it a lot.
And the thought he thinks but can never complete
Is his long dark thought of something to eat.
Most anything does, and I have to add
That when he eats his manners are bad.
He's a gulper, a ripper, a snatcher, a grabber.
Yes, his manners are drab. But his thought
    is drabber.
That one dark thought he can never complete
Of something — anything — somehow to eat.

Be careful where you swim, my sweet.

— *John Ciardi*

It's All the Same to the Clam

You may leave the clam on the ocean's floor,
It's all the same to the clam.
For a hundred thousand years or more,
It's all the same to the clam.
You may bury him deep in mud and muck
Or carry him 'round to bring you luck,
Or use him for a hockey puck,
It's all the same to the clam.

You may call him Jim or Frank or Nell,
It's all the same to the clam.
Or make an ashtray from his shell,
It's all the same to the clam.
You may take him riding on the train
Or leave him sitting in the rain.
You'll never hear the clam complain,
It's all the same to the clam.

Yes, the world may stop or the world may spin,
It's all the same to the clam.
And the sky may come a-fallin' in,
It's all the same to the clam.
And man may sing his endless songs
Of wronging rights and righting wrongs.
The clam just sets — and gets along,
It's all the same to the clam.

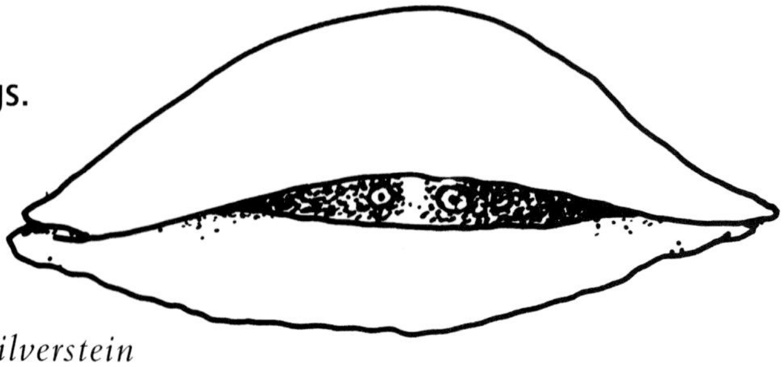

— *Shel Silverstein*

244

THE BAT

By day the bat is cousin to the mouse.
He likes the attic of an aging house.

His fingers make a hat about his head.
His pulse beat is so slow we think him dead.

He loops in crazy figures half the night
Among the trees that face the corner light.

But when he brushes up against a screen,
We are afraid of what our eyes have seen:

For something is amiss or out of place
When mice with wings can wear a human face.

— *Theodore Roethke*

People

CAMPFIRE

Just think —
when Mother was my age,
she could build a fire
with sparks from rocks,
catch a bunch of
grasshoppers and
roast them whole
for a summer
night's snack!

"Get me a good stick,"
she says, "thin but strong,"
and I bring her one
from the woods
behind our tent.
On the way back
I see a brown bag
by her feet —
could it be?

When the fire is spitting ready,
she reaches
in the bag, rustling,
and hands me
one big, fat, luscious
marshmallow.

— *Janet Wong*

Be Glad Your Nose Is on Your Face

Be glad your nose is on your face,
not pasted on some other place,
for if it were where it is not,
you might dislike your nose a lot.

Imagine if your precious nose
were sandwiched in between your toes,
that clearly would not be a treat,
for you'd be forced to smell your feet.

Your nose would be a source of dread
were it attached atop your head,
it soon would drive you to despair,
forever tickled by your hair.

Within your ear, your nose would be
an absolute catastrophe,
for when you were obliged to sneeze,
your brain would rattle from the breeze.

Your nose, instead, through thick and thin,
remains between your eyes and chin,
not pasted on some other place —
be glad your nose is on your face!

— *Jack Prelutsky*

Reggie

It's summertime
And Reggie doesn't live here anymore
He lives across the street
Spends his time with the round ball
Jump, turn, shoot
Through the hoop
Spends his time with arguments
     and sweaty friends
And not with us
He's moved away
Comes here just to eat and sleep
     and sometimes pat my head
Then goes back home
To run and dribble and jump and stretch
And stretch
And shoot
Thinks he's Kareem
And not my brother

— *Eloise Greenfield*

WHAT ARE POCKETS FOR?

What are pockets for?
An old piece of sash cord,
a knob from a door;
a small U magnet,
if you can find it;
a sprung clock spring,
with the key to wind it;
oodles of marbles,
a twist of copper wire;
a baseball calendar,
a flint for fire;
one soiled jack of hearts
or the five of spades;
that unshown copy of
your last month's grades;
two colored pebbles,
one hickory nut;
a shell, some fish line
with three feet of gut;
a cog out of something
which never did run;
a cellophane of candy —
I'll give you one;

your first circus ticket stub,
the snap you took
of the clown on the slack
wire before it shook;
a flashlight bulb,
a dirty green stamp;
the long-missing part of
your bicycle lamp;
one thin pair of pliers
to ply or to nip;
one old zipper fastener
with nothing to zip;
that half-busted harness-
bell you found inside
the barn on the farm,
and the buckle too wide
for its three-inch strap;
and a whole lot more
of stuff. Did you say,
What are pockets for?

— *David McCord*

249

Ode to Pablo's Tennis Shoes

They wait under Pablo's bed,
Rain-beaten, sun-beaten,
A scuff of green
At their tips
From when he fell
In the school yard.
He fell leaping for a football
That sailed his way.
But Pablo fell and got up,
Green on his shoes,
With the football
Out of reach.

Now it's night.
Pablo is in bed listening
To his mother laughing
To the Mexican *novelas* on TV.
His shoes, twin pets
That snuggle his toes,
Are under his bed.
He should have bathed,
But he didn't.
(Dirt rolls from his palm,
Blades of grass
Tumble from his hair.)

He wants to be
Like his shoes,
A little dirty
From the road,
A little worn
From racing to the drinking fountain
A hundred times in one day.
It takes water
To make him go,
And his shoes to get him
There. He loves his shoes,
Cloth like a sail,
Rubber like
A lifeboat on rough sea.
Pablo is tired,
Sinking into the mattress.
His eyes sting from
Grass and long words in books.
He needs eight hours
Of sleep
To cool his shoes,
The tongues hanging
Out, exhausted.

— *Gary Soto*

Dream Variation

To fling my arms wide
In some place of the sun,
To whirl and to dance
Till the white day is done.
Then rest at cool evening
Beneath a tall tree
While night comes on gently,
    Dark like me —
That is my dream!

To fling my arms wide
In the face of the sun,
Dance! Whirl! Whirl!
Till the quick day is done.
Rest at a pale evening. . . .
A tall, slim tree. . . .
Night coming tenderly
    Black like me.

— Langston Hughes

Creating

Write a Poem

Write a poem that begins with the words "I wish" or "I see" or "I remember." Repeat the opening phrase on every line or on alternating lines. Be as free and imaginative as you like. Do not try to make the poem rhyme.

Variation: Choose another phrase of your own to begin the poem.

Tips

- If you need help getting started, work with a partner. Take turns adding lines.
- Try adding a color, a place name, or an animal to each line of the poem.
- Wait to correct your spelling and punctuation until after the poem is finished.

Read On Your Own

Falling Up

by Shel Silverstein (Harper)

Silverstein's last collection contains over a hundred poems and drawings, all in his distinctive style.

The Earth Under Sky Bear's Feet

by Joseph Bruchac (Philomel)

These poems of the land represent the Mohawk, Pima, Pawnee, Navajo, and other Native peoples.

Soul Looks Back in Wonder

by Tom Feelings (Dial)

Langston Hughes, Mari Evans, and Lucille Clifton are among the African American poets featured in this collection.

Joyful Noise

by Paul Fleischman (Harper)

The fourteen poems in this Newbery-winning collection are meant to be read aloud by two voices.

Peeling the Onion

by Ruth Gordon (Harper)

This collection contains poems by Roethke, Whitman, Paz, Rexroth, and many others.

Voices
of the
Revolution

*"We always had governed ourselves,
and we always meant to."*
farmer at the Battle of Lexington, April 1775

*"The flame is kindled and like lightning
it catches from Soul to Soul."*
Abigail Adams

*"I know not what course others
may take, but as for me, give me
liberty or give me death!"*
Patrick Henry

Pulling Down the Statue of George III at Bowling Green (New York City), by William Walcutt

Voices of the Revolution

Contents

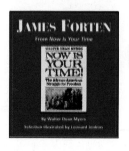

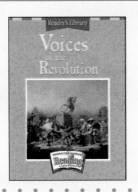

Reader's Library

- **Bunker's Cove**
- **The Drummer Boy**
- **Deborah Sampson: Soldier of the Revolution**

Theme Paperbacks

Daughter of Liberty
by Robert Quackenbush

Phoebe the Spy
by Judith Berry Griffin

Guns for General Washington
by Seymour Reit

Book Links

And Then What Happened, Paul Revere?

by Jean Fritz

Katie's Trunk
by Ann Turner

Then try . . .

Can't You Make Them Behave, King George?

by Jean Fritz (Putnam)
The colonists' rebellion is seen from the perspective of King George III, who imposed taxes that enraged the colonists.

A Young Patriot

by Jim Murphy (Clarion)
Using the original journal entries of a soldier in the Continental army, the author records the hardships of war.

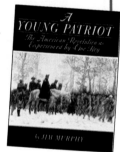

Then try . . .

Toliver's Secret

by Esther Wood Brady (Random)
Dressed as a boy, ten-year-old Toliver slips past British sentries to deliver secret military information for her Patriot uncle.

If You Lived at the Time of the American Revolution

by Kay Moore (Scholastic)
Discover what life was like, especially for children, during the Revolution, when some families were Patriots and others were Loyalists, supporting King George III.

258

If you like . . .

James Forten
by Walter Dean Myers

Then try . . .

Samuel's Choice

by Richard Berleth (Whitman)

A young African American slave in Brooklyn Heights must decide what to do when the fighting gets closer, and only he can help the rebels against the British.

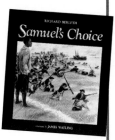

The Fighting Ground

by Avi (Harper)

Thirteen-year-old Jonathan, eager to fight the British, discovers that war is not all fame and glory.

Internet

Do you want to find out about these books and more? Visit Education Place:

www.eduplace.com/kids

- Look up reviews by readers around the country for these and other books about the Revolutionary War.

- Post your own *Voices of the Revolution* book review.

Win cool prizes for reading great books. Go to:

www.bookadventure.org

AND THEN WHAT HAPPENED,
PAUL REVERE?
by JEAN FRITZ
PICTURES BY MARGOT TOMES

On the
Brink of War

Between 1765 and 1770, people in the thirteen American colonies grew tired of being ruled by England. When the English king ordered more taxes, the colonists found ways to oppose him. *And Then What Happened, Paul Revere?* shows how one American Patriot helped begin a revolution to end English rule.

◄ The colonists showed their hatred of unfair taxes wherever possible — even on teapots!

No Stamp Act.

A VIEW OF PART OF ... OF BOSTON IN NEW ENGLAND AND BRITISH SHIPS OF WAR

▲
King George III sent soldiers to make the colonists obey his laws. In protest, Paul Revere created this picture of English ships arriving in Boston Harbor in 1768.

New England farmers prepared to fight the British on a moment's notice. That moment arrived on April 19, 1775, when the first shots of the American Revolution were fired in Lexington, Massachusetts.

◀ The Patriots came from many backgrounds and professions. Paul Revere, shown in this portrait by John Singleton Copley, was a silversmith and an **express** rider, spreading news of Patriot and British activities.

Courtesy, Museum of Fine Arts, Boston. Reproduced with permission.
©1999 Museum of Fine Arts, Boston. All Rights Reserved.

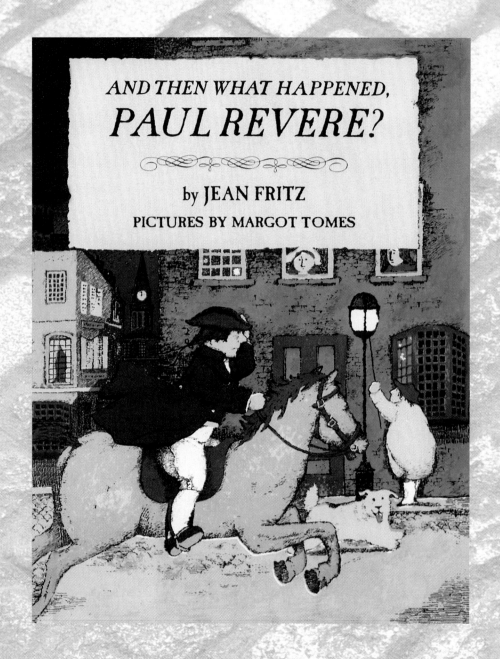

AND THEN WHAT HAPPENED, PAUL REVERE?

by JEAN FRITZ

PICTURES BY MARGOT TOMES

Strategy Focus

As you read, **evaluate** the way Jean Fritz describes Paul Revere. How well do you think she tells the story of his life?

262

In 1735 there were in Boston 42 streets, 36 lanes, 22 alleys, 4,000 houses, 12 churches, 4 schools, 418 horses (at the last count), and so many dogs that a law was passed prohibiting people from having dogs that were more than 10 inches high. But it was difficult to keep dogs from growing more than 10 inches, and few people cared to part with their 11- and 12-inch dogs, so they paid little attention to the law. In any case there were too many dogs to count.

Along with the horses, streets, and alleys, there were, of course, people in Boston — about 15,000. Four of them lived in a small wooden house on North Street near Love Lane. They were Mr. Revere, a gold and silversmith; his wife, Deborah; their daughter, Deborah; and their young son, Paul Revere, born the first day of the new year.

Of all the busy people in Boston, Paul Revere would turn out to be one of the busiest. All his life he found that there was more to do, more to make, more to see, more to hear, more to say, more places to go, more to learn than there were hours in the day.

In Boston there was always plenty to see. Ships were constantly coming and going, unloading everything from turtles to chandeliers. Street vendors were constantly crying their wares — everything from fever pills to hair oil to oysters. From time to time there were traveling acrobats, performing monkeys, parades, firework displays, and fistfights.

Once there was a pickled pirate's head on exhibit; once there was a polar bear.

And there was plenty for Paul to do. When he was a teenager, his father died, and Paul took over the silversmithing business. He made beads, rings, lockets, bracelets, buttons, medals, pitchers, teapots, spoons, sugar baskets, cups, ewers, porringers, shoe buckles, and candlesticks.

Once he made a silver collar for a man's pet squirrel.

To make extra money, he took a job ringing the bells in Christ Church. In Boston, church bells were rung not just on Sundays but three times a day on weekdays, at special hours on holidays and anniversaries, for fires and emergencies, whenever a member of the congregation died, and whenever there was especially good news or especially bad news to announce. Sometimes at a moment's notice word would come that the bells were to be rung, and off Paul would run, his hat clapped to his head, his coattails flying.

Busy as he was, Paul liked to do new things. If there was excitement around, he liked to find it. In the spring of 1756, when Paul was twenty-one years old, there was, as it happened, a war close by, and Paul didn't want to miss it. French soldiers, along with Indians, were attacking the borders of the colonies. So Paul grabbed his rifle, buckled on his sword, clapped his hat to his head, and off he went — coattails flying — to defend Fort William Henry on Lake George.

And what happened?

Paul spent the summer sitting around, cleaning his rifle and polishing his sword. And swatting flies. There were thousands of flies at Lake George that summer. But there were no French or Indians.

In November the Massachusetts men were sent home. Paul went back to Boston, married Sarah Orne, and began filling up his house with children. There were Deborah, Paul, Sarah, Mary, Frances, and Elizabeth (in addition to two babies who died young). Then Sarah died, and Paul married Rachel Walker, and along came Joshua, Joseph, Harriet, Maria, and John (in addition to three more babies who died young).

Paul kept putting up new chairs at the kitchen table, and now in addition to making buckles, spoons, cups, and all the other silver items, Paul had to find new ways to make money. So he engraved portraits, produced bookplates, sold pictures, made picture frames, brought out hymnbooks, and became a dentist. "Artificial Teeth. Paul Revere," he advertised. "He fixes them in such a Manner that they are not only an Ornament, but of real Use in Speaking and Eating."

You would think that with all Paul Revere did, he would make mistakes. But he always remembered to put spouts on his teapots and handles on his cups.

The false teeth that he whittled out of hippopotamus tusk looked just fine.

Generally when he did arithmetic in his Day Book, he got the right answers.

Of course, sometimes there were so many different things to do that he forgot what he was doing. In the beginning of a new Day Book, he wrote, "This is my book for me to —", but he never finished the sentence.

Sometimes he was in such a hurry that his writing looked sloppy. At the end of a letter he would write, "Pray excuse my scrawl."

Sometimes he was late for his work. There was a hymnbook, for instance, that didn't come out until eighteen months after he promised it.

Once he built a barn and by mistake put part of it on a neighbor's property.

Still, Paul Revere wasn't always at work. Occasionally he just dreamed. There was one page in his Day Book that he used simply for doodling.

But beginning in 1765, there was no time for doodling. The French had stopped bothering America, but now the English were causing trouble, telling the colonies they couldn't do this and couldn't do that, slapping on taxes, one after another. First there was a tax on printed matter — newspapers, diplomas, marriage licenses. When this was withdrawn, there was a tax on tea, glass, printers' colors, and paper. The one tax England would never give up was the tax on tea.

And what did Paul Revere do about it?

He became a leader of the Sons of Liberty, a secret club that found interesting ways to oppose the English.

One of Paul's busiest nights was December 16, 1773. He prepared for it by smearing his face with red paint and lampblack, pulling a tight stockinglike covering over his head, and draping a ragged blanket over his shoulders. Then he picked up his ax and joined other Sons of Liberty, all pretending to be Indians, all carrying axes.

And what were they up to?

They were going to make sure that no one in Boston would pay taxes on the three shiploads of tea that had just arrived from England. So they marched on board the ships, hauled the chests of tea onto the decks, broke them open with their axes, and dumped the tea — 10,000 pounds of it — into Boston Harbor. It was all done in an orderly fashion. No one was hurt; no other cargo was touched; the ships were unharmed. (There was only one minor incident when a man, found stuffing tea into the lining of his coat, had to be punished.)

When the Sons of Liberty finished, they marched home, washed their faces, and went to bed.

But not Paul Revere. Someone had to ride to New York and Philadelphia and spread the news. And Paul was picked to do it.

So off he galloped, his hat clapped to his head, his coattails flying. From Boston to Cambridge to Watertown to Worcester to Hartford *(watch out, dogs on the road! watch out, chickens!)* to New York to Philadelphia he went. And back. 63 miles a day. (This was not swatting flies!)

He was back in Boston on the eleventh day, long before anyone expected him.

Paul Revere became Massachusetts' Number One express rider between Boston and Philadelphia. He also became a secret agent. In the winter of 1774 it looked more and more as if the English soldiers in Boston meant to make war on America, and Paul's job was to try to find out the English plans.

He was far too busy now to write in his Day Book. He was too busy to make many silver teapots or to whittle many teeth. Instead, he patrolled the streets at night, delivered messages to Philadelphia, and kept himself ready at all times to warn the countryside.

Sometimes on his missions things went just right. He got past the sentries, got through the snow, kept his horse on the road, and kept himself on his horse.

Sometimes things went poorly. Once the English found him in a rowboat snooping around Castle Island in Boston Harbor. So they stopped him, questioned him, and locked him up. He stayed locked up for two days and three nights.

But all his rides, Paul knew, were small compared to the Big Ride that lay ahead. Nothing should go wrong with this one. In the spring, everyone agreed, the English would march into the countryside and really start fighting. And when they did, Paul Revere would have to be ahead of them.

On Saturday, April 15, spring, it seemed, had arrived. Boats for moving troops had been seen on the Charles River. English scouts had been observed on the road to Lexington and Concord. A stableboy had overheard two officers making plans.

At about 10 o'clock on Tuesday night, April 18, Dr. Joseph Warren, who was directing Patriot activities in Boston, sent for Paul Revere. Other messengers had been dispatched for Lexington and Concord by longer routes. Paul was to go, as planned, the same way the English were going — across the Charles River. He was to alarm the citizens so they could arm themselves, and he was to inform John Hancock and Samuel Adams, Boston's two Patriot leaders who were staying in Lexington. And Paul was to leave now.

He had already arranged a quick way of warning the people of Charlestown across the river. Two lanterns were to be hung in the steeple of the North Church if the English were coming by water; one lantern if they were coming by land.

So Paul asked a friend to rush to the North Church. "Two lanterns," he told him. "Now."

Then he ran home, flung open the door, pulled on his boots, grabbed his coat, kissed his wife, told the children to be good, and off he went — his hat clapped to his head, his coattails flying. He was in such a hurry that he left the door open, and his dog got out.

On the way to the river Paul picked up two friends, who had promised to row him to the other side. Then all three ran to a dock near the Charlestown ferry where Paul had kept a boat hidden during the winter. Paul's dog ran with them.

The night was pleasant, and the moon was bright. Too bright. In the path of moonlight across the river lay an armed English transport. Paul and his friends would have to row past it.

Then Paul realized his first mistake. He had meant to bring cloth to wrap around the oars so the sound would be muffled. He had left the cloth at home.

That wasn't all he had left behind. Paul Revere had started out for his Big Ride without his spurs.

What could be done?

Luckily, one of Paul's friends knew a lady who lived nearby. He ran to her house, called at her window, and asked for some cloth. This lady was not a time waster. She stepped out of the flannel petticoat she was wearing and threw it out the window.

Then for the spurs. Luckily, Paul's dog was there, and luckily, he was well trained. Paul wrote a note to his wife, tied it around the dog's neck, and told the dog to go home. By the time Paul and his friends had ripped the petticoat in two, wrapped each half around an oar, and launched the boat the dog was back with Paul's spurs around his neck.

Paul and his two friends rowed softly across the Charles River, they slipped carefully past the English transport with its 64 guns, and they landed in the shadows on the other side. Safely. There a group of men from Charlestown who had seen the signal in the church steeple had a horse waiting for Paul.

And off Paul Revere rode on his Big Ride.

He kept his horse on the road and himself on his horse, and all went well until suddenly he saw two men on horseback under a tree. They were English officers. One officer sprang out and tried to get ahead of Paul. The other tried to overtake him from behind, but Paul turned his horse quickly and galloped across country, past a muddy pond, toward another road to Lexington.

And what happened to the officers?

One of them galloped straight into the mud and got stuck; the other gave up the chase.

Paul continued to Lexington, beating on doors as he went, arousing the citizens. At Lexington he woke up John Hancock and Samuel Adams and advised them to leave town. He had a quick bite to eat, and then, in the company of two other riders, he continued to Concord, warning farmers along the way.

For a while all went well. And then suddenly from out of the shadows appeared six English officers. They rode up with their pistols in their hands and ordered Paul to stop. But Paul didn't stop immediately.

"Stop!" one of the officers shouted. "If you go an inch farther, you are a dead man."

Paul and his companions tried to ride through the group, but they were surrounded and ordered into a pasture at one side of the road.

In the pasture six other officers appeared with pistols in their hands.

One of them spoke like a gentleman. He took Paul's horse by the reins and asked Paul where he came from.

Paul told him, "Boston."

The officer asked what time he had left Boston.

Paul told him.

The officer said, "Sir, may I crave your name?"

Paul answered that his name was Revere.

"What! *Paul* Revere?"

Paul said, "Yes."

Now the English officers certainly did not want to let Paul Revere loose, so they put him, along with other prisoners, at the center of their group, and they rode off toward Lexington. As they approached town, they heard a volley of gunfire.

"What was that?" the officer said.

Paul said it was a signal to alarm the countryside.

With this piece of news, the English decided they'd like to get back to their own troops in a hurry. Indeed, they were in such a hurry that they no longer wanted to be bothered with prisoners. So after relieving the prisoners of their horses, they set them free.

And then what happened?

Paul Revere felt bad, of course, to be on his Big Ride without a horse. He felt uneasy to be on a moonlit road on foot. So he struck out through the country, across stone walls, through pastures, over graveyards, back into Lexington to see if John Hancock and Samuel Adams were still there.

They were. They were just preparing to leave town in John Hancock's carriage. Paul and Hancock's clerk, John Lowell, went with them.

All went well. They rode about two miles into the countryside, and then suddenly John Hancock remembered that he had left a trunk full of important papers in a Lexington tavern. This was a mistake. He didn't want the English to find those papers.

So what happened?

Paul Revere and John Lowell got out of the carriage and walked back to Lexington.

It was morning now. From all over the area farmers were gathering on Lexington Green. As Paul crossed the green to the tavern, there were between 50 and 60 armed men preparing to take a stand against the English. The troops were said to be near.

Paul went into the tavern, had a bite to eat, found the trunk, and carried it out, holding one end while John Lowell held the other. As they stepped on the green, the troops appeared.

And then what happened?

274

Paul and John held onto the trunk. They walked right through the American lines, holding onto the trunk. They were still holding on when a gun was fired. Then there were two guns, then a succession of guns firing back and forth. Paul did not pay any attention to who was firing or who fired first. He did not stop to think that this might be the first battle of a war. His job was to move a trunk to safety, and that's what he did.

The battles of Lexington and Concord did, of course, begin the Revolutionary War. And they were victories for the Americans who have talked ever since about Paul Revere's ride. Some things went well on Paul's ride, some things went poorly, but people have always agreed that the ride was a success.

But now that the war had started, what did Paul Revere do?

Naturally, he kept busy. He rode express for the Committee of Safety, for which he was paid 4 shillings a day. (He had asked for 5.) He printed paper money for the colony, engraved its official seal, supervised the setting up of a powder mill, learned how to make brass and iron cannon, and took part in two military engagements — one in Rhode Island, one in Maine. And as a lieutenant colonel in the Massachusetts militia, he was put in command of the fort at Castle Island.

Some things went well for Paul during the war. Some things went poorly — the same as always.

At the end of the war Paul was 48 years old. He went back to silver-smithing, but this wasn't enough to keep him occupied. So he opened a hardware store. In addition to hardware, he sold sandpaper, playing cards, woolen cloth, sealing wax, fish lines, wallpaper, pumice stones, pencils, and spectacles. (Once he sold Samuel Adams two dozen sleigh bells.)

Later he set up a foundry and made stoves, anvils, forge hammers, bolts, cogs, braces and pumps.

Then he began to make church bells. He made 398 bells, most of them weighing at least 500 pounds. He charged 42 cents a pound for them and often had trouble collecting his bills. (75 of his bells still ring in New England steeples.)

Still later he learned how to roll sheet copper, set up a rolling mill, and made copper sheathing for ships. And when the dome of Boston's new Statehouse was built, Paul gave it a shiny copper covering.

But Paul Revere was not always at work. Sometimes he just dreamed. Sometimes he would go back in his mind to the days when he was Massachusetts' Number One express rider. Then, if anyone were around, Paul would talk about his Big Ride. He even wrote out the story of his ride — in a hurry, of course, for the writing looked sloppy.

Boston was not the same as it had been when Paul was a young man.

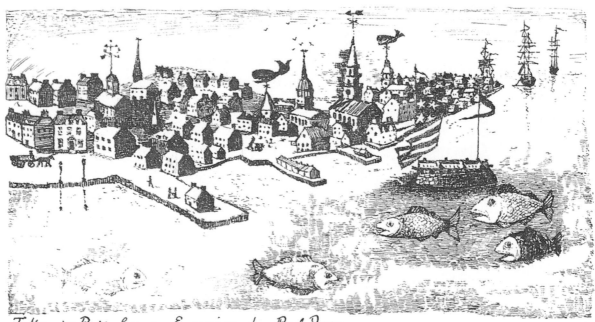

Taken, in Part, from an Engraving by Paul Revere

No one bothered now to count the streets and the alleys, the horses and houses. They were too busy putting up new buildings, tearing down hills, filling in ponds, building bridges, and making the city bigger. They still did count the people, however. In 1810, when Paul was 75 years old, there were 33,787 people in Boston. Nineteen of these were Paul's grandchildren. He also had great-grandchildren, but no one bothered to keep a record of them. But it was the great-grandchildren, more than anyone else, who liked being around when Paul told his story. If he paused or if he appeared to be reaching an end, they would urge him to keep on.

"And then what happened?" they would ask.
"And *then* what happened?"

Meet the Author

Jean Fritz

Home: Dobbs Ferry, New York

Accomplishments: Fritz has written more than forty-four books for children and adults.

Childhood: Fritz was born in China where her parents were missionaries. She came to the United States at age thirteen and found her American roots by reading about American heroes.

Reasons for writing about history: Fritz likes to show the human side of famous people. She believes that truth is often funnier than fiction.

Sampler of her books: *Where Was Patrick Henry on the 29th of May?*, *What's the Big Idea, Ben Franklin?*, *Won't You Sign Here, John Hancock?*

Meet the Illustrator

Margot Tomes

Accomplishments: Before her death in 1991, Tomes illustrated more than sixty-six books, four of them by Jean Fritz.

Childhood: Tomes was born in 1917 in Yonkers, New York. She loved old books and fairy tales, even though her fascination with monsters kept her awake at night.

Reasons for becoming an illustrator: Tomes called herself a "pre-television person." She preferred to spend her time reading and looking at book illustrations.

Find out more about Jean Fritz and Margot Tomes at Education Place.

www.eduplace.com/kids

Responding

Think About the Selection

1. Which word best describes Paul Revere for you: *smart, ambitious, busy, lucky, energetic, accomplished,* or some other word? Explain your choice.

2. Find examples in the selection to prove or disprove this statement: Paul Revere could not have carried out his famous midnight ride without help from others.

3. Jean Fritz writes that Paul Revere sometimes was forgetful, daydreamed, and made mistakes. Why do you think she included this information?

4. If Paul Revere were alive today, what would he be interested in? What kind of job do you think he might have? Explain your answer.

5. Compare Paul Revere's busy schedule with your own. Do you like to do many different things? Do you prefer to have just a few activities? Why?

6. Paul Revere used to tell his grandchildren stories about his life. If you were one of his grandchildren, what questions would you want to ask him?

7. **Connecting/Comparing** Of all Paul Revere's contributions to the American Revolution, which do you think is his most valuable one and why?

Write a Message

Paul Revere carried news of the Boston Tea Party to New York and Philadelphia. Write a message that he might have carried, giving details about the event and explaining its importance.

Tips

- **Begin the message with the most important facts.**
- **Include details that tell who, what, when, where, why, and how.**

Math

Compute Revere's Earnings

On p. 276, Jean Fritz tells us that Paul Revere made church bells. If each bell weighed 500 pounds, how much money did he earn making bells? If everyone paid their bills, how much did he earn from the bells that are still ringing in New England?

PAUL REVERE & SON,

No. 13, Lynn Street, North End, BOSTON,

Science

Compare Metals

Paul Revere made objects from many different metals: silver, copper, brass, and iron. Review the text to see how Revere used these metals. Choose one of the metals and explain how that metal is used today.

Bonus **Find out more about one of the metals listed above. Report your findings to the class.**

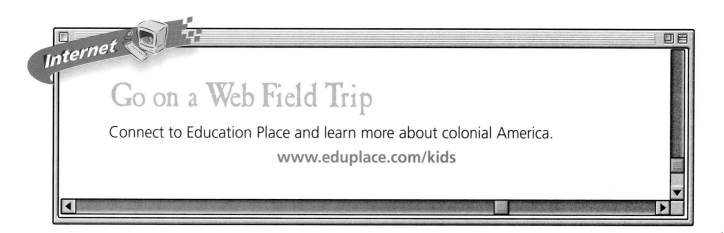

Go on a Web Field Trip

Connect to Education Place and learn more about colonial America.

www.eduplace.com/kids

Skill: How to Read Song Lyrics

❶ Look for these parts of a song:

Lyrics: all the words of a song.

Chorus: part that is repeated.

Stanzas: two or more lines of verse.

❷ Read the **lyrics** above or below the lines of musical notes. Notice the rhythm of the words.

❸ Read the remaining **stanzas**. Repeat the **chorus** at the end of each stanza.

Yankee Doodle

by Jerry Silverman

The surest way to popularize an idea in song is to set new words to a familiar melody. As early as 1767, there was mention in Philadelphia of a comic song called "Yankee Doodle."

When the word "yankee" first appeared in print, people were not quite sure what it meant. To this day there is some confusion about its origin. Some people believe it comes from an Indian word; others think it is based on a French word. The strongest possibility is that it comes from the Dutch name for the English colonists: "Jan Kaas," or "Jan Kees." Jan (yan) is Dutch for John; kees means cheese. "John Cheese" was not meant as a compliment. Neither was "Doodle," which means a fool.

"Yankee Doodle" first appeared in print in a London broadside in 1775. Its subtitle was "The Lexington March." The British band played it on the march to Lexington. In those days, European armies played loud music on the way into battle. It cheered up the soldiers and gave them courage. In this case, the strains of the music let the Minutemen know exactly where the British were.

The Minutemen also realized that the British were trying to make fun of them by calling them "Yankee Doodles." In the true spirit of the times, the familiar melody was taken up by the Americans (with new words by a Harvard College student, Edward Bangs) and sung right back at them. It is this version of "Yankee Doodle" that has gone down in American history.

In verse one, a boy visits a rebel, or patriot, camp with his father. The entire song is a light-hearted description of his impressions of the soldiers, captains, and arms. "Hasty pudding" was a quickly prepared cornmeal mush.

Yankee Doodle went to town
Riding on a pony;
Stuck a feather in his cap
And called it macaroni.

This well-known verse doesn't seem to have anything to do with the rest of the song. Most people who sing it probably assume that it is just a bit of Revolutionary War nonsense. Not at all!

This verse was sung by the British to taunt the patriots. In eighteenth-century England, a "macaroni" was a gentleman who wore overly fancy clothes in what he thought was the "Italian style," to try and make himself look more important than he really was. In other words, a macaroni was a dandy.

And just what was Yankee Doodle trying to do? He was, from the British point of view, getting "all dressed up" and "putting on airs." Yankee Doodle, in this verse, represents the colonies and their foolish desire to be free of Great Britain.

General Washington in military uniform on a white horse, painted around 1835.

283

Yankee Doodle

1. Fath'r and I went down to camp, A - long with Cap - tain Good - ing, And

there we saw the men and boys As thick as ha - sty pud - ding.

Chorus

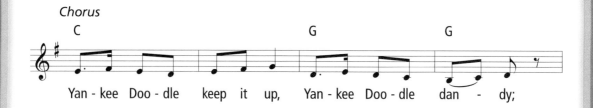

Yan - kee Doo - dle keep it up, Yan - kee Doo - dle dan - dy;

Mind the mu - sic and the step, And with the girls be han - dy.

2. And there we see a thousand men
   As rich as Squire David,
   And what they wasted every day,
   I wish it could be saved. *Chorus*

3. I see a little barrel, too,
   The heads were made of leather,
   They knocked upon with little clubs,
   And called the folks together. *Chorus*

4. And there was Captain Washington,
   And gentle folks about him;
   They say he's grown so tarnal proud
   He will not ride without them. *Chorus*

5. He got him on his meeting-clothes,
   Upon a slapping stallion,
   He set the world along in rows,
   In hundreds and in millions. *Chorus*

Fighting with Fife and Drum

Songs like "Yankee Doodle" were made popular by boys who signed up with the colonial army to play the drum or the fife, a wind instrument that looks like a flute.

Army leaders depended on the young fifers and drummers to give commands to the troops during a battle. Each drumbeat or tune had a different meaning. The drum's loud rattle could be heard over the roar of muskets and cannons. The fife's shrill notes could carry a long distance.

After a battle, the fifers and drummers helped to gather the scattered company together. On the way back to camp, they kept up the soldiers' spirits with lively marching tunes. In camp, they signaled when it was time to eat or to take a break.

The musicians often wore a different uniform from the soldiers so that officers could locate them quickly. But the different uniforms enabled the enemy to locate them also. Because of their important role, the boys were key targets, and many did not survive to see the outcome of the war.

The Spirit of '76, from the painting by Archibald Willard

A Story

A story is a narrative made up by the author. Use this student's writing as a model when you write a story of your own.

A good story has a clear **plot** with a **problem.**

It's important to introduce the **characters** and the **setting** right away.

The Boston Tea Party

My father, James Codder, was going to throw tea off the boat. "Dad, please don't go to Boston Harbor. You might get arrested," I begged him.

He simply said, "No, Drew, the taxes are way too high. I have to stand up for what I think is right. You'll understand when you're older."

"I don't think I will," I told him. He didn't listen to me. "One more day," I said to myself while I was getting into my bed.

The day came when my dad was going to Boston Harbor. "Drew," he said, "You're coming. We need a lookout." I didn't even want to argue because I'd have to go anyway. I kept saying to myself, "I'm too young to go to jail. I'm too young to go to jail." I was living in fear practically the whole day!

When we were eating dinner, my father and I were dressed in black, and my father said with pride, "Tonight's the night!" I got my coat and my scarf, and went outside shaking with fear.

"It's going to be about an hour's walk," he told me. I almost fainted. I hated the thought of my dad going to Boston Harbor in the first place, and now I had to walk three miles with him to get there. It just wasn't fair. I didn't want to argue, or I'd be grounded forever. We talked about what we would do when we got to Boston Harbor. We were going to meet the other people at a boat called the *Beaver*, which was filled with tea from England. I was exhausted, but my father was marching with pride.

After about ten minutes, I asked, "Are we there yet?" When I heard that it would be about ten more minutes, I felt relieved; at that point, I couldn't even feel my legs. We got there in time so I didn't collapse. We got to the boat, and everyone else was already there.

Dialogue makes the story real for the reader.

Details create mental pictures for the reader.

287

"This is my son Drew," my father said as he introduced me to his friends.

They looked at the boat and stared at it for a long time. Then someone said, "Let's do it! Let's throw this tea into the harbor!"

When everyone was getting into the boat, my father said, "You'll have to stay here." I nodded my head, and then I sat on a bench. It was freezing near the harbor. The men put on Native American clothing. I thought it was odd, but then my dad explained to me that they didn't want to get caught. I couldn't help thinking that this wasn't really fair. I hoped no one would get caught or be blamed.

I sat on the bench, terrified. After about ten minutes, I called up to my father, "Can we go? I'm cold and scared!" My father didn't hear me, so I just closed my eyes. I wondered if we were going to get caught. I tried to forget about it. I looked at my father. He looked back at me and smiled. I looked at the boxes, and there were only ten boxes left! I was so relieved!

> A good story often has suspense.

I went up to the boat and asked my dad, "Can I throw the last box off the boat?" He nodded his head. I climbed aboard and took the box from my dad's hands, and threw it as hard as I could. It made a big splash. I felt very important.

Everyone got out of their disguises and got off the boat. We were about to walk home, but one of my dad's friends said, "Need a ride?" My dad delightedly nodded his head. We got into the carriage and rode into the night.

A good ending **resolves** the story's problem.

Meet the Author

Drew W.
Grade: five
State: Massachusetts
Hobbies: skateboarding
What he wants to be when he grows up: a skateboarder

KATIE'S TRUNK
by Ann Turner

illustrations by Ron Himler

Who Were the Tories?

At the time of the American Revolution, nearly one third of all colonists were Tories, or Loyalists, who remained loyal to the king of England and believed that English laws were fair and just. They opposed the rebels who were arming and drilling to prepare for war. The story of *Katie's Trunk* shows how neighbor turned against neighbor in the growing trouble with England.

George III became king of England in 1760, shortly before he posed for this portrait by the English painter Allan Ramsay.

Even some famous Patriot families included Tories. Benjamin Franklin's son, William, the governor of colonial New Jersey, sided with the British.

Benjamin Franklin

William Franklin

The American Revolution caused between 75,000 and 100,000 Loyalists to leave the colonies. Most fled to Canada. This sketch shows a Tory family camping on its way up the St. Lawrence River in 1784.

Meet the Author
Ann Turner

When she writes historical fiction, Ann Turner tries to imagine herself as a child, alive in a particular time and place. She asks herself, "What would I do then? How would I feel and react?"

The story for *Katie's Trunk* came from a conversation between Turner and her aunt about an old trunk that used to be in her grandmother's basement. "'One of our ancestors hid in it when the Revolutionary soldiers came,' she told me one day. I was astonished. 'You mean we were *Tories*?' I had to write a story about it, and the character of Katie came to mind — a rebellious, spirited girl (as I was) who would have wanted to protect her family's things from the rebels." Turner's other books include *Dakota Dugout, Dust for Dinner, Red Flower Goes West,* and *Mississippi Mud: Three Prairie Journals.*

Meet the Illustrator
Ron Himler

As a child in Cleveland, Ohio, Ron Himler spent many hours each week drawing at his grandmother's house. Since then, in a career that spans three decades, he has illustrated more than eighty books.

Himler lives in the American Southwest, where his special interest is researching and painting the ceremonies of Native Americans.

To find out more about Ann Turner and Ron Himler, visit Education Place. **www.eduplace.com/kids**

KATIE'S TRUNK
by Ann Turner

illustrations by Ron Himler

Strategy Focus

What would it be like to be a Tory if your neighbors were Patriots? When you read, **summarize** the conflict between Katie's family and their neighbors.

293

When I'd been bad all day long,
hiding Hattie's doll under the sofa
and never telling where it went,
Mama sighed and said, "I should sit you down
to sew long seams all day
and get the goodness straight inside,
Katie. What is wrong with you?"

I couldn't tell it with a name,
though I felt it inside,
the way a horse knows a storm is near.
I could feel the itchiness in the air,
the wind bringing cold,
the clouds tumbling over the trees
bringing rain — a sour rain.

"Must be," Mama sighed and sat down to tea,
"must be all this trouble and fighting.
Why, it makes me skittish as a newborn calf,
all this marching and talking,
these letters your Papa speaks of,
that tea they dumped in the harbor."

Mama's hand shook.

"Tea! In the harbor! Wasting God's good food."

Brother Walter said, "That's not the least of it.
It will get worse."

She peered at him.

"How could it be worse, Walter?"

Then she shut her lips on the words.

Already we had lost friends, neighbors,
families we had played with on the green
and helped with building their new barns.

Celia Warren no longer spoke to me.
Her brother, Ralph, no longer spoke to Walter.
Sometimes I heard that word hissed, "Tory!"
like a snake about to bite.
The rebels were arming, brother told me,
marching and drilling beyond the meadows.

I'll never forget the day they came.
The sun was hot on the mill pond
and Walter, Hattie, and I watched the dragonflies
peel their skins off on the long grass
and fly away.
Something like smoke rose over the road
and out of it Papa came running. "Get your mother!
Hide in the woods. The rebels are coming!"

We ran to the house,
Mama's face like a white handkerchief.
She shoved a piece of pork pie in our hands
and ran us out to the thick woods
where we could hide.
Crouched in the underbrush,
I felt like an animal in a trap. And suddenly
I was so mad I could not still myself.

I raced for the house,
Mama's fierce whisper trying to call me back.
I would not let John Warren and Reuben Otis
hurt our house and things. It was not right,
it was not just, it was not fair.

Inside our parlor, I touched each thing
I loved: Mama's pineapple teapot,
the silver tray, shining like a moon,
the pictures of all our kin
ranged across the wall — home.

Then I heard voices by the door,
Reuben Otis, John Warren, Harold Smith
and others, not our neighbors.
"This'll be fine pickings!"
They paused on the front step
and ripped the knocker off the wood.

I ran into Mama and Papa's room,
looking for a place to hide.
If they could steal, they could hurt as well.
There was Mama's wedding trunk,
big and black and domed.
I pulled up the trunk lid and hid under the dresses.
In the shut down darkness everything
was muffled and faraway. The door slamming.
Their footsteps next door in the parlor.

"English goods!" someone spat
and something hit the floor and broke.
My breath stuck in my throat.
I heard Reuben say,
"Mr. Gray has money here. Look hard for it."
John Warren spoke of arms they would buy.
The air closed around my mouth
like a black cloth.

I bit my hand and prayed,
though I was never much good at that.
I thought my words might go up to God
like bubbles in a pond to the silver top
where they would burst. "Please, God,
don't let them find me, don't let them hurt us,
let me breathe."
The footsteps came closer, someone leaned against
the trunk. My breath got caught somewhere midst
my stomach and chest, and I could not
get it back. There wasn't enough air.
John Warren said, "Fine dresses and silver here."
He pulled up the lid and the sweet air rushed in.
I sucked in a breath as a dress was snatched out.
The rustlings drowned their words,
another dress went, and a hand touched me.
I wanted to bite it, to make him jump and shout,
but I stilled myself. Maybe he didn't know.
Suddenly, he shouted, "Out! The Tories
are coming. Back to the road! Hurry!"
He did not close the lid, and footsteps sounded
out the door.

Sudden quiet. My heart beat loud
as the horses galloping down the road.
Quiet as quiet, I crept
to the window and looked out. No one.
Puffs of smoke far down on the green.

A horse thudding past, riderless;
someone's hat blowing by in the gusty wind.
Would I ever play with Celia again?
Would I always wear this name, Tory, as if
it were written on my chest?

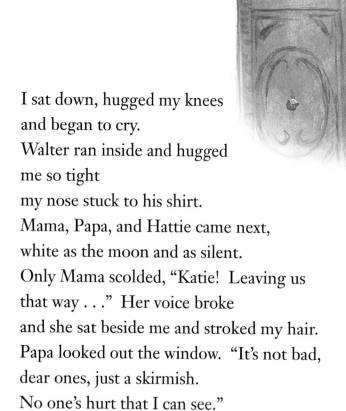

I sat down, hugged my knees
and began to cry.
Walter ran inside and hugged
me so tight
my nose stuck to his shirt.
Mama, Papa, and Hattie came next,
white as the moon and as silent.
Only Mama scolded, "Katie! Leaving us
that way . . ." Her voice broke
and she sat beside me and stroked my hair.
Papa looked out the window. "It's not bad,
dear ones, just a skirmish.
No one's hurt that I can see."

Walter's mouth snapped open and then
shut tight. I wiped my eyes on his sleeve.
A sudden thread like a song
ran through my head. When Mama asked me
to sew straight seams to get the goodness straight
I knew I couldn't do it.
But John Warren had. When I hid
in the black stuffy trunk,
when my breath got lost in Mama's dresses,
he left the trunk lid up to let me breathe
and called the others away.

He'd left one seam of goodness there,
and we were all tied to it:
Papa, Mama, Walter, Hattie
and me.

Responding

KATIE'S TRUNK
by Ann Turner

illustrations by Ron Himler

Think About the Selection

1. What is it like for Katie to be a member of a Tory family living among rebel neighbors? How does the conflict make her feel?

2. If you were Katie's friend Celia Warren, would you stop speaking to Katie? Explain what you would do and why.

3. Katie says "It was not fair" for rebels to break into her house. Do you agree with her? Why or why not?

4. Do you think Katie was right or wrong to run back to her house? Explain your answer. Find evidence from the selection that supports your opinion.

5. What causes John Warren to leave the trunk lid open and call the other rebels away? What effect does his action have on Katie?

6. Katie says that John Warren left a "seam of goodness there, and we were all tied to it" on page 303. What does she mean? What effect might that "seam of goodness" have on her family?

7. **Connecting/Comparing** Both Katie and Paul Revere face challenges caused by the conflict with England. What do you think is the biggest challenge each one faces? How does each respond to that challenge?

Creating

Write a Scene for a Screenplay

Assume that *Katie's Trunk* is going to be made into a movie. Write a screenplay for one scene. For example, you might choose the scene in which Katie hides after hearing the rebels at the door.

Tips
- Write each character's name before his or her lines.
- Write instructions telling the actors where to move and how to say their lines.

Art

Make a Mobile

On p. 298, Katie notices things that represent home for her. Create a mobile using cardboard, magazine photographs, drawings, or foil to show things that represent home for you. Thread string through your creations and tie them to a hanger.

Bonus **Write a poem about your family to hang from your mobile.**

Listening and Speaking

Hold a Debate

Reread what Katie's mother says about the Boston Tea Party and other conflicts. Do you agree with her? With a partner or small group, make a list of reasons supporting the Patriot or Tory point of view. Invite another group to take the opposite point of view. Present your opinions to the class in a debate.

Tips

- **Be sure each group has equal time to speak.**
- **Support your opinion with strong reasons.**
- **Give a summary at the end of the debate.**

Internet

Write a Review

Write your own review of *Katie's Trunk*. What did you like? What didn't you like? Explain why. Then post your review on Education Place.

www.eduplace.com/kids

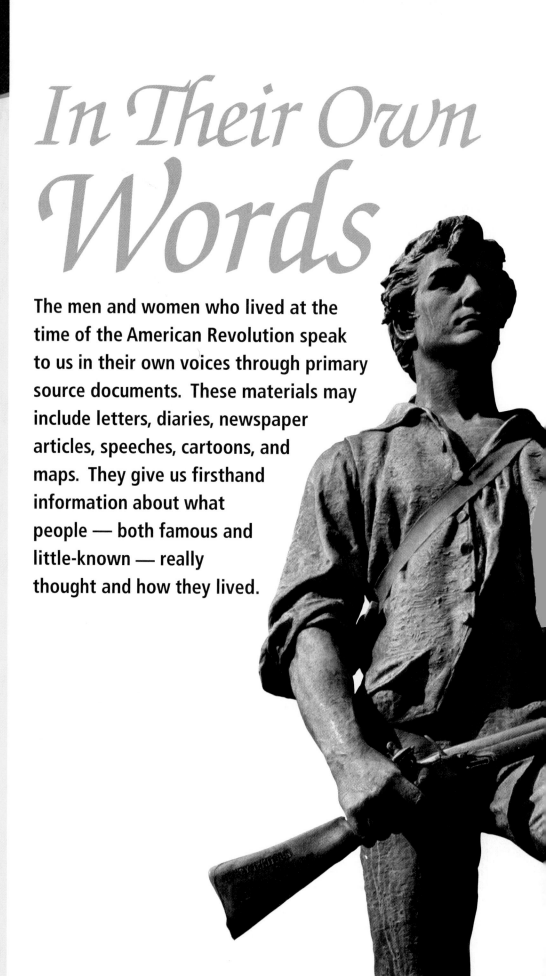

In Their Own Words

The men and women who lived at the time of the American Revolution speak to us in their own voices through primary source documents. These materials may include letters, diaries, newspaper articles, speeches, cartoons, and maps. They give us firsthand information about what people — both famous and little-known — really thought and how they lived.

When war began, the American army urgently needed soldiers. Notices like this one were posted to persuade men to enlist.

....

Cambridge, April 28, 1775

To: The Massachusetts Committee of Safety

An Appeal for Help

Gentlemen:

The barbarous murders committed on our innocent brethren on Wednesday the 19th . . . have made it absolutely necessary that we immediately raise an army to defend our wives and children from the butchering hands of an inhuman soldiery. . . . [They] will, without doubt, take the first opportunity in their power to ravage this devoted country with fire and sword.

Death and devastation are the certain consequences of delay. . . . Hasten and encourage, by all possible means, the enlistment of men to form the army, and send them forward to headquarters at Cambridge.

....

◀ This statue at Lexington, Massachusetts, honors the farmers who stood their ground against the British in April of 1775.

After the clash between the colonists and the British on April 19, 1775, a British officer wrote this letter to his father. What is his opinion of the Yankees?

Boston, April 23, 1775

My Dear Sir,

It is impossible [for you not to] hear an account, and probably a most exaggerated one, of the little fracas that happened here a few days ago between us and the Yankee scoundrels. Our bickerings and heart-burnings, as might naturally be expected, came at length to blows, and both sides have lost some men . . . The rebels, you know, have [for] a long time been making preparations as if to frighten us . . . Though they are the most absolute cowards on the face of the earth, yet they are just now worked up to such a degree of enthusiasm and madness that they are easily persuaded . . . that they must be invincible.

from the Memoir and Letters of Captain Evelyn

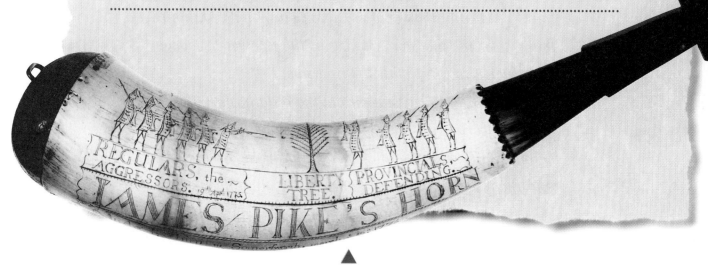

▲ Most Revolutionary soldiers carried powder horns, which held gunpowder for firing rifles. Made from animal horn and wood, some powder horns were elaborately carved, like this one made by James Pike of New Hampshire. "Regulars" were British soldiers; the Liberty Tree was a popular symbol of the rebellion; and "Provincials" were American soldiers.

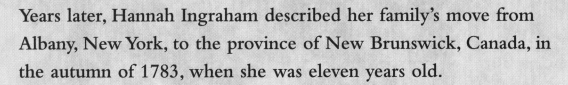

An encampment of Loyalists on the banks of the St. Lawrence River in Ontario, Canada. ▶

The Ingraham family, like thousands of other Loyalists, fled to Canada after the American Revolution. Years later, Hannah Ingraham described her family's move from Albany, New York, to the province of New Brunswick, Canada, in the autumn of 1783, when she was eleven years old.

....

It was a sad, sick time after we landed in Saint John. We had to live in tents. The government gave them to us and rations, too. It was just at the first snow then, and the melting snow and the rain would soak up into our beds as we lay. Mother got so chilled and developed rheumatism and was never well afterwards.

[Later we went] up the river in a schooner and were nine days getting to St. Anne's. . . . We lived in a tent at St. Anne's until Father got a house ready.

One morning when we awoke, we found the snow lying deep on the ground all around us. Then Father came wading through it and told us the house was ready and not to stop to light a fire and not to mind the weather, but follow his tracks through the trees. . . . It was snowing fast and oh, so cold. Father carried a chest and we all took something and followed him up the hill.

There was no floor laid, no windows, no chimney, no door, but we had a roof. . . . We toasted bread [around a small fire] and all sat around and ate our breakfast that morning. Mother said . . . "This is the sweetest meal I ever tasted for many a day."

....

Fighting for Freedom

Many African Americans played important roles in the American Revolution. Some, like James Forten, a sailmaker from Philadelphia, fought at sea. Others served as soldiers or spies, or smuggled food through British lines. In all, more than 5000 black soldiers, both free and enslaved men, risked their lives for America's independence. Many fought to gain their own freedom as well.

▲ This painting is widely believed to be a portrait of James Forten (1766–1842). After the Revolution, Forten was **influential** in the fight to free slaves.

◀ This Philadelphia school, which James Forten attended, was founded by Quakers, who were **abolitionists**. They wanted to get rid of slavery and **assisted** African Americans in getting an education and finding good jobs.

310

Hundreds of African American men served in the Continental navy. The sailor in this 1779 portrait may have been on the crew of a **privateer**, a private ship used in naval **conflict**. James Forten also served on a privateer.

By 1778, Rhode Island and Massachusetts each had an African American army unit. The Patriot leader John Hancock presented this flag to the Massachusetts troop in honor of its bravery. ▼

Meet the Author Walter Dean Myers

Growing up in New York City, Walter Dean Myers read and wrote constantly, filling one notebook after another with stories and poems. In his twenties, Myers entered a contest for picture book writers. He won. Today, he has published more than thirty-five books for children and young adults. *Now Is Your Time* describes the important roles that African Americans played in our nation's history. "History has made me an African American," says Myers. "What we understand of our history is what we understand of ourselves."

Myers's novels about young people include *Me, Mop, and the Moondance Kid,* and *Mop, Moondance, and the Nagasaki Knights.*

Meet the Illustrator
Leonard Jenkins

Leonard Jenkins was born in Chicago, Illinois. By the time he was in high school, he was exhibiting his paintings and selling them to admirers.

Jenkins believes that talent and hard work are essential for an artist. But he adds, "Your art must go beyond how well you can paint. It has to go to the soul."

Find out more about Walter Dean Myers and Leonard Jenkins at Education Place. **www.eduplace.com/kids**

312

JAMES FORTEN

From *Now Is Your Time*

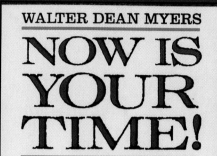

By Walter Dean Myers

Selection illustrated by Leonard Jenkins

James Forten served on a ship during the Revolution. As you read, think of **questions** to discuss with classmates about his experiences.

313

It was early morning on Tuesday, September 2, 1766, in the city of Philadelphia. The roads into the city were already filling with farmers bringing in produce to sell. Windows in the city were coming alive with the glow of lamplight. Small factory owners trudged through the winding streets to small shops. Printers, shoemakers, blacksmiths, candle makers, bakers — all began the business of the day. For Philadelphia was indeed a city of business.

As day broke over the harbor, the masts of the ships loomed against the gray skies. The ships rocked at their moorings as if they, too, were ready for the new day.

Hundreds of free men of African descent lived in Philadelphia. The city

314

was the home of a number of noted abolitionists — people who wanted to abolish, or do away with, the practice of slavery — including the Quakers, a powerful and influential religious group. More important was the fact that Africans could find work in Philadelphia.

Many of the Africans worked the docks, loading and unloading the ships that brought products to the colonies from all over the world. Others were tradesmen and seamstresses, cooks, barbers, and common laborers. All along the eastern seaboard, from Baltimore to New England, free Africans worked on boats, hauling loads, carrying passengers, and fishing. Many opened restaurants. Others bought their own boats and tried their luck on the brisk waterfronts.

Thomas Forten, a free African, was employed by Robert Bridges, a sail-maker in Philadelphia. Sail making was a profitable but difficult job. Sewing the coarse cloth was brutal on the hands. The heavy thread had to be waxed and handled with dexterity. A person trying to break the thread with his hands could see it cut through his flesh like a knife. But Forten appreciated his job. It paid reasonably well and the work was steady.

Forten helped in all aspects of sail making and assisted in installing the sails on the ships the firm serviced. With the income from his work he had purchased his wife's freedom. Now, on this early Tuesday morning, a new baby was due. The baby, born later that day, was James Forten.

Young James Forten's early life was not that different from that of other poor children living in Philadelphia. He played marbles and blindman's bluff, and he raced in the streets. When he was old enough, he would go down to the docks to see the ships.

Sometimes James went to the shop where his father worked and did odd jobs. Bridges liked him and let him work as much as he could, but he also encouraged Thomas Forten to make sure that his son learned to read and write.

The Fortens sent their son to the small school that had been created for African children by a Quaker, Anthony Benezet. He believed that the only way the Africans would ever take a meaningful place in the colonies would be through education.

Thomas Forten was working on a ship when he fell to his death. James Forten was only seven at the time. His mother was devastated, but still insisted that her son continue school. He did so for two more years, after which he took a job working in a small store.

What James wanted to do was to go to sea. He was fourteen in 1781 when his mother finally relented and gave her permission. America was fighting for its freedom, and James Forten would be fighting, too.

He knew about the difficulties between the British and the American colonists. He had seen first British soldiers and then American soldiers marching through the streets of Philadelphia. Among the American soldiers were men of color.

A black child in Philadelphia in the 1700's had to be careful. There were stories of free Africans being kidnapped and sold into slavery. He had seen the captives on the ships. They looked like him: the same dark skin, the same wide nose; but there was a sadness about them that both touched his heart and frightened him. He had seen Africans in chains being

marched through the streets, on their way to the South. He never forgot the sight of his people in bondage, or accepted it as natural that black people should be slaves.

But the black soldiers Forten saw were something special. Marching with muskets on their shoulders, they seemed taller and blacker than any men he had ever seen. And there were African sailors, too. He knew some of these men. They had been fishermen and haulers before the conflict with Great Britain; now they worked on privateers and navy ships. Sometimes he heard talk about naval battles, and he tried to imagine what they must have been like.

In the summer of 1781, James Forten signed onto the privateer *Royal Louis,* commanded by Stephen Decatur, Sr. The colonies had few ships of their own to fight against the powerful British navy and issued "letters of marque" to private parties. These allowed the ships, under the flag of the United States, to attack British ships and to profit from the sale of any vessel captured.

The *Royal Louis* sailed out of Philadelphia in August and was quickly engaged by the British vessel *Active,* a heavy armed brig sent from England to protect its trade ships.

The *Royal Louis's* guns were loaded with gunpowder that was tamped down by an assistant gunner. Then the cannonball was put into the barrel and pushed against the powder. Then the powder would be ignited. The powder had to be kept belowdecks in case of a hit by an enemy ship.

Forten's job was to carry the powder from below to the guns. Up and down the stairs he raced with the powder as shots from the British ship whistled overhead. There were large holes in the sails and men screaming as they were hit with grapeshot that splintered the sides of the ship. The smell of gunpowder filled the air as Captain Decatur turned his ship to keep his broadside guns trained on the *Active.* Sailors all about Forten were falling, some dying even as others cried for more powder.

Again he went belowdecks, knowing that if a shot ripped through to the powder kegs, or if any of the burning planks fell down into the hold, he would be killed instantly in the explosion. Up he came again with as much powder as he could carry.

After what must have seemed forever with the two ships tacking about each other like angry cats, the *Active* lowered its flag. It had surrendered!

Decatur brought his ship into Philadelphia, its guns still trained on the limping *Active.*

The crowd on the dock cheered wildly as they recognized the American flag on the *Royal Louis.* On board the victorious ship James Forten had mixed feelings as he saw so many of his comrades wounded, some mortally.

The *Royal Louis* turned its prisoners over to military authorities. On the 27th of September, the *Active* was sold; the proceeds were split among the owners of the *Royal Louis* and the crew.

The sailors with the worst wounds were sent off to be cared for. The others, their own wounds treated, were soon about the business of repairing the ship. Forten must have been excited. Once the fear of the battle had subsided and the wounded were taken off, it was easy to think about the dangerous encounter in terms of adventure. And they had won.

The missing crew was replaced. The ship was checked carefully by its captain and found to be in fine fighting condition. The crew carried more ammunition aboard, more powder, and fresh provisions. Once more they sailed for open waters.

On the 16th of October, 1781, they sighted a ship, recognized it as British, and made for it instantly. As they neared, a second ship was spotted, and then a third. Decatur turned to escape the trap, but it was already too late. The three British ships, the *Amphyon,* the *Nymph,* and the sloop *Pomona,* closed in. It was soon clear that the *Royal Louis* had two choices: to surrender or to be sunk.

The *Royal Louis* lowered its flag. It had surrendered, and its crew were now prisoners. Forten was terrified. He had heard the stories of the British sending captured Africans to the West Indies to be sold into slavery. He knew the *Pomona* had sailed back and forth from the colonies to the island of Barbados, where many Africans already languished in bondage. It was a time for dread.

James was taken aboard the *Amphyon* with others from his crew. On board the British ship Captain Beasley inspected the prisoners. There were several boys among the American crew, and he separated them from the older men.

Captain Beasley's son looked over the boys who had been captured. Many of them were younger than he was. Although still prisoners, the boys were given more freedom than the men, and Beasley's son saw the Americans playing marbles. He joined in the game, and it was during this playing that he befriended Forten.

The result of this tentative friendship was that Captain Beasley did not, as he might have done, send Forten to a ship bound for the West Indies and slavery. Instead he was treated as a regular prisoner of war and sent to the prison ship the *Jersey*.

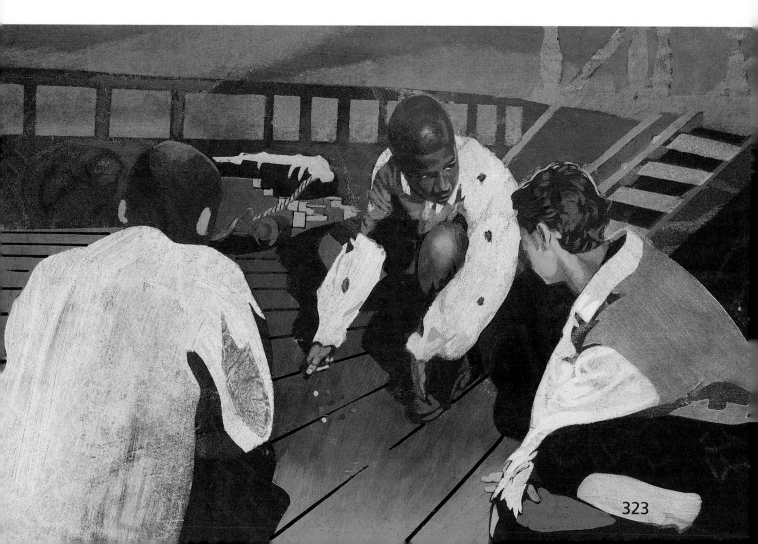

Dark and forbidding, the *Jersey* was a sixty-gunner anchored off Long Island, in New York. It had been too old to use in the war and had been refitted first as a hospital ship and then as a ship for prisoners. The portholes had been sealed and twenty-inch squares carved into her sides. Across these squares iron bars were placed.

The captain of the *Jersey* greeted the prisoners with a sneer. All were searched under the watchful eyes of British marines. The wounded were unattended, the sick ignored. The pitiful cries of other prisoners came from belowdecks. A few pale, sickly prisoners, covered with sores, were huddled around a water cask. Then came the cry that some would hear for months, others for years.

"Down, Rebels, down!"

They were rebels against the king, to be despised, perhaps to be hanged. Traitors, they were being called, not soldiers of America. James was pushed into a line on deck. The line shuffled toward the water cask, where each man could fill a canteen with a pint of water. Then they were pushed roughly belowdecks.

The hold of the ship was dark. What little light there was came from the small squares along the hull. The air was dank as men relieved themselves where they lay. Some of the prisoners were moaning. Others manned pumps to remove the water from the bottom of the boat.

Sleep was hard coming, and James wasn't sure if he wouldn't still be sold into slavery. Beasley's son had liked him, he remembered, and the boy had offered to persuade his father to take James to England. It would have been better than the hold of the *Jersey*.

In the morning the first thing the crew did was to check to see how many prisoners had died during the night. Many of the prisoners were sick with yellow fever. For these death would be just a matter of time.

Forten later claimed that the game of marbles with Beasley's son had saved him from a life of slavery in the West Indies. But on November 1, two weeks after the capture of the *Royal Louis,* the news reached New York that Brigadier General Charles Cornwallis, commander of the British army in Virginia, had surrendered to George Washington. Washington had strongly protested the British practice of sending prisoners to the West Indies. It was probably the news of his victory, more than the game of marbles, that saved the young sailor.

James Forten was not a hero. He did not single-handedly defeat the British, or sink a ship. But he fought, like so many other Africans, for the freedom of America, and he fought well. He was only one of thousands of Africans who helped to create the country known as the United States of America.

In Philadelphia, after the war, James Forten became an apprentice to the man his father had worked for, Robert Bridges. Like his father, James was a hard worker. Eventually he would run the business for Robert Bridges, and by 1798 he owned it. At its height the business employed forty workers, both black and white. Forten became one of the wealthiest men in Philadelphia. He married and raised a family, passing on to them the values of hard work he had learned from his father. Forten made several major contributions to the sail-making business, among them a method of handling the huge sails in a shop, which allowed sails to be repaired much faster and saved precious time for ship owners. In the coming years he would use his great wealth to support both antislavery groups and the right of women to vote — at a time when over 90 percent of all Africans in America were still in a state of enslavement.

James Forten became one of the most influential of the African abolitionists. He spent much of his life pleading for the freedom of his people in the country his people had helped to create.

327

Responding

Think About the Selection

1. We remember James Forten more for his life after the American Revolution than for his role during the war. Use the selection to discuss whether this statement is true or false.

2. Do you think James Forten was treated fairly when he was a prisoner? How do you think prisoners of war should be treated?

3. After the British ship, the *Active,* surrendered, James Forten had "mixed feelings" about the victory. Why? Describe the feelings he may have had.

4. James Forten and Captain Beasley's son shared an interest in playing marbles. What interests do you have that might help build a friendship?

5. Choose one of the events that helped shape James Forten's life. What do you think he learned from this experience?

6. Walter Dean Myers writes that James Forten was "not a hero." Do you agree or disagree? Explain why. What do you think it means to be a hero?

7. **Connecting/Comparing** Many people, both Patriots and Tories, risked their lives during the American Revolution. Compare the dangers that Paul Revere, Katie Gray, and James Forten each faced during the war.

Persuading

Write a Dialogue

What do you think James Forten said to persuade his mother to let him go to sea? What might she have said in reply? Write a dialogue between Forten and his mother that shows how each feels.

Tips

- Be sure that each character states his or her opinion clearly and backs it up with strong reasons.
- Use correct punctuation and capitalization.

Social Studies

Create a Pamphlet

Based on what you have read about Philadelphia in this selection, create a pamphlet that tells about the city's strong points in 1781. Try to persuade people to move to the city.

Viewing

Write a Caption

Look back at the illustrations in the selection. Choose one that you find interesting or exciting. Then write a caption that provides a short explanation of what is happening in the illustration.

Take an Online Quiz

In this theme, *Voices of the Revolution,* you read about people who helped create the United States. Take our online quiz at Education Place to see what you remember. **www.eduplace.com/kids**

Games of Young America

Skill: How to
Follow Directions

❶ Read through the
directions, noting
materials needed
and the sequence of
steps. Pay special
attention to **order
words** such as *first,
next, then, after,* or
finally. Study pic-
tures or diagrams, if
provided.

❷ **Gather** the materi-
als. **Reread** the
steps, one at a time,
and **follow** each in
sequence.

❸ If you don't under-
stand a step, **reread**
the directions.
Check diagrams
again.

When James Forten and Captain Beasley's son played marbles on the deck of the British ship *Amphyon*, they were taking part in a game that has been popular for more than 2000 years.

Many games from the time of the American Revolution are still with us, such as tag, leap frog, and hide-and-seek. Other games have changed only slightly. Jackstraws, quoits, and the game battledore and shuttle-cock are known today as pick-up sticks, horseshoes, and badminton.

Most colonial games relied on simple objects found at home. One of the most popular games of the revolutionary period, hoop-rolling, used the wood or metal hoops that held barrels together.

The games described here would look very familiar to James Forten and his friends. When you play them you will be keeping alive traditions that are hundreds of years old.

Marbles, or "Ring Taw"

As you will discover, hitting the marbles in the circle requires practice and skill!

Players: 2 to 5
Materials: 6 marbles or cranberries per player
Object of the Game: To win marbles belonging to other players

How to Play

1. Draw a circle, three feet in diameter, on a level surface.
2. Draw another circle, one foot in diameter, in the center of the first circle.
3. Place marbles inside the smaller circle, five marbles for each player. Save the sixth marble as the "shooter."
4. To choose the first player, take turns shooting from the outside circle. To shoot, cradle the marble in one hand and release it with a fast flick of the thumb. The player whose shooter lands closest to the inside circle has the first turn.
5. Take turns trying to shoot marbles out of the inside circle. Players keep all the marbles they shoot out. A turn ends when a player misses.
6. Play until all the marbles have been shot from the circle. The player with the most marbles is the winner.

Snail

In the 1700s, children often scratched the pattern for this game in the dirt with a stick.

Players: 2 to 4

Materials: Number cube; up to four different kinds of markers (beans or buttons); a game board, as shown.

Object of the Game: To be the first player to arrive at the center of the spiral.

How to Play

1. Choose markers — a different marker for each player.
2. Take turns rolling a number cube. The highest number goes first.
3. The first player rolls a number cube and moves the number of spaces shown. The next player rolls and moves. Take turns to the left around the circle.
4. No player may land in an occupied space. If a player rolls a three and that space is occupied, he or she must give up that turn.
5. The winner is the first to land on the last spot in the center of the spiral. A player close to the last spot cannot move if he or she rolls a number higher than the remaining spaces.

Eleven Men's Morris

This game may remind you of tic-tac-toe.

Players: 2

Materials: Two different kinds of markers such as beans or pennies; eleven markers for each player. A game board, as shown, copied on paper or poster board.

Object of the Game: To make the most rows of three markers in a line and remove opponent's markers from the board.

How to Play

1. Choose markers. Decide who goes first.

2. Take turns putting down one marker at a time, always placing markers at a point where lines cross or meet. Markers can be placed horizontally, vertically, or diagonally. Three markers in a straight line make a row. When a player makes a row, he or she can remove the opponent's marker if it is not already part of a row.

3. When all the markers have been placed on the board, continue to try to make rows by moving a marker in any direction to the next vacant point.

4. The game ends when one player has only two markers left, or when no one can make another move. The player with more markers left on the board wins.

✔ Writing a Personal Response

Some tests ask you to choose one of two topics and write a personal response to it. Here is a sample. Use the tips when you write this kind of answer.

Tips

- Read the directions carefully. Look for key words that tell you what to write about.
- Decide which topic you'll write about.
- Plan your response before you begin to write. Think about the topic and list supporting reasons and examples.
- After you have finished writing, proofread for errors.

Write one or two paragraphs about one of the topics below.

a. In the theme *Voices of the Revolution*, you learned about different trades or jobs. What trade do you think you might have wanted to learn during the time of the American Revolution? Why?

b. In *Katie's Trunk*, you saw the American Revolution from the Tory side. Which side would you have supported during the Revolution, the Tories or the Patriots? Why?

Now look at a good answer that one student wrote, and the features that make this a good response.

In the Revolution I would have supported the Patriots. Even though the British paid for the colonists' trip over, I don't think the British had the right to do the things that they did that led up to the Revolutionary War.

The British taxed everything and had soldiers on patrol. It's not as if the British were supplying the colonists with essential living products, such as food and water. If the British had done that then the colonists would not have gotten mad. The British were basically saying we're not going to help you survive, but we're still going to rule and tax you.

The response focuses on the topic throughout.

Details support the answer.

The writer uses vivid and exact words.

There are few grammar, spelling, capitalization, or punctuation errors.

Person to Person

*Cuando ayudamos a otro,
ambos nos fortalecemos.*

When one helps another,
both gain in strength.

— Ecuadorian proverb

Person to Person

Contents

Reader's Library

- **Something for Everyone**
- **Pretty Cool, for a Cat**
- **Trevor from Trinidad**
- **Upstate Autumn**

Theme Paperbacks

The Junior Thunder Lord

by Laurence Yep

Frindle

by Andrew Clements

Where the Flame Trees Bloom

by Alma Flor Ada

Book Links

If you like . . .

Mariah Keeps Cool
by Mildred Pitts Walter

Then try . . .

Ernestine and Amanda

by Sandra Belton (Simon)
When their paths keep crossing, two girls reluctantly form a fragile friendship.

The Kid in the Red Jacket

by Barbara Park (Random)
Ten-year-old Howard thinks a move across country is bad enough, but he hadn't counted on a six-year-old neighbor determined to become his best friend.

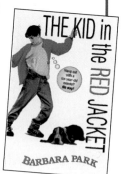

If you like . . .

Mom's Best Friend
by Sally Hobart Alexander

Then try . . .

Like Jake and Me

by Mavis Jukes (Knopf)
Alex wants to be like his rugged cowboy stepfather, but they don't seem to have much in common.

A Letter to Mrs. Roosevelt

by C. Coco De Young (Delacorte)
When her family faces losing its home during the Depression, Margo believes a letter to Eleanor Roosevelt is their only hope.

Yang the Second and Her Secret Admirers

by Lensey Namioka

Thank You, Jackie Robinson

by Barbara Cohen (Beech Tree)

A boy and an old man of different races and religions become friends through their admiration for Jackie Robinson.

Thief of Hearts

by Laurence Yep (Harper)

Chinese American Stacy resents having to look after the new Chinese girl at school, until the girl is accused of theft.

Dear Mr. Henshaw

by Beverly Cleary

Strider

by Beverly Cleary (Morrow)

In the sequel to *Dear Mr. Henshaw,* Leigh Botts and a friend care for an abandoned dog they name Strider.

Chevrolet Saturdays

by Candy Dawson Boyd (Puffin)

Joey's difficulties at school with an unsympathetic teacher and coach may bring him closer to his new stepfather.

Internet

For more great books, visit **www.eduplace.com/kids** and **www.bookadventure.org**

Volunteering

To **volunteer** is to give your time and energy freely, not because you have to, but because you want to.

In *Mariah Keeps Cool,* one of the characters volunteers her time at a shelter for the homeless. Other characters organize a party to benefit the shelter.

Have you ever volunteered to do something? What did you do? How did you feel while you were helping?

Maybe you've been part of a team of volunteers. People can be **amazingly** productive when they're all working together, whether it's to perform in a play, clean up litter on a beach, or **decorate** a wall with a mural.

Members of a team of volunteers don't **compete** with each other. They're working together for a common goal: to finish a job, to create something, to help people. And at the end, there's often a **celebration** to say: We did it!

These students in St. Paul, Minnesota are helping to clean up their neighborhood.

Mildred Pitts Walter

Born: Sweetville, Louisiana, 1922

Home: Denver, Colorado

Work: Shipwright helper during World War II; elementary school teacher; children's book writer since 1969

How her writing career began: Looking for books by and about African Americans for her students, Walter was challenged by a publisher to write one herself. The result was her first book, *Lillie of Watts: A Birthday Discovery*.

Family: "I think family is everything within the lives of human beings. Not just the nuclear family, but the extended family — grandmothers, uncles, cousins, friends, community, city, country."

Booklist: *Justin and the Best Biscuits in the World*; *Kwanzaa: A Family Affair*; *Have a Happy*; *Mississippi Challenge*; *The Suitcase*

Nneka Bennett

Born: New Jersey, 1972

Favorite art materials: Watercolor paints and colored pencil

Illustrators she especially admires: Leo and Diane Dillon

To young artists: "You can take my mom's advice: Follow your heart and don't let anyone sway you away from your dreams."

To find out more about Mildred Pitts Walter and Nneka Bennett, visit Education Place. **www.eduplace.com/kids**

MARIAH KEEPS COOL

by Mildred Pitts Walter

Read the selection title and the introduction. What do you **infer** about Mariah? How do you **predict** her plans will turn out?

*Mariah and her pals — the Friendly Five — are getting
ready for a big swim meet, with the help of their classmate
and coach, Brandon. Meanwhile, Mariah is planning
a surprise birthday party for her sister Lynn, with guests
bringing donations for the homeless shelter where Lynn
volunteers. Organizing the party has also brought Mariah
closer to her half sister, Denise.*

Only four days before Lynn's birthday and nine days before
the swim meet. Mariah felt there were not enough hours
in the day for all she had to do. Lynn's party took time, but
the hardest work continued to be getting ready for the meet. Each step
she took as she walked down the street was measured to the approach
on the springboard. She often thought about Lorobeth and wondered if
all this work was worth it. Maybe she could never compete and win.

Besides now having to spend four hours a day swimming, instead
of two, she had to spend time on the party. Each afternoon she worked
with Brandon, members of the Friendly Five, and Denise at Brandon's
house getting everything ready. Denise was more helpful than Mariah
had imagined. Today she was going to show the Friendly Five how to
make paper flowers to decorate their yard for the party.

Everything seemed under control except Lynn. Mariah felt that
Lynn suspected something unusual was going on when Lynn sometimes
suggested that Denise do things with her. Whenever Denise begged off,
Lynn, sometimes offended, wanted to know just what Denise was up to.

Mariah was grateful that Mama often stepped in and insisted that
Lynn do things with, or for, her.

That afternoon when Mariah was leaving for Brandon's she called,
"See you later, Denise."

"Where y'all going?" Lynn wanted to know.

Realizing she had made a mistake, Mariah quickly said, "I'm going
to Brandon's to swim."

"So where will you see Denise later?"

"At home. Same time I'll see you. When I get back."

As soon as Mariah reached Brandon's she called and asked her mama to please call home and send Lynn on an errand so Denise could more easily join them at Brandon's.

Finally Denise arrived. In Brandon's room they all got busy cutting colorful paper flower petals and clipping thin wire, wrapping it with strips of green paper to make flower stems. Mariah was surprised at how quickly Denise shaped the petals and stems into beautiful flowers. Soon all the girls were turning out flowers while Brandon worked on signs and banners.

"I think Lynn suspects something," Denise said.

"She better not know. This has to be a surprise," Cynthia said.

Just then Brandon's mother rushed to the door. "Hurry, get out to the pool. Lynn is coming."

They all started up. "Not you, Denise," Mariah commanded. "You hide in here."

"Oh, we don't have on our suits," Trina whispered as they all raced through the house.

"Take off your shoes," Mariah demanded. "Sit on the edge of the pool. Splash your feet."

Mariah listened as Brandon's mama talked to detain Lynn, and when Lynn entered the backyard Mariah called out as if surprised, "Lynn, what you doing here?"

"I was on an errand this way and thought I'd stop to see how you guys are doing with your strokes for the meet. You're not swimming today?"

"I'm letting them rest for a little while," Brandon said. "They'll be at it pretty soon."

"Please, Brandon, give us the day off," Nikki suggested.

"No way. We gotta work. And Lynn, you had better go."

"Let me see them for a little while. Just once," Lynn pleaded.

"No spectators when we work. Rules. Suit up, girls," Brandon ordered.

"Bye, Lynn," they all sang as they marched inside.

When Lynn had gone they rushed back to Brandon's room. "Whew!" Mariah exclaimed. "Brandon, you saved the day."

"Something's up," Trina said.

"Yeah. But who could've told?" Jerri asked.

"I really don't think she knows," Denise said. "I think maybe she suspects something."

"We better hurry and finish all this stuff," Mariah said. "This is getting to be hard on the nerves."

At dinner on the day before her birthday Lynn announced, "I just want to do nothing on my birthday but rest in bed all day."

Oh, no, Mariah thought as she glanced at Mama and then at Denise. Did Lynn know? Was she going to make it impossible for them to pull the party off as a surprise? Lynn really could be a pain.

"Fine," Denise agreed with Lynn. "Mariah and I will make breakfast and serve you in bed."

"You and Riah make breakfast?" Lynn laughed.

"Sure. We can fix fruit and cold cereal, huh, Riah?"

"You can make your specialty, Denise," Mariah suggested.

"She wouldn't want corn muffins for breakfast." Denise laughed. That was the only thing Denise made successfully since she had started to learn to cook.

"Yours are so good, Denise, maybe," Lynn said.

"We'll give you millet cereal for sure," Mariah said, and they all laughed.

Mariah went to bed worried. How would they ever get ready for the party? If only her sister were not so weird!

Early the next morning Mariah and Denise took a tray to Lynn's room, followed by Mama and Daddy. They sang "Happy Birthday" and as they were leaving Lynn to eat alone, Mama asked, "Lynn, are you sure you want to stay in bed all day?"

"I'm sure."

"Aw, Lynn . . ."

Mama quickly raised a hand. "Riah, we must honor that."

In the kitchen Mariah argued. "She can't be here. We'll never get things done. Do something, Mama. Take off from work and get her out of here."

"I had planned to take half a day off," Mama said.

"Hey, remember, Lynn said she wanted some books," Denise reminded them.

"She'd never refuse to shop for books," Mariah said. "And take her to lunch and to a movie, Mama."

"What if she won't go?" Denise suggested.

"She will," Mama said. "She'd better."

352

Mariah joined her friends at the rec center. They all wanted to know what time to come to get ready for the party.

"Might not be a party." Mariah told them about Lynn's decision to stay in bed all day.

"Somebody talked and she's being cool, huh?" Trina suggested.

"She makes me sick even if she is my sister," Mariah fumed.

"We told you. She's weird," Jerri said.

"I can say that, but you can't, okay?"

Mariah returned home just before noon and Lynn was still in her room. "I don't think she's gonna get up," Mariah said to Denise.

Denise responded quickly, "If she wants to act that way, I don't care. There'll be no surprise. We'll have to tell her."

Just then Mama came home. She went to Lynn's room. Mariah heard her say, "Lynn, I know you don't want a celebration, but I took off so you and I can do something."

"I don't want anything special."

"This isn't special. We'll go to the bookstore. How about that?"

"If we go maybe Riah and Denise would like to come, too."

Mariah wanted to shout *No!* but Mama said it for her, "No, no. We said no big thing. Just me and you. Get up and get ready."

As soon as they were out of the house, Mariah rushed to the phone. "Lynn's left the house. The surprise is on."

By three o'clock that afternoon Daddy had picked up all the things from Brandon's and everyone was there ready to work. Brandon's mother and Cynthia's grandmother came to help, too.

Mariah liked the way Denise had mixed and matched the colorful paper that covered the boxes. Only Denise and Lynn would dare mix those colors, she thought. The boxes were amazingly attractive.

Brandon put his handmade signs on the boxes: MEN'S AND BOYS' CLOTHING; WOMEN'S AND GIRLS' CLOTHING; and there was a box with the sign: CLOTHING FOR SMALL CHILDREN. Then he helped Mariah's daddy string the big banners across the yard so that they could not be seen from the street.

"Where's the music?" Brandon asked.

"Oh, I forgot the music," Mariah shouted.

"What's a party without music?" Trina asked.

"Don't worry," Daddy said. "I'll call Brandon's dad. He'll rig it up." Brandon's father supplied equipment for concerts and big parties.

Soon everything was ready. The yard looked festive as people began to arrive. The Friendly Five worked collecting food to put in boxes marked: CANNED GOODS and STAPLES AND DRIED FOODS. Denise worked with Brandon's mother and Cynthia's grandmother separating clothing and filling boxes.

Mariah looked around. The yard looked like a magic garden with the flowers and colorful boxes, the lights and banners. People stood together talking softly, waiting. Where was Lynn? Mariah worried. Had something happened?

Brandon's father set up the musical equipment and went to help Mariah's daddy get the grill ready for the hot dogs and bring out the tub of ice for the soft drinks. The cake, hot dog buns, chips, and all the relishes were on the table. Why didn't Mama bring Lynn?

Finally, Mariah heard the car in the driveway. She became so excited she could hardly say softly with force, "Quiet, everybody. She's here."

Lynn entered the backyard and they all shouted, *"SURPRISE!"*

Lynn's eyes widened, her mouth opened, she quickly covered it to stifle the sound and then spun around and tried to escape. Mama held her there until she came to herself.

Mariah beamed. She rushed to Lynn and threw her arms around her. "We did it," she cried. Lynn looked stunned, truly surprised. Mariah watched as Lynn looked at the banners: HAPPY BIRTHDAY, LYNN, WE LOVE YOU and SHARING IS CARING. Then Lynn saw the boxes filled with food and clothing for St. Martin's Shelter. Mariah knew she was fighting back tears when she said, "I didn't want a party, but I'm so glad all of you are here. I know my friends at St. Martin's will be happy to know that you care." She looked at Mariah, "Why didn't I think of this? I bet this was your idea, Riah."

"She's guilty!" a member of the Friendly Five shouted.

"And my friends and our sister, Denise, made it happen," Mariah said proudly. "Give them a hand." After everyone applauded, Mariah shouted, "Let's party."

Brandon picked a record, with some help from the Friendly Five. The music and the smell of hot dogs roasting filled the air. Mariah moved about making sure everyone was getting enough to eat and was having a good time.

Soon she had nothing to do. She stood with her friends watching Lynn and all of her friends dancing. No one asked her or the other Friendly Five members to dance.

"Go ask Brandon to come and dance with us," Jerri suggested.

"Not me," they all cried.

"I'll ask him," Mariah volunteered.

She came back without him. "His excuse is that he's playing the music."

"And Lynn's friends all think we're too young," Trina complained.

"We don't need them. Let's dance together, or by ourselves," Mariah said.

Later everyone sang "Happy Birthday" and shared Lynn's birthday cake and ice cream. After that, the crowd stayed on, reluctant to leave.

After midnight, when all the guests were gone, Mariah, still happy, did not even notice how tired she felt. The Friendly Five huddled with Brandon. "Now on to the meet," Mariah cried. With joined hands raised they shouted, "One down and one to go!"

"We did it once," Mariah said, "and we'll do it again."

MARIAH
KEEPS COOL

by Mildred Pitts Walter

Think About the Selection

1. Why do you think Mariah chooses the gift she does for Lynn? Do you think it was the right choice? Why or why not?

2. Would you like to receive, or give, the kind of gift Lynn received? Why or why not?

3. When Jerri says that Lynn is weird, Mariah replies, "I can say that but you can't, okay?" Why does Mariah say this?

4. Is Lynn surprised by the party, or did she know that something was up? Find details in the story that support your answer.

5. How would you describe Mariah? Would you like to have a friend like her? Explain.

6. How do the Friendly Five show that they are good problem solvers?

7. **Comparing/Contrasting** How do you think this selection fits the theme *Person to Person*? What do people do for each other?

Write an Invitation

In planning Lynn's party, Mariah might have sent invitations to the guests. Write an invitation Mariah might have sent. Give all the important information a party guest would need to know, including the surprise.

Tips

- Tell when and where the party is, and for whom.
- Include details about what to bring and why.
- Capitalize proper nouns and check for correct punctuation.

Plan a Healthy Diet

With a partner, review the categories of food that Lynn's guests collected for the homeless shelter on page 354. Note that *staples* means "important basic foods," such as flour or rice. Under each category, make a list of foods that you think would contribute to a healthy diet.

Bonus Plan a meal using the foods in your list.

Review an Illustration

Choose one of the illustrations in *Mariah Keeps Cool*. With a partner, discuss your thoughts about it. How does it fit with the words on the page? Is it a scene you would have chosen to illustrate? Why do you think the illustrator made the choices she did? If you wish, review more illustrations.

Internet

Take an Online Poll

In a group, brainstorm a list of ways you could help people in your community. Then take an online poll at Education Place to find out how other students your age have helped out in their communities. **www.eduplace.com/kids**

One Pair of Shoes
and a lot of good souls!

*by Ms. Ginsberg's fifth grade class
at the Ramaz School in New York City, New York*

Many people in the world are less fortunate than you or me. They don't have shoes or even a house. My school decided to do something to help.

— *Samantha Springer, age 11*

How it all started

One day on Zev Alpert's way to school, he saw a homeless man walking on the street without shoes. Zev didn't like the fact that it was close to winter and people who didn't have shoes would freeze their feet, so when he got to school he asked Ms. Ginsberg (our teacher) if he could start a shoe drive. She asked "Why?" Zev explained how he saw a man without shoes and Ms. Ginsberg said, "We're already doing City Harvest. Sorry, I don't think we can do it with everything else we have to do." Ms. Ginsberg thought about what Zev told her and started to regret the answer that she gave to him, so she went over to Zev and said "You know what? We will do the shoe drive and I regret what I said to you." That is how it got started.

— *Jonathan Robin*

How it all works

We get the shoes by giving out flyers to different people in the school building. Shoes come in from parents and kids. When we get to the school in the morning we always hang up our coat and books. But there's one thing different: We know that when we finish, if we have time left, we will polish and tie shoes. We buy different kinds of polish and make old shoes new again. It seems as though there's no end to them!

— *Jacob Savage*

To make the shoe drive successful we made posters and hung up advertisements.

— Eric Rechschaffen, age 11

Every Friday I go to the shoe stores to pick up shoes. I tell people every 2 pairs of shoes they bring in they get 15% off. This way it will help the shoe stores get more customers and help us get more shoes.

— Hannah Zimet, age 11

What we do with the shoes

A call came in from a drop-in shelter named Peter's Place on 23rd St. and 7th Ave. Our class delivered the shoes to Peter's Place. We had gotten 136 pairs of women's shoes and 62 pairs of men's shoes. We delivered the shoes and stayed for about two hours. In those two hours we played with the people, who were mostly seniors, watched television, and played ping-pong, chess, and checkers.

When we got back to school, we made plans to return. We decided to go have lunch at Peter's Place. We also decided to bring some gifts to the people at the shelter. Another class had an even greater task. They had to collect children's shoes and give them to a shelter for the children.

— Jess Mermelstein, age 10

The word *mitzvah* means a good deed in Hebrew. The project of giving shoes to those who need them is a big mitzvah.

— *Samuel Jesselson*

Every morning when I go to school, I always see a lot of people working with the shoes. They wash the shoes, polish them, and tie them, and much more. This has been going on since November and I still don't get bored helping and watching the shoes in motion. It's just amazing that so many kids get involved and want to help.

— *David Pollack, age 11*

So far we have collected about 800 pairs of shoes and we hope to reach at least 1,500!

— *Samantha Springer, age 11*

A Personal Narrative

A personal narrative gives a first-person account of a true experience. Use this student's writing as a model when you write a personal narrative of your own.

Grand Slam!

"Smack!" It looks like it's going all the way past the pale silver fence, 135 yards away from the plate.

"Oh man," I said, as the ball plopped down on the ground just before the fence. "Nick almost had a homer!"

Then I heard coach John say, "Shepard, you're up!"

Nervous and dripping with sweat, I got up to the plate. There were two outs and three men on: Ron, Nick, and Mike.

"Strike one!" called the ump. "Ball one! . . . Ball two!" Then again, "Strike two!"

The pressure was on as my teammates cheered, "Let's go, Tim. Let's go!" The pitch was there. It was a big, fat meat ball. I swung as hard as I could.

"Crack!" I hit the microscopic ball. As I ran to first, I saw my first base coach signaling me to go to second. As I touched second, I saw the ball glide over the fence. Then I heard a bang. "Beep! Boop! Boop! Beep! Beep! Boop! Beep! Boop!" I had hit a car, but I was still happy. It was a grand slam. I slowed down to a trot.

As I touched the dirty home plate, my team crowded around me. They were screaming and cheering. I tried desperately to run from them, but they kept chasing me around the field. I gave up the chase and they dog-piled me. I was so happy that my cheeks felt bright red.

Then I noticed something. My grand slam had just won us, the Vipers, the championship game! We had won 9 to 8. WE WERE THE CHAMPS!

Details help the reader follow the narrative.

A good **ending** ties the narrative together.

Meet the Author

Tim S.
Grade: five
State: Florida
Hobbies: sports, reading, and writing
What he'd like to be when he grows up: a lawyer

Mom's
Best
Friend

Sally Hobart Alexander
Photographs by George Ancona

Background and Vocabulary

A Special Relationship

Mom's Best Friend describes the special attachment between Sally Hobart Alexander and her dog guide, Ursula.

Visiting dogs help cheer up people in hospitals.

Dogs were probably the first animals to be tamed and trained by people. Their original role may have been to help people hunt. Since then dogs have **mastered** such jobs as guiding blind and hearing-impaired people, rescuing accident victims, and visiting and cheering up hospital patients.

366

German shepherds and Labrador retrievers are popular dog guides for the blind.

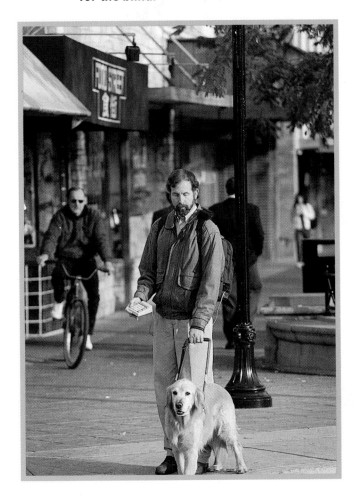

Hearing dogs act as ears for the hearing-impaired.

You will read about the **obedience training** Ursula goes through to learn her job. But **memorizing** routines and learning to avoid **obstacles** is only half of that special relationship between dog and human. The other half is a dog's **instinct** for being a pal.

When both halves of the relationship fit together — the learning and the love — something nice happens. The trained helper becomes a best friend.

Many dogs are specially trained for finding and rescuing people.

Meet the Author
Sally Hobart Alexander

Sally Hobart Alexander grew up in rural Pennsylvania where she hiked, swam, and acted out stories with her friends. Alexander was in her twenties, teaching third grade in California, when she lost her eyesight to a rare disease. The next year, she was teaching again, at a center for the blind in Pittsburgh. Making up stories for her two children led Alexander to a career as a children's book author. Her first book, *Mom Can't See Me*, was also illustrated by photographer George Ancona.

Meet the Photographer
George Ancona

George Ancona grew up near Coney Island in Brooklyn, New York. He learned photography from his father, and began to draw by copying photographs. After traveling in Mexico, his parents' birthplace, Ancona studied in art school and worked as a designer for magazines and television. Since then he has kept busy as a photographer and author of children's books.

To find out more about Sally Hobart Alexander and George Ancona, visit Education Place. **www.eduplace.com/kids**

Mom's Best Friend

Sally Hobart Alexander

Photographs by George Ancona

Strategy Focus

As you read about Mom and her dog guide, Ursula, **monitor** your understanding of Ursula's training. If necessary, reread and use the photographs to **clarify**.

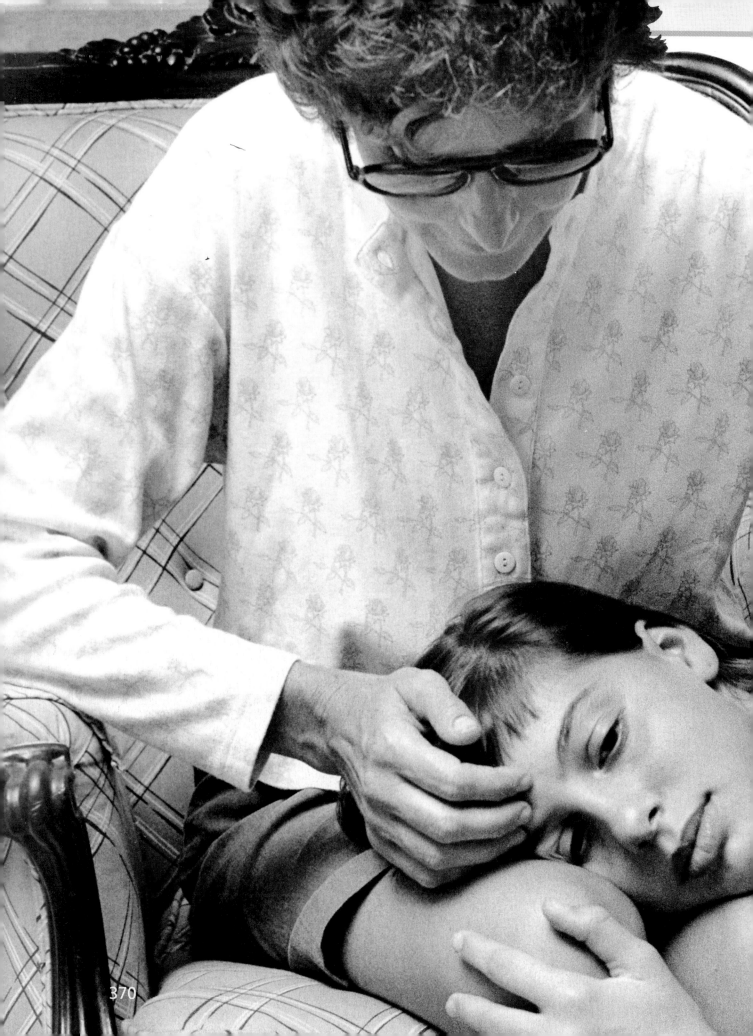

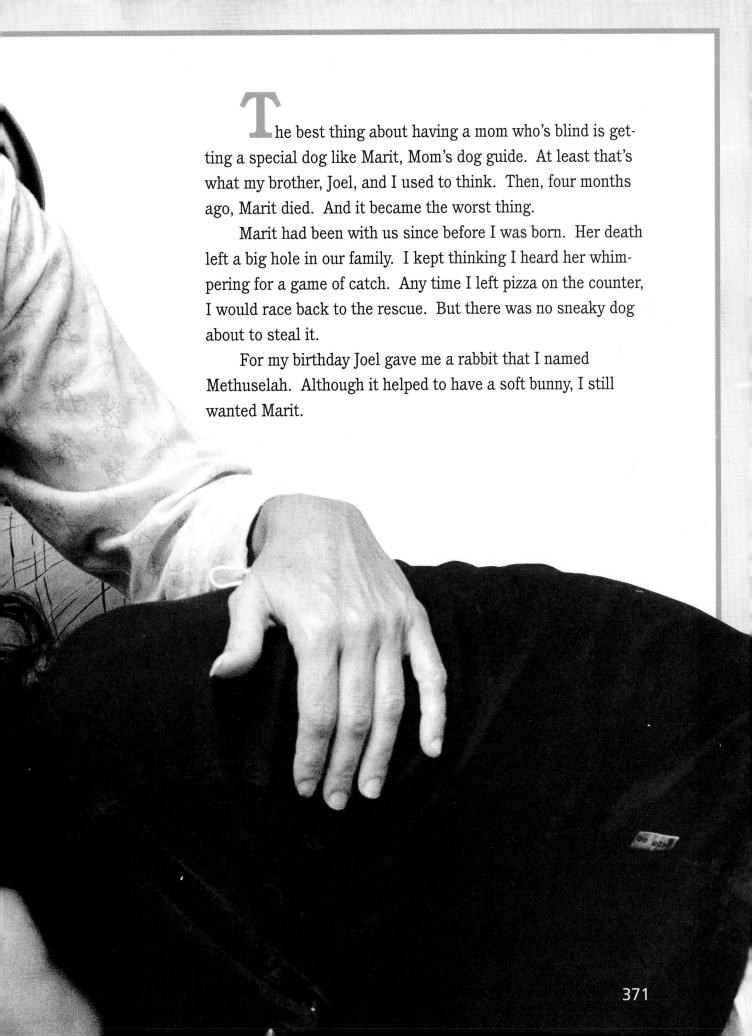

The best thing about having a mom who's blind is getting a special dog like Marit, Mom's dog guide. At least that's what my brother, Joel, and I used to think. Then, four months ago, Marit died. And it became the worst thing.

Marit had been with us since before I was born. Her death left a big hole in our family. I kept thinking I heard her whimpering for a game of catch. Any time I left pizza on the counter, I would race back to the rescue. But there was no sneaky dog about to steal it.

For my birthday Joel gave me a rabbit that I named Methuselah. Although it helped to have a soft bunny, I still wanted Marit.

Mom missed her even more. She didn't lose just a sweet, furry pet. She lost her favorite way of traveling, too. She had to use her cane again, and crept along the sidewalk like a snail. Once, when she crossed the street, she missed the opposite curb and kept walking toward the traffic. I had to holler to get her onto the sidewalk.

After that, I worried about her running errands by herself. I asked her to "go sighted guide," holding Dad's, Joel's, or my arm. Sometimes she did. But mostly she used the cane. She didn't want to depend on us — or on anybody.

A lot of blind people do fine with a cane. It's like a real long arm to help them feel what's around: walkways, hedges, mailboxes.

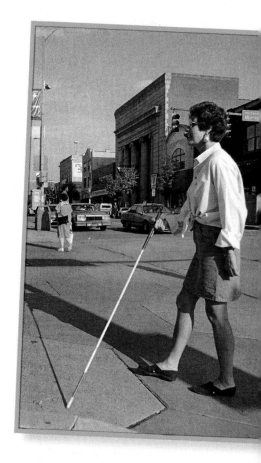

With a dog guide, blind people use their hearing more than touch. Mom has trained her ears. It's amazing: she can tell when something, like a movie marquee, is above her head, and when she passes a lamppost. She knows from the change in the sound of her footsteps.

In spite of Mom's special hearing, I worried. I was relieved when she decided to go back to The Seeing Eye for a new dog guide.

Before Mom left, I told her I wouldn't be able to love the new dog as much as Marit. Mom hugged me and said, "The night before you were born, I wondered how I could love a second child as much as your brother. Then you came, and like magic, I was just as crazy about you."

373

The Seeing Eye, in Morristown, New Jersey, was the first dog guide school in the United States. (Now there are nine others.) It trains German shepherds and Labrador and golden retrievers for three months. Then, for about a month, it teaches blind people to use the dogs.

When Mom arrived at The Seeing Eye, she was met by her instructor, Pete Jackson.

I missed Mom as much as I missed Marit, but at least Mom called every night. She also wrote letters and sent pictures.

Mom's first day was a cinch. She'd gone to Seeing Eye twelve years before to get Marit, and still remembered her way around. Usually when she's in a new place she has to move from room to room with her cane, memorizing the layout.

In the morning Mom walked with Pete Jackson so that he could check her pace. He wanted to choose the dog that would suit her best. Then she was free to play the piano, exercise . . . and worry. Would she get along with the new dog? Would they work well together?

The next day she got Ursula. What a strange name! The staff at Seeing Eye's breeding station had named Ursula when she was born. (Ursula's brothers and sisters were also given names starting with *U*.) Dog guides need a name right away so that Seeing Eye can keep track of the four hundred or so pups born each year. At two months of age, the pups go to Seeing Eye puppy-raising families to learn how to live with people. At fifteen months, they are mature enough to return to Seeing Eye for the three-month training program.

Dad said that Ursula means "bear." But in the pictures Mom sent, Ursula looked too pipsqueaky to be called bear. Mom explained that Seeing

Eye is now breeding some smaller dogs. They are easier to handle and fit better on buses and in cars.

My friends thought dog guides were little machines that zoomed blind people around. Until Mom went away, even I didn't understand all the things these dogs were taught.

But on Mom's first lesson in Morristown, Ursula seemed to forget her training. She veered on a street crossing and brushed Mom into a bush. Mom had to make her correct herself by backing up and walking around the bush. Then Mom praised her.

After ten practice runs with Pete, Mom and Ursula soloed. Ursula didn't stop at a curb, so Mom had to scold her and snap her leash, calling, "Pfui." Later Ursula crashed Mom into a low-hanging branch. "Ursula will have to start thinking tall," Mom said that night, "or I'll have to carry hedge clippers in my purse."

Even though Ursula had walked in Morristown a lot with Pete, she was nervous when Mom's hand was on the harness. Mom talked and walked differently. And Mom was nervous, too. Ursula moved so much faster than old Marit had, and Mom didn't trust her.

Every day Mom and Ursula made two trips. Every week they mastered new routes. Each route got longer and more complicated, and Mom had less time to learn it. Every night Mom gave Ursula obedience training: "Come. Sit down. Rest. Fetch." I thought she should try obedience training on Joel.

While Mom worked hard, Dad, Joel, and I went on with our normal lives — school, homework, soccer, piano, spending time with friends. We divided Mom's chores: Dad did the cooking, Joel, the vacuuming and laundry, and I did the dishes, dusting, weeding. The first two weeks were easy.

In a phone call Mom said that things were getting easier for her, too. "Remember how tough curb ramps have been for me?" she asked. "They feel like any other slope in the sidewalk, so I can't always tell that I've reached the street. Well, Ursula stopped perfectly at every ramp. And she guided me around, not under, a ladder and right past a huge parking lot without angling into it. But best of all, she actually saved my life. A jackhammer was making so much noise that I couldn't hear whether the light was green or red. When I told Ursula, 'Forward!' she refused to move and kept me from stepping in front of a car. (Of course, Pete would have saved me if Ursula hadn't.)"

Mom barely asked about us. It was all Ursula, Ursula, Ursula! She seemed to be forgetting Marit, too. When a letter came a few days later, I was sure she didn't miss anyone.

Dear Bob, Joel, and Leslie,

Today Ursula and I faced several disasters! She tried hard to ignore a boxer dog who wanted to play. A few minutes later, a great Dane lunged out from nowhere, jumped all over her, and loped off. Ursula's instinct is to chase dogs, but she didn't move a paw after that one. As if the dogs weren't enough trouble, fire engine sirens went off. Ursula just strolled down the sidewalk.

Mostly, life is smooth here. Seeing Eye is a vacation — no cooking, no cleaning, lots of time to talk to new friends, like Dr. Holle, the veterinarian. And since I don't have many blind friends, it's a treat to be with my roommate and the twenty other students. We laugh about the same things, like the great enemy of the blind — trash collection day! Every twenty feet there's a garbage can reeking of pizza, hoagies, old cheese. Usually Ursula snakes me around these smelly obstacles. But sometimes the temptation to her nose wins out, and I have to correct her, all the while holding my own nose.

Some trainees really inspire me, like Julie Hensley, who became blind from diabetes at twenty-two. Even though she's been blind for twelve years, she still teaches horses to do stunts. She judges her location from a radio playing music in the center of the pen, and gallops around as fast as she ever did when she could see.

Bob Pacheco used to race motorcycles and hunt. Then, two years ago, when he was twenty-nine, he developed optic atrophy and became blind two months later. He took up fishing, swimming, even trapping. But something was missing. He couldn't get around quickly enough. After the first trip with his dog guide, he was overjoyed. "Sally!" He grabbed my hand. "I don't feel blind any more."

The dogs are wonderful, and the people here are very special. So are you.

Love, Mom

Well, life at home wasn't very wonderful or special. Dad ran out of the casseroles Mom had frozen ahead of time, and although his meals were okay, I missed Mom's cooking. Worse, the dishes kept piling up. I never knew Joel ate so much.

Then things got really bad. While Dad was teaching his American literature night class, Joel and I faced a disaster Mom and Ursula couldn't have dreamed of: the toilet bowl overflowed! We wiped the floor with towels. As Joel took the towels down to the washing machine, he found water dripping through the ceiling — all over the dining room table, all over the carpet. He ran for more towels, and I ran for the furniture polish and rug shampoo. When Dad got home, everything looked perfect. But I wrote a braille letter.

Dear Mom,

Come home soon. The house misses you.

Love,

Exhausted in Pittsburgh

Mom wrote back.

Dear Exhausted,

Hang on. We'll be home to "hound" you Thursday. Be prepared. When you see me, I will have grown four more feet.

Mom

I couldn't laugh. I was too tired and worried. What if I couldn't love Ursula? Marit was the best dog ever.

Soon they arrived. Ursula yanked at her leash and sprang up on me. She pawed my shoulders, stomach, and arms just the way Marit used to, nearly knocking me over. She leaped onto Joel, licking him all over. As she bounded up onto me again, I realized Mom was right. Like magic, I was crazy about this shrimpy new dog.

But by the end of the day, I had a new worry. Was *Ursula* going to love *me*? She seemed friendly enough, but keyed up, even lost in our house.

Mom explained that Ursula had already given her heart away three times: first to her mother, then to the Seeing Eye puppy-raising family, and finally to Pete. Mom said we had to be patient.

"Remember how Marit loved you, Leslie? When you were little, she let you stand on her back to see out the window. Ursula will be just as nuts about you. Love is the whole reason this dog guide business works."

So I tried to be patient and watched Mom work hard. First she showed one route in our neighborhood to Ursula and walked it over and over. Then she taught her a new route, repeated that, and reviewed the old one. Every day she took Ursula on two trips, walking two or three miles. She fed her, groomed her, gave her obedience training. Twice a week Mom cleaned Ursula's ears and brushed her teeth.

"I'm as busy as I was when you and Joel were little!" she said.

Mom and Ursula played for forty-five minutes each day. Joel, Dad, and I were only allowed to watch. Ursula needed to form her biggest attachment to Mom.

Mom made Ursula her shadow. When she showered or slept, Ursula was right there.

Still, Ursula didn't eat well — only half the amount she'd been eating at Seeing Eye. And she tested Mom, pulling her into branches, stepping off curbs. Once she tried to take a shortcut home. Another time, because she was nervous, she crossed a new street diagonally.

Crossing streets is tricky. Ursula doesn't know when the light is green. Mom knows. If she hears the cars moving beside her in the direction in which she's walking, the light is green. If they're moving right and left in front of her, it's red.

I worried about Ursula's mistakes, but Mom said they were normal. She kept in touch with her classmates and knew that their dog guides were goofing, too. One kept eating grass, grazing like a cow. Another chased squirrels, pigeons, and cats. Still another always stopped in the middle of the street, ten feet from the curb. Once in a while her friends got lost, just like Mom, and had to ask for help.

Mom said it takes four to six months for the dogs to settle down. But no matter how long she and Ursula are teamed up together, Ursula will need some correcting. For instance, Ursula might act so cute that a passerby will reach out to pet her. Then Mom will have to scold Ursula and ask the person not to pet a dog guide. If people give Ursula attention while she's working, she forgets to do her job.

After a month at home, Ursula emptied her food bowl every time. She knew all the routes, and Mom could zip around as easily as she had with Marit.

"Now it's time to start the loneliness training," Mom said. She left Ursula alone in the house, at first for a short time while she went jogging with Dad. Ursula will never be able to take Mom jogging because she can't guide at high speeds.

Each week Mom increased the amount of time Ursula was alone. I felt sorry for our pooch, but she did well: no barking, no chewing on furniture.

Then Mom said Joel and I could introduce Ursula to our friends, one at a time. They could pet her when she was out of harness.

Every morning Ursula woke Joel and me. Every night she sneaked into my bed for a snooze.

Finally Mom allowed Joel and me to play with Ursula, and I knew: shrimpy little Ursula had fallen for us, and we were even crazier about her.

But we haven't forgotten Marit. Joel says that Ursula is the best dog alive. And I always say she's the best dog in this world.

Think About the Selection

1. What can you tell about the family in *Mom's Best Friend* from the way the family members manage while Mom is away?

2. What are other relationships in *Mom's Best Friend* besides the one between Mom and Ursula? Review the selection and report what you find.

3. What traits does a person need to be a good trainer of dog guides? Tell why you would or would not be good at this job.

4. Why do you think Ursula needs to form her strongest attachment to Mom?

5. Why do you think it takes so long for Ursula to settle down after moving to her new home?

6. Explain what Mom means when she says on page 381, "Love is the whole reason this dog guide business works."

7. **Connecting/Comparing** Compare the family described in this selection with Mariah's family in *Mariah Keeps Cool*. Think about how the members work together, and what is important to each family.

Write an Audiotape Message

Suppose the family sent audiotape messages back and forth to stay in touch. Write the text of an audio greeting Mom might have sent, or write a message her family might have sent to her. Tell what the sender's day-to-day life is like. If you like, tape-record your message.

 Tips

- Use language and a tone you might use in everyday speech.
- Add humor or emotion.

Science

Compare How Sounds Are Absorbed

Reread the description of Mom's hearing on page 372. What does it tell about how objects absorb, or muffle, sounds? Make a list of the different places Mom goes in the selection and note how sounds might be absorbed, or not, by her surroundings. Which places might be louder? Which might be quieter? Why?

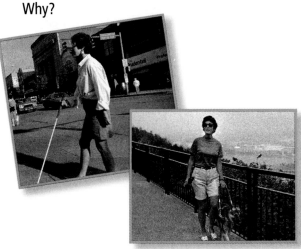

Math

Map a Route

Make a map of a two-mile route Mom and Ursula could take to practice Ursula's dog guide skills. Draw your route to scale. Use a formula in which one inch equals a fraction of a mile. Find information in the selection to help you figure out what obstacles to include, such as low branches and traffic lights.

Bonus Number each obstacle. Below the map, write what Ursula should do when she encounters each obstacle.

Post a Review

What would you like to tell others about *Mom's Best Friend*? What did you learn while reading it? Post your review at Education Place. **www.eduplace.com/kids**

Monkeys with

Well-trained monkeys shine at helping human friends overcome limits.

A man is thirsty and wants a drink of water, but he can't get it for himself. The man, George Boyle of Cleveland, Alabama, can't move his arms or legs because his neck was broken in a car accident. So his good friend Gizmo gets the drink for him.

Gizmo is a helpful, playful monkey. Here Gizmo gets ready to place a water bottle in a holder, open it, and insert a straw. Gizmo does other tasks for Boyle, who gets around using a wheelchair.

a Mission

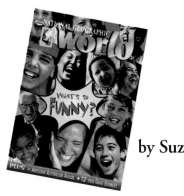

by Suzanne Wilson

Gizmo, 14, is a capuchin (kuh-PYOO-shun) monkey. She comes from Helping Hands, an organization in Boston, Massachusetts, that trains capuchins to help people with disabilities. In South America capuchins live in the wild. But the monkeys from Helping Hands are born at a special breeding facility near Boston. Intelligent and small, capuchins easily form relationships with people.

Family First

"She's like my sister," says Elizabeth Ford, 13, about Sadie. The capuchin has lived with Elizabeth's family in Norton, Massachusetts, for three years. Sadie will spend another two or three years there, getting used to living with people. Then she'll be trained to help a person with a disability.

Like Elizabeth, Sadie enjoys eating snacks. Unlike Elizabeth, though, her favorite hangout is on the roof (right). Elizabeth will be sad when Sadie leaves to start her training, but says, "I know she'll be helping somebody."

389

Learning to Help

Training follows the family stay. At Helping Hands, a monkey called Patty learns to turn the pages of a magazine (above). "The monkeys are so curious, and they love doing the tasks," says trainer Sue Costa.

Using a laser pointer, Costa indicates objects a monkey must work with or fetch. First the monkeys learn the basics — getting food and drinks or retrieving dropped objects. Then they learn special tasks, such as loading a computer disk, putting a cassette into a VCR, or punching telephone buttons. After about 18 months, most monkeys are ready for work. Then Helping Hands carefully matches humans to monkeys, based on personality.

Living 30 to 40 years, a capuchin is a long-term companion. People don't have to pay for their capuchin helpers. But training and caring for the monkeys is costly. Helping Hands can afford to place only six to ten monkeys a year.

Lunch is served when Kimba opens a sandwich holder.

A red laser light shows Patty which switch to flip.

Working

Gizmo finished her training. Now she doesn't monkey around when she's busy at work. She knows she'll earn a reward when she positions the magazine Boyle wants to read (right). Boyle blows through a straw to dispense fruit juice treats to Gizmo. While he reads, Gizmo watches traffic from the window, plays, or sits in the sun. She likes musical toys and watching TV commercials. At night she sleeps in a big cage with her stuffed animals and a blanket.

Every morning a health-care worker helps Boyle bathe and dress. Then Boyle and Gizmo spend the day together. "She's a lot like a child," says Boyle. He gives Gizmo presents on her birthday and knows when she's happy by the way she chirps. Gizmo often knows what Boyle wants before he asks her. Friends for five years, they will be together for many more.

Gizmo comes to the rescue when Boyle asks her to scratch his nose.

Honoring Your Heritage

What is a **heritage**? Where does it come from? Why is it important?

A heritage is a collection of **traditions** passed down through many generations. It includes the special customs and values that children learn from their parents and grandparents.

In *Yang the Second and Her Secret Admirers*, one character deeply values her Chinese heritage. Eating *dim sum*, listening to Chinese **opera**, wearing Chinese clothes — these traditions are all part of her heritage.

In the Chinese meal called *dim sum*, diners are served a wide variety of small dishes, one after the other.

392

Think about the culture of your grandparents — or of their grandparents. What traditions have you learned from them? Perhaps there is a dish from a family recipe, an old song you sing, or a dance that you perform on holidays.

Sometimes many cultures may contribute to your heritage. Think about the sports you play, the foods you eat, the music you listen to, and the languages you speak. How many different cultures are part of who *you* are?

The Chinese characters *Chuán Tŏng* mean "heritage."

传统

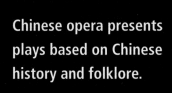

Chinese opera presents plays based on Chinese history and folklore.

Traditional Chinese instruments include the *erhu*, a stringed instrument related to the violin.

Lensey Namioka

Yang the Second and Her Secret Admirers

Illustrated by Kees de Kiefte

Who is Yang the Second? Who secretly admires her?
As you read the selection, use what you discover
about characters and events to create more **questions**
that you can ask your classmates.

As the oldest daughter in her family, Second Sister clings to her Chinese heritage and refuses to make any friends. But her younger brother and sister have a plan, which they have practiced at the home of their friend, Kim O'Meara. What if Second Sister overhears them saying that Paul Eng, her classmate, likes her? And what if Paul overhears them saying that Second Sister likes him? Who knows what might happen next?

By the next day I was beginning to have second thoughts about our plot. It could turn out to be really embarrassing for Second Sister.

She looked so unhappy sometimes that I thought it might be mean to play a trick on her. Once, Second Sister, Third Sister, and I were at a shopping mall, and we went into a restaurant for refreshments. Third Sister saw some of her friends there, and she went over to their table. Soon we heard them talking and laughing.

Second Sister sat with her head down, sipping her drink, and she suddenly looked very forlorn. In China she had lots of friends, and she would be sitting with them, talking and laughing. She could have made friends here, too, but she preferred to stay home like a grouch.

But Second Sister isn't always a grouch, and I remembered the times when she was kind to me. Like the days when my family still wanted me to play the violin, for instance. Father, Mother, and Eldest Brother had all thought that I played so badly because I wasn't trying hard enough. Second Sister wasn't like the rest of them. She thought that I had it in me to be a good musician, but that I gave up playing so that my friend Matthew could play in our family string quartet. We all knew that Matthew had real musical talent. Second Sister thought I was being noble and letting Matthew take my place because of our friendship. It was just the kind of thing she would do for her own friends. She simply refused to believe that a member of the Yang family would have a terrible ear. It wasn't in our genes.

I wanted to get Third Sister alone and discuss whether we should go on with our trick. But I didn't get a chance. Third Sister came home just before dinner, and we all sat down around the dinner table. Mother had cooked my favorite dish: pork stewed with yellow turnips. Normally I eat so much of this dish that I get scolded for hogging it (can you hog a dish of pork?).

But I was too busy with my thoughts to eat much. I jumped when Mother said, "What's the matter, Yingtao? Aren't you feeling well? You aren't eating your favorite."

"I'm fine," I muttered. Hurriedly, I took a big helping.

Eldest Brother began to ask Second Sister about the demonstration she had given that day in school. Her class was studying different types of entertainment in countries all over the world, and she had offered to talk about Chinese opera.

To demonstrate background music in opera, Second Sister brought in an *erhu*, a kind of Chinese violin with two strings, and played it to her class. She usually played a viola, but she jumped at this chance to show how a traditional Chinese instrument sounded.

Father beamed. "I'm glad you did it. We concentrate so hard on playing Western music that sometimes we forget there is a long tradition of music in China."

"Did the class enjoy your demonstration?" asked Eldest Brother.

"A few of the kids made faces when I hit the high notes on the *erhu*," said Second Sister. "But most were very interested. Afterward some of them came up and wanted to try it."

Then she frowned. "You know that boy Paul Eng? He told me he had never seen or heard the instrument before!"

I had to defend Paul. "What's so strange about that? I bet very few people in this country have seen one!"

Second Sister's lips curled scornfully. "Maybe that's true of your average American. But you'd think somebody like Paul Eng would care more about his Chinese heritage!"

Lately Second Sister has been using the word *heritage* a lot. I'm not quite sure what she means by our Chinese heritage. Does she mean being as Chinese as possible? But her own instrument is a viola, a Western instrument. Or does she mean clothes? Is that why she likes to wear her cloth jacket with the high collar and buttons down the front? Maybe she means eating Chinese food with chopsticks. But Paul ate Chinese food — the whole Eng family had been eating *dim sum* in Chinatown just the other day.

Listening to the scornful way Second Sister talked about Paul, I decided it would be a great joke after all to get the two of them together, like that couple in the movie. My eyes met Third Sister's, and we nodded to each other.

*I*n our family Third Sister and I do the dishes, while Second Sister and Eldest Brother help Mother with some of the cooking. As Third Sister scraped the garbage into the disposal, I filled a big pan with hot, sudsy water and began putting the dishes in.

The chopsticks I washed by rubbing them against one another: You hold a bunch of them and roll them between your two hands, making a *burrrr* sound. The rubbing makes the chopsticks really clean.

Once I even did it in time to music. Eldest Brother was practicing a piece, and I added a rhythmic part with the chopsticks. I have a terrible ear for pitch — that is, I'm no good at telling high from low. But I've got pretty good rhythm. Eldest Brother enjoyed my chopsticks accompaniment. It was the only time he ever said anything good about my music making.

"Shh! Not so loud with the chopsticks," whispered Third Sister. "I think Second Sister is finished in the pantry. Let's start when she goes up the stairs."

I dropped the chopsticks into the pan, and after a minute Third Sister winked at me in a signal to begin our act.

"Isn't it touching," said Third Sister in a loud whisper, "the way Paul Eng went up to Second Sister after her demonstration?"

This wasn't the opening line we had planned, but it was a good one. I did my best to play up to it. "Yeah, he must have been really hurt when she didn't say anything friendly back to him."

We paused and listened. Second Sister's steps paused at the foot of the stairs. Instead of going up to her room to practice, she was stopping to hear more.

"Are you sure he likes her?" asked Third Sister. Now we were using the lines we had rehearsed. "After all, she hasn't been nice to him at all. In fact she's been awfully mean every time his name comes up."

There was no sound from Second Sister. She must have been listening intently. I risked a short pause, and washed a few plates. Then I sighed heavily. "Poor Paul. I asked him once about his batting stance. He was very nice to me and explained everything patiently." I paused to wash a couple of rice bowls before continuing. "Then he looked at me sort of anxiously. He asked me whether Second Sister ever went out with boys — you know, on dates."

"So that *proves* he likes her!" exclaimed Third Sister. "What did you tell him?"

"I had to tell him the truth," I said, and sighed again. "I told him Second Sister wouldn't look at a boy who didn't speak Chinese."

"Poor Paul!" Third Sister said. The two of us were beginning to repeat ourselves, so we didn't say anything more and went on washing dishes. Besides, we had said enough.

Our ears were eagerly cocked, and sure enough, we could hear Second Sister's steps going slowly up the stairs. They sounded thoughtful.

*A*rranging for Paul to overhear Kim and Third Sister wasn't easy. The trouble was that neither our family nor the O'Mearas knew the Engs outside of school. Besides, Third Sister, Kim, and I went to elementary school, while Paul went to the same high school as Eldest Brother and Second Sister. Except at school concerts or baseball games, we just didn't run into the Engs much.

Days passed, and I almost gave up hope. I noticed that Second Sister sometimes had on a peculiar expression. Her face would be screwed up, like she was trying to get a piece of gristle out from between her teeth. She must have been chewing over our remarks she had overheard.

That meant the first part of our scheme was working. But what good did it do if we couldn't carry out the second part?

Our chance came at last. It was our spring vacation, and as a treat Mrs. O'Meara took Kim, Third Sister, and me to visit the Pacific Science Center.

Mrs. O'Meara said she was sick and tired of having kids underfoot all the time. "Jason is acting really strange," she said. "He goes around mooning and bumping into things!" So she chased him out of the house with orders to practice soccer with his friends. It was the first time she ever had to order him to practice.

Mrs. O'Meara offered to drop Kim and Third Sister at the Science Center. I had hoped to play with my friend Matthew, but he had to go to the dentist. He protested that it was totally unfair for someone to see a dentist during vacation. "Life *is* totally unfair," said his mother as she dragged him off.

So Mrs. O'Meara took me along with Kim and Third Sister, who didn't mind me tagging along. It turned out to be a good thing we went together.

The Science Center is a big museum with lots of buttons to push. Things go squirting and squeaking and beeping and gurgling. We're supposed to learn important scientific facts from all this. In spite of that, it's loads of fun.

While Kim and Third Sister played with machines that speeded up their voices and made them sound like Donald Duck, I went over to look at a box containing poisonous spiders. Next to that was a tall glass case with a section of a beehive in it. I was just about to go over when I saw Paul Eng standing behind the case, looking at the bees.

I rushed over to Third Sister and grabbed her arm. "I saw Paul over there!" I whispered. "Come on! This is our chance to carry out our plan!"

Third Sister and I hurried over to the case of bees, and she began her speech. Then she stopped. Kim had to be in the act, too, and she was still back at the sound machine, making like Donald Duck!

We ran back and got Kim over, but by then Paul had already gone.

Looking around frantically, we spotted him going into the dinosaur exhibit room. He stopped and peered at a tyrannosaurus, which roared menacingly.

We quickly positioned ourselves behind the dinosaur. Third Sister and Kim opened their mouths and tried to start our script.

ROAR, went the tyrannosaurus. The three of us looked at one another and shook our heads. This wasn't going to work.

I waited until I saw Paul reach one of the quiet dinosaurs, an armored stegosaurus. There was no time to be lost. "Come on!" I hissed to the other two.

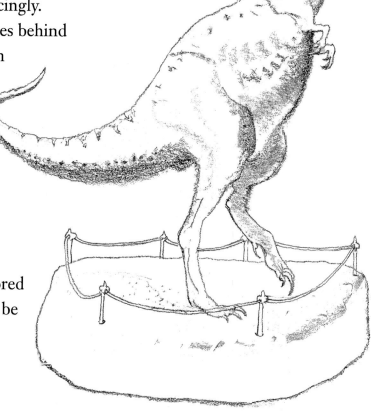

Again we got ourselves into position, and Kim cleared her throat. "So what makes you think your sister likes Paul Eng?" she asked.

"Well, she was impressed by the way he played in that ball game," said Third Sister, "and she isn't usually interested in American sports."

I came in with my lines. "And I thought she didn't like him! I thought she only liked boys who spoke Chinese."

"That's what I thought, too," said Third Sister. "Second Sister told me what really changed her mind was how good he is in math. He's in her math class, you know."

As I listened to our act, the lines suddenly sounded really stiff and unnatural. How could anyone believe something as lame as this?

Maybe Kim and Third Sister felt that way, too. Their voices petered out and stopped. Then without another word, we began to shuffle off. I didn't dare to look behind me at Paul to see how he had taken our words.

We went to the food court, where we were supposed to wait for Mrs. O'Meara to pick us up. For a while the three of us sipped our drinks without saying anything. I broke the silence and got the last drop of my drink with a loud slurp. "Do you think he fell for the act?"

"I don't know," muttered Kim. "It was okay when we were practicing the other day, but it sounded awfully phony just now."

Third Sister and I nodded. We both knew what she meant. In a way, I was almost relieved.

Suddenly Third Sister grabbed my arm. "Isn't that him over there?" she hissed.

She was right. Paul was standing at the pie counter, buying some refreshments. He was also buying something for his companion, the girl standing next to him.

It seemed that we had been wasting our time: Paul already had a girlfriend!

I felt a kick on my leg from Third Sister. She had seen Paul's girlfriend, too. I nodded and pointed out the couple to Kim.

The three of us sighed in unison. "I'm sorry," I said. "I should have found out whether Paul already had a girlfriend before we started all this."

We sat around glumly and thought about all the time and energy we had wasted. Then I heard a step behind me, and a soft cough.

"Hello," said Paul Eng's voice.

I spun around and stared. Paul and his girlfriend were standing by our table.

"Hi, Paul," I said weakly. Then I said the first thing that came into my head, "I'd give anything to hit a home run!"

Third Sister had better manners. "Hi, I don't know if you remember me. I'm Mary, and this is my friend Kim."

Paul looked embarrassed. That wasn't surprising, after the conversation he had overheard. In his place, I would have avoided the Yang family like chicken pox.

But for some strange reason, Paul didn't go away. He just stood there. Three months seemed to go by as we all waited and squirmed.

Finally the girl with Paul poked him. He cleared his throat, swallowed, and said, "This is my sister, Melanie. You met her at the *dim sum* restaurant, didn't you?"

Now I realized that the girl looked familiar. She wasn't his girlfriend at all. She was his sister! There was still hope our trick might work.

Melanie poked her brother again, and again Paul cleared his throat. "You have another sister, don't you? Her name is Yinglan, right?" His voice sort of died off.

Third Sister and I nodded solemnly. "That's right," I acknowledged. "I do have another sister, called Yinglan."

There was a pause. The five of us stared at one another some more, and three more months passed.

*I*t's hard for Americans to remember Chinese names. Unlike Third Sister, Second Sister refused to give herself an English name. I thought it was a good sign that Paul knew Second Sister's name, since that meant he had really paid attention to her — even before we played our trick.

Melanie poked Paul for the third time, and for the third time he cleared his throat. A family of frogs must have set up housekeeping with his tonsils. "Er . . . I noticed Yinglan in my math class," he began. "But she's only a sophomore, isn't she?"

"She got put a year ahead," admitted Third Sister. Then she added quickly, "It's not that she's a math genius, or anything. It's just that Chinese schools are more advanced in math."

"Very good, very good . . . ," said Paul absently. Then he must have realized that he sounded foolish, and his voice faded. Suddenly he took a deep breath and said in a rush, "Does your sister ever go out with boys, you know, on dates?"

We did it! Our trick had worked. I caught Third Sister's eye, and we both smothered an urge to laugh. Paul's words were almost exactly the same as the ones Second Sister had overheard while we were doing dishes!

Paul must have seen the laughter in our eyes. He turned red as a sunset. Dragging Melanie after him, he rushed out of the food court. He almost crashed into Mrs. O'Meara, who had come to pick us up.

"Who was that?" asked Mrs. O'Meara, staring after the Engs. "Friends of yours?"

"I hope so," Third Sister said slowly. She looked at me and then at Kim. The three of us beamed at one another and silently congratulated ourselves on our success.

MEET THE AUTHOR
Lensey Namioka

Chinese Heritage: Born in Beijing, China, Namioka moved to the United States at the age of nine. She started school before she could speak English.

Like Author, Like Character: Namioka, like Second Sister, excelled at math in school. She went on to teach math at Cornell University.

Hobby: Music. She says: "[I] prefer to make it myself badly than to hear it performed superbly."

Bylines: Namioka began her literary career by writing humorous articles for a newspaper. She then turned to children's books. Read her other books about the Yang family: *Yang the Youngest and His Terrible Ear*; *Yang the Third and Her Impossible Family*; and *Yang the Eldest and His Odd Jobs*.

MEET THE ILLUSTRATOR
Kees de Kiefte

Dutch Heritage: "I was born in a small medieval town alongside a river in Holland a long time ago."

Advice: "Sit down in a city center and observe people, sometimes making note-like drawings and adding word-like notes. . . . Doing this you LOOK as well as REMEMBER."

On Himself: "I am a clumsy dreamer coming to life while drawing."

Internet

To find out more about Lensey Namioka and Kees de Kiefte, visit Education Place. **www.eduplace.com/kids**

Think About the Selection

1. If you moved to a new country, like Second Sister, what reminders of your heritage would you hold on to? What traditions would you miss?

2. What advice would you give Second Sister to help her feel more comfortable with life in the United States?

3. Compare and contrast the way Second Sister and Paul Eng react after they hear the false rumor.

4. Do you think Yingtao and his sister should have tricked Second Sister and Paul as they did? Explain.

5. On page 405, the author writes: "The five of us stared at one another some more, and three more months passed." Explain this silence.

6. What do you think will happen next in the story? Why?

7. **Connecting/Comparing** Yingtao plays a trick on Second Sister. Mariah misleads Lynn in *Mariah Keeps Cool*. How are these two kinds of trickery alike and different?

Summarizing

Write a Personal Introduction

It is your job to introduce Paul Eng to Second Sister. Write an introduction of one or two paragraphs, telling one of the characters what the other is like.

Tips

- **Begin by listing the characters' interests and talents.**
- **Decide which features should get the most emphasis.**
- **Be sure your introduction includes each character's name, grade, and age.**

Social Studies

Learn About Traditions

Second Sister plays an *erhu*, a Chinese violin with two strings. Look through the story to find other details about Chinese traditions. With a partner, do research to learn more about these traditions. Then write and illustrate a report sharing what you learned.

Listening and Speaking

Act It Out

With five classmates, act out the end of the selection, beginning with the scene at the Science Center. Decide who will play the parts of Yingtao, Third Sister, Kim, Paul, Melanie, and Mrs. O'Meara. Look for clues in the story to help you figure out what each character says or does.

Internet

E-mail a Friend

Would you recommend *Yang the Second and Her Secret Admirers* to a friend? Send an e-mail to a friend telling what you liked or didn't like about it.

Hands&

The orange crane Lauren is holding takes her about 15 minutes to fold. It's worth the effort, though, says Lauren. According to her grandmother, cranes bring good luck!

Hearts

By Candace Purdom

Read about three girls and their grandmothers who, like Yinglan, keep alive skills that are part of their heritage.

Folds & Creases

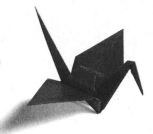

Lauren Okada can turn a piece of paper into a duck! She does it through *origami* (or-uh-GAH-mee), the Japanese art of paper folding. Two years ago, Lauren's grandmother Mary began teaching Lauren how to fold, tuck, and crease colorful paper to make an origami box. "At first it was pretty hard," says the ten-year-old from Ohio. "If you don't fold it evenly, it comes out pretty bad!" But Lauren loved making the shapes appear as if by magic. So she spent many more hours with her grandmother, learning to fold stars, birds, balloons, and other intricate shapes.

Lauren's grandmother learned origami from *her* mother, who brought the art with her from Japan. As a girl, Mary often gave her friends the paper objects she made. Now Lauren does the same thing! For one birthday party, Lauren folded each guest a box that she filled with candy. She and her grandmother also made origami ornaments to hang on their Christmas tree. They have a colorful collection that they add to each year. It's a tradition Lauren and her grandmother love to share.

411

Grandy Jean, Morgan, and a fellow quilter, Louise Carter, add stitches to a Double Wedding Ring quilt, a design often made for new brides.

Bits & Pieces

More than a century ago, Morgan Friday's great-great-grandmother stitched together pieces of fabric to make colorful patchwork quilts. Today, Morgan and her grandmother, Grandy Jean, carry on the tradition at old-fashioned quilting bees in their Texas town.

When Morgan, 12, first joined the quilters, she helped out by threading needles and organizing the quilting supply cabinet. But soon the women invited her to sew. In the beginning, Morgan was nervous. She remembers asking, "What if I mess up?" The women answered, "Just take out the stitches and start again!"

During bees, Morgan helps connect the top, middle, and bottom layers of the quilt with tiny stitches. Sewing around every piece on the top layer can take the group 20 to 24 hours! But Morgan loves sitting and listening to the stories the women share as they stitch.

Morgan's grandmother has a saying: "When you give somebody a quilt, tell them to count the stitches and they'll know how much you love them." Morgan agrees; "It means a lot because you put a lot of work into it!"

Twists & Coils

Cynthia Burns, 10, loves going to the Charleston Market with her grandmother. That's where they make and sell sweetgrass baskets, a craft that's been in her family for centuries. Cynthia's ancestors came to South Carolina from Africa as slaves. They brought with them the special basket-making technique that her family still uses today.

Sweetgrass grows in nearby marshes and is known for its sweet smell. Cynthia began twisting the grass into baskets when she was seven. Her Grandma Helen starts each one by tying a bundle of long pine needles in a knot — needles that she and Cynthia rake up together in the forest. Cynthia then twists bunches of sweetgrass and bulrushes. She connects the coils of twisted grass, one row on top of the other, using skinny palm leaves.

Most baskets take Cynthia a few weeks to complete. She signs the bottom of each one she makes. Cynthia is proud of her talent and her family tradition. "My grandma always tells me to pass it down," she says, "and to someday tell my daughter to pass it down, too!"

Cynthia learned to make sweetgrass baskets by watching her grandmother (right) and her mother. The first basket Cynthia made sold for $35!

413

Dear Mr. Henshaw

BEVERLY CLEARY
Dear
Mr.Henshaw

ILLUSTRATED BY PAUL O. ZELINSKY

Background and Vocabulary

room which
th some help
sn't sure B
r house wh
s, but
m cook
gs like gr
matoes and
Barry said
ouse becau

414

A World of Writing

Writing plays a big part in the life of Leigh Botts, the main character in *Dear Mr. Henshaw*. Consider the kinds of writing you do, at home or at school. Then ask yourself how writing makes a difference in your life.

Do you keep a diary or journal? If so, how is it valuable to you? Maybe you use it to record your deepest thoughts and feelings. Maybe you use a journal to keep a record of your travels or other experiences. Writers also jot down ideas in journals and notebooks, and develop those ideas later. Does that sound like you?

Letter writing can be a good way to appreciate the events of your life. Writing a description of something you did or saw can make old memories and feelings fresh again. The person who receives your letter will enjoy reading it, too.

Have you written a story, or some other kind of creative prose or poetry? Leigh Botts tries writing different stories — first a fantasy, then a mystery — before he finds a kind of writing that he feels comfortable with. Think about the stories *you* have to tell.

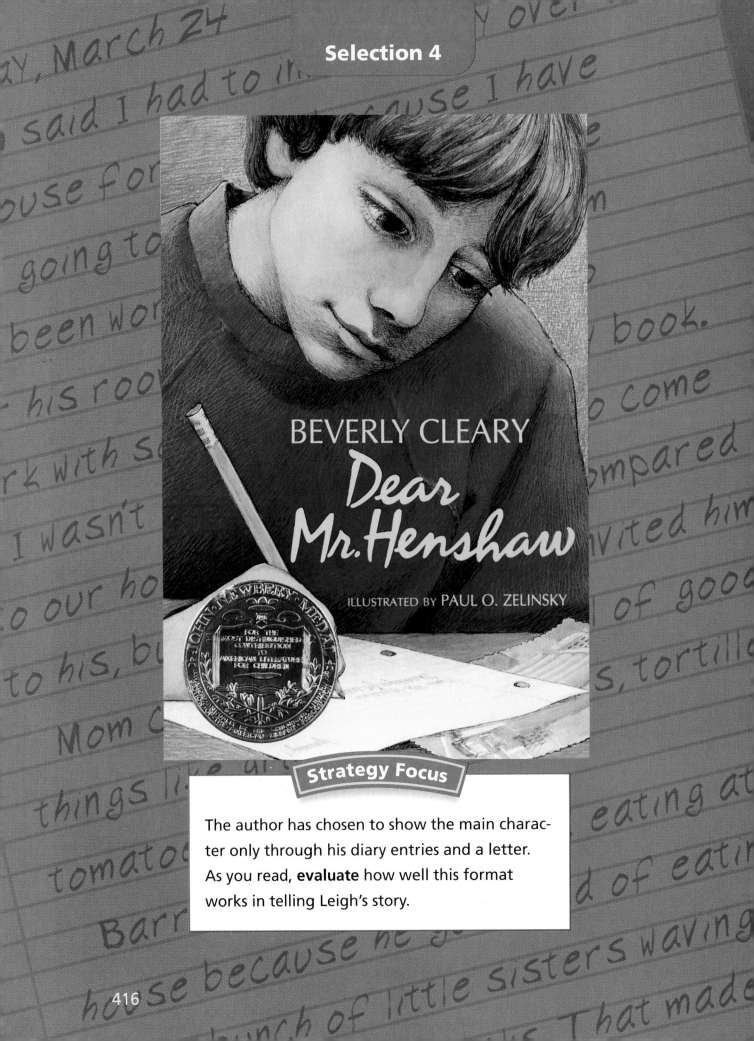

BEVERLY CLEARY

Dear Mr. Henshaw

ILLUSTRATED BY PAUL O. ZELINSKY

The author has chosen to show the main character only through his diary entries and a letter. As you read, **evaluate** how well this format works in telling Leigh's story.

416

*S*ince the second grade, Leigh Botts has been writing to Boyd Henshaw, a children's book author. First in those letters, and now in his diary, Leigh has been describing his life in a house beside a gas station in Pacific Grove, California, a town known mainly for the monarch butterflies who spend the winter there. Leigh's parents are divorced and he seldom sees his dad, a long-distance truck driver. When they spoke on the phone recently, his dad was about to go out for pizza with a lady and her son, and Leigh is worried that his dad might get married again. At school, Leigh has had to cope with an unknown thief who was stealing from his lunchbox. But he has made his first friend, Barry. And there's a writing contest Leigh is thinking about entering: the winners get to have lunch with a famous children's book author.

Saturday, March 17

Today is Saturday, so this morning I walked to the butterfly trees again. The grove was quiet and peaceful, and because the sun was shining, I stood there a long time, looking at the orange butterflies floating through the gray and green leaves and listening to the sound of the ocean on the rocks. There aren't as many butterflies now. Maybe they are starting to go north for the summer. I thought I might write about them in prose instead of poetry, but on the way home I got to thinking about Dad and one time when he took me along when he was hauling grapes and what a great day it had been.

Tuesday, March 20

Yesterday Miss Neely, the librarian, asked if I had written anything for the Young Writers' Yearbook, because all writing had to be turned in by tomorrow. When I told her I hadn't, she said I still had twenty-four hours and why didn't I get busy? So I did, because I really would like to meet a Famous Author. My story about the ten-foot wax man went into the wastebasket. Next I tried to start a story called *The Great Lunchbox Mystery*, but I couldn't seem to turn my lunchbox experience into a story because I don't know who the thief (thieves) was (were), and I don't want to know.

Finally I dashed off a description of the time I rode with my father when he was trucking the load of grapes down Highway 152 through Pacheco Pass. I put in things like the signs that said STEEP GRADE, TRUCKS USE LOW GEAR and how Dad down-shifted and how skillful he was handling a long, heavy load on the curves. I put in about the hawks on the telephone wires and about that high peak where Black Bart's lookout used to watch for travelers coming through the pass so he could signal to Black Bart to rob them, and how the leaves on the trees along the stream at the bottom of the pass were turning yellow and how good tons of grapes smelled in the sun. Then I copied the whole thing over in case neatness counts and gave it to Miss Neely.

Saturday, March 24

Mom said I had to invite Barry over to our house for supper because I have been going to his house after school so often. We had been working on a burglar alarm for his room which we finally got to work with some help from a library book.

I wasn't sure Barry would like to come to our house which is so small compared to his, but he accepted when I invited him.

Mom cooked a casserole full of good things like ground beef, chilies, tortillas, tomatoes and cheese. Barry said he really liked eating at our house because he got tired of eating with a bunch of little sisters waving spoons and drumsticks. That made me happy. It helps to have a friend.

Barry says his burglar alarm still works. The trouble is, his little sisters think it's fun to open his door to set it off. Then they giggle and hide. This was driving his mother crazy, so he finally had to disconnect it. We all laughed about this. Barry and I felt good about making something that worked even if he can't use it.

Barry saw the sign on my door that said KEEP OUT MOM THAT MEANS YOU. He asked if my Mom really stays out of my room. I said, "Sure, if I keep things picked up." Mom is not a snoop.

Barry said he wished he could have a room nobody ever went into. I was glad Barry didn't ask to use the bathroom. Maybe I'll start scrubbing off the mildew after all.

Sunday, March 25

I keep thinking about Dad and how lonely he sounded and wondering what happened to the pizza boy. I don't like to think about Dad being lonesome, but I don't like to think about the pizza boy cheering him up either.

Tonight at supper (beans and franks) I got up my courage to ask Mom if she thought Dad would get married again. She thought awhile and then said, "I don't see how he could afford to. He has big payments to make on the truck, and the price of diesel oil goes up all the time, and when people can't afford to build houses or buy cars, he won't be hauling lumber or cars."

I thought this over. I know that a license for a truck like his costs over a thousand dollars a year. "But he always sends my support payments," I said, "even if he is late sometimes."

"Yes, he does that," agreed my mother. "Your father isn't a bad man by any means."

Suddenly I was mad and disgusted with the whole thing. "Then why don't you two get married again?" I guess I wasn't very nice about the way I said it.

Mom looked me straight in the eye. "Because your father will never grow up," she said. I knew that was all she would ever say about it.

Tomorrow they give out the Young Writers' Yearbook! Maybe I will be lucky and get to go have lunch with the Famous Author.

Monday, March 26

Today wasn't the greatest day of my life. When our class went to the library, I saw a stack of Yearbooks and could hardly wait for Miss Neely to hand them out. When I finally got mine and opened it to the first page, there was a monster story, and I saw I hadn't won first prize.

I kept turning. I didn't win second prize which went to a poem, and I didn't win third or fourth prize, either. Then I turned another page and saw Honorable Mention and under it:

A Day on Dad's Rig
by
Leigh M. Botts

There was my title with my name under it in print, even if it was mimeographed print. I can't say I wasn't disappointed because I hadn't won a prize, I was. I was really disappointed about not getting to meet the mysterious Famous Author, but I liked seeing my name in print. Some kids were mad because they didn't win or even get something printed. They said they wouldn't ever try to write again which I think is pretty dumb. I have heard that real authors sometimes have their books turned down. I figure you win some, you lose some.

Then Miss Neely announced that the Famous Author the winners would get to have lunch with was Angela Badger. The girls were more excited than the boys because Angela Badger writes mostly about girls with problems like big feet or pimples or something. I would still like to meet her because she is, as

423

they say, a real live author, and I've never met a real live author. I am glad Mr. Henshaw isn't the author because then I would *really* be disappointed that I didn't get to meet him.

Friday, March 30

Today turned out to be exciting. In the middle of second period Miss Neely called me out of class and asked if I would like to go have lunch with Angela Badger. I said, "Sure, how come?"

Miss Neely explained that the teachers discovered that the winning poem had been copied out of a book and wasn't original so the girl who submitted it would not be allowed to go and would I like to go in her place? Would I!

Miss Neely telephoned Mom at work for permission and I gave my lunch to Barry because my lunches are better than his. The other winners were all dressed up, but I didn't care. I have noticed that authors like Mr. Henshaw usually wear old plaid shirts in the pictures on the back of their books. My shirt is just as old as his, so I knew it was OK.

Miss Neely drove us in her own car to the hotel, where some other librarians and their winners were waiting in the lobby. Then Angela Badger arrived with Mr. Badger, and we were all led into the dining room which was pretty crowded. One of the librarians who was a sort of Super Librarian told the winners to sit at a long table with a sign that said Reserved. Angela Badger sat in the middle and some of the girls pushed to sit beside her. I sat across from her. Super

Librarian explained that we could choose our lunch from the
salad bar. Then all the librarians went off and sat at a table
with Mr. Badger.

There I was face to face with a real live author who seemed
like a nice lady, plump with wild hair, and I couldn't think of a
thing to say because I hadn't read her books. Some girls told
her how much they loved her books, but some of the boys and
girls were too shy to say anything. Nothing seemed to happen
until Mrs. Badger said, "Why don't we all go help ourselves to
lunch at the salad bar?"

What a mess! Some people didn't understand about salad bars, but Mrs. Badger led the way and we helped ourselves to lettuce and bean salad and potato salad and all the usual stuff they lay out on salad bars. A few of the younger kids were too short to reach anything but the bowls on the first rows. They weren't doing too well until Mrs. Badger helped them out.

Getting lunch took a long time, longer than in a school cafeteria, and when we carried our plates back to our table, people at other tables ducked and dodged as if they expected us to dump our lunches on their heads. All one boy had on his plate was a piece of lettuce and a slice of tomato because he thought he was going to get to go back for roast beef and fried chicken. We had to straighten him out and explain that all we got was salad. He turned red and went back for more salad.

I was still trying to think of something interesting to say to Mrs. Badger while I chased garbanzo beans around my plate with a fork. A couple of girls did all the talking, telling Mrs. Badger how they wanted to write books exactly like hers. The other librarians were busy talking and laughing with Mr. Badger who seemed to be a lot of fun.

Mrs. Badger tried to get some of the shy people to say something without much luck, and I still couldn't think of anything to say to a lady who wrote books about girls with big feet or pimples. Finally Mrs. Badger looked straight at me and asked, "What did you write for the Yearbook?"

I felt myself turn red and answered, "Just something about a ride on a truck."

"Oh!" said Mrs. Badger. "So you're the author of 'A Day on Dad's Rig!'"

Everyone was quiet. None of us had known the real live author would have read what we had written, but she had and she remembered my title.

"I just got honorable mention," I said, but I was thinking, She called me an author. *A real live author called me an author.*

"What difference does that make?" asked Mrs. Badger. "Judges never agree. I happened to like 'A Day on Dad's Rig' because it was written by a boy who wrote honestly about something he knew and had strong feelings about. You made me feel what it was like to ride down a steep grade with tons of grapes behind me."

"But I couldn't make it into a story," I said, feeling a whole lot braver.

"Who cares?" said Mrs. Badger with a wave of her hand. She's the kind of person who wears rings on her forefingers. "What do you expect? The ability to write stories comes later, when you have lived longer and have more understanding. 'A Day on Dad's Rig' was splendid work for a boy your age. You wrote like *you*, and you did not try to imitate someone else. This is one mark of a good writer. Keep it up."

I noticed a couple of girls who had been saying they wanted to write books exactly like Angela Badger exchange embarrassed looks.

"Gee, thanks," was all I could say. The waitress began to plunk down dishes of ice cream. Everyone got over being shy and began to ask Mrs. Badger if she wrote in pencil or on the typewriter and did she ever have books rejected and were her characters real people and did she ever have pimples when she was a girl like the girl in her book and what did it feel like to be a famous author?

I didn't think answers to those questions were very important, but I did have one question I wanted to ask which I finally managed to get in at the last minute when Mrs. Badger was autographing some books people had brought.

"Mrs. Badger," I said, "did you ever meet Boyd Henshaw?"

"Why, yes," she said, scribbling away in someone's book. "I once met him at a meeting of librarians where we were on the same program."

"What's he like?" I asked over the head of a girl crowding up with her book.

"He's a very nice young man with a wicked twinkle in his eye," she answered. I think I have known that since the time he answered my questions when Miss Martinez made us write to an author.

On the ride home everybody was chattering about Mrs. Badger this, and Mrs. Badger that. I didn't want to talk. I just wanted to think. A real live author had called *me* an author. A real live author had told me to keep it up. Mom was proud of me when I told her.

The gas station stopped pinging a long time ago, but I wanted to write all this down while I remembered. I'm glad tomorrow is Saturday. If I had to go to school I would yawn. I wish Dad was here so I could tell him all about today.

March 31

Dear Mr. Henshaw,

I'll keep this short to save you time reading it. I had to tell you something. You were right. I wasn't ready to write an imaginary story. But guess what! I wrote a true story which won Honorable Mention in the Yearbook. Maybe next year I'll write something that will win first or second place. Maybe by then I will be able to write an imaginary story.

I just thought you would like to know. Thank you for your help. If it hadn't been for you, I might have handed in that dumb story about the melting wax trucker.

Your friend, the author,
Leigh Botts

P.S. I still write in the diary you started me on.

MEET THE AUTHOR *Beverly Cleary*

Beverly Cleary took up writing because, like Mildred Pitts Walter, she couldn't find enough books about the kids she knew — "plain, ordinary boys and girls," as she called them. Since 1950 Cleary has introduced dozens of extraordinary characters to readers, including Henry Huggins, Ramona Quimby, and Leigh Botts. Cleary's mother once started a lending library in Oregon, and Cleary went on to become a librarian herself, in Yakima, Washington. Telling stories and thinking about characters led directly to her first book, *Henry Huggins*.

Dear Mr. Henshaw was a change for Cleary to a more serious character, and critics approved. The book won the Newbery Medal in 1984. You can read more about Leigh Botts in Cleary's book *Strider*.

MEET THE ILLUSTRATOR *Nancy Carpenter*

Nancy Carpenter grew up in Philadelphia, Pennsylvania. She says that she learned how to draw princesses and ballerinas before she learned how to talk.

In elementary school, Carpenter's mother was her art teacher, and she often felt that her mom was hard to impress. It turns out that her mom had always liked Carpenter's artwork, but hadn't wanted to appear to be playing favorites in class!

To find out more about Beverly Cleary and Nancy Carpenter, visit Education Place. **www.eduplace.com/kids**

Think About the Selection

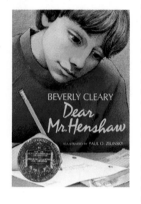

1. Why do you think Leigh decides to write "A Day on Dad's Rig" instead of using his other story ideas?

2. Writing is important to Leigh. In what ways do you think writing helps him?

3. On page 420, Leigh says: "It helps to have a friend." Helps how? Describe a time when having a friend has helped you.

4. What kind of person is Angela Badger? Name some story details that help reveal her personality.

5. How would you sum up the advice Angela Badger gives Leigh about writing stories?

6. What does Leigh's behavior at the luncheon tell you about him?

7. **Connecting/Comparing** Leigh Botts uses his writing to connect with people. How do Mariah, Mom, and Yingtao make connections with people?

Expressing

Write a Letter

Like Leigh, write a letter to the author of your favorite book. Tell why you liked the book and describe what you like to write about.

Tips

- Use details from the book to tell what you liked.
- Begin a new paragraph for each new subject.
- Be sure to use correct letter form when you write your letter.

Art

Design a Book Jacket

What if Leigh's story, "A Day on Dad's Rig," were made into a book? Design a book jacket for it. Include the title, the author's name, and illustrations. View some real book jackets before you begin to find out what information to include on the front, back, and spine.

Bonus Write a description of the book and a brief author biography for the two side flaps.

Listening and Speaking

Perform a Radio Show

Picture Angela Badger hosting a radio show in which young writers call her for advice. In a group, prepare a script for the show. Create questions and answers for Mrs. Badger. Write an introduction that an announcer might say at the beginning. Then perform the radio show.

Internet

Send an E-Postcard

What books have you been reading during this theme? Which ones would you recommend? Send an electronic postcard to a friend. You'll find one at Education Place. **www.eduplace.com/kids**

433

More Young Writers

Write honestly about what you know and feel strongly about, says Mrs. Badger in *Dear Mr. Henshaw*. Here are five students who have done just that.

Los ojos de mi gente

Los ojos de mi gente son brillantes
Cuando están tristes o felices
Los ojos de mi gente son las estrellas
De la media noche en el firmamento

The Eyes of My People

The eyes of my people are bright
They are sad, they are glad
The eyes of my people are stars
In the arch of the midnight sky
— *DaMonique Domínguez, 11, California*

To Mother

I remember those days at the old house
the house where my life began
You would weed the small garden
of blue-starry forget-me-nots and violets
tending those delicate dahlias
you so loved
I frolicked on the grass, in the sprinkler
running in and out of the junipers
both of us building —
me building forts and imaginary worlds
you building reality, building the garden
building me
— *Aaron Wells, 11, Oregon*

Problems

As my life comes to a mountain
I climb it
As my life comes to a river
I swim across it
As my life comes to an obstacle
I overcome it
And as my life comes to a stop sign
I rest a while
— *Kevin A. Zuniga, 12, Texas*

Swish

My basketball springs
like a tumbleweed jumping up and down
in the dusty afternoon
the ball goes up and up
till it encircles
the rim like a
hurricane or a tornado
beginning
the net tickles its side
as it swishes through
another three-pointer makes the day
— *Chance Yellowhair, Arizona*

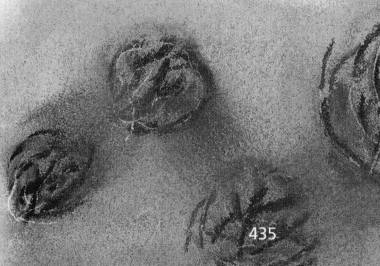

435

Maputo Saturday Craft Market

It's Friday afternoon,
nearly evening.
The whir of my bike is comforting in the silence.
One or two late workers hurrying home.
I stop my bike,
breathing in the cool evening air.
The plaza.
Today it is a barren stone circle
Patches of grass and a tree or two
is all it has to offer.
But for me, the plaza is special
My heart leaps in anticipation
of Saturday morning
when the plaza comes alive.

At first, just a vendor.
Then two,
then three.
Mostly young boys and men
Cloths are spread out on the sidewalk
Gentle hands unwrap intricate wooden carvings,
handsome wooden chests,
and hand-painted toys.
Red wooden cars, green airplanes, and multi-colored motorcycles
Most are small enough to fit in the palm of your hand.
Batiks are unfurled and carefully examined
Young boys push their way through the crowd
displaying the vividly dyed cloths.
Sellers hawk their merchandise in loud persistent voices
to buyers who argue in equally loud persistent tones
each trying to get the best price.

The market bustles with activity
enveloping me.
I become a part of it,
bargaining with vendors,
admiring the finely carved masks and jewelry,
Beaded necklaces, bracelets and earrings.
Comparing and choosing until midday.

I can't wait until tomorrow!
The plaza will come alive again,
with me swept up along into it.
I pedal off into the glowing darkness
thinking of and anticipating
the Saturday morning craft market.
        — *Rebecca Beatriz Chavez, 11, Virginia*
Rebecca was living in Maputo, Mozambique,
        in Africa, when she wrote this poem.

Vocabulary Items

Some test items ask you to identify a word that has more than one meaning and can fit in two sentences. You are given three to five answer choices. How do you choose the correct answer? Below is a sample item. The correct answer is shown. Use the tips to help you answer this kind of test item.

Tips

- Read the directions carefully. Make sure you understand what to do.
- Read the sentences and all the answer choices.
- Try each word in both sentences. Ask yourself which word makes sense in both sentences.

Read the sentences below. Then choose the word that correctly completes both sentences.

1   Leigh wanted to _____ a sandwich for lunch.

Mariah had to _____ the flat tire on her bicycle.

A   prepare

B   fix

C   make

D   repair

ANSWER ROW 1   Ⓐ ● ⓒ ⓓ

Now see how one student figured out the correct answer.

I am looking for the word that fits in both sentences. I know it isn't **D** because *repair* doesn't fit in the first sentence. I see that *prepare, fix,* and *make* all work in the first sentence.

I won't choose **A** or **C** because they don't fit in the second sentence. Only **B** works in both the first and second sentences. Now I see why **B** is the correct answer.

PLAYS

A play can take place on the stage or on the page.

On the stage, characters appear, speaking and acting in **scenes**, or sections, of the play. Whenever the place or time in the play changes, there is a new scene.

On the page, the play is a **script**, a plan for the performance. Each scene is numbered, with a description of the place or time. The names of characters are followed by their lines, or **dialogue**. Descriptions of the action or how a character feels are often written in *italics*. Those are the **stage directions**.

As you read the following play, *The Case of the Runaway Appetite*, you'll see that it's just a story in a new form. You may want to compare the written version with a stage version by performing the play with your classmates.

You will also be invited to write the opening scene of your own play.

And now — curtain up!

Contents

The Case of the Runaway Appetite

A JOE GILES MYSTERY

by Rob Hale

Main Characters

Joe Giles: Head and sole employee of Finders Keepers
Detective Agency, age eleven

Veronica: Princess of the Grand Duchy of Isselburg, age
eleven

Mrs. Bibby: Veronica's chaperone, in her forties

Secondary Characters

Voice on the phone

TV Anchor Kathy Keen

TV Reporter Mike Macintosh

Leo the Limo Driver

Mario

Celia

Sheriff McGrew

Deputy Fisk

Child

Babysitter

Girl

Moviegoer 1

Moviegoer 2

Veronica's Appetite

Newspaper Reporters

Setting

The little town of Riverton, present day

‖‖

SCENE 1

(Joe Giles's office, which is really the family kitchen. Joe is sitting at a kitchen table, partly in the shadows, addressing the audience in a confiding way, as if he's telling a story.)

Joe: My name is Giles. Joe Giles. Maybe you've heard of me. I've got my ads up on bulletin boards all over town: Finders Keepers Detective Agency. You lose it — we find it. "We" means me. I've got this talent for finding things. Lost socks. Lost glasses. Lost car keys. . . .

(Telephone rings.)

Joe: Excuse me. . . . *(He picks up the phone.)* Finders Keepers, Joe speaking.
Voice: Is this the guy who finds lost things?
Joe *(Cautiously)*: Yes. . . .
Voice: Great! I just lost a game of tic-tac-toe! Do you think you can find it??
(Voice laughs and hangs up.)

Joe: *(He hangs up and resumes talking to the audience.)* I get a lot of that. The fact is, it's been a while since my last case. Mostly I've been hanging around my office — actually it's my mom and dad's kitchen — waiting for a client. Sometimes when the phone's no help, I turn on the TV and try the news.

(Joe turns on TV. The following scene can be performed on video, live, or with puppets and backdrops.)

TV Anchor: Next — Royalty in Riverton! Princess Veronica comes to town. News 4's Mike Macintosh is live at the Riverton Inn. . . .

Joe *(Getting interested)***:** Oh, that's right — Princess Veronica of some Grand Duchy or other is in town to dedicate a museum. Actually, this is a big deal. We almost never get celebrities in Riverton.

Mike Macintosh: This is Mike Macintosh at the Riverton Inn where Princess Veronica has just arrived with her entourage. I'll see if I can ask her a few questions. Princess Veronica!

Veronica: *(She speaks with a slight accent.)* Yes. How do you do?

Mike Macintosh: Princess, how are you enjoying your visit to our country so far? How do you like our customs? Our music? Our shopping malls? What do you think of American food?

Veronica: Well, I am enjoying my visit, but I have been kept very busy attending to my duties as my country's representative.

Joe: She needs to get out more.

Veronica: As for American food, I am sorry to say I have — what is the phrase? — "lost my appetite." But I hope I find it soon, so that I can enjoy your delicious hot dog and apple pie! Thank you. *(She leaves.)*

Mike Macintosh: Well, she may have lost her appetite, but she hasn't lost her charm. Back to you, Kathy.

Joe: I turn off the TV. *(He does so.)* I stand up. Suddenly I know what I have to do. It will be the greatest challenge of my career. I, Joe Giles, Riverton's smartest detective, will find Princess Veronica's appetite!

SCENE 2

(The lobby of the Riverton Inn. Reporters are taking pictures of Veronica.*)*

Joe: I'm in luck. When I arrive at the Riverton Inn, there's the Princess sitting in the lobby surrounded by photographers. I make my move and present my card. Unfortunately, this lady gets in the way.

Mrs. Bibby *(Taking his card)***:** I'll take that.

Veronica: Is it another reporter, Mrs. Bibby?

Mrs. Bibby: I can't tell. *(to* Joe*)* What's "Finders Keepers"?

Joe: Just what it says, ma'am. You lose, we find. Well, actually, I do. My name's Joe Giles. And I understand you've lost something very important, Princess.

Veronica: I have?

Joe: Yes, I believe you said you've lost your appetite. And I would consider it an honor and a privilege to find it for you. At no cost, of course.

(Long silence. Then Veronica *bursts out laughing.)*

Mrs. Bibby: Young man, either you have no manners at all or a very bad sense of humor. In any case, Princess Veronica has a dinner to get ready for in two hours.

Veronica *(Sobering up at the thought)*: Dinner? Oh, dear. I wish I were a bit hungrier.

Joe: Aha! You see? This is serious! We can't waste any time! Princess, please tell me, if you can. Where were you when you lost your appetite?

Mrs. Bibby: Of all the ridiculous . . .

Veronica: No, I can tell you exactly where I was. I was in the limousine coming in from the airport. I happened to glance out the window and see a billboard. It said: "Have you had your mush today?" I have always had a great disliking for mush. It was then that I lost my appetite.

Joe: I know that billboard! Princess, I'll need your help! Would you be willing to go on a little expedition?

Mrs. Bibby: All right, young man, this has gone far enough. As Princess Veronica's chaperone, I must insist —

Veronica: Actually, I *would* enjoy seeing a bit more of America, Mrs. Bibby. And we do have a few hours. And of course you'll come, too.

Joe: There you go.

Mrs. Bibby: Hm. *(She thinks a while.)* Well, I suppose the fresh air might do you good. You *are* looking a little pale. Very well. But two hours, young man! Not a second longer!

Veronica: Lead the way, Mr. Giles.

Joe: "Mr. Giles." *(He looks pleased.)* I could get used to that. *(He leads the way offstage.)*

SCENE 3

(Inside Veronica's limousine, with Leo the Limo Driver behind the wheel)

Joe: So here we are, me and the Princess and Mrs. B, riding along in the Princess's limo. I've never been in a limo before. It's amazing.

Mrs. Bibby: Who on earth are you talking to?

Joe: Nobody. It's just something detectives do. Say, Princess, would you happen to have a sheet of paper and a pen?

Veronica: Yes. In the writing desk. First drawer on the right.

(Joe opens a drawer.)

Joe: Wow, gold markers, embossed stationery. . . . Here you go, Princess. (*He hands her markers and paper.*) I want you to draw a picture of your appetite.

Veronica: Excuse me?

Mrs. Bibby: (*She shakes her head.*) Now I know he's balmy.

Joe: Don't think about it. Just draw what you think your appetite looks like, real quickly.

(Veronica *draws a quick sketch, using different colored markers.*)

Mrs. Bibby (*To both of them*): It's just an expression! "To lose your appetite!" It's a figure of speech!

Joe: I know. (*He takes completed sketch from* Veronica.) Interesting. Green hair?

(Veronica *nods.*)

Leo the Limo Driver: Here we are, kids. Corner of Washington and Fourteenth.

Joe: Let's just hope the trail hasn't gone cold. Leo, meet us here in two hours.

Leo: You got it, chief.

(*They get out of limo; it drives off.*)

Joe: Okay, here's the billboard where you lost your appetite, Princess. Better not look up. Now the first thing to do is ask ourselves: Where would I go if I were a runaway appetite?

Mrs. Bibby (*Dryly*): Somewhere delicious, I suppose.

Joe: Exactly! Like for instance that place right over there. The Napoli Pizza Palace.

Veronica (*Innocently*): Is pizza delicious?

Joe: You're kidding me. You've never eaten a pizza?

Veronica: Not to my knowledge.

(Joe *looks disapprovingly at* Mrs. Bibby.)

Mrs. Bibby: Don't blame me. I don't make up the menus.

Joe: (*He shakes his head, sighs.*) Follow me.

††

SCENE 4

(Napoli Pizza Palace. Music is playing in the background.)

Celia: Hey, Mario, look who's back!

Mario: Who? *(He looks at* Veronica.*)* No way, that's not her.

Celia: Sure it's her. So, sugar, did you make up your mind? What'll it be, the pepperoni or the black olive?

(Joe, Veronica, and Mrs. Bibby *look at each other, baffled.)*

Veronica: Are you talking to me?

Celia: Well, of course, sugar.

Veronica: I believe you've confused me with someone else.

Mario: See, I told you. This one looks entirely different. Different hair, different clothes.

Celia: And I'm telling you that I never forget a face.

Joe: Wait a minute! (Joe *takes the sketch of* Veronica's Appetite *and hands it to* Mario.) Is this the person you saw?

Mario: Yeah, that's her. You've definitely captured the green hair and orange beret. (*Looks at* Veronica.) Now that you mention it, you do look alike.

Celia: I've got it. She was your twin sister, right?

Veronica: I believe I . . . need to sit down.

Joe: Quick! A glass of water!

(Mario *gets* Veronica *a glass of water.*)

Mrs. Bibby: (*She fans* Veronica *with a paper plate while turning to* Joe.) Listen to me, boy wonder. If this is a practical joke, you'll be running around trying to find your *head*!

Joe (*To* Mario *and* Celia): This other girl you saw — how did she act? Do you have any idea where she went?

Mario: Well, for the longest time she was just standing in the door, sniffing the aromas. Then she started turning all her pockets inside out, looking for change, I guess.

Celia: Poor kid. I was going to *give* her a slice of pizza, but she just kind of growled and took off. That way. (*She points.*) Toward the mall.

Joe: The mall?!

Veronica (*Reviving a bit*): Is that bad?

Joe: I don't know. So far she's kept herself under control. I'm not sure what a runaway appetite will do when she's in a food court surrounded by a dozen restaurants.

Veronica: We'd better hurry! Mrs. Bibby, let's go!

Mrs. Bibby: Will someone kindly explain to me what's going on?

(*They exit.*)

Celia: You know, for a day when we haven't had any customers, it's been pretty busy.

Mario: Yeah.

SCENE 5

(Outside the Riverton Mall)

Veronica: But how could this happen? I've never heard of an appetite getting up and walking away before.

Joe: Hey, you're a princess. I'm a detective. Weird stuff always happens to people like us.

(Sound of sirens and car doors slamming. Enter Sheriff McGrew *and* Deputy Fisk.*)*

Mrs. Bibby: *Now* what?

McGrew: Well, look who it is! Mr. Finders Keepers himself! How's it going, kid? Find any lost kitty-cats lately?

Joe: No, sir. Are you out on a call?

McGrew *(Chuckles)*: A regular Junior Crimestopper, isn't he? Yeah, we're answering a Code 12: Disturbing the Peace.

Joe: Sounds dangerous.

McGrew: Not really. Seems as though someone's been bothering people in the food court.

Fisk: *(He takes out his pad and reads aloud.)* "Running around, sniffing people's plates . . . making funny yum-yum noises . . . loudest stomach grumbling I ever heard." Then someone offered her a french fry and she took off.

Veronica: Oh, the poor thing.

McGrew: Don't worry, miss. We'll — *(He looks at her and* Mrs. Bibby *closely.)* Say, it's the Princess and her chaperone, isn't it? *(He frowns.)* Giles, I don't recall anyone appointing *you* tour guide.

Joe *(At a sudden loss for words)*: Uh, well . . .

Mrs. Bibby *(Taking pity on* Joe*)*: Not to worry, Sheriff. It was my decision. I wanted to find someone who can offer the Princess a young person's point of view.

McGrew (*Smiling again*): I see. Well, that's okay then. Fine young man, our Joe here. He'll make a crackerjack detective some day.

Joe: Thank you, sir.

(*Exit* McGrew *and* Fisk.)

Joe: I owe you one, Mrs. B.

Mrs. Bibby (*Tartly*): Never mind that. We've got to find the Princess's appetite before she disturbs someone else's peace!

Joe: Maybe she's still in the mall. Come on! (*He starts to exit stage right.*)

Veronica: Wait.

(*Joe stops, turns.*)

Veronica: She's my appetite. *I'll* lead the way. *This* way. (*They exit stage left.*)

SCENE 6

(Inside the Riverton Mall, beside a fountain)

Joe: What makes you so sure she went this way?

Veronica: I can't explain it. I just know.

(Babysitter *and* Child *are arguing beside fountain.)*

Child: I want to go swimming! I want to go swimming!

Babysitter: I already told you: you can't go in the fountain!

Child: No fair! That girl got to go in!

Babysitter: That was a no-no. Remember how the security man ran after her?

Joe: It sounds like your Appetite was here, all right. Maybe she was trying to cool off a little. Now where?

Mrs. Bibby: That's easy. Follow the wet sneakerprints.

(Veronica runs off, stage left, unnoticed by *Joe.)*

Joe: Hey, you're right, she did leave tracks. *(He looks around.)* Where did the Princess go?

Mrs. Bibby: She's way ahead of you. *(She points off-stage.)* Halfway up the escalator.

(They exit stage left.)

SCENE 7

(Riverton Mall, one floor up)

Joe *(Looking around)*: Oh, great. Now we've lost the Princess *and* her Appetite.

Mrs. Bibby: Maybe that young lady saw her.

Joe *(to* Girl*)*: Excuse me, did you happen to notice a girl who looked sort of like a princess who was chasing after a girl with spiky green hair and an orange beret, only if you looked closely they each had the same face?

(Girl calmly points to stage left.)

Joe: Thanks! *(He stops.)* Oh, no. I was afraid of that.

Mrs. Bibby: What's wrong?

Joe: There's only one place in that direction. The Multiplex. The Princess and her Appetite could be in any one of six different movies!

Mrs. Bibby: Well, Mr. Giles, you're the detective. Which movie do *you* think they went to?

Joe: Let's see. *(He reads off the marquee.)* *The Search for Delicious, Willy Wonka and the Chocolate Factory, Jaws . . .*

Mrs. Bibby: *James and the Giant Peach, The Apple Dumpling Gang,* and *The Creature That Ate Philadelphia.* They all sound like they'd appeal to an appetite.

(Scream off-stage. Mrs. Bibby and Joe look at each other.)

Joe: I think it came from *The Creature That Ate Philadelphia*!

(They exit stage left.)

SCENE 8

(Inside the movie theater of Cinema 8)

Moviegoer 1: She tried to eat my popcorn!

Moviegoer 2: She tried to eat mine, too! It was awful!

Moviegoer 1: What, the popcorn?

Moviegoer 2: No, the Creature! She's the one who eats Philadelphia, right?

Moviegoer 1: I don't know. But these are amazing special effects!

Moviegoer 2: Look! There she is again! She's up on the stage by the movie screen!

(Veronica's Appetite, wearing a green wig, an orange beret, and other colorful clothes, is standing against the movie screen, looking baffled.)

(Enter Sheriff McGrew and Deputy Fisk.)

McGrew *(Speaking through a bullhorn)*: All right, everybody. The situation is under control. I repeat — the situation — is —

Fisk *(Yelling)*: UNDER CONTROL!

McGrew *(He gives Fisk a "Do you mind?" look. Then, to Appetite)*: Come on down off the stage now. No one is going to hurt you.

Appetite *(Growls)*: Hungry!

McGrew: I understand that. But you can't just help yourself to other people's food, can you? Now I'm going to ask you one more time, real nicely, to come on down off the stage.

Appetite *(Growls louder)*: Hungry!!

Veronica *(Entering from stage left)*: Can't you see you're scaring her? *(She's holding a giant tub of popcorn.)*

Mrs. Bibby: Veronica!

McGrew: Princess, I'm going to have to ask you to stay out of this —

Joe: Um, actually, Sheriff, the princess and that girl are sort of related to each other. Isn't that right, Mrs. Bibby?

Mrs. Bibby: Yes! They *are* extremely close, Sheriff. Don't worry, I'm sure the Princess can deal with this situation.

(McGrew *looks at her, hesitates, then backs off.*)

Veronica (*Coaxing*): See? I've got a big tub of popcorn. We can share it.

(*She gets up on the stage with the* Appetite, *who backs off a little.*)

Veronica: Don't be afraid. It's delicious. It's got real butter. And it's hot, too. Try some.

(*She takes a handful for herself and hands the popcorn to the* Appetite. *The* Appetite *eats some. She smiles, and says "Mmm." Then* Veronica *and the* Appetite *walk off-stage together, sharing the tub of popcorn and making* Mmm *sounds together.*)

(Moviegoers, Fisk, Joe, *and* Mrs. Bibby *applaud, as at the end of a movie.*)

McGrew (*Moved, but hiding it under a gruff show*): Okay, folks. The excitement's over. Get your refunds at the box office.

(*Exit* Moviegoers.)

(Veronica *returns alone, tossing up popcorn and catching it in her mouth.*)

McGrew: Nice job, Princess. You'd make a first-class negotiator. Now, where's your friend?

Veronica: (*She smiles.*) It's okay. She's safe and sound. I sent her home.

McGrew (*Pausing in disbelief*): You did *what*?? But that's interfering with police procedure, Princess! Your cousin violated a Code 12, a Code 28, and possibly a Code 81! Fisk, search the mall. Princess, I'm afraid I'm going to have to —

(Deputy Fisk *whispers in* McGrew's *ear.*)

McGrew (*Listening*): What? Oh, right. International incident. Highly embarrassing. The Mayor will not be pleased. (*He smiles.*) Well, we don't want to spoil the relations between our two countries, do we? (*He pauses.*) Just make sure your friend has a nice hot meal, okay, Princess?

Veronica: Okay, Sheriff. *(She gives the tub of popcorn to McGrew.)* Here. I'd better not spoil my appetite, now that I've got it back.

McGrew: Oh, sure, whatever you say. Can I give you folks a ride?

Mrs. Bibby *(Taking McGrew's arm)*: We'll settle for a police escort, Sheriff McGrew.

(Exit McGrew, Mrs. Bibby, and Fisk.)

Veronica: Thanks for finding my appetite, Mr. Giles.

Joe: That's Joe, Princess. And you're really the one who found her. I just found the trail.

Veronica: That's Veronica, Joe. Let's just call it a team effort. *(They exchange high fives.)* Will you be my guest at the museum dinner?

Joe: Glad to, Veronica. I just have to do one more thing. *(He moves upstage to address the audience.)* Well, I guess that closes the book on the Case of the Runaway Appetite. It had a little of everything. Movies, pizza, royalty. . . . And for Finders Keepers, it was a double success. Not only did I find an appetite, I found a friend.

Veronica *(Pulling him by the arm)*: Let's go, Joe. I'm starved!

Joe: Okay!

(Exit Veronica and Joe.)

●◖◗◖◗◖◗◖◗◖◗◖◗◖◗ CURTAIN ◖◗◖◗◖◗◖◗◖◗◖◗◖◗◖◗●

Narrating

Write the Opening Scene for a Play

Now that you've read *The Case of the Runaway Appetite*, write the opening scene for your own play. That scene might even lead you to write the whole play. If you wish, work with a partner.

Remember that a play has the same elements a story has: characters, a setting, a problem and solution, and events. But in a play, you show events only through the dialogue of the characters and stage directions.

Tips

- **Begin by thinking of a problem and a solution.**
- **Decide on the main characters and the setting of the play.**
- **Think about the place and time in which you want your play to begin.**

Characters:

Setting:

Problem:

Read On Your Own

Thirty Plays from Favorite Stories

edited by Sylvia Kamerman and Sylvia Burack (Plays)
This lively collection offers something for everyone.

Read-Aloud Plays: Pioneers

by Dallas Murphy (Scholastic)
Included in this collection are plays about Thomas
Jefferson, Laura Ingalls Wilder, and a family traveling the
Oregon Trail.

James and the Giant Peach

by Richard R. George (Puffin)
Roald Dahl's well-known story is presented as a play.

WKID: Easy Radio Plays

by Carol Adorjan (Whitman)
Included with these four radio scripts are practical tips
for acting and producing.

You're On!

selected by Lori Marie Carlson (Morrow)
These seven plays by Latino authors are presented in
English and in Spanish.

One Land, Many Trails

I have heard of a land

Where the earth is red with promises . . .

Where the imagination has no fences

Where what is dreamed one night

Is accomplished the next day

Joyce Carol Thomas

from *I Have Heard of a Land*

One Land, Many Trails

Contents

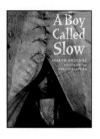
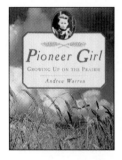

 Writing an Answer to a Question 570

Reader's Library

- **Shell-Flower**
- **Journey to a Free Town**
- **Zachary's Ride**
- **America: A Dream**

Theme Paperbacks

Meet the Wards on the Oregon Trail
by John J. Loper

Children of the Wild West
by Russell Freedman

High Elk's Treasure
by Virginia Driving Hawk Sneve

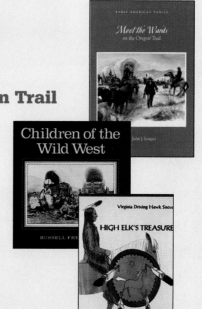

Book Links

If you like . . .

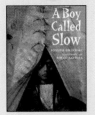

A Boy Called Slow
by Joseph Bruchac

If you like . . .

Pioneer Girl
by Andrea Warren

Then try . . .

My Name Is York
by Elizabeth Van Steenwyck
(Rising Moon)

York, an enslaved man who accompanied Lewis and Clark on their expedition, tells his story.

Off the Map: The Journals of Lewis and Clark
edited by Peter and Connie Roop
(Walker)

The story of Lewis and Clark's 1806 expedition is told through their journal entries.

Then try . . .

Dandelions
by Eve Bunting (Harcourt)

After her family arrives in the Nebraska Territory, Zoe plants dandelions on their sod house as a landmark.

The Way West: Journal of a Pioneer Woman
by Amelia Stewart Knight (Aladdin)

The author's diary reveals her experiences with her family while traveling by covered wagon to the Oregon Territory.

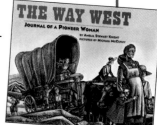

If you like . . .

Black Cowboy, Wild Horses

by Julius Lester

If you like . . .

Elena

by Diane Stanley

Then try . . .

The Buffalo Jump

by Peter Roop (Rising Moon)
Little Blaze is unhappy when his older brother is chosen to lead the herd in the buffalo jump.

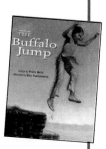

West by Covered Wagon: Retracing the Pioneer Trails

by Dorothy Hinshaw Patent (Walker)
A modern-day wagon train journey is compared with such a journey a hundred years earlier.

Then try . . .

I Have Heard of a Land

by Joyce Carol Thomas (Harper)
The author draws on her family's history in this account of African Americans settling in the Oklahoma Territory.

Willow Chase: Kansas Territory, 1847

by Kathleen Duey (Aladdin)
When she becomes separated from her family on their way to Kansas, Willow must find her way alone.

Internet

For more great books, visit **www.eduplace.com/kids** and **www.bookadventure.org**.

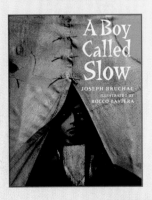

FIRST TRAVELERS OF THE PLAINS

Long before European settlers came, the Great Plains were home to some thirty Native American tribes, including the Lakota Sioux and the Crow, the people you will read about in *A Boy Called Slow*. Each tribe had its own language and customs. Each traveled the plains, following the buffalo herds, trading with other tribes and sometimes raiding them for horses and weapons. In a raid, a warrior hoped to establish a reputation for bravery.

Few chiefs among the Plains Indians earned as much respect for courage and determination as did Sitting Bull (1831–1890) of the Lakota Sioux.

◀ A warrior might show his bravery by riding up to an enemy and touching him with a coup stick.

Buffalo herds numbering in the millions provided the Plains Indians with food, clothing, and shelter. When the Plains were settled in 1900, fewer than fifty wild buffalo were left.

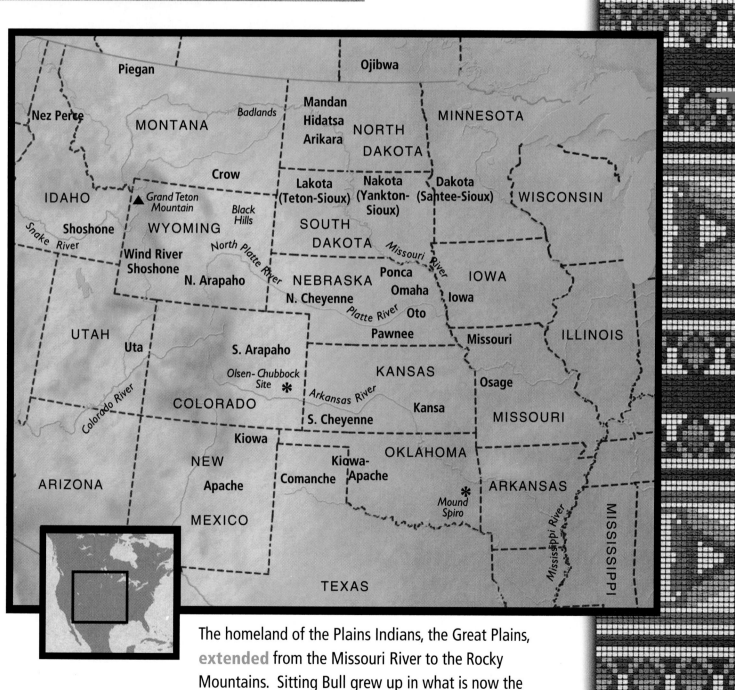

The homeland of the Plains Indians, the Great Plains, **extended** from the Missouri River to the Rocky Mountains. Sitting Bull grew up in what is now the state of South Dakota.

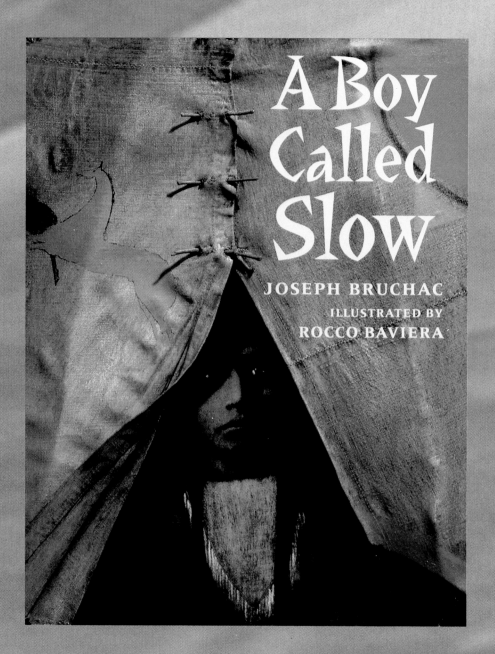

A Boy Called Slow

JOSEPH BRUCHAC

ILLUSTRATED BY
ROCCO BAVIERA

Think about the selection title and review the
illustrations. What can you **infer** about the main
character? What do you **predict** will happen?

Many years ago, in the winter of 1831, a boy was born to the family of Returns Again of the Hunkpapa band of the Lakota Sioux.

Though Returns Again loved his daughters — knowing well that women are the heart of the nation — both he and his wife gave thanks to Wakan-Tanka for at last giving them a son. "Now," Returns Again said, "we have one who will hunt for his Hunkpapa people and help to protect them."

But his wife smiled. "Han!" she said. "We have one to follow his father's path."

It was the custom in those days to give a childhood name. Such names came from the way a child acted. So it had been with Returns Again and his father before him.

So the parents of this boy and the other relatives in his tiyospaye, his extended family, watched the first son of Returns Again closely.

If he had tried to swallow everything he could get hold of — as was the case with one of his cousins — they might have called him "Hungry Mouth." But that was not so for this boy.

"If he were to take much longer eating," his uncle Four Horns said, "the food would bite him before he bites it!"

Perhaps, his mother thought, if he were quick in his movements and always watching things they might call him "Mouse." But that was not the case for this boy. He never did anything quickly. This son of Returns Again was always slow.

"U we!" his mother said. "Come here, quickly!" But her son only looked at her.

"Nihwa hwo?" Returns Again would say. "Are you sleepy?" But it was not sleep that made their son act as he did. It was simply the way he was. Every action he took was slow.

"Slon-he," his father said. "That is the name for our son."

His mother agreed. "We will call him Slow."

So that became his name.

Slow's uncle Four Horns would tell Slow how the horses came to the plains only in the time of Slow's grandparents, and how the horses made their lives easier than they had been in the old days. Some said that the horses were brought by the wasicun, the white man. But Four Horns told him a different story.

"Our Creator, Wakan-Tanka, loves the Lakota people," his uncle would tell him. "Wakan-Tanka saw that we had only our dogs to help us pull our travois and hunt buffalo. So Wakan-Tanka sent us a new animal as faithful as our dogs but able to pull our loads and carry us as quick as the whirlwind into the hunt, the Shoog-Ton'kah, the 'Spirit Dog.'"

As Slow grew up, he was not happy with his name. Few boys were given names they wanted to keep. No one wanted to be known as "Hungry Mouth" or "Curly" or "Runny Nose" or "Slow" all of his life. But until a child earned a new name by having a powerful dream or by doing some brave or special deed, it could not be changed.

472

Slow wished for this vision of bravery to come to him. He wished for a vision that would allow him to prove himself to his people.

Slow longed to have a name like his uncle Four Horns, or like the strong name his father had earned — Returns Again to Strike the Enemy.

"Your father," Slow's mother said, "was given his name because of his courage in battle. When the Crows raided our village, the others were

ready to retreat, but your father was the one who returned. Because of his bravery, the enemies were driven away.

"You must always help and protect your people," she continued. "A true Lakota shares everything with the people."

Slow listened to his mother's words, knowing how true they were. He had often seen his father return from hunting and share what he brought

back with the poorest people in the village. He remembered two winters ago when his father returned from a raid and brought back many horses. Returns Again had given all of those horses away except for one strong gray pony, which he saved for his son.

"The best way," Returns Again told him, "to gain the respect of your people is to be both brave and wise."

Slow understood those words. By the time Slow reached his seventh winter, he had gained a reputation as one of the strongest of the boys. And when it came to riding, none of the small children was more at ease on the back of a pony than the boy called Slow.

Returns Again was a man who could sometimes understand the speech of the animals and the birds. Slow, too, inherited some of his father's gift. He knew that his gray pony understood him, and when he was on its back, it was as if the two of them were one. Slow knew that many of his Lakota people could speak with the birds and animals, and hear their speech as clearly as human words; and the animals understood them, as well. And because he listened to the animals, Returns Again was given four more names.

One summer, Returns Again went hunting with some friends. As they camped at night beside their fire not far from the place called Smoky Butte, they heard a sound approaching them. It was a low sound, like a deep voice talking. Someone was coming along the trail which led

between the low hills. The other men reached for their weapons, but
Returns Again stopped them. There, coming slowly along the trail toward
them, was a big bull buffalo, its head close to the ground. The deep mur-
muring sound came from its throat. The other men could not make out
what the buffalo was saying, but Returns Again heard it clearly. Returns
Again listened carefully as the buffalo spoke, for the words it spoke
were names:

Tatan'ka Iyota'ke,
Tatan'ka Psi'ca,
Tatan'ka Winyu'ha Najin,
Tatan'ka Wanji'la.

Those were the four names spoken by the great bull buffalo. They were powerful names. As the buffalo slowly passed them and continued on along the trail until it was over the hill and out of sight, Returns Again knew that those names had been given to him. From that day on, he owned not only the name Returns Again to Strike the Enemy, he also owned those four names given him by the old bull buffalo.

Slow was proud to have a father with such names as Returns Again and Tatan'ka Iyota'ke. One day, he promised himself, he too would have such a strong name. But he knew that it would not be easy. So, as Slow wrestled with his friends, as he hunted with his bow and arrows, as he raced his gray pony, he always tried to do his best so that one day he would become a good warrior.

Slow was careful and deliberate in everything he did. It might take him a while to decide, but once he put his head down and went forward, he would not turn back.

At the age of ten, he killed his first buffalo — a yearling calf. His mother skinned the buffalo calf and, with his two sisters helping, tanned its skin and made it into a robe for him to wear. Though he was still called Slow, no one teased him any longer. His name now meant determination and courage to those who knew him.

As the winters passed, Slow grew. He was not as tall as some of the boys his age, but his shoulders were broad and strong.

One evening, he heard word in the camp that his father and some other men were going to ride out against the Crow, who his father called his favorite enemies. Slow knew that the Crow were great warriors and had some of the best horses on the plains. Slow had now seen fourteen winters and was old enough to go along.

He wrapped his robe made of the skin of the buffalo calf around his shoulders. He picked up his bow and his quiver full of blunt-pointed arrows that he used for hunting birds. He quickly brushed his gray pony's tail and plucked a burr from its mane. "Mitakola," he said, "my friend, we are ready to help protect the people."

Determined, he rode through the cottonwood trees until he reached the trail his father's war party had taken. Before long, Slow came to the place where they had chosen to gather and make plans. He rode into their midst and before his father or any of the other men could speak, he jumped from his pony's back and put his arm over the animal's neck.

"We are going," Slow said.

Returns Again looked around at the other men and then looked at his son with pride.

"Han," he said.

The war party began to ride to the place where the Red River meets the Missouri River.

When at last they were close to the place, the men who had been sent ahead as scouts came back.

"Upelo," the scouts said. "They are coming!"

The men began to make preparations. They put on their best clothing and brought out their paint to mark their faces and their horses. They uncovered their war shields and took out their coup sticks and their lances. From behind a small hill, they had a good view of the plain before them and could see the enemy coming from a long way off.

Closer and closer the enemy came, ready for attack.

Everyone waited for Slow's father to give the word. But as he waited, Slow's father looked over to his right. There, already mounted on his horse, was Slow. All that he wore were his moccasins and his breech cloth and he held a coup stick in his hand. He looked over at his father and then he kicked his horse's sides.

"Hiyu'wo!" the boy shouted. His horse leaped forward and over the top of the hill, down toward the enemy. His father and the rest of the war party tried to catch up, but Slow's horse was too far ahead.

480

481

The Crow war party at the base of the hill looked up to see many men galloping down.

One of the Crow warriors drew an arrow to his bowstring, but before he could let it go, Slow had reached him and struck his arm with the coup stick, spoiling his aim. "Oh-hey," Slow cried in triumph.

At the sight of Slow and the men, the Crow warriors fled.

"Hiyu'wo, Hiyu'wo!"

When the fight was over, not one Hunkpapa warrior had been injured. The Lakota people brought back many horses and weapons from the Crow. The raid was a success.

482

Slow was a hero.

When they returned to their village, all of the men spoke in loud voices of the brave deeds they had done. But the loudest voice of all was the voice of Slow's father. He painted his son with black paint — a sign of victory.

"My son is brave," he said. "His determination has won the battle for us. I give him a new name. I give him the name that was mine. He is no longer Slon-he. He is now Tatan'ka Iyota'ke."

And so it was that the boy who was once called "Slow" gained the name Tatan'ka Iyota'ke, a name which is known well, for Tatan'ka Iyota'ke means Sitting Bull — one of the greatest of all the Lakota warriors.

And this is his story.

Meet the Author Joseph Bruchac

Joseph Bruchac's books show the influence of his Native American roots. His grandfather was Abenaki, a member of a Native American group from the Northeastern United States and Canada.

Bruchac has published stories, poetry, and novels including *Eagle Song, The Great Ball Game: A Muskogee Story, Children of the Longhouse,* and *Flying with the Eagle, Racing the Great Bear.* Some of his books draw on his Abenaki heritage. Others, such as *A Boy Called Slow,* deal with Native American cultures very different from his own.

In his writing Bruchac frequently celebrates nature and being true to yourself. He says: "Have pride in what you are and recognize that we as human beings make ourselves. Our possibilities are not limited by what our family was or by what other people say we are."

Meet the Illustrator Rocco Baviera

In addition to *A Boy Called Slow,* Rocco Baviera has collaborated with Joseph Bruchac on *The Song of the Buffalo.* The illustrator of two other books for children, Baviera lives with his wife in Ontario, Canada.

Internet

To learn more about Joseph Bruchac and Rocco Baviera, visit Education Place.
www.eduplace.com/kids

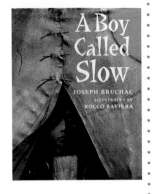

Think About the Selection

1. If you could give yourself a name in the Lakota way, what name would best suit you? Why?

2. Think about Slow's boyhood goals. How are they similar to those of a child today? How are they different?

3. Do you agree with Returns Again about the best way to gain the respect of others? Why or why not?

4. Slow's father calls the Crow his "favorite enemies." What do you think he means?

5. What childhood actions and character traits were clues that Slow might grow up to be a great warrior and leader?

6. Why do you think Slow used a coup stick in the raid? What did it show about him?

7. **Connecting/Comparing** Both Slow and Leigh Botts in *Dear Mr. Henshaw* got advice from older people. Compare the kinds of advice and how they made sense for each boy's life.

Write a Story

Think about how Four Horns might have gotten his name. Then write a story about how it happened. Use what you learned in the selection about Lakota names to help you.

Tips
- Put the story's events in order.
- Use details to make the setting real for your readers.
- Include dialogue that suits your characters and the time.

Social Studies

Make a Card Quiz

A *Boy Called Slow* contains many facts about the Lakota Sioux and their traditions. Use the selection to create a series of Question and Answer cards giving information about the Lakota and Slow. Challenge classmates to come up with the answers.

Answer: _____

Question: _____
_____
_____
_____

Bonus Find out more about the history and traditions of the Plains Indians. Make an illustrated report showing what you learned. Present your findings to the class.

Vocabulary

Make a Word Banner

Find words in the selection that describe important character traits, such as *determined*. Choose one of those traits and design a word banner on paper or cardboard that defines and illustrates the word. You might choose to draw a scene from the selection or from your own life.

Internet

Complete a Web Word Find

Rediscover some of the words you learned about the Lakota Sioux. You can find them in a puzzle that can be printed from the Education Place Web site.

www.eduplace.com/kids

Drawn from History

Skill: How to Look at Fine Art

As you look . . .

Ask yourself these questions:

- **What** does the artwork show? Look at the whole scene, figure, or portrait. Notice the details.

- **How** did the artist create the artwork? What materials were used? What colors, shapes, lines, and patterns do you notice?

- **Where** and **when** did the artist create the artwork? What does it tell you about that place and period in history?

The Indians of the Great Plains have long recorded their lives, visions, and history by drawing and painting. They first painted on rocks and animal hides using paints made from natural pigments and brushes made from bones and sticks. But by the 1860s, Plains Indians were using new materials on a new surface: paper.

Explorers and traders who traveled across the Great Plains brought ledger books and other notebooks with them. Plains Indians began to trade for these notebooks, as well as for colored pencils, crayons, and watercolor paints. Soon, ledger pages once used for lists of numbers became, in the hands of the Lakota, Kiowa, and other Plains tribes, a new art form called Ledger Art.

As you view these drawings, you may notice that the earlier ones, like Sitting Bull's, are simpler in form. By the 1880s, as artists had a wider variety of art supplies to work with, they added scenery and other details. Today the full range of these drawings serves as a valuable record of American Indian life on the Great Plains.

◀ On what is known as the Julian Scott Ledger, an unknown Kiowa artist drew this portrait entitled "Kiowa Couples" in 1880 using pencil, ink, and colored pencil.

▲ This sketch, created by Sitting Bull and copied by his uncle, shows the 14-year-old Slow striking a Crow warrior with his coup stick. The buffalo bull is Sitting Bull's signature.

◀ In 1877, Kiowa artist Wohow represented the new art of photography in "Kiowa Portraits" using pencil and crayon.

489

The Kiowa artist who drew "Kiowa Couples" also created this group portrait, "Twelve High-Ranking Kiowa Men," in 1880 using pencil, ink, and colored pencil.

◀ This pencil-and-ink drawing was created before 1868 by Little Shield of the Arapaho. It is entitled "Pen-na-tak-er Co-manch."

▲ A Cheyenne artist, Squint Eyes, made this
1876 drawing, "Buffalo Hunt," using pencil
and colored pencil.

▲ The artist Black Hawk, of the Sans-arc Lakota, drew this untitled
group portrait from an unusual perspective in 1881 using ink and
colored pencil.

A Research Report

A research report presents facts about a particular topic. Use this student's writing as a model when you write a research report of your own.

Pioneers

The **introduction** helps to capture the attention of the reader.

The **main idea** and **topic sentences** are usually placed at the beginning.

Being a pioneer was an exciting adventure and involved plenty of hard work for men, women, boys, and girls. Pioneers from 1780 to 1850 traveled in wagon trains on a long, hazardous journey to the American West. They had oxen, horses, and even dogs tied to their wagons. Some also traveled by large boats, called flatboats, that carried two or three families down a river, along with their livestock and everything else they owned. More than a million people and animals traveled. Lots of them died on their journey.

The pioneers always helped one another while they traveled. Once they reached their destination, they continued this practice. They worked together as a team. The men made tools, carried water, and sawed wood. The women made candles and clothing. The boys and girls ground corn. The pioneers usually ate vegetables such as beans, squash, turnips, potatoes, and cabbages, but they mostly ate corn. They shared their food with one another.

The pioneers needed shelter during their journey and after they reached their destination. The wagons and flatboats provided shelter for the travelers. The flatboats had a large boxlike structure in the center, which the families used as a house when they traveled. Once they reached the end of their journey, the pioneers usually built log cabins, which they could put together quickly.

> **Supporting details** show that the writer is using facts.

Clothing was harder to provide on the frontier than either food or shelter, because clothing materials were expensive and difficult to get. Linsey-woolsey, a coarse cloth, woven with wool and cotton, was the favorite material of the pioneer housewife for making clothes for herself, her husband, and her children.

When the pioneers farmed, they made their own tools, such as rakes, hoes, and plows. They also built themselves workshops, where they made their tools and household items.

Almost every large pioneer settlement had a church. Parents taught prayers and songs to their children, and kept Sunday as a day of rest and worship.

Pioneering was challenging, exciting, and very difficult. Only the strong and persistent were able to answer the challenge to find and settle in new territories.

List of Sources

"Frontier Life." <u>Encyclopedia Americana.</u> 1995 ed.

"Pioneer Life in America." <u>World Book Encyclopedia</u>. 1992 ed.

Youngberg, Florence C., ed. <u>Conquerors of the West: Stalwart Mormon Pioneers,</u> Vol. 1. Agreka Books. 1998.

Meet the Author

Cora L.
Grade: five
State: Massachusetts
Hobbies: cooking, baking cakes with her dad
What she'd like to be when she grows up: a movie star or a famous singer

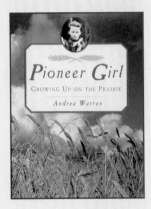

Pioneer Girl
GROWING UP ON THE PRAIRIE
Andrea Warren

Claiming the Land

For years, European **pioneers** thought of the Great Plains as a place to cross, not a place to live. Then in 1862 a new law was passed — the Homestead Act. Settlers could claim a **homestead** on 160 acres of **prairie** land. If they lived on their claims and farmed the land for five years, they would become the owners. Thousands of homesteaders like the family you will meet in *Pioneer Girl* eagerly rushed to settle in Kansas, Nebraska, and the Dakota Territories. Among them were recent **immigrants** from Sweden, Norway, Denmark, France, Germany, and Russia.

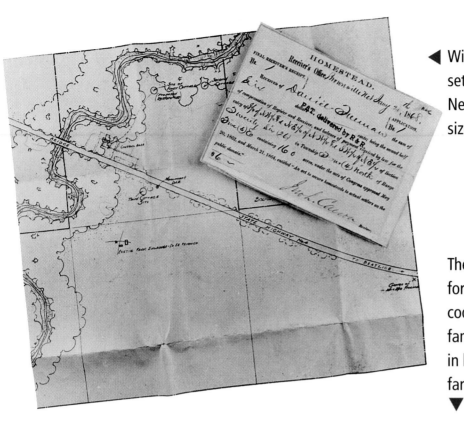

With this receipt for a filing fee, a settler officially owned a **claim** on a Nebraska lot — a piece of land the size of eighty city blocks.

The grasslands were **fertile** for growing crops, if the weather cooperated. But many farm families grew **discouraged** living in houses of **sod**, or earth blocks, far from neighbors.
▼

MEET THE AUTHOR
Andrea Warren

Childhood: Warren grew up in a small Nebraska town on the edge of the Great Plains, where she spent hours reading at the local library. Although she loved to read as a child, she didn't think about becoming a writer until she was an adult.

Work: Warren had several jobs before she decided to write full time, including teaching, editing, and newspaper reporting. She says that each of those jobs has "in some way connected me to words and the joy of writing, or teaching writing."

Writing: Warren has written books for several age groups, including novels for adults and young adults, and books for younger readers. *Pioneer Girl* is her second nonfiction book for children. Her first was *Orphan Train Rider: One Boy's True Story,* which won the *Boston Globe–Horn Book* Award.

To find out more about Andrea Warren, visit Education Place. **www.eduplace.com/kids**

Pioneer Girl

GROWING UP ON THE PRAIRIE

Andrea Warren

As you read about a pioneer family in the 1880s, think of **questions** that you can ask your classmates about details of their life.

RICH FARMING LANDS!

ON THE LINE OF THE

Union Pacific Railroad!

Located in the GREAT CENTRAL BELT of POPULATION, COMMERCE and WEALTH, and adjoining the WORLD'S HIGHWAY from OCEAN TO OCEAN.

12,000,000 ACRES!

3.000,000 Acres in Central and Eastern Nebraska, in the Platte Valley, now for sale!

We invite the attention of all parties seeking a HOME, to the LANDS offered for sale by this Company.

The Vast Quantity of Land from which to select, enables every one to secure such a location as he desires, suitable to any branch of farming or stock raising.

The Prices are Extremely Low. The amount of land owned by the Company is so large that they are determined to sell at the cheapest possible rates, ranging from $1.50 to $8.00 per acre.

The Terms of Payment are Easy. Ten years' credit at six per cent interest. A deduction of ten per cent for cash.

The Location is Central, along the 41st parallel, the favorite latitude of America. Equally well adapted to corn or wheat; free from the long, cold winters of the Northern, and the hot, unhealthy influences of the Southern States.

The Face of the Country is diversified with hill and dale, grain land and meadow, rich bottoms, low bluffs, and undulating tables, all covered with a thick growth of sweet nutritious grasses.

The Soil is a dark loam, slightly impregnated with lime, free from stone and gravel, and eminently adapted to grass, grain and root crops; the subsoil is usually light and porous, retaining moisture with wonderful tenacity.

The Climate is mild and healthful; the atmosphere dry and pure. Epidemic diseases never prevail; Fever and Ague are unknown. The greatest amount of rain falls between March and October. The Winters are dry with but little snow.

The Productions are wheat, corn, oats, barley, rye and root crops, and vegetables generally. Flax, sweet potatoes, sorghum, etc., etc., do well and yield largely.

Fruits, both Wild and Cultivated, do remarkably well, The freedom from frosts in May and September, in connection with the dry Winters and warm soil, renders this State eminently adapted to fruit culture.

Stock Raising in all its branches, is particularly profitable on the wide ranges of rich pasturage. Cattle and sheep feed with avidity and fatten upon the nutritious grasses without grain; hogs thrive well, and wool growing is exceedingly remunerative.

Timber is found on the streams and grows rapidly.

Coal of excellent quality, exists in vast quantities on the line of the road in Wyoming, and is furnished to settlers at reduced rates.

Market Facilities are the best in the West; the great mining regions of Wyoming, Colorado, Utah and Nevada, are supplied by the farmers of Platte Valley.

The Title given the purchaser is absolute, in fee simple, and free from all incumbrances, derived directly from the United States.

Soldiers of the Late War are entitled to a Homestead of one hundred and sixy acres, within Railroad limits, which is equal to a bounty of $400.

Persons of Foreign Birth are also entitled to the benefits of the Free Homestead Law, on declaring their intentions of becoming citizens of the United States; this they may do immediately on their arrival in this country.

For Colonies, the lands on the line of the Union Pacific Railroad afford the *best locations* in the West.

TOWN LOTS FOR SALE VERY CHEAP in the most important towns on the line of the Road, affording excellent opportunities for business or investments.

Full information in regard to lands, prices, terms of sale, &c., together with pamphlets, circulars and maps, may be obtained from all the Agents of the Department, also the

"PIONEER."

A handsome ILLUSTRATED PAPER, with maps, etc., and containing the HOMESTEAD LAW. *Mailed free* to all applicants. Address

O. F. DAVIS,
Land Commissioner, U. P. R. R.
OMAHA, NEB.

Posters like this one, advertising land for sale by the railroad, drew settlers to the prairie.

In 1885, the McCance family of Missouri filed a claim on 160 acres of land in central Nebraska, headed west, and became "homesteaders." Poppie McCance built a house on the windswept prairie out of blocks of earth, or sod. The new farm brought both adventures and hardships for the McCance children – Grace, Florry, and Stella – and their hardworking parents. Grace had a remarkable memory and could recall details from even her very early years. Whenever she is quoted, the words are directly from her memoir.

During the fall, Grace and Florry played outside whenever they could. Their favorite place was the old buffalo trail that wound over the prairie and out of sight from the house. Their cat liked to go with them. Sometimes they found tiny shells in the soil and would bring them home to Mama. She explained how, millions of years ago, glaciers covered the land. When they melted, they created a sea. That's where the shells had come from.

Later Grace learned that the Midwest was dry because the Rocky Mountains in Colorado blocked moisture blowing inland from the Pacific Ocean. Nebraska was one of the driest Midwest states. The few trees grew mostly along the rivers. Rainfall also affected how tall the grass grew. Travelers going west noticed that the closer they got to the Rocky Mountains, the shorter the grass was. "Shortgrass" grew only six to twelve inches tall.

The McCance family reunion, 1892: Mama and Poppie are standing to the far right. In front of them are babies Elsie and Nelie.

On the eastern side of the Midwest, known as the "tallgrass" prairie, native grasses got enough rain to grow six to twelve feet in height. In the shortgrass area where the McCances lived, Poppie planted types of wheat and corn that needed little rainfall. His crops still had to have some rain, however, and like all farmers he kept one eye on the weather.

The weather was always a concern. Hailstorms could pound crops to pieces in a matter of minutes, and injure or kill birds and animals. Hailstones even killed people caught without shelter. Lightning was another danger. Grace once saw a horse that had been killed by lightning. When the weather was dry, lightning, a spark from a campfire, or a gun discharge could start prairie fires, and the wind would spread them.

Settlers banded together to fight the fires. Sometimes they tried setting backfires — burning a strip of land in the fire's path so that when the fire reached the strip, it either burned out or turned in a different direction. Like every settler, Poppie tried to keep firebreaks — grassless ditches the fires could not cross — plowed around his land. But sometimes, if prairie fires

*S*eated to the far right are (left to right) Stella, Florry, Grace, and Ethel.

were moving fast enough, they could jump firebreaks and be stopped only by a river or a creek.

Grace never forgot her first prairie fire. As soon as Poppie saw smoke in the far hills, he took off in the wagon with a barrel of water. Mama, Florry, and Grace watched all morning as the fire drew closer to their land. Grace was frightened.

Mama told the girls that if the fire jumped the firebreak they would run to the middle of the big bare field where the fire would have nothing to burn and would either go around them or die out. When the flames reached the firebreaks, Grace was ready to run. Then she saw that the fire was going out. When Poppie finally came home, his clothes and skin were black from soot.

A few months after the fire, a rainstorm struck the homestead. The howling of the wind woke everyone up. Suddenly "the darkness, black and thick as velvet, was ripped apart by a terrible blue flash of lightning," Grace remembered. "Then there was a cracking, tearing sound, and the soddy seemed to quiver."

The noise was the roof being torn off the kitchen. When the storm finally stopped, the house was "a sorry-looking mess. Every last thing had blown off the walls, and all Mama's little shelves, brackets, whatnots, and pictures were either smashed to bits or gone entirely." Grace remembered that "Mama went around in a kind of a daze, picking some of her torn and broken things out of the hash on the floor and sweeping out the worst of the mud. The hot sun was pouring down on our heads when Poppie, hard put to keep a cheerful expression on his face, offered thanks for the cornmeal mush and fried eggs we finally sat down to."

The girls helped Mama carry water to clean up. Poppie hunted for roof boards that had blown away and set to work rebuilding the roof. Grace and her mother walked through the fields looking for their belongings. They "found half of the marriage certificate, but no part of the frame or glass. Just that half, ripped from the rest, its doves and cupids hardly stained by the mud and rain."

Storms could destroy a pioneer family's house and fields.

*W*indmills built over wells pumped water to the surface and also showed travelers where houses were located.

Still, Poppie was not discouraged. Like most farmers, he lived on hope, always convinced that the next year would be better.

When early November's chill made it too cold to play outside, Grace and Florry gathered up their cob dolls and settled into the sod house for the winter. "Flour sacks full of beans and dried corn hung in the kitchen corner that winter, and heaps of onions, turnips, pumpkins, cabbage, and potatoes filled the cellar cave."

Just before Thanksgiving, Poppie came home from one of his weekly trips to town with three barrels in the back of the wagon. They had come by railroad from Grandma and Grandpa Blaine, Mama's parents back in Missouri. Grace and Florry and even little Stella were almost beside themselves with excitement when Poppie started to pry off the lids.

A rare photograph of the crowded interior of a one-room sod house.

The first one was filled with molasses to sweeten their cereal and Mama's baked goods. The second was full of red apples from Grandpa Blaine's orchard behind the big white house. Grace saw the faraway look in Mama's eyes when she took one and held it in her hands.

The third barrel was the best. First they pulled out bags of black walnuts from Grandpa's nut trees and sweet potatoes from his garden. Then came Grandma's bundles. One contained a dress length of new calico fabric for Mama and each of the girls. The other held clothes from Mama's younger sister, Aunt Ollie, who always wore the latest styles. She had sent along jackets, dresses, and petticoats she did not want anymore.

Mama laid everything out on the bed, and Grace and Florry gazed at the lovely garments. Mama would make over the clothes so the girls would have new outfits. And she promised to have their new calico dresses made in time for Christmas dinner.

506

That first Christmas, Mama and Poppie could not afford any presents, but Poppie cut down a little wild plum bush and Grace and Florry decorated it with paper chains and strings of popcorn. All three girls wore their new dresses when the neighbors came to feast on a roast turkey dinner. Grace's only complaint was that the table was not big enough. She and Florry and the neighbors' children had to wait until the adults finished at "first table" before it was their turn to eat. "While hard knots of hunger grew and grew inside us, we had to sit back, smelling the good smells, and hoping there would be enough of everything left for us," she recalled. "Homestead children had to put up with a lot of hard things, but one of the hardest was waiting for second table."

Spring came again, and the prairie turned soft green.

Grace was now four and lingered outside. "The first day of going barefoot was almost as good as Christmas, or the Fourth of July," she recalled. "There is almost no describing it; the good feeling to tender, bare soles of cushiony new buffalo grass, or of the fine, warm dust of a cow trail."

Everything on the homestead was humming and growing. The horse gave birth to a colt. Pearlie the cow had a calf. Little chicks followed the fussy old turkey. Poppie planted his wheat, and then had to use his shotgun to fight off flocks of geese flying north that kept stealing the precious seeds. Mama planted her garden again, a bigger one this year. "Poppie said, for the hundredth time, that he had never seen such a land as this, so rich, so fertile. But Mama said only that she wished we had a well in our own yard."

Poppie kept after the well men, but they had so much business from all the new homesteaders in the area that they raised their rates. Poppie said they did not have enough money. He would have to keep hauling water until he could dig the well himself.

Their second year on the prairie passed much as the first. Grace and Florry still begged to go whenever Poppie loaded up the water barrels. If Mama would relent, "we had fun, jouncing along in the wagon and singing

Pioneers used buffalo or cow chips for fuel because there were few trees on the prairie. The little girl is holding her corn husk doll.

with Poppie above the rattle and bang of the empty barrels. . . . When we pulled up at the well, our neighbor, Mrs. Totten, would come out to visit with us while Poppie filled the barrels, or maybe she would take us to the house with her."

The Tottens were only a few miles away, but Mama still felt as if she lived in the middle of nowhere. That changed when the Yoders, who had been the McCances' neighbors in Missouri, took a claim nearby. "Their arrival made Mama happier than anything that had happened since we came to Nebraska," Grace realized.

On Mama's birthday in April, Mama decided the family should visit the Yoders since their son's birthday was the same day. Mama began preparing food to take with them. Grace and Florry did their chores and took baths, put on their best petticoats, and tried to stand still while Mama braided their long hair. Then Mama brushed her own hair and arranged it stylishly on her head. Just as they all finished dressing, Mama glanced out the window and cried, "'Merciful heavens, there's the Yoders, the whole family, and look at this house!'"

Immigrants, like this French family who pioneered in Kansas, played an important role in helping to settle the Midwest.

Grace and Florry looked — at a tub of cold dirty bathwater, clothes strewn everywhere, and the kitchen not yet tidied from breakfast. While Mama hurriedly picked up, Grace and Florry grabbed the bath basin and dragged it outside, just as their unexpected guests came to the door. They had brought a birthday dinner for Mama and their son, all ready to eat.

The homesteaders settling around the McCances were mostly Swedish immigrants. When the farmers gathered together to help harvest one another's wheat crops, Poppie, whose ancestors were Scottish and Irish, missed out on most of the conversation, which was in Swedish.

Immigrants who settled in the Midwest usually came for the rich farmland. In the countries they left behind, they either could not afford to own land or were not allowed to. Some also came to find religious freedom, to escape paying unfair taxes, or to avoid serving in the military. So many Germans settled in Kansas during the 1860s and 1870s that one tribe of Kansas Indians spoke German as a second language instead of English. In 1870, over half of Nebraska's population was made up of foreign-born immigrants and their American-born children.

Like Poppie, many people born in the United States also wanted to homestead. Some had lost their homes in the Civil War or thought the East was getting too crowded. Freed slaves came because they wanted to leave the South, and homesteading was a way they could own land. Sometimes freed slaves established a community, such as the little Kansas town of Nicodemus.

Most homesteaders were poor. Children were often barefoot because they owned no shoes. One child remembered that his parents used kegs for chairs during family meals and the children stood. Before they had those kegs, they sat on pumpkins.

Everyone worked six days a week, including small children. Three-year-olds could act as human scarecrows to chase grain-eating birds out of the fields and help gather chips for fuel. Four-year-olds ran errands, took water to field-workers, and gathered eggs. Five-year-olds helped break up clods in the fields, pull weeds, feed the cookstove, milk cows, and even plow. One six-year-old boy sent to find stray cattle was gone several days before his father set out to search for him and found him not far from home, returning with the lost cows.

Grace and Florry had always helped out. Grace was five and Florry was seven when they were given a new chore: looking for turkey nests. When chicken and turkey hens turned "broody" in the spring, they stopped laying for several weeks so they could sit on one batch of eggs long enough for them to hatch into baby chicks. But they often laid their eggs far from home, where skunks and snakes could get them and where coyotes could kill the hens. The girls' job was to find the nests and get the hens to "brood" them back at the stable. Grace recalled, "The hens would stroll the prairie for hours, acting as if they had nowhere to go and nothing to do. Sometimes we sat watching a hen for a solid half day, and then somehow missed her when she slipped, like the shadow of a cloud, into some patch of brush or tall grass and disappeared."

The fall of 1887, Poppie bought a small herd of cattle. Since there were no boys in the family, he called on five-year-old Grace, nicknaming her Pete because she would be doing work usually done by a boy. He said, "'You'll have to be my herd boy now, Pete. Mommie needs Florry to help her in the house and you'll have to do it all alone. Think you can?'" Grace was thrilled. She disliked housework and far preferred to work outdoors.

Her job was to drive the cattle to the fields in the morning, stay with them all day, and bring them home in the evening. Herding would have gone fine, had it not been for one mean-tempered heifer who constantly threatened Grace with her sharp horns. Grace had to carry a stout stick to protect herself. One evening the cows turned contrary and wanted to stay inside the cave they had created in the big haystack: "No matter how much I ran and yelled and whacked, they outran me and dodged back into the cave. Finally, I pushed past them into the hole and began pounding on their heads with my stick. The older cows gave up and backed out together, leaving me suddenly face-to-face with the long-nosed, ornery heifer."

Boys helped bring in the crops.

As the heifer rushed her, Grace flattened herself against the hay, but the heifer gouged a deep cut from her hip to armpit. As much as it hurt, Grace got the cows home, even the heifer. When she was finally in the house, she burst into tears. Mama cared for her, then told Poppie he had to get rid of the heifer or Grace could no longer herd. Poppie said he would sell the heifer the next time he went to town. In the meantime, he would keep her in the corral.

A few days later, when Grace was in the barn helping with the milking, she heard a snort behind her. She whirled around and saw the heifer, head down, coming straight for her. Grace made a mad dash, ducking under one of the cows and rolling under the barbed-wire fence. She was unhurt, but she was wearing her favorite calico dress and ripped it so badly it was ruined. That made her cry more than the scare. Poppie sold the heifer in town the next day.

Even very young pioneer children helped feed animals, milk cows, and do other chores.

GRACE McCANCE SNYDER
1882–1982

When I was growing up in Newman Grove, Nebraska, I could see a cornfield from my bedroom window, and I marked the seasons by its growth and colors. My view now is of city streets, and I sometimes wish I could still see that cornfield every day as a reminder of the pioneer families who settled the Midwest.

Many pioneer children grew up on hardscrabble homesteads, working alongside their parents in harsh conditions to nurture the growth of crops and cattle. In researching the lives of children on the prairie, however, I did not hear many complaints. These children were needed by their families and had a strong sense of purpose. Because they knew no other life, they did not feel deprived. The prairie was their home. Their optimism, steadfastness, and hard work have given those of us fortunate enough to live in this beautiful part of the world a proud legacy.

When I first read Grace McCance Snyder's memoir, *No Time on My Hands*, I knew I wanted to write about her pioneer childhood. I liked her spunk and spirit. She dared to dream, and she saw her dreams come true.

I hope readers will enjoy her story as it is told here and, through her, will gain new appreciation of what it meant to grow up on the prairie.

— Andrea Warren

Grace posed on horseback for her ninetieth birthday.

513

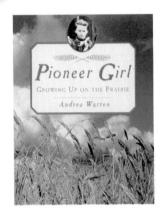

Think About the Selection

1. How do Grace and Florry's chores compare with the chores you do at home?

2. The author writes that Poppie and the other farmers "lived on hope." Give examples from the selection that show this.

3. What do you think would have been the best and worst things about being a child in a homesteading family? Explain your answer.

4. Based on the information in the selection, would you expect the McCance family's farm to become successful? Why or why not?

5. Do you think it was fair to lure homesteaders to the prairie with ads promising rich farmland? Explain.

6. What can Americans today learn from the experiences of ordinary people of earlier generations, like Grace McCance Snyder?

7. **Connecting/Comparing** Compare how the Lakota people in *A Boy Called Slow* and the McCance family in *Pioneer Girl* adapted to life on the Great Plains.

Write Instructions

Think about the chores a child would have to do in a homesteading family. Someone who took over those chores for a few days might need instructions. Write instructions for two of the chores, telling how to do each one.

Tips

- Use imperative sentences when giving directions.
- Use words such as *first, then, next,* and *last* to make the order of the steps clear.

514

MATH

Make a Diagram

Draw a diagram of a sod house and the furniture inside it. Use information from the selection to help you decide the size of the living area and the objects in it. Include the approximate measurements of each room.

Bonus Suppose you were building a sod house out of sod blocks 3' long by 1' wide by 4" thick. How many blocks would you need for a one-foot-thick wall measuring 12' long by 9' high?

ART

Create an Illustration

Use the photographs, events, and descriptions in *Pioneer Girl* to create your own illustration for the story. Think about the clothes the characters might have worn and other details of the landscape and weather.

Send an E-Postcard

Send a friend an e-postcard telling about the McCance homestead. You might give a few details from the selection, and invite your friend to read *Pioneer Girl*. You'll find the postcard at Education Place. **www.eduplace.com/kids**

Nicodemus Stakes a Claim In History

By Angela Bates-Tompkins

In 1877, 350 former slaves moved from Kentucky to northwest
Kansas. The town in which they settled was given the name
Nicodemus. It was named after the first slave to purchase his
freedom in the United States. W.R. Hill, a white town builder,
and W.H. Smith, an African American homesteader, were
partners in organizing this all–black settlement.

A buffalo soldier demonstration in Nicodemus in 1998.

The townspeople of Nicodemus, Kansas, gather on Main Street around 1885 (left). Today fewer than thirty people live in the town.

This October 1, 1879 homestead application (below) was submitted by S.P. Roundtree, one of the founders of Nicodemus.

Hill and Smith were joined by five African American ministers who had been living in Topeka, Kansas. In April 1877, the group founded the Nicodemus Town Company and sought settlers from Kentucky to move to Kansas.

The first 350 recruits arrived in Nicodemus in September 1877 with high hopes. They were soon disappointed. They found themselves surrounded by a treeless landscape. Some of the town organizers even were living in dugouts. As many as sixty families returned to Kentucky. Those who stayed had brought only a few belongings with them. Their supplies soon ran out. Fortunately, some Osage Indians stopped at Nicodemus while on a hunting trip and gave the settlers food to survive the winter.

Though the first year was a struggle, several other groups of settlers soon joined the original bands. By 1885, the population of Nicodemus had grown to nearly seven hundred people. The town had two newspapers, livery stables, a post office, a general store, a doctor, hotels, restaurants, schools, and churches. From the late 1800s to the 1940s, the largest number of black farmers and African American–owned farmland in Kansas was in Graham County, of which Nicodemus was the central city.

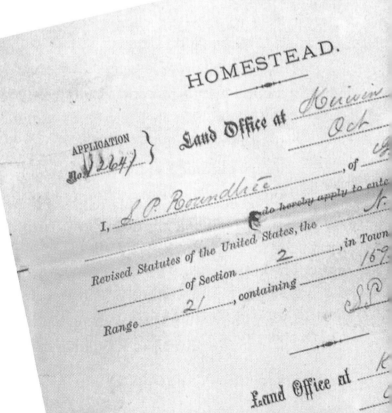

HOMESTEAD.

APPLICATION No. 2647

Land Office at Kirwin

Oct

I, S. P. Roundtree, of do hereby apply to ente

Revised Statutes of the United States, the N

of Section 2, in Town 15

Range 21, containing S. P.

Land Office at K

In 1887, residents of Nicodemus raised money to try to help bring a railroad through their town. Trains and railroads meant progress. The townspeople hoped that a train station would carry people and goods to the town. The railroad bypassed the town, however. Many settlers became discouraged and began to leave. Some merchants moved their businesses to the newly organized railroad town of Bogue, just six miles to the west.

Difficult years followed, but Nicodemus residents still hoped to succeed. A drought came, making it hard to grow crops. When the crops did flourish, locusts ate them.

In the 1930s, the United States was faced with the Great Depression. In Nicodemus, as elsewhere in the country, people lost their jobs and new jobs were almost impossible to find. Townspeople left for what they hoped would be new starts in better places.

Despite the decline in population, Nicodemus remained a cultural center for African American life. And although people left the town, they did not forget it. They still return for the annual Emancipation Celebration, held during the last weekend of July. Descendants of those first settlers come from all over the United States to reconnect with family and friends.

In 1976, Nicodemus was put on the National Register of Historic Places as a National Historic Landmark. In 1991, efforts by the Nicodemus Historical Society resulted in a proposal to establish Nicodemus as a National Historic Site/Park. The bill was passed by Congress and signed by President Bill Clinton on November 12, 1996. The town is now receiving funds to help restore its five historic buildings.

The National Park Service is providing assistance in interpreting the town's rich African American history and its unique contribution to the economic, social, and political development of Kansas and the West.

Nicodemus is the oldest and only remaining all-African American town west of the Mississippi River. On August 1, 1998, during the 120th Emancipation Celebration, Nicodemus was dedicated as a National Historic Site/Park.

**Black
Cowboy,
Wild Horses**

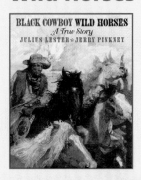

Galloping Free

Horses were once native to North America. Long ago they disappeared from the landscape, only to return in the 1500s with explorers from Spain. Many of these horses escaped, ran free out into the plains, and lost their tame ways. They became wild horses, or **mustangs**. Before long, **herds** of mustangs were roaming the **bluffs** and **ravines** of the Great Plains and the Southwest, much like the herd in *Black Cowboy, Wild Horses*.

Wild horses are smaller than domestic horses, with harder hooves, to help them survive outdoors. Each herd contains one male, a **stallion**, who leads several females, or **mares**, and their youngsters, or foals. Another stallion may challenge the leader to a fight. If the challenger wins, he becomes the new leader.

Horses were especially valuable to the cattlemen of the plains in the 1870s. Without horses, cowboys could not move their cattle to market. Many cowboys had a talent for rounding up and taming mustangs.

One of the most famous horsemen was Bob Lemmons. In Lemmons's time — especially the 1870s and 1880s — one out of three cowboys was African American or Mexican.

Meet the Author
Julius Lester

Birthplace: St. Louis, Missouri
Writing for children: Lester's own children had a big influence on his writing. He says, "I want them to have books that I would have liked to have had when I was growing up."
Odd jobs: Lester was once a professional musician and singer and the host of a radio show in New York.

Meet the Illustrator
Jerry Pinkney

Birthplace: Philadelphia, Pennsylvania
Odd job: Pinkney once worked as a designer and illustrator for a greeting card company.
Family ties: Pinkney's wife, Gloria Jean, and his daughter-in-law, Angela Davis Pinkney, are both writers. His son, Brian, is a children's book writer and illustrator, and his son Myles is a photographer whose work also appears in children's books.
Collaborators: Lester and Pinkney have worked together on *John Henry* and five books of *The Tales of Uncle Remus*.

To learn more about Julius Lester and Jerry Pinkney, visit Education Place. **www.eduplace.com/kids**

BLACK COWBOY WILD HORSES
A True Story
JULIUS LESTER ☆ JERRY PINKNEY

The author tells a true story using words to create pictures in a poetic way. As you read, **evaluate** how well those word pictures help to tell that story.

523

FIRST LIGHT. Bob Lemmons rode his horse slowly up the rise. When he reached the top, he stopped at the edge of the bluff. He looked down at the corral where the other cowboys were beginning the morning chores, then turned away and stared at the land stretching as wide as love in every direction. The sky was curved as if it were a lap on which the earth lay napping like a curled cat. High above, a hawk was suspended on cold threads of unseen winds. Far, far away, at what looked to be the edge of the world, land and sky kissed.

He guided Warrior, his black stallion, slowly down the bluff. When they reached the bottom, the horse reared, eager to run across the vastness of the plains until he reached forever. Bob smiled and patted him gently on the neck. "Easy. Easy," he whispered. "We'll have time for that. But not yet."

He let the horse trot for a while, then slowed him and began peering intently at the ground as if looking for the answer to a question he scarcely understood.

It was late afternoon when he saw them — the hoofprints of mustangs, the wild horses that lived on the plains. He stopped, dismounted, and walked around carefully until he had seen all the prints. Then he got down on his hands and knees to examine them more closely.

Some people learned from books. Bob had been a slave and never learned to read words. But he could look at the ground and read what animals had walked on it, their size and weight, when they had passed by, and where they were going. No one he knew could bring in mustangs by themselves, but Bob could make horses think he was one of them — because he was.

He stood, reached into his saddlebag, took out an apple, and gave it to Warrior, who chewed with noisy enthusiasm. It was a herd of eight mares, a colt, and a stallion. They had passed there two days ago. He would see them soon. But he needed to smell of sun, moon, stars, and wind before the mustangs would accept him.

The sun went down and the chilly night air came quickly. Bob took the saddle, saddlebag, and blanket off Warrior. He was cold, but could not make a fire. The mustangs would smell the smoke in his clothes from miles away. He draped a thick blanket around himself, then took the cotton sack of dried fruit, beef jerky, and nuts from his saddlebag and ate. When he was done, he lay his head on his saddle and was quickly asleep. Warrior grazed in the tall, sweet grasses.

As soon as the sun's round shoulders came over the horizon, Bob awoke. He ate, filled his canteen, and saddling Warrior, rode away. All day he followed the tracks without hurrying.

Near dusk, clouds appeared, piled atop each other like mountains made of fear. Lightning flickered from within them like candle flames shivering in a breeze. Bob heard the faint but distinct rumbling of thunder. Suddenly lightning vaulted from cloud to cloud across the curved heavens.

Warrior reared, his front hooves pawing as if trying to knock the white streaks of fire from the night sky. Bob raced Warrior to a nearby ravine as the sky exploded sheets of light. And there, in the distance, beneath the ghostly light, Bob saw the herd of mustangs. As if sensing their presence, Warrior rose into the air once again, this time not challenging the heavens but almost in greeting. Bob thought he saw the mustang stallion rise in response as the earth shuddered from the sound of thunder.

Then the rain came as hard and stinging as remorse. Quickly Bob put on his poncho, and turning Warrior away from the wind and the rain, waited. The storm would pass soon. Or it wouldn't. There was nothing to do but wait.

Finally the rain slowed and then stopped. The clouds thinned, and there, high in the sky, the moon appeared as white as grief. Bob slept in the saddle while Warrior grazed on the wet grasses.

The sun rose into a clear sky and Bob was awake immediately. The storm would have washed away the tracks, but they had been going toward the big river. He would go there and wait.

By mid-afternoon he could see the ribbon of river shining in the distance. He stopped, needing only to be close enough to see the horses when they came to drink. Toward evening he saw a trail of rolling, dusty clouds.

In front was the mustang herd. As it reached the water, the stallion slowed and stopped. He looked around, his head raised, nostrils flared, smelling the air. He turned in Bob's direction and sniffed the air again.

Bob tensed. Had he come too close too soon? If the stallion smelled anything new, he and the herd would be gone and Bob would never find them again. The stallion seemed to be looking directly at him. Bob was too far away to be seen, but he did not even blink his eyes, afraid the stallion would hear the sound. Finally the stallion began drinking and the other horses followed. Bob let his breath out slowly. He had been accepted.

The next morning he crossed the river and picked up the herd's trail. He moved Warrior slowly, without sound, without dust. Soon he saw them grazing. He stopped. The horses did not notice him. After a while he moved forward, slowly, quietly. The stallion raised his head. Bob stopped.

When the stallion went back to grazing, Bob moved forward again. All day Bob watched the herd, moving only when it moved but always coming closer. The mustangs sensed his presence. They thought he was a horse.

So did he.

The following morning Bob and Warrior walked into the herd. The stallion eyed them for a moment. Then, as if to test this newcomer, he led the herd off in a gallop. Bob lay flat across Warrior's back and moved with the herd. If anyone had been watching, they would not have noticed a man among the horses.

534

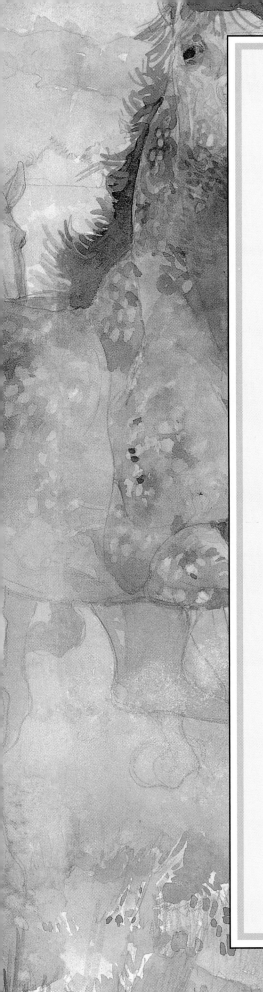

When the herd set out early the next day, it was moving slowly. If the horses had been going faster, it would not have happened.

The colt fell to the ground as if she had stepped into a hole and broken her leg. Bob and the horses heard the chilling sound of the rattles. Rattlesnakes didn't always give a warning before they struck. Sometimes, when someone or something came too close, they bit with the fury of fear.

The horses whinnied and pranced nervously, smelling the snake and death among them. Bob saw the rattler, as beautiful as a necklace, sliding silently through the tall grasses. He made no move to kill it. Everything in nature had the right to protect itself, especially when it was afraid.

The stallion galloped to the colt. He pushed at her. The colt struggled to get up, but fell to her side, shivering and kicking feebly with her thin legs. Quickly she was dead.

Already vultures circled high in the sky. The mustangs milled aimlessly. The colt's mother whinnied, refusing to leave the side of her colt. The stallion wanted to move the herd from there, and pushed the mare with his head. She refused to budge, and he nipped her on the rump. She skittered away. Before she could return to the colt, the stallion bit her again, this time harder. She ran toward the herd. He bit her a third time, and the herd was off. As they galloped away, Bob looked back. The vultures were descending from the sky as gracefully as dusk.

It was time to take over the herd. The stallion would not have the heart to fight fiercely so soon after the death of the colt. Bob galloped Warrior to the front and wheeled around, forcing the stallion to stop quickly. The herd, confused, slowed and stopped also.

Bob raised Warrior to stand high on his back legs, fetlocks pawing and kicking the air. The stallion's eyes widened. He snorted and pawed the ground, surprised and uncertain. Bob charged at the stallion.

Both horses rose on hind legs, teeth bared as they kicked at each other. When they came down, Bob charged Warrior at the stallion again, pushing him backward. Bob rushed yet again.

The stallion neighed loudly, and nipped Warrior on the neck. Warrior snorted angrily, reared, and kicked out with his forelegs, striking the stallion on the nose. Still maintaining his balance, Warrior struck again and again. The mustang stallion cried out in pain. Warrior pushed hard against the stallion. The stallion lost his footing and fell to the earth. Warrior rose, neighing triumphantly, his front legs pawing as if seeking for the rungs on which he could climb a ladder into the sky.

The mustang scrambled to his feet, beaten. He snorted weakly. When Warrior made as if to attack again, the stallion turned, whinnied weakly, and trotted away.

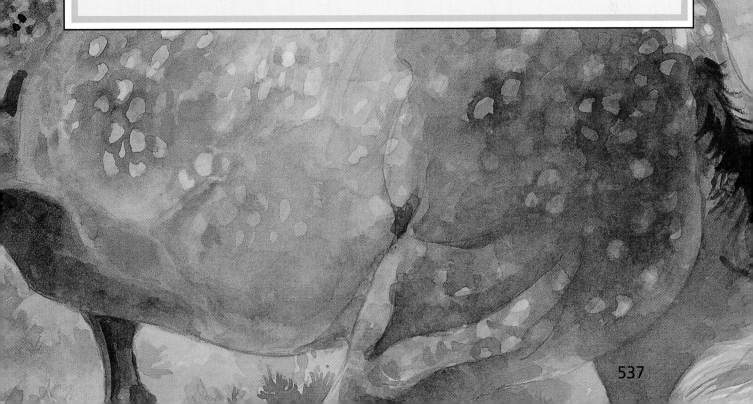

Bob was now the herd's leader, but would they follow him? He rode slowly at first, then faster and faster. The mustangs followed as if being led on ropes.

Throughout that day and the next he rode with the horses. For Bob there was only the bulging of the horses' dark eyes, the quivering of their flesh, the rippling of muscles and bending of bones in their bodies. He was now sky and plains and grass and river and horse.

When his food was almost gone, Bob led the horses on one last ride, a dark surge of flesh flashing across the plains like black lightning. Toward evening he led the herd up the steep hillside, onto the bluff, and down the slope toward the big corral. The cowboys heard him coming and opened the corral gate. Bob led the herd, but at the last moment he swerved Warrior aside, and the mustangs flowed into the fenced enclosure. The cowboys leaped and shouted as they quickly closed the gate.

Bob rode away from them and back up to the bluff. He stopped and stared out onto the plains. Warrior reared and whinnied loudly. "I know," Bob whispered. "I know. Maybe someday." Maybe someday they would ride with the mustangs, ride to that forever place where land and sky kissed, and then ride on. Maybe someday.

Responding

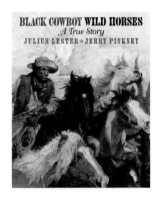

Think About the Selection

1. Choose one of the author's descriptions of nature that you like best. Explain what this description helps you imagine.

2. How do you think Bob might have "read" the mustang hoof-prints? How did they provide him with clues about the herd?

3. Do you agree with Bob's reason for letting the rattlesnake go after it killed the colt? Why or why not?

4. Do you think people should be allowed to round up wild horses or should we not interfere with them? Explain your answer.

5. What would you find most difficult about what Bob does for a living? Most rewarding?

6. What do you think the author means when he says, "Bob could make horses think he was one of them — because he was."

7. **Connecting/Comparing** How are Bob Lemmons and Returns Again alike in their understanding of animals? Compare and contrast their experiences with animals.

Write a Description

The author uses similes and metaphors to create vivid descriptions. Write a colorful description of a scene or detail from the selection. Use similes and metaphors to enliven your description.

Tips

- Remember that a simile uses *like* or *as* to compare two things. A metaphor compares two things by stating that one thing is the other.
- Use vivid, exact words.

Explain How an Ecosystem Works

Living things, together with the environment they live in, form ecosystems. Use the illustrations and text to write an explanation of the ecosystem in *Black Cowboy, Wild Horses*. What animals, plants, and features of the environment are part of it? How do the horses depend on it?

Bonus Draw a diagram to illustrate your explanation.

Ecosystem of Wild Horses

Animals

Plants

Environmental Features

Review Illustrations

With a partner, present an oral review of the illustrations in *Black Cowboy, Wild Horses*. Choose ones you especially like and tell what you like about them. How do they help tell Bob Lemmons's story?

Internet

Take an Online Poll

Think about the following statement: *It is wrong for people to herd and tame wild horses.* Do you agree or disagree? Find out what other students your age think. Visit Education Place and add your opinion to a poll.

www.eduplace.com/kids

Home on

Technology has changed life on this giant 145-year-old Texas ranch. But not much.

by Johnny D. Boggs

Calves bawl as a handful of cowboys send the scared animals through narrow, wooden chutes to separate them for tomorrow's branding.

The dust is thick and suffocating, and the afternoon sun bakes man and beast. Saddle leather creaks, spurs jingle, horses snort and sweat-soaked cowboys yell in Spanish and English to keep the cattle moving.

Out of nowhere, high-pitched beeps suddenly sound. In a pickup truck, a cowboy's phone-radio is ringing.

Hey, it's the 1990s — not the 1870s.

the Range

A Short History of a BIG Place

Welcome to the King Ranch in south Texas. At 825,000 acres, it's the largest privately owned ranch in the world. How big? At almost 1,300 square miles, it's larger than Rhode Island. Wire fences along the ranch's boundaries could stretch from Denver, Colo., to Boston, Mass.

Riverboat pilot Richard King founded the ranch in 1853. The captain bought cattle in Mexico and convinced an entire village to move to Texas to work for him. These workers became known as *Kiñenos*, Spanish for King's Men.

Today, the King Ranch is run by the heirs of Captain King, and *Kiñenos* still work here. Fourth-generation *Kiñeno* Faustino Montalvo was born on the ranch. "No hospital, no doctor," the 55-year-old says.

Times have changed, though. A public school district falls within the ranch's boundaries, and the town of Kingsville, founded in 1904 and built partly on land donated by Mrs. King, includes a state university and modern facilities. The ranch itself is diverse, with oil exploration, wildlife management and farming.

But cattle remain the ranch's centerpiece. And it still takes real cowboys to look after some 60,000 cattle.

The "Running W" brand marks the Santa Cruz cattle of the King Ranch.

Photographs © 1998 by David Nance

545

The Cowboy Way

Today, nearly 50 cowboys work on the King Ranch, and some things haven't changed since the 1800s. Many hands still live on the ranch. They answer to nicknames like "Chito," "Gallo" and "Leon."

Cowboys still wear leather chaps over their jeans, spurs on their boots and well-worn straw cowboy hats. Some opt for baseball caps and, occasionally, athletic shoes.

Calves get branded with the same "Running W" mark Captain King first used in 1869, using the old, heavy irons. Sometimes the cattle are vaccinated and branded in the chutes.

Often, though, it's done the old-fashioned way. Calves are roped and held down — it's where the calf-roping contest in rodeos comes from — while a cowboy slaps a hot iron above the animal's rear leg. Smoke and dust burn the nostrils. It's a dirty job, just as it was in the 1800s.

"It's not a job you get into for the money," cowboy Steve Shermer says. Indeed. Cowboys don't get paid overtime, and their workday can begin before sunrise and end after dark. "You just work until the job's done," Shermer says.

And there's usually a lot to be done, whether it's checking stock, mending fences or working with horses.

High-Tech Cowboys

Technology has changed the ways of the ranch. While cowboys continue to drive cattle to the corral on horseback, a pickup truck — air-conditioned, of course — also helps. And though they don't plug branding irons into electrical

Cowboy Jonathan Hawkins, 19, helps round up the cattle.

Photographs © 1998 by David Nance

Although technology can help with some tasks, cowboys still rely on the help of dogs to herd cattle (far left). Cowboys (left) lead calves into wooden chutes in order to give them medicine.

outlets, propane tanks make lighting fires and heating branding irons easier.

"It used to take seven to ten days to work the cattle," says Alfredo "Chito" Mendietta. "Now we can work them in two days."

Computers log inventory and keep track of wildlife. Hal Hawkins, King Ranch's animal physiologist, monitors herd research and development with a laptop computer.

Technology's Drawbacks

Shermer compares the job of today's cowboy to that of a factory worker. "The land's the factory and the cattle are your product," he says. "In a factory, you try to get the most out of your product. And that's what we try to do as land managers."

Technology goes only so far. Computers can't make it rain. Droughts were rough on cowboys and cattle in the 1800s, and they're just as hard today.

"It's tough," unit manager Robert Silguero says. "It can make you think of doing something else."

But not really. The weather can be tough, but cowboys are tougher.

City Slickers Are Welcome

So you want to be a cowboy? Silguero, Mendietta and Montalvo have been at the King Ranch all of their lives. Others, like Hawkins, Shermer and Knudsen, come from rural areas.

"We've had quite a few hands come out of the city, though," Shermer says. "The trick is you've just got to be willing to learn. I pretty much learn something new every day."

You also have to be willing to spend long days in the sun, working livestock. And it's not all fun and games.

Mendietta certainly didn't think so when a horse landed on his leg and left him in a hospital for ten days.

"This," Shermer says, "is really a job that you have to love."

A Revolution in Mexico

Rebel leader Pancho Villa was both cheered and feared throughout Mexico.

The year was 1910. For more than thirty years, the nation of Mexico had suffered under a cruel **dictator**, President Porfirio Díaz. He had taken land from the peasants, or *campesinos*, and given it to wealthy friends, leaving most Mexicans poor and hungry.

Finally, the people had had enough. Rebel leaders all over Mexico, including the **notorious** former **bandit**, Pancho Villa, rose up to overthrow President Díaz. It was the beginning of the Mexican Revolution, but it was far from the end.

For the next ten years, Mexico was **transformed** into a country at war. Groups of Mexicans bitterly fought one another. No one was in charge for long. Innocent people lost their homes and lives.

Tens of thousands of **frantic** citizens fled to the United States with their few possessions. Among them was the family in *Elena,* which is a true story of that dangerous time.

Many refugees left Mexico for California, following the same route as the one taken by Elena's family. ▶

A group of revolutionaries gathers in Mexico City, Mexico in 1915. ▼

549

Strategy Focus

As you read, think about the characters, their problem, and how they solve it to **summarize** the events of the story.

Growing up in a wealthy family in rural Mexico, Elena insists on learning to read and do math, skills denied most girls a hundred years ago. She also wins her parents' permission to marry the man she loves — Pablo, a famous sombrero maker. But just before the Mexican Revolution, her peaceful life is disrupted. Elena's true story is told by Rosa, one of Pablo and Elena's four children.

In the year 1910, when I was about five years old, my father had to go to Guadalajara on business. He went there once or twice a year. It was nothing unusual. As he mounted his horse, my mother went out to say goodbye. "Be careful," she told him. She was worried about who he might meet on the road. We had heard talk of a revolution. There were said to be rough soldiers and armed *campesinos* about. They were dangerous men. But Father just squeezed her hand and smiled. "I will be careful," he said.

Father was joined by several villagers who were making the trip with him. They waved to us and headed off across the rugged countryside, for there were no proper roads. It was just at the end of the rainy season and the path was wet. About an hour after they left, the ground under Father's horse suddenly gave way, creating a landslide. Down they plunged into the ravine below.

The villagers raced back for help, and many men hurried off with ropes to haul my father up to safety.

They brought him to our house and laid him on the bed. The doctor came and dressed my father's wounds. As he was leaving, we asked the doctor, "Will he live?" He shrugged his shoulders. "Who can tell?" he said. "Perhaps Pablo knows."

My mother stood and watched the doctor walk away from our house. "He is right," she thought to herself. "Pablo knows." So she went into the darkened room and knelt down beside the bed. She took his big hand and gently stroked it.

"Husband," she whispered, "how is it? Do you think you will recover?"

For a long time he did not look at her and he did not answer. At last he turned his head and spoke. "No," he said. Then in a weak but steady voice he told her what he knew. He named the very day and hour in which he would die. He said there would be war and that she and the children must leave their home.

"You will always be in my heart," he said. He never spoke again.

Three days later, at the very hour he had spoken, my father died.

Mother went crazy with grief. She ran weeping into the patio, and with a big stick began to swing wildly, knocking down her beautiful flowers. Then she opened all the cages and let the birds free.

After that, my mother grew quiet. Though she went on caring for us just as before, that *chispa*, the bright spark that was always a part of her, went out. Papá's absence filled our house with emptiness. I could not really understand what had happened, because I was so young. It seemed to me that Papá had just gone to where I couldn't see him — perhaps he was in the next room. I kept expecting him to walk in our door one day and make everything good again. But he never came, of course, and in time I understood that he never would.

I remember that it was warm and beautiful at that time, the skies a brilliant cloudless blue, day after day. It was as if nature were mocking us.

One day I was playing upstairs with my brother Luis. I heard the loud clop-clop of horses on the stone pavement outside — not one, but many horses. So I ran to the window to see. Looking down, I saw our street transformed into a river of sombreros. The revolution had reached our little village — it was the army of Pancho Villa riding by! With a gasp, Mother pulled me away from the window, for Pancho Villa was a notorious man. It was true that he was fighting to help free Mexico from the dictator Porfirio Díaz and that he wanted to give back to the campesinos the land that had been stolen from them. He was, in fact, on his way to becoming a genuine folk hero, the Robin Hood of Mexico. But it was also well known that he had once been a bandit and that his men were just as bad as the government soldiers. Neither army respected the law. Wherever they went, they stole from the people, killed anyone who challenged them, and left burned villages in their wake. What would happen to us?

Mother knelt down and gathered us in her arms. She understood in a flash that everything that had happened to her before had been for a reason. The books she had read, the hard numbers she had conquered, the battle she had won over her marriage — all this had made her strong. Now she had no father and no husband to help her. She had, instead, great courage and determination. Had there not always been wars? And in every country and every age, brave men and women had faced terrible dangers. She could do it, too. We saw this understanding pass across her face like a ripple of light. "Children," she said urgently, "we must find Esteban."

She knew that soldiers often took older boys and forced them into the army. My brother was sixteen.

None of us had seen him for hours. We searched the house for him, but he wasn't there. A book lay open on his bed. He had put it down and gone off somewhere. Maybe he was out in the streets among all those men. Maybe they had already taken him. At last María found him — up on the roof watching the soldiers. Boys are so foolish sometimes!

We made a hiding place for him in a kitchen cabinet, behind the big clay pots. Then Mother had another thought — the horses. They were sure to steal the horses. But maybe if they found the stable empty, they would think the horses had already been seized. They would certainly not think to look for them in the kitchen, so she brought the horses in there, too.

Before my mother could hide anything else, there was a loud knock on the door. We could hear deep voices laughing and talking outside. Mother hesitated a moment, wondering what to do. Then she sent us into the back room. We did as we were told but opened the door a crack so we could see what happened. Mother took a deep breath and opened the door.

There stood four or five soldiers, rough men who smelled of sweat and horses. The man in front was stout and wore a huge drooping mustache. *Bandoleras* crossed his chest. We had seen his face before, on a government poster. It was Pancho Villa himself!

"Señora," he said, "is this the house of Pablo, the famous maker of sombreros?" It was the last thing she expected to hear.

"It is," she said. "I am his widow."

"Then please accept my sincere condolences," said the leader of the rebel army, bowing slightly. He paused for a moment and then added almost shyly, "And the hats? The fine hats? Are there no more left?"

My mother actually smiled. "Excuse me a minute," she said. She went to a cupboard in her bedroom and returned with one of Father's beautiful silver-trimmed sombreros. "This is the last one," my mother said.

Pancho Villa was delighted. He put it on right away and actually paid her for it. Not only that, he posted a guard outside our house. As long as Villa's army was there, we were not harmed.

"Pablo was surely watching over us this day," my mother told us later. "But it may not always be so. Before your father died, he told me there would be soldiers. He told me we must leave our home. I wonder how I could have forgotten it."

"You were sad, *Mamacita*," María said.

When the *Villistas* had gone, Mother went to the plaza and opened the shop to the people of the village. She emptied the store of everything, taking down great bolts of manta and giving them to people who had nothing. We took only our money, some clothes, and food for the journey. We were leaving behind our aunts and uncles, our little house, the furniture, the pictures, the pots and pans and dishes. We said good-bye to the friends of a lifetime.

Everyone urged us not to go. "It is not proper for a woman to travel unprotected like that," they said. "It is not safe."

"The world is changing around us," Mother answered. "We must change, too."

We left the village early in the morning. When we reached the train station, we found that it was packed with frantic, pushing people. It seemed as though everyone in Mexico was trying to get on that train. Mother and María managed to make it inside. Then before Esteban got on, he handed Luis and me in through the window, along with the basket of food.

We were lucky to have benches to sit on. Most of the people were in boxcars or crowded in the aisles.

For five days the train chugged north. Through the open windows came soot, dust, and flies. I had worn a beautiful lacy white dress for the trip. Soon it was damp with sweat and covered with dirt.

When we reached Ciudad Juárez, we faced a new problem. What were we to do with Esteban? He was tall, almost a man. The soldiers at the border crossing would not treat him as a child. They might detain him for days, together with the rough men from the train. They might take him for the army.

"I think the answer will come to me," Mother told us. "We must be patient."

So we waited while she thought, but it was not a good place to be. The town was rough and lawless. With thousands of refugees pouring in, desperate to flee homes that were no longer safe, thieves and pickpockets roamed the streets. Hotels and shops charged ridiculous prices that people had to pay, because they had no other choice but to starve or sleep in the streets. For days we ate nothing but fruit.

Mother befriended a Chinese fruit seller who was honest and kind. One day she told him our problem. He smiled, for he knew exactly how to help us. Every day he crossed the border with his fruit wagon. We could dress Esteban in the man's clothes and straw hat. He would pretend to be the fruit seller's helper.

That afternoon we went over the bridge to El Paso together, Mother and the three of us walking along next to the fruit wagon. The cost was one penny each. At last we were safely in the United States.

We headed for California because we had a cousin, Trinidad, who lived there. We didn't have his address, though. In fact, we didn't even know what town he lived in. So we went to San Francisco, which was famous. We made our way to the *barrio*, where many people from Mexico lived. We asked everyone we met there, "Do you know our cousin Trinidad?" No one did. And besides, we didn't like it there. It was damp and cold. In Los Angeles, no one had heard of Trinidad, either. We were happier there, because the weather was warmer. But the city was too big, not like our lovely little village in Mexico. We heard about a place called Santa Ana. There were lemon and orange and walnut groves there and good schools for the children. So that is where we went and that is where we stayed. We never did find Trinidad.

By then, we had spent most of our money. So Esteban got a job picking fruit. Sometimes he was gone for weeks, living in the camps near the farms. When he came home he was sore and tired. He didn't laugh and play with me the way he had before.

Mother ran a boardinghouse, which was hard work. She did the cleaning, made the beds, mopped the floors, and scrubbed the bathtub. She washed and ironed the boarders' clothes. After all that, she went into the kitchen and cooked mountains of rice and beans and *tortillas* and *enchiladas* for them to eat. We all sat down to dinner together at a long pine table. Sometimes the boarders were very nice and became our friends. Some even came from the same part of Mexico as our family had. It made me feel like I wasn't so far from home.

María and I did what we could. We hung the laundry out on the clothesline, and we brought it back in if it rained. We helped wash the dishes and changed all the sheets once a week. And we looked after little Luis.

But Mother said that our real job was to get an education. School and homework always came first. When we were done with that, she said, we could help. I felt bad sometimes, sitting in a chair with a book in my lap while Mother was never still, always bustling about at her chores. She did it with a good spirit, though. If I said to her, "You work too hard, Mamacita," she would just shake her head and smile.

"And what is so bad about work?" she would say. "Work is how I take care of my family. Work is how I keep busy. Work is how I am useful. It is not so bad."

At school we learned to speak English and heard all about George Washington crossing the Delaware and Thomas Jefferson writing the Declaration of Independence. We wrote essays on the American Revolution and the American Civil War, and one day it dawned on me that Americans had suffered in terrible wars just as we had. And not long after that, I realized that Americans weren't "they" anymore. After all, we wore American clothes, read American books, knew American songs, and ate American candy. We had all become *real* Americans — all of us, that is, but Mamá.

She never quite knew what she was. Part of her was still back in Mexico and part of her was with us in California. Sometimes in the evening, after the dishes were done, we all went out on the porch to sit and enjoy the cool night air. At those times, Mother liked to talk about the old days. She told us about growing up in her father's great house in the beautiful mountains of Mexico. She talked of her gentle sisters who sang so beautifully to the guitar. She remembered her own little house full of flowers and birds. But she especially loved to talk about Father — how they fell in love first and got to know each other later, how he was such an artist, making beautiful sombreros, and how he knew things it was impossible to know, yet he knew them just the same. I had been so small when Father died, I could scarcely remember him. Those stories gave him back to me.

In all those years she talked only of happy times. It was much later that we learned what had happened in our little village. Only when we were grown — strong and full of hope — did we find out that it was gone, burned to the ground by the soldiers. And when we heard about the people who had died, people we had known, then we understood what our mother had done. With her courage and daring, she had saved us all.

Meet the Author Diane Stanley

Diane Stanley is best known as an author and illustrator of biographies of historical figures. She was born in Abilene, Texas, and spent her childhood there, in New York City, and Southern California. Although moving was a challenge, she feels that it helped her become a writer by presenting her with new situations and keeping her from looking at things in only one way. *Elena*, Stanley's first work of historical fiction, is based on the family story of one of her grandmother's friends during the Mexican Revolution.

Stanley's other books include: *Shaka: King of the Zulus*, *Cleopatra*, and *Leonardo Da Vinci*.

Meet the Illustrator Raúl Colón

Before he began illustrating children's books, Raúl Colón worked in animation, designed puppets, and created theater posters and CD covers. Part of the unique look of Colón's illustrations comes from his use of a tool called a "scratcher" to etch lines and patterns into his paintings and drawings. Colón lives in New York City with his wife and two children.

 *Internet*

To find out more about Diane Stanley and Raúl Colón, visit Education Place.

www.eduplace.com/kids

Think About the Selection

1. Compare the way you expected the outlaw Pancho Villa to act with the way he did act in *Elena*. Why do you think he acted this way?

2. What part of the family's troubles in *Elena* would you have found most difficult? Why?

3. Rosa says that she and her brothers and sister became "*real Americans*" in Santa Ana. What do you think she means by that?

4. Mamá says, "The world is changing around us. We must change, too." Do you agree with her? Why or why not?

5. Why do you think Mamá believes so strongly in the importance of education? How is your education important to you?

6. What do you think Rosa learned from her experiences in *Elena*?

7. **Connecting/Comparing** All the main characters in *One Land, Many Trails* demonstrate courage and determination. Compare Elena's courage to that of Slow, Grace McCance, or Bob Lemmons.

Reflecting

Write a Journal Entry

Think about a scene in *Elena* in which the characters have to make an important decision. Then write a journal entry describing a time in your life when you had to make a decision of similar importance.

Tips

- Remember that keeping a journal is a way of recording events, facts, feelings, and ideas.
- Use the first-person point of view when writing a journal entry.

Social Studies

Create a Wanted Poster

Think about the descriptions of Porfirio Díaz and Pancho Villa on page 554. Use them to create a wanted poster for either Díaz or Villa. Include a picture of your choice and list the reasons why you think he should be brought to justice.

Bonus Work with a partner to find out more about Pancho Villa or Porfirio Díaz. Give an oral report to the class on what you learn.

Listening and Speaking

Role-Play a Telephone Conversation

Suppose that Mamá and the children finally locate their cousin Trinidad. With a partner, role-play the first telephone conversation between Trinidad and Mamá, Rosa, or Esteban. Include their stories and their feelings.

Tips

- Speak clearly and not too fast.
- Be careful not to interrupt while another is talking.
- Pay attention to what is being said or asked.

Internet

Take an Online Quiz

In this theme, you have read about some of the people who have shaped the United States, and about some of the journeys that helped shape their lives. See how much you learned by taking our online theme quiz at Education Place.

www.eduplace.com/kids

Skill: How to Take Notes

As you read . . .

- Write down the **topic** or title.

- Note the most important ideas.

- Write down **key words** and phrases as headings. Use a separate note card for each heading, or leave several lines between headings on your paper.

- Write **details** about each key word or phrase beneath the heading.

- Write down the **source** of the information.

COMING TO GOLDEN MOUNTAIN

Not all of the trails to California started in the eastern United States or Mexico. Another path for emigrants began in China.

Gold! In 1848, word went out about the discovery of gold near Sutter's Mill, California. From around the world, people flocked to the territory of California — newly acquired from Mexico, but not yet a state — hoping to strike it rich.

The lure of the gold mines was especially strong in China.

During the mid-1800s, millions of Chinese were living in poverty. Chinese farmers were having trouble producing enough food to meet the needs of China's population. And from 1850 to 1864, China was wracked by a civil war that claimed over twenty million lives.

A ship carrying Chinese workers arrives in the United States.

With life in China so difficult, the idea of finding a fortune in America sounded very appealing. Many Chinese were encouraged by newspaper advertisements that confidently stated, "Money is in great plenty and to spare in America." Even the popular Chinese name for California, *Gum Shan*, or "Golden Mountain," gave the impression that riches were there for the taking.

The cost of boat passage from ports such as Guangzhou to San Francisco was very high by the standards of most Chinese. Some managed to save enough to pay for the journey themselves; others borrowed from banks or wealthier family members. Later emigrants from China had the option of working to pay the cost of their tickets once they arrived in America.

The first Chinese gold-seekers arrived in California in 1848, the same year as the gold strike. By 1852, there were around 25,000 Chinese living in the state. Almost all were men. Many had left their wives and children back in China and hoped to return home one day with enough money to live in comfort.

At first the Chinese enjoyed some success in the gold fields. Most worked for Chinese or American mining companies; a few worked on their own claims. Some gained a reputation as skillful miners who could extract gold from claims

Chinese miners join in the search for gold in California.

Railroad workers (above) build a trestle to support train tracks.

Records for track laying (below) were achieved at the cost of many lives.

that other miners had given up as worthless. One story told of a Chinese man who bought a miner's shack for $25, and then collected $300 worth of gold dust that the previous inhabitants had spilled on the floor.

But many American miners resented this success. They used threats and intimidation to force Chinese miners to take up other kinds of work. Some Chinese became merchants. Others took on jobs as cooks or launderers in mining camps.

Starting in 1864, many Chinese laborers began working to help complete the transcontinental railroad, connecting the east and west coasts of the United States. The work was very hard and dangerous. Especially in the mountains, the weather could be harsh, leading to frostbite and death by exposure. In addition, the Chinese were often assigned to blasting crews, whose job it was to clear rock out of the path of the railroad. Accidental explosions were responsible for the death and injury of hundreds

10 MILES OF TRACK, LAID IN ONE DAY. APRIL 28TH 1869.

568

of Chinese workers. No group gave so much to the building of the railroad and received so little credit at the time.

There would be more disappointments from Golden Mountain.

New federal laws made it difficult for Chinese to become American citizens. More laws banned all Chinese immigration — laws that were not lifted until 1943. In addition, the hostility that the Chinese faced in the countryside caused most to settle in "Chinatowns" in large cities such as San Francisco and Los Angeles.

Despite the difficulties of life on Golden Mountain, most Chinese-Americans stayed, many relying on their own small businesses to make a living. People helped one another as they had in China. Family or clan associations rose up to help new arrivals find homes and jobs. Through theater, art, holiday celebration, and many other traditions, the Chinese heritage continued.

And the Chinese-Americans who stayed — along with the people of many other countries who followed the Gold Rush — made the state of California culturally all the richer.

Children in San Francisco welcome the Chinese new year.

✓ Writing an Answer to a Question

Many tests ask you to write an answer to a question about something you have read. Usually you can answer these questions with a few sentences. Here's a sample test question for *Elena*. Use the tips to help you answer this kind of test item.

Tips

- Read the directions and the question carefully.
- Think about your answer before you write.
- Look back through the selection if you need help.
- Write only as much as you need to answer the question directly.
- Check your answer if you have time.

Write your answer to this question.

1   In the story *Elena*, what are three examples that show how brave Rosa's mother was?

Now read one student's answer, and see how he planned it.

> Rosa's mother shows how brave she is when she talks to Pancho Villa, when she moves her family from the village, and when she takes her family across the border in the fruit wagon.

This is a good answer. It gives three clear examples from the selection that show how brave Rosa's mother was.

I remember that Rosa's mother showed bravery when Pancho Villa came to her house. I need two more examples. I can look in the selection if I have to.

I remember when Rosa's mother hides the horses in the kitchen. But that shows cleverness more than bravery. Maybe there's a better example.

Focus on

Autobiography

Autobiography is the story of a person's life as told by that person. The writer shares his or her memories, often adding new insights about the original events.

Autobiographies usually begin with the writer's childhood and work their way up to the present day. The life story might include people, animals, places, or events that were important to the writer. The selections you will read give some examples. But the final autobiographical piece will be yours. You'll be invited to write about an important event from your life.

Contents

In this selection from her autobiography, poet and author Eloise Greenfield describes a place that has played an important part in her life, the neighborhood where she grew up.

Langston Terrace
by Eloise Greenfield

I fell in love with Langston
Terrace the very first time I saw it.
Our family had been living in two
rooms of a three-story house when
Mama and Daddy saw the newspaper article telling of the plans to
build it. It was going to be a low-
rent housing project in northeast
Washington, and it would be named
in honor of John Mercer Langston,
the famous black lawyer, educator,
and congressman.

So many people needed housing and wanted to live
there, many more than there would be room for. They
were all filling out applications, hoping to be one of the 274
families chosen. My parents filled out one, too.

I didn't want to move. I knew our house was crowded — there were eleven of us, six adults and five children — but I didn't want to leave my friends, and I didn't want to go to a strange place and be the new person in a neighborhood and a school where most of the other children already knew each other. I was eight years old, and I had been to three schools. We had moved five times since we'd been in Washington, each time trying to get more space and a better place to live. But rent was high so we'd always lived in a house with relatives and friends, and shared the rent.

One of the people in our big household was Lillie, Daddy's cousin and Mama's best friend. She and her husband also applied for a place in the new project, and during the months that it was being built, Lillie and Mama would sometimes walk fifteen blocks just to stand and watch the workmen digging holes and laying bricks. They'd just stand there watching and wishing. And at home, that was all they could talk about. "When we get our new place . . ." "If we get our new place . . ."

Lillie got her good news first. I can still see her and Mama standing at the bottom of the hall steps, hugging and laughing and crying, happy for Lillie, then sitting on the steps, worrying and wishing again for Mama.

Eloise with her brother and father at Langston Terrace in 1938.

Finally, one evening, a woman came to the house with our good news, and Mama and Daddy went over and picked out the house they wanted. We moved on my ninth birthday. Wilbur, Gerald, and I went to school that morning from one house, and when Daddy came to pick us up, he took us home to another one. All the furniture had been moved while we were in school.

Eloise's sisters Vera (left) and Vedie Little, at Langston Terrace in 1949.

Langston Terrace was a lovely birthday present. It was built on a hill, a group of tan brick houses and apartments with a playground as its center. The red mud surrounding the concrete walks had not yet been covered with black soil and grass seed, and the holes that would soon be homes for young trees were filled with rainwater. But it still looked beautiful to me.

We had a whole house all to ourselves. Upstairs and downstairs. Two bedrooms, and the living room would be my bedroom at night. Best of all, I wasn't the only new person. Everybody was new to this new little community, and by the time school opened in the fall, we had gotten used to each other and had made friends with other children in the neighborhood, too.

I guess most of the parents thought of the new place as an in-between place. They were glad to be there, but their dream was to save enough money to pay for a house that would be their own. Saving was hard, though, and slow, because each time somebody in a family got a raise on the job, it had to be reported to the manager of the project so that the rent could be raised, too. Most people stayed years longer than they had planned to, but they didn't let that stop them from enjoying life.

They formed a resident council to look into any neighborhood problems that might come up. They started a choral group and presented music and poetry programs on Sunday evenings in the social room or on the playground. On weekends, they played horseshoes and softball and other games. They had a reading club that met once a week at the Langston branch of the public library, after it opened in the basement of one of the apartment buildings.

Eloise with her future husband, Bobby Greenfield, in 1948.

The library was very close to my house. I could leave by my back door and be there in two minutes. The playground was right in front of my house, and after my sister Vedie was born and we moved a few doors down to a three-bedroom house, I could just look out of my bedroom window to see if any of my friends were out playing.

There were so many games to play and things to do. We played hide-and-seek at the lamppost, paddle tennis and shuffleboard, dodge ball and jacks. We danced in fireplug showers, jumped rope to rhymes, played "Bouncy, Bouncy, Bally," swinging one leg over a bouncing ball, played baseball on a nearby field, had parties in the social room and bus trips to the beach. In the playroom, we played Ping-Pong and pool, learned to sew and embroider and crochet.

For us, Langston Terrace wasn't an in-between place. It was a growing-up place, a good growing-up place. Neighbors who cared, family and friends, and a lot of fun. Life was good. Not perfect, but good. We knew about problems, heard about them, saw them, lived through some hard ones ourselves, but our community wrapped itself around us, put itself between us and the hard knocks, to cushion the blows.

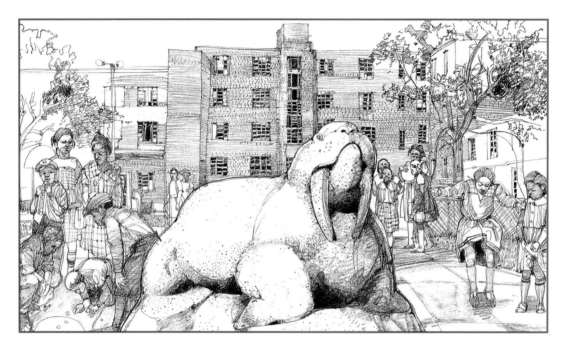

It's been many years since I moved away, but every once in a long while I go back, just to look at things and remember. The large stone animals that decorated the playground are still there. A walrus, a hippo, a frog, and two horses. They've started to crack now, but I remember when they first came to live with us. They were friends, to climb on or to lean against, or to gather around in the evening. You could sit on the frog's head and look way out over the city at the tall trees and rooftops.

Nowadays, whenever I run into old friends, mostly at a funeral, or maybe a wedding, after we've talked about how we've been and what we've been doing, and how old our children are, we always end up talking about our childtime in our old neighborhood. And somebody will say, "One of these days we ought to have a Langston reunion." That's what we always called it, just "Langston," without the "Terrace." I guess because it sounded more homey. And that's what Langston was. It was home.

In this brief autobiography, Jane Goodall, one of the world's foremost experts on chimpanzees, tells how her childhood interest in animals led her to doing research in Africa.

Jane Goodall

I have been interested in animals since before I can remember. From the time I was very small, I was fascinated with creepy, crawling, furry, flying creatures. When I was quite young, my mother found me in my room with a handful of worms in my bed, watching as they went around and around. She didn't say, "Yuk!" and threw them out the window. She said, "Jane, if you leave them in here, they'll die. They need the air." And so I let them go free.

In fact, my mother is the most important reason for my doing what I've done and being who I've been. When I was four years old, I stayed on a farm, where I helped collect hens' eggs. I became puzzled and asked those around me, "Where is the hole big enough for the eggs to come out?" When no one answered to my satisfaction, I hid in a small, stuffy henhouse for four hours to find out. While I watched and waited, my mother looked frantically for me in the house and garden. She even called the police to help locate me. But when my mother saw me rushing toward the house in excitement, she didn't scold me for disappearing for so long. She sat down and listened to me tell the wonderful story of how a hen lays eggs.

Two orphaned chimpanzees (above) make friends in the Congo's Tchimpounga Sanctuary.

Goodall's study of chimpanzees, which began in 1960, is now in its fifth decade.

Even my first books were about animals. I read *The Story of Dr. Doolittle, The Jungle Book*, and *Tarzan.* Looking back, I see that the original Tarzan was terribly hard on animals. But I didn't realize it then. Books are a great source of inspiration. They lure your mind to be imaginative. By the time I was eight or nine, I was dreaming of going to Africa. And my mother, a very special person, would say, "Jane, if you really want something and if you work hard, take advantage of opportunities, and never give up, you will somehow find a way."

In those days you had to learn a foreign language to get a schol-arship to a university. But I couldn't do it — I couldn't speak French, couldn't speak German, couldn't speak Latin. So Mum said, "Why not take a secretarial course, then you can get a job anywhere in the world." So that's what I did.

But that didn't lead me directly to Africa. After I finished my sec-retarial class I began working for a documentary film company — a wonderful job, but with very low pay. When a school friend invited me to visit her family in Kenya, I readily accepted. I quit my job with the film company to begin work as a waitress in order to save the money. Finally, at age 23, with only enough money for boat fare to Africa (that was the cheapest way to travel in those days), I went off by myself to an unknown continent.

After two months in Africa I met the man who made all my dreams come true. Louis Leakey was an anthropologist and paleontologist who was interested in animals and early man. I made an appointment to meet him. Because I had studied animals throughout my childhood, I was able to answer many of his questions about the natural world, and he gave me a job as his assistant. I traveled with Louis and his wife, Mary, on one of their fossil-hunting expeditions to Olduvai Gorge. After some time, Louis decided I was the person he had been looking for to study the chimpanzees living near the shore of Lake Tanganyika, in what is now called Tanzania. And when the British authorities refused to let a young, untrained girl venture into the wilds of Africa on her own, who should volunteer to accompany me for the first three months but my own amazing mother.

Louis Leakey (1903-1972)

And so my work began. After several years in Africa I returned to England to work for my Ph.D. in ethology from Cambridge University, and then I returned to the paradise of Gombe Stream, Tanzania, to continue my research.

Goodall extends a hand to a young chimpanzee named Flint.

Before becoming a children's author and illustrator, Bill Peet worked as an animator at Walt Disney Studios. In this excerpt, Peet has just arrived in Los Angeles. His fiancée, Margaret, is back in Indiana. Peet's hope for a job rests on a letter from Disney inviting him to participate in a tryout.

BILL PEET:
AN AUTOBIOGRAPHY

The Disney Studios were closed in by a high cement wall, and the only view was through the wrought-iron front gate. What I could see of the complex looked most inviting. There was a flagstone walk across a grass courtyard to an archway in front of what appeared to be the main building —

a quaint, cozy look appropriate for a company dealing with fun and fantasy.

Just a block from the studios I ran across a rooming house, a big barn of a place with the second floor and the attic sectioned off into narrow compartments with a small cot in each one. The landlady was a little mouse of a woman who explained apologetically that the two dollars a week rent need not be paid until I could afford it.

Her tenants were mostly Disney beginners or else newcomers like me who had no guarantee of a job. That dear little lady, Mrs. Beson, was well aware of our situation, and no doubt she had seen many come and go who could never pay the rent.

The next morning at the appointed time of nine o'clock I was at the Disney front gate. It was the wrong place. I was told to check in at a one-story stucco building across the street called the Disney Annex. The tryout group had already lined up at the front door to sign in, and I was the last of the fifteen to arrive.

Most of them were fresh out of art school as I was, and they came from all parts of the country in response to the special delivery letter, not knowing what to expect.

The boss of the Annex, George Drake, was a tall, scrawny fellow with a shock of rusty hair and extremely large ears.

583

He started things off with a stern lecture warning us that the one-month tryout would be no bed of roses. And more than once he reminded us how fortunate we were to get an opportunity to work for Disney. "There are plenty of people waiting out on the street to get a job here" was his last warning.

After the lecture we were given model sheets, guides to drawing Mickey, Donald, and Goofy so we could practice the roundish Disney drawing style. During that one-month period Drake kept us on edge by continually pacing the hall and popping in on us at odd moments. Every few days one or two of the group were let go, and as it came down to the last week we wondered if Drake would fire all of us. I was warned many times about leaving the buttons off of Mickey's pants, but even so I was one of the three survivors at the end of the month.

We were put to work as in-betweeners, with the tedious, painstaking job of adding hundreds of drawings in between hundreds of other drawings to move Donald or Mickey from here to there.

It was a matter of enduring the job with the hope of making it to the promised land across the street where big

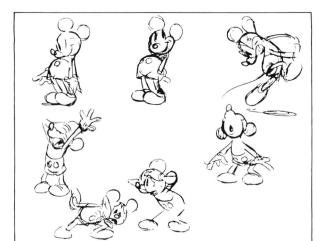

exciting things were going on. They were making *Snow White and the Seven Dwarfs,* the very first feature-length animated film.

I wrote to Margaret immediately to let her know I made it through the tryouts and was on the job. And even though it was assembly-line work there would be all kinds of opportunities if *Snow White* was a success.

I didn't mention all the dire predictions coming from Hollywood bigwigs and movie columnists. They called *Snow White* Disney's Folly. The picture would be a box-office flop! People would never sit through a full-length cartoon feature! Disney was getting too big for his britches! And so on.

Those ominous predictions made me wonder if I had arrived just in time to board the Disney *Titanic*. And I'm sure those voices of doom haunted the people working with a frenzy to complete *Snow White* in time for the grand première before Christmas. I even got in on the last-minute effort, working nights tracing dwarves on something called a rotoscope machine.

Margaret came out on the train the last week of November and we were married on the thirtieth, then moved into a dingy little apartment about a half-hour walk from the studio. A few weeks later, we attended the gala première of *Snow White*. All Disney employees and their wives or husbands were invited, along with hundreds of special guests and newspeople. As we moved through the mob toward the marquee of the Carthay Circle Theater, I caught my first glimpse of Walt Disney. He was addressing the crowd from a podium, but his voice was lost in all the hubbub.

Very few people who worked on the film had seen it all in one piece, so it was a new experience for most of the audience. Of course the overwhelming success of *Snow White* is motion picture history, and as I write about it now, it is out in the theaters for the seventh time, having celebrated its fiftieth anniversary in 1987.

I believe everyone in that first *Snow White* audience could have predicted the enormous success of the film. They were carried away by the picture from the very beginning, and as it went along everyone was bubbling over with enthusiasm and frequently bursting into spontaneous applause. At the end, the audience exploded into a thunderous ovation — and the voices of doom were silenced for good.

In this selection, athlete Alex Rodriguez tells about an important period in his career, his first two years in professional baseball with the Seattle Mariners organization.

Hit a Grand Slam!
by Alex Rodriguez

My first spring training opened my eyes to how hard pro athletes work. The posted time for practice was ten o'clock in the morning. Every day for a month I showed up at 9:30, figuring being early would show my dedication. One day I decided to arrive at 7:00 A.M. I walked in and saw a few guys already in the clubhouse.

I turned the corner into the weight room and saw second baseman Joey Cora pumping iron. I then went to the batting cage and found two-time batting champion Edgar Martinez hitting off a batting tee into a net.

"Edgar, what are you doing here so early?"

"I have to hit. I have to work!"

Most guys would go home at about two o'clock in the afternoon. One day I forgot my pager. I returned to the clubhouse and found Edgar in the batting cage at 6:00 P.M. Those veterans showed me that success in anything begins with dedication and hard work. I met NBA coach Pat Riley recently, and he told me a key to success is enjoying your sweat. That means you have to find joy in practice and working out to reach your highest athletic potential.

I started my first season at the bottom of the Mariners' minor leagues with Wisconsin's Class A Appleton Foxes. Players tell horror stories about the minor leagues, but playing in Appleton gave me cherished memories.

The town embraced me with a welcoming hug.

Within two months, I moved up to Class AA at Jacksonville. Three weeks later, I got the call to join the big-league team, that week playing in Boston.

I stayed up late calling family, friends, and old coaches — "I'm going to the show!"

At 18, I became the youngest Major League player in a decade. The lights, reporters, and crowds were unbelievable.

I remember preparing for my first at-bat in the on-deck circle. Ken Griffey, Jr. walked by and said: "It's showtime."

My body felt jittery, and my knees buckled. I could barely stand. I went hitless in three tries that first night, but I had a solid fielding night.

The next night I broke out with two hits. Still, I was nervous for days. I didn't want to make a mistake. I arrived early at the ballpark, hoping not to be noticed.

After 26 days, the Mariners sent me down to their Class AAA team in Calgary, Canada. That gave me the rare glimpse of playing in all four pro levels in one season.

I started the 1995 season with the Tacoma Rainiers, the M's new Class AAA affiliate. The 31-mile trip between Tacoma and Seattle became all too familiar. I was called up to Seattle on May 6th and stayed 21 days, enduring the rookie razzing.

The Mariners have a special rookie tradition for the team's first series in Kansas City. When I got out of the shower after the last game, all my clothes were gone. Instead, I had to sign 30 autographs while wearing a silver dress and balancing in high-heeled shoes. If that wasn't bad enough, I had to wear them on the flight home and listen to all the teasing jokes. I laughed along with them.

Much of that season was no laughing matter to me. I became a human yo-yo going between Tacoma and Seattle. Three times the M's sent me back to Tacoma. Each demotion chipped away at me. The last time, in mid-August, I sat at my Seattle locker with my head down, in tears. I felt drained, defeated.

"Come on, relax, you're going to get through this," teammates said.

Hurt and angry, I seriously thought about driving back to Miami. Instead, I called Mom.

"Forget them. I hate them all. I don't want to be here. I'm coming home," I said.

"No you're not!" Mom answered. "You don't have a house here if you come home. You have to stay out there. You are GOING TO MAKE IT!"

Wanting to quit during tough times is natural. There are times you should quit and try something else. But quitting out of frustration is rarely the right time. I'm so thankful Mom talked me out of it. I know now the adversity made me stronger.

If I had quit, I would have missed the Mariners' remarkable "Refuse To Lose" playoff run. In August, Seattle trailed California by 13 games. A magical string of victories closed the gap as I rejoined the team August 31st.

The playoff race excited me as much as the guys playing.

I saw it as a learning experience. I prepared myself each day to play. I paid attention to every detail, as if my life depended on it.

The season ended with us tied with California. We won the one-game playoff in dramatic fashion for the M's first-ever playoff spot.

I hit three times in the hard-fought playoff series against New York. What a thrill! What I'll remember most, though, is being on-deck in the roaring Kingdome when Edgar drove home Junior in the 11th inning to beat New York 6-5 in the deciding division playoff game. That's the best feeling I've had in baseball. There's nothing like winning. The same could be said for losing.

Cleveland dashed our World Series visions 4–2 in the American League Championship Series.

With the season-ending loss at the Kingdome, Seattle fans gave us a thunderous moving ovation after the game to show their thanks for the season's incredible ride.

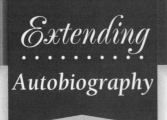

Extending

Autobiography

Narrating

Write a Chapter of Your Autobiography

You've read a few examples of autobiography. Now write a chapter from your own autobiography. Focus on a time or event in your life that has been important to you. Choose something that you think other people would be interested in reading about.

Tips

- Before beginning, try to remember as much about your topic as you can. Write down things that you think would make interesting reading.

- Be specific when choosing a topic. Think about how you will begin and end your chapter.

- Provide details for your readers. People and places that are familiar to you will not necessarily be to them.

Read On Your Own

Knots in My Yo-Yo String:
The Autobiography of a Kid
by Jerry Spinelli (Knopf)
Black-and-white family photos accompany Spinelli's
recollections of his childhood.

The Abracadabra Kid
by Sid Fleischman (Greenwillow)
In his witty autobiography, Sid Fleischman
includes tips for young writers.

The Moon and I
by Betsy Byars (Simon)
Byars recalls family anecdotes and fun
with her pet blacksnake, Moon.

Boy: Tales of Childhood
by Roald Dahl (Puffin)
Dahl's childhood in England and Norway
influenced his later writing.

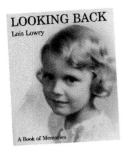

Looking Back: A Book of Memories
by Lois Lowry (Houghton)
Lowry recalls childhood memories as well as
experiences from her adult years.

Theme **6**

Animal
Encounters

The great hurrah about wild animals is that they exist at all, and the greater hurrah is the actual moment of seeing them.

— Annie Dillard
Pilgrim at Tinker Creek

594

Animal
Encounters

Contents

Reader's Library

- **The Hyrax of Top-Knot Island**
- **Saving Sea Turtles**
- **Kat the Curious**

Theme Paperbacks

Dolphin Adventure
by Wayne Grover

The Tarantula in My Purse: and 172 Other Wild Pets
by Jean Craighead George

To the Top of the World
by Jim Brandenburg

Book Links

If you like . . .

The Grizzly Bear Family Book

by Michio Hoshino

Then try . . .

The Leopard Family Book

by Jonathan Scott (North-South)

With accompanying photographs, the author explains how the leopard is able to survive in the wild.

Back to the Wild

by Dorothy Hinshaw Patent (Harcourt)

Many endangered animals are born in captivity, taught survival skills, and released to the wild.

If you like . . .

The Golden Lion Tamarin Comes Home

by George Ancona

Then try . . .

Sea Otter Rescue

by Roland Smith (Dutton)

After a disastrous oil spill in Alaska's Prince William Sound, a team of animal rescue experts rushes to the aid of oil-covered sea otters.

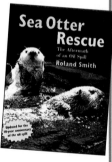

Once a Wolf

by Stephen R. Swinburne (Houghton)

Wildlife biologists work to bring the gray wolf back to Yellowstone National Park.

If you like . . .

My Side of the Mountain
by Jean Craighead George

Then try . . .

Frightful's Mountain

by Jean Craighead George (Dutton) Frightful, Sam Gribley's peregrine falcon from *My Side of the Mountain,* must now try to survive in the wilderness on her own.

The House of Wings

by Betsy Byars (Viking) Caring for an injured crane helps bring a boy and his grandfather closer.

Internet

Do you want to find out about these books and more? Log on to Education Place:

www.eduplace.com/kids

- Look up reviews by readers around the country for these and other books about encounters with animals.

- Post your own *Animal Encounters* book review.

For more good books to read, go to:

www.bookadventure.org

Background and Vocabulary

Wild Alaska

The state of Alaska, the setting of *The Grizzly Bear Family Book*, includes huge areas of wilderness. Two great mountain ranges span the state.

The Brooks Range, in the north, lies above the Arctic Circle. The Alaska Range, in the south, arcs up to include Mt. McKinley, also called Denali, the highest mountain in North America, located in Denali National Park. At over 7,300 square miles, the park is larger than Connecticut and Rhode Island combined.

The land in the park is a rich environment of mountains, glaciers, and grassy, treeless Arctic tundra, home to abundant wildlife. Over thirty species of mammals live there, ranging in size from tiny shrews and voles to the grizzly bears featured in the selection. Other large animals in the park include Dall sheep, moose, and caribou, also known as reindeer.

Human beings who visit the wild habitats of Alaska need to remember that they are entering the territory of wild animals. The creatures who make their homes there are likely to view humans with wariness. In return, the humans should view the wild inhabitants with respect.

Caribou

Dall Sheep

Grizzly Bears

601

The Grizzly Bear Family Book

Michio Hoshino

The author of this selection spent a year photographing grizzly bears. As you read, **evaluate** how his personal involvement enhances the story he tells.

Imagine meeting a grizzly bear in the wild. Not at the zoo, not in a book, but out in the open — a chance encounter with the real thing. Just you and the bear, face to face.

It happened to me once, when I was camping near Mount McKinley in Alaska. For more than half of each year, I hike through the mountains and plains of Alaska, the Great Land, with my tent on my back, taking pictures of the land which has attracted me since my teens.

Around four o'clock one morning I was awakened by something brushing against my tent. Wondering what it was, I rubbed my eyes and opened the tent flap. There, right in front of me, was a bear's face. I was startled, but the bear must have been even more surprised. It took one look at me and clumped hastily away.

I had never before been so close to a bear. And I knew that I wanted to use my camera to record one year in the lives of the Alaskan grizzlies.

In midwinter the temperature here may fall to fifty degrees below zero. During this harsh time, a grizzly bear will sleep in a snug underground den, the entrance covered by a blanket of snow.

While the mother bear sleeps, her tiny cubs are born. They nurse and snuggle next to her until longer days and warmer temperatures signal the arrival of spring.

One day in April, as I hiked through the mountains called the Alaska Range, I noticed fresh bear tracks on the snowy slope. Following them with my binoculars, I spotted a mother bear and her cub walking through the snow.

The cold, biting wind was already giving way to spring breezes. When the bears come out of their dens, it's a sure sign that the long winter is over.

As the snow melts and shrinks into patches of crusty ice, wildflowers push their faces towards the sky. In the far north, the flowers are very small. But each blossom possesses tremendous strength. I am moved when I come upon these tiny shapes, living their lives to the fullest extent.

In early spring, grizzly bears also enjoy life to its fullest. Once I watched as a mother and her cub played tag on a slope across from me. The mother chased her cub across the grassy hillside. When she caught the youngster, she took it in her arms and hugged it to her gently, and they began to roll down the slope together. They seemed to be having such a wonderful time, I couldn't help but burst out laughing.

A nursing bear will often lie on her back and offer milk to her cub. If she has two, she will cradle one in each arm. I'm not sure that nursing tires her out, but afterwards the mother often spread-eagles on the ground, sound asleep.

People have such fearful images of bears. But is the affection and care of a human mother for her children so different from the love and tenderness the mother bear shows her cubs?

Grizzlies just emerging from their winter dens are as thin as they will be all year. They have not eaten for months, and in the snow-covered landscape, their first meal may be the carcass of a moose or caribou that did not survive the winter. Near the sea, bears may find a beached whale, or a dead sea lion or walrus.

After the snow melts and the earth turns green, bears begin to eat roots and grasses. Sedges — grasses that grow in wetlands — are particularly important, because they grow rapidly in the early spring and are rich in protein.

Arctic ground squirrels are a popular food for bears, but it takes real work to catch one. An 850-pound bear chasing a 2-pound squirrel is a truly comical sight. When the squirrel dives into its hole, the bear begins digging furiously with its front paws. But there may be many holes, all connected underground. Sometimes the squirrel will pop out of a hole behind the bear and watch it dig away.

Of course, many squirrels do get caught and eaten by bears. Scientists at Denali National Park in Alaska found that each grizzly bear eats about 400 ground squirrels a year.

Caribou, wolves, Dall sheep, moose, and many other animals give birth in the spring. They must keep constant watch over their newborns to protect them from danger.

One June afternoon I was sitting on a mountain slope looking down at a moose with her two young calves. For some reason the moose was uneasy, her ears pulled far back to the sides. A bear suddenly appeared from the bushes and rushed towards the calves.

The moose turned to confront the powerful bear. The bear stopped and the two faced off, staring at each other intently. A moment later the moose charged. The startled bear took off, with the moose close behind.

The moose had risked her life to protect her calves. And the bear retreated rather than risk being injured by the slashing hooves of the determined cow.

The bear will try again, of course, and next time it may be successful. But I have come to understand that when a bear catches a moose calf, it is not a sad event. The bear may have cubs of her own who will share in the meal. There will be new moose calves and new bear cubs next year, and life in the wilderness will go on. In nature, all living things, including humans, depend on other lives for their existence.

As summer nears, the daylight hours lengthen quickly until the nights are completely gone.

Imagine having no night at all. The sun moves around the sky in a big circle, always staying just above the horizon. Without a watch, it's hard to know when one day ends and the next begins. You may forget what day of the week it is, and even what month. And all the while, the sun's energy feeds the trees, grasses, and shrubs of the Alaskan wilderness.

In June salmon swim upstream in Alaska's rivers and streams, and bears are drawn to choice fishing spots. Grizzlies avoid contact with other bears during most of the year, but fishing season brings them shoulder to shoulder along the streams. With food temporarily abundant, they seem to tolerate one another more, but first a dominance order — an understanding of who bosses whom — must be established.

The stronger, more aggressive bears, usually males, command the best places. When a new bear joins a group, a brief struggle for dominance is often the result. Bears avoid fighting if at all possible, but two bears of nearly equal strength may wage a fierce battle. When two bears who have already fought meet again, the loser will automatically give up its place to the victor, avoiding another fight.

Bears use body language to express dominance or subservience within the temporary community at the river. By observing bears as they fish, I have learned some useful clues about the safest way to behave around bears in the wild.

One time I watched a mother bear with one cub, and another mother with two cubs, approach a river. While the mothers fished for salmon in the river, the cubs waited on the riverbank. Curiosity drew all three cubs together. Suddenly the mother of the two cubs rushed up the bank. Would she kill the stranger? But the mother bear simply sniffed the cub that was not her own. Then the mother of the single cub realized what was happening, and charged out of the water to defend her young. Again it seemed as if there might be trouble. The cubs looked on nervously, staying near their mothers. In the end, the two families parted peacefully. Mother bears are usually quite tolerant of the cubs of others, even to the point of adopting strays and orphans.

I was surprised the first time I saw a bear catch a salmon, hold it briefly as if examining it, and then release it in the river. When salmon are rare, grizzlies will hungrily devour every one they catch. But at the height of the salmon season, a bear may capture ten salmon an hour and can afford to be selective. Sometimes bears just eat the head and eggs, discarding the rest. The uneaten portion of the fish doesn't go to waste, however, because gulls swarm nearby, ready to grab the leftovers.

When a bear catches a salmon with its paws and mouth, it can probably smell the difference between a male fish and a female fish. The bear I saw catching and releasing salmon may have been selecting only the female fish with their delicious eggs.

610

First-year cubs wait on the riverbank for their mothers to bring freshly caught salmon. By their second year, cubs wade in to fish for themselves. Although rarely successful at first, they learn by watching and imitating their mothers.

With the end of the salmon run, the bears' temporary society breaks up, each bear returning to its own mountain territory, where autumn food sources are now maturing.

The bugling of sandhill cranes sweeping south in great ragged Vs announces autumn across Alaska. The animals of the Arctic grow lovely, thick winter coats. Moose and caribou antlers are now very large. Aspen and birch forests turn golden, and the tundra blazes red.

Blueberry, cranberry, and crowberry bushes blanket the ground, offering a rich harvest for bears.

"Don't bump heads with a bear when you go blueberry picking!" This frequently heard advice is no joke in Alaska. Both humans and bears become so engrossed in berry picking that they scarcely take a moment to lift their heads and look around. While you probably won't actually bump heads with a bear, it's wise to check your surroundings now and then.

Bears seem to like soapberries best of all. Wondering how they taste, I picked a ripe red one and popped it in my mouth. It didn't taste very good to me, but then I don't like fish heads, either.

It's wonderful to observe a huge bear holding a thin soapberry branch, gently stripping it of the delicate fruit.

As the days shorten, bears must put on a large store of fat to take them through winter. Berries are high in sugar, and the autumn feast can be critical to a bear's survival. With their shiny coats rippling as they move across the tundra, grizzlies consume an enormous amount of berries.

How many berries would you guess a grizzly can eat in one day? The bears in Denali National Park eat berries for twenty hours a day in late summer, hardly stopping to sleep. One bear may consume 200,000 berries in a single day! Bear droppings at this time of year consist mainly of partially digested berries. From the seeds in these droppings new bushes will grow to feed a new generation of bears.

One autumn day as I was hiking through the Brooks Range near the Arctic Circle, I suddenly noticed two bears running towards me from a riverbank. Were they coming at me on purpose, or did they not realize I was there? They appeared to be siblings, just old enough to leave their mother's care, but already powerful. Closer and closer they came, loping gracefully. My heart beat like a drum. When they were about twenty yards away, I raised my arms and shouted, *"Stop!"*

The two bears skidded to a halt as if in complete surprise. They stood up on their hind legs, wagging their heads from side to side, sniffing the air. I was so excited, I thought my heart would burst.

Then, as if they had finally become aware of my existence, they turned and raced off in the direction they'd come from. It had been a pretty frightening experience for me, but it must have been equally startling for the bears.

That night I couldn't fall asleep. The two grizzlies might be close by. Very few bears are interested in pursuing people, but still I felt somewhat uneasy. Unable to sleep, I thought about bears, about people, and about Alaska.

If there wasn't a single bear in all of Alaska, I could hike through the mountains with complete peace of mind. I could camp without worry. But what a dull place Alaska would be!

Here people share the land with bears. There is a certain wariness between people and bears. And that wariness forces upon us a valuable sense of humility.

People continue to tame and subjugate nature. But when we visit the few remaining scraps of wilderness where bears roam free, we can still feel an instinctive fear. How precious that feeling is. And how precious these places, and these bears, are.

Trophy hunters from the lower United States and from Europe come to Alaska to shoot grizzlies. They smile for the camera and stand, gun in hand, over the body of a dead bear. They hang their trophy on the wall — the head of a bear with its fangs bared, as if it was killed while attacking the heroic hunter. In truth, a high-powered rifle was fired from a great distance at a bear that was peacefully eating berries.

Just imagine: You're alone and unarmed on the Arctic plain with a bear. You and the bear feel the same breeze pass over your faces. You — a human being — are on an equal footing with the bear.

How wonderful that would be. No matter how many books you read, no matter how much television you watch, there is no substitute for experiencing nature firsthand. If you cannot meet a bear in the wild, then you must try to imagine it — for even if you only imagine it, the feeling can be real. And it is the feeling that is important.

Today's snowfall marks the advent of winter. The daylight hours are shorter now. The aurora dances in the clear night sky. A mother bear and her half-grown cubs trace footprints in the new snow as they climb up the mountain to their den. The cubs will spend the long winter with their mother snug beneath the snow.

The snow continues to fall, and finally the tracks are gone. Alaska, the Great Land, settles down for a quiet winter sleep.

Meet the Author/Photographer
Michio Hoshino

Michio Hoshino grew up in Tokyo, Japan. When he was a young man he saw a picture of a remote Inuit village in a book. He sent a letter to the village's mayor, who invited him to Alaska to spend the summer living with a family in the village. He accepted.

Hoshino was fascinated by the Alaskan wilderness, and his photographs of the state's wildlife were published in many books, and in magazines including *National Geographic* and *Smithsonian*. In addition, Hoshino wrote several books, including *Grizzly*, an award-winning book of bear photography.

After a career of almost twenty years as a wildlife photographer, Hoshino's life was cut short. In the early morning of August 8th, 1996, he was pulled from his tent and killed by a brown bear at a camp in a wildlife refuge in Siberia. Witnesses said the bear had begun behaving aggressively towards human beings as a result of being given food by visitors to the refuge.

Learn more about Michio Hoshino by visiting Education Place. **www.eduplace.com/kids**

Think About the Selection

1. A surprise encounter caused the author to want to learn more about grizzlies. Would you have had the same reaction? Explain.

2. Why do you think the author compares bear mothers to human mothers on page 605?

3. Why do you think the author includes so much information about the grizzly bears' habitat?

4. The author writes on page 607: ". . . when a bear catches a moose calf, it is not a sad event." Do you agree? Why or why not?

5. Based on the selection, what generalizations can you make about bears? Think about their family life, growth, and feeding habits.

6. Has reading this selection changed your feelings about bears? Why or why not?

7. Connecting/Comparing Compare the relationship of Michio Hoshino and the bears he photographs with that of Bob Lemmons and the horses he rounds up in *Black Cowboy, Wild Horses*.

 Describing

Write About Bears

Choose two photographs of grizzly bears from the selection. Write a paragraph about each photograph. Describe the setting and season, how fully grown the bears are, and what the bears are doing.

 Tips

- **Include a topic sentence in each paragraph.**
- **Make each paragraph more interesting by using different sentence types and lengths.**

Math

Make a Graph

Make a list of all the animals mentioned in the selection. Then take a poll of your class or school. Find out how many people have seen each kind of animal the author mentions. Create a graph that shows the results.

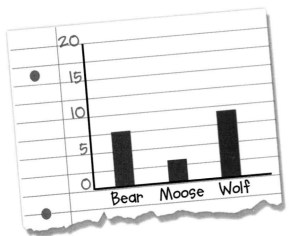

Health and Safety

Make a Safety Poster

Humans in bear territory need to be educated about grizzlies, for both their own and the bears' protection. Use information from the selection about bear behavior to make a safety poster especially for people who pick wild berries or people who fish for salmon.

Go on a Web Field Trip

Connect to Education Place and explore a part of the world where grizzlies roam.

www.eduplace.com/kids

Three Poems
by Joseph Bruchac

Skill: How to Compare Poems

When you read two or more poems together, ask yourself these questions:

- What is the **subject** of each poem? How are the subjects or images in the poems alike or different?

- What is the **mood** of each poem? Light and funny? Dark and serious? How are the moods alike or different?

- How are the **sounds** and **rhythms** of the poems alike or different?

- If the poems are by the same poet, what **elements** in the poems — subject, sound, images, mood — tell you that the same person wrote them?

Above Jackson Pond

Long-winged, it circled
slow as a heron
yet shoulders broader in flight.

Seeking an updraft
to lift it higher,
it flapped wings
darker than clouds,
tail fanned, catching light.

An Eagle.

I whistled its way
and on my third whistle
it folded wings,
dove and rolled in answer
before flying on
past the tallest pines
which sentinel
the hill above Jackson Pond.

Valleys widen with green,
with the flow of spring,
rivers and lakes
veins pulsing the heart
of the land
held under those wide wings.

Thinking now of that great bird
praising its return,
my own vision opens
to see this earth
more gift than we humans
can give.

Raccoons on the Shore at Paradox Lake

From the lake shore
greyed in by trails of mist
from the warm evening water
bright eyes flash at me
in the beam of the lantern
as I lift my paddle
and let the boat drift.

Six small raccoons, cubs of this year.
One curious one edges too close
and, nudged by a brother or a sister,
splashes off the dock,
comes up like a cork
and scrambles back onto the land.

They watch me,
until the canoe bumps in
to the dock, then after
a quick glance at each other,
they scoot to the base
of the big basswood tree
and hand over hand
up to its thin branches
which arch over water.

Their small paws
break free twigs
which rain about me
as a sudden wind
cuts across the lake,
cutting through the low
grey clouds above me,
so that there,
above their lifting heads I see
the shoulder of the mountain
and then, just before the mist
closes in again, high above
on the night trail of the Milky Way.

There, too, beyond Great Bear
and The Hunter
are the Northern Lights,
the ones my old people
called the spirits who dance.
They ripple the edge of the sky.

Stars reflect around me
in the lake's dark mirror
and between the shapes of the dancing stars
and that rippling form of my canoe cutting its wake
across the stars, I see again
those small raccoons,
looking up and down
in wonder.

A Thousand Geese

Geese have flown over
for twelve days now.
I've counted each flock
lying on my back
at the edge of the old field
where sumacs edge in.

All that they carry
is all that they are.
They travel far
in need of nothing
but fair weather,
food and a safe place to rest,
their wide wings linking
winter and spring.

As the last flight passes
they take with them
my weariness
which had no reason
yet held me back
from doing the real work
half of my life.

Now, like those geese,
today all I seek
is warmth enough,
food and light enough
to sustain myself and
those whose lives
are close to mine
as we journey
the seasons.

A Persuasive Essay

The purpose of a persuasive essay is to convince the reader to think or act in a particular way. Use this student's writing as a model when you write a persuasive essay of your own.

Why People Should Get a Dog

I think people should get dogs because they are good companions. I also think pets, especially dogs, help you and improve your life. Some people say their dogs changed their lives because when you take care of a dog you need to learn to be unselfish. People also say dogs help them communicate better. When you have a dog, you have to try to find out what it wants, and that can help you find out how to talk to other people.

An important thing about getting a dog is to find one that suits you. When I had my dog Simba, he was my best friend. He was my favorite mammal to be with besides my mom. He always made my family and me laugh. Sometimes he got all mixed up and ran into the wall. When we played music, he tried to sing. I loved him very much. I could tell him anything in the world as if he was my best friend.

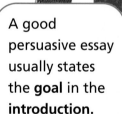

A good persuasive essay usually states the **goal** in the **introduction.**

The persuasive goal should be supported by **strong reasons.**

624

Dogs help you because your personality is one of the many important parts of your life, and dogs help improve it. My dog helped me improve my personality by making me be more open because it wasn't always about me. He also improved my knowledge because I did not know dogs needed so many things to be satisfied. I had to learn how to react to him and find out when to feed him and what he liked to eat.

Some people say that dogs need too much care. You have to feed them and take them for walks. My dog Simba was worth any work I had to do because he was my friend.

I think everyone should have a dog because they may improve your life. Simba and every other pet I had taught me a valuable lesson I will need to know later in life. By getting a dog, you too can learn a valuable lesson or two.

It's important to state **facts** and give **examples**.

A good persuasive essay **answers objections**.

The **conclusion** should bring the essay to a satisfactory close.

Meet the Author

Michiala L.
Grade: five
State: Massachusetts
Hobbies: playing softball, making friendship bracelets, listening to music, and riding her bike
What she wants to be when she grows up: a veterinarian

Rescue in the Rain Forest

The "home" in *The Golden Lion Tamarin Comes Home* is the coastal rain forest of Brazil. It provides a habitat for a great variety of animals, even though, as the map on the right shows, the rain forest has been reduced to a fraction of its original size. How did this happen?

When human beings move into an area, their need for food and shelter may conflict with the needs of animals who make their home there. As they lose their habitat to human development, animals like the golden lion tamarin may even face extinction. This creates a dilemma: how to allow for development without threatening wildlife?

There is hope. The reintroduction of captive tamarins into the wild may help their numbers grow in what remains of the rain forest. Who is doing this work? Where does the work begin and end? The answers are in *The Golden Lion Tamarin Comes Home*.

South America
Brazil

Coastal Rain Forest of Brazil
■ Before Europeans arrived
■ Today

627

Meet the Author/Photographer
George Ancona

Future Traveler: As a boy, Ancona visited the East River docks in New York City with his father. Watching freighters from around the world sparked an interest in other countries.

Study Abroad: While in art school, Ancona traveled to southern Mexico, where he met his parents' families for the first time.

Early Work: Before Ancona became a photographer, he worked for a carpenter, a mechanic, and at an amusement park.

In His Own Words: "I think people are fascinating and I love to find myself in strange places, meeting people, getting to know them and learning about them. This helps me to learn about myself."

Other Titles: Ancona's books reflect his love of travel and other cultures. *Turtle Watch* and *Carnaval* also take place in Brazil, and *Pablo Remembers* was photographed in Mexico.

Internet

To find out more about George Ancona, log on to Education Place. **www.eduplace.com/kids**

Selection 2

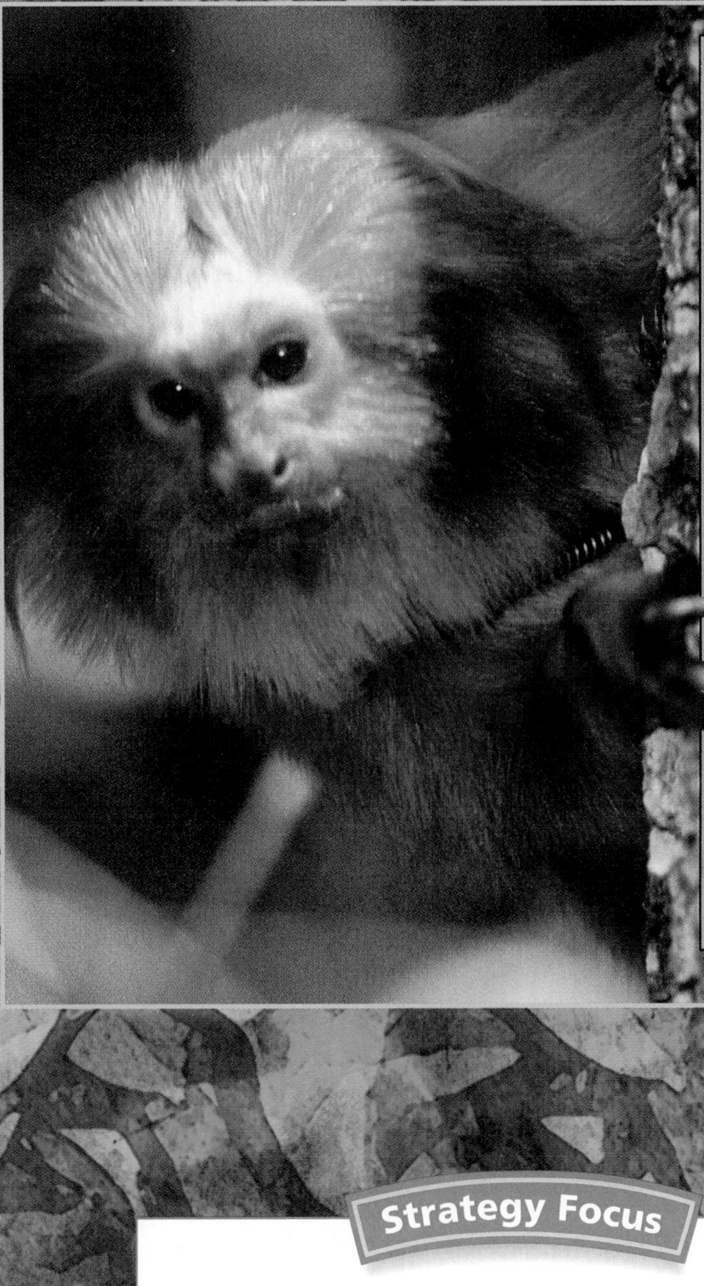

THE GOLDEN LION TAMARIN COMES HOME

George Ancona

Strategy Focus

As you read, **monitor** your understanding of how people are trying to help the golden lion tamarin. If necessary, reread or read ahead to **clarify**.

Whistling softly as she scans the upper canopy of leaves, Andreia Martins leads her sister Carolina and brother Renato through the rain forest. It is hot and humid. The small group is surrounded by the teeming life of the tropical forest.

Birds sing, insects buzz, cicadas chirp. Nearby they hear a tractor engine, cattle lowing, a rooster, and men at work on a *fazenda*, or "farm." They pick their way carefully along the narrow path to avoid the sharp spines of leaves and the tangle of vines underfoot.

Andreia raises her hand, and the group stops. Above them the leaves rustle and branches sway as streaks of orange-gold flash in the speckles of sunlight. "*Micos*," she whispers to the children, and points to the cluster of golden lion tamarins staring down at them from the branches of the trees. Their high-pitched whistles and squeaks pierce the air.

"Mico" is short for *mico leão dourado*, the Portuguese name for the golden lion tamarin of Brazil. About the size of a squirrel, the monkey is named for its color and lionlike mane.

The golden lion tamarin is found only in the coastal rain forest of southeastern Brazil. Flanked by a mountain range on the west and the Atlantic Ocean on the east, the forest once stretched for 1,500 miles.

When the first Europeans arrived, they cut down the trees to build their homes and towns. They burned the rest of the forest to clear the land for settlements, for coffee and sugar plantations, and for pastures on which to graze livestock. The city of Rio de Janeiro grew and spread. Today only 2 percent of the original rain forest remains, scattered like small islands in a sea of farms and towns.

As its native habitat disappeared, so did the golden lion tamarin. By 1960 there were so few left that Dr. A. Coimbra-Filho, a Brazilian biologist, warned of its imminent extinction. He urged the Brazilian government to set aside the remaining forest as a wildlife refuge. The Poço das Antas Biological Reserve, a protected habitat, was established in 1973.

The tall trees in the tropical rain forest offer the tamarins food, protection from predators, and a network of routes through their territories. The cupped centers of bromeliads, plants that live in host trees, hold water and insects for the monkeys to drink and eat. Tamarins are omnivorous. They eat not only fruits, seeds, and nuts but also bird eggs, insects, frogs, and snakes, which provide additional protein.

The rain forest is alive both day and night with a diversity of wildlife. Among the trees can be seen sloths and other species of monkeys.

Tamarins must always be on guard for predators. Above them fly owls, while on the ground prowl ocelots, feral dogs, and — the most dangerous of all — humans. Poachers trap the tamarins and sell them in illegal animal markets for high prices. If discovered, these pets are confiscated and returned to the reserve.

Today golden lion tamarins are bred in many zoos around the world. These animals do not have the skills to survive in the wild on their own. A captive tamarin lives in a confined space, climbs sturdy poles that don't move, and is served its food in a bowl at regular hours by a familiar keeper. It has never leaped from a vine to a delicate tree branch that sways under its weight. It doesn't know how to forage for its food. It hasn't experienced weather changes — cold, rain, thunder, and lightning. It would be killed by predators or get lost and starve. It needs the help of humans and that of native-born tamarins to learn to survive independently in its original habitat.

Since 1983, Dr. Benjamin Beck and his staff at the National Zoological Park in Washington, D.C., have been trying to find ways to prepare captive-born tamarins for their return to the rain forest. Dr. Beck coordinates the reintroduction of the tamarins into their natural habitat for the Golden Lion Tamarin Conservation Program.

The tamarins being reintroduced often come from other zoos and are examined carefully when they arrive at the National Zoo. A different number is tattooed onto each animal's leg and entered into a record of all the tamarins born in captivity.

As an experiment, tamarins are being permitted to live free in a wooded section of the zoo. Because they are territorial, they stay close to their nesting boxes, which are wired vertically high in the trees. The nesting box is a modified picnic cooler with two chambers inside, one above the other. In the top chamber is a hole through which the tamarins enter and leave. Should a predator attack, the tamarins huddle in the lower chamber, where a groping paw cannot reach them.

A tamarin claims its territory by rubbing a scent from its body onto tree limbs. The ones that will someday be reintroduced into the wild wear radio collars that transmit a constant beep, enabling the keepers to locate them in the woods. The tamarins are fed by food trays raised to the height of their nesting boxes.

Ropes are hung to simulate vines and to provide a network of treetop highways for the monkeys. The ropes and the nesting boxes are often changed while the tamarins are asleep to help prepare them for the unexpected.

The dilemma for the zoo is how to protect the animals and still expose them to the experiences and dangers they will meet in the wild.

Observers watch and record everything the monkeys do. To tell the tamarins apart, they mark the tails with hair dye. Each member of the tamarin family has its own distinctive tail marking.

When the time is right, the monkeys are shipped by air from Washington, D.C., to Rio de Janeiro.

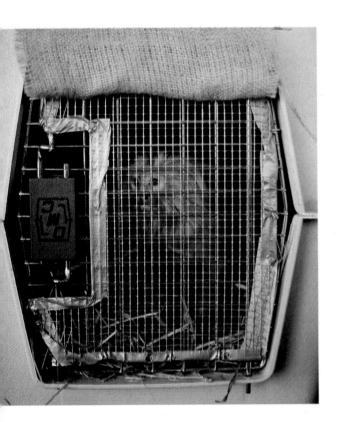

Andreia Martins is one of the many people in Brazil and abroad working to save the golden lion tamarin. She coordinates a team of observers who roam the rain forest, tracking tamarins and observing their behavior. The team's notes are sent to the National Zoo, where scientists in the conservation program use them to help prepare captive-born tamarins for their reintroduction into the rain forest.

In Rio de Janeiro, Andreia and Dionizio Moraes Pessamilio, director of the reserve, carry bags of fruit when they meet a shipment of seven tamarins that arrives from Washington, D.C.

After the overnight flight, the squealing monkeys are hungry, and they gobble up the pieces of fruit that Andreia and Dionizio squeeze into the cages. Then the noisy cages are loaded into a van for the two-hour trip to the reserve.

Golden lion tamarins tend to be monogamous, which means a male and female will live together and mate only with each other. This shipment includes a family of four from one zoo: the mother, the father, and a pair of one-year-old twins, one male and one female. The other three tamarins come from three different zoos and will be used to create new families.

Because there are so few tamarins left in the wild, they keep reproducing among themselves. Introducing animals that are born in distant zoos helps to strengthen the gene pool of the native tamarins. Genes carry the characteristics of a species from one generation to the next.

The van and the observation team meet on a narrow road in the forest. The tamarins are unloaded and carried into the woods, where large cages await the immigrants. They are released into the cages, where they will grow accustomed to their new surroundings.

635

Everything is different: the heat, the tall trees, the noises. The tamarins will get to know their potential prey, such as the insects and small reptiles and mammals that scoot in and out of their cages. Beyond the cages stalk their predators, which they must learn to avoid.

The reserve is located a few kilometers from the town of Silva Jardim, where Andreia lives with her mother and ten brothers and sisters. Every morning Andreia and her sister Arleia, who is also an observer, cut up fruit and canned marmoset food. The canned food, which provides needed protein, is exactly what the tamarins ate in the zoo.

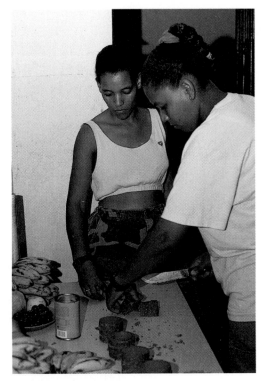

The pieces of food are then stuffed into feeders made of plastic tubes wired together to make a square, with holes drilled along the tubes. Andreia crams bits of food into the holes. This encourages the tamarins to use their long fingers and nails to extract the food, just as they will probe in trees and rotted logs once they are released.

Meanwhile, Arleia fills canteens with water. By 7:30 A.M. the van is loaded with feeders and canteens. The sisters tuck their camouflage pants into their socks to keep out insects and jump into the van.

The Golden Lion Tamarin Conservation Program has provided many jobs for people in Silva Jardim. A small town, it is located near the main highway to Rio. The *praça*, or "plaza," with its tall shade trees, bandstand, and playground, sits in the center of town.

Andreia stops at the plaza to pick up more of the observation team. While waiting for them to arrive, she works out the assignment for each one. Every day, an observer is assigned to a different group of tamarins.

637

The observation team is split into two groups. One group goes to the reserve, while the other goes to the fazendas where tamarins have been reintroduced. Originally the *fazenderos*, or "farmers," were hesitant about accepting the monkeys on their forest-land. But now they speak of them as "my micos."

Andreia drives through the forest, stopping every so often to drop off an observer. Each carries a canteen and a machete on a belt, as well as a backpack with food, rain gear, a snakebite kit, and mosquito repellent. Everyone carries a compass, a digital watch, a notebook, and an antenna and radio receiver for tracking the tamarins. A full tamarin feeder, carried on the shoulder, completes the equipment each observer takes into the woods.

Today the newly arrived tamarin family of four will be released. They have spent enough time in the large cage to become accustomed to the climate of the rain forest. In addition to its own tail marking, each monkey has another mark on its body that identifies the family to which it belongs. One tamarin in the group wears a new radio collar.

Andreia and Paulo Caesar, another observer, carry the nesting box into the woods. They have selected a tree in an area that the tamarin family can claim as its own. Paulo Caesar nimbly climbs the tree with a rope and wire on his shoulder. When he reaches a fork about twenty feet above the ground, he drops one end of the rope to Andreia. She ties the end to the nesting box, and Paulo Caesar hoists it up and wires it in place. With the rope draped over a branch, he drops both ends to Andreia so she can raise a feeder up to the box. Finally, Paulo Caesar uncovers the opening of the nesting box and slides down to the ground. Then they both sit down to see what will happen.

A young tamarin pokes its head out of the box, looks around, and squeals. Then the other golden heads appear to take a look. After some tentative moves, the juvenile darts out to the feeder, pokes into it, and stuffs food into its mouth.

Below, Andreia glances at her watch and writes in her notebook. For the first hour, she describes what the entire group is doing — the way they eat, socialize, and rest, and the sounds they make. Then she notes what each member of the family does.

In order not to give the tamarins human characteristics, the observers do not give them names. Instead they identify the monkeys by letters that represent the zoo they came from and numbers that symbolize their position in the group. For example, KO1 is the adult female from the zoo in Cologne, Germany, KO2 is the adult male, and KO3 and KO4 are their offspring.

At first the newcomers stay close to their nesting box. Away from their new home, they may become disoriented and get lost. Alone, a newly reintroduced tamarin can die of starvation, become injured, or fall prey to a predator.

This is when the tamarins need the most help. They are given plenty of food and water. Oranges and bananas are hung on branches for them. Because the tamarins have always eaten chopped fruit, they don't know how to peel whole fruit. The bananas are partially opened for them, and the oranges have "windows" cut into them.

As the months go by, the feeder is placed farther from the nesting box. Fruits are placed on saplings that will sway when the tamarins leap onto them.

When the tamarins begin to forage and eat natural foods, the observers reduce their visits to three times a week, then to once a week, and finally to once a month. When the tamarins become independent, all feeding is stopped.

Bit by bit, the family becomes familiar with the rain forest, the younger ones adapting faster than the parents. But only about 30 percent of all reintroduced tamarins survive more than two years. Some die by eating poisonous fruits or snakes. Some are killed by Africanized, or "killer," bees, which sometimes take over a nesting box to make a hive. The infants that are born in the wild fare much better than the reintroduced tamarins. They are more acrobatic and confident as they leap from limb to limb. They are able to deal with surprises, and they don't have to unlearn behaviors that were adequate for zoo life but are useless in the forest.

The goal of the Golden Lion Tamarin Conservation Program is to have two thousand tamarins living in the wild by the year 2025. For this to happen, the people who live in and around the rain forest have to help protect the tamarins and their environment. That way, human beings and tamarins will be able to share the Brazilian landscape for years to come.

641

Responding

Think About the Selection

1. Do you think the settlers' reasons for cutting down the rain forest were good ones? Why or why not?

2. Why do you think tamarins born in the wild do better than tamarins who return to the rain forest after living in captivity?

3. Find evidence in the text to support this idea: Tamarins need the most help just after they return to the rain forest.

4. Do you agree with the observers' decision on page 639 not to name the tamarins? Why or why not?

5. Would you want to be part of a conservation program? If so, what would you like to do? If not, why not?

6. Do you think the efforts to return tamarins to the forest are worthwhile, even though only 30% of them survive? Explain.

7. Connecting/Comparing Which animal's survival do you feel more hopeful about — the grizzly's or the golden lion tamarin's? Why?

Write a Fax Message

A conservation team leader might send a fax to tamarin observers. Write a fax that tells what jobs they will do, what equipment they will need, and where and when they will be picked up.

Tips

- Keep your message brief and clear.
- Include a cover page giving your name and the name of the person you're faxing.

642

Make a Fact Chart

Use the information in the selection to make a chart of facts about the golden lion tamarin. Create rows with category headings such as *Size, Color, Habitat, Food, Predators,* and *Family*. Then fill in the rows to show what you have learned.

Bonus Make a similar fact chart for another kind of monkey, and then compare the two animals.

Golden Lion Tamarin

Size	
Food	
Color	

Give a Talk

Are you concerned about the golden lion tamarin? Do you agree that it should be returned to the rain forest? Use the selection to prepare a talk about the Golden Lion Tamarin Conservation Program and present it to your class.

Tips

- Use note cards instead of writing out your whole talk. Practice using your notes.
- Speak at an even pace. Be sure that everyone in your audience can hear you.

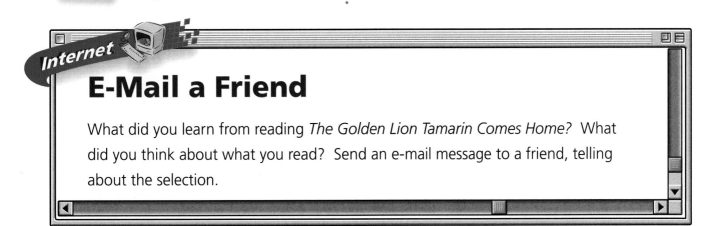

Internet

E-Mail a Friend

What did you learn from reading *The Golden Lion Tamarin Comes Home?* What did you think about what you read? Send an e-mail message to a friend, telling about the selection.

Skill: How to Read a Technology Article

Before you read . . .

- Identify the **topic** of the article.

- Look through the article for **diagrams** or **illustrations** that help explain the technology.

As you read . . .

- If you come to an unfamiliar **term**, try rereading or reading ahead to find its definition.

- If you come to an unfamiliar **abbreviation**, scan back to the first time it appears. The full name is usually given there.

Tuning in on Animals

Golden lion tamarins are not the only species scientists are listening to. New technologies have changed the way we keep in touch with animals, and have taught us surprising things about their behavior.

In the fall of 1994, a Florida manatee, an endangered sea mammal, was spotted off the coast of Maryland. Scientists know that manatees migrate north over the summer, but they were puzzled that this one had not returned south yet. Clearly there was a lot more they needed to know about manatees. They caught the animal, but before bringing it back to Florida waters, they fitted it with a special radio collar around the base of its tail. From this collar, the scientists could track the manatee's movements and location and learn more about manatee migration.

Animal tracking means following the location of an animal as it walks, runs, swims, or flies. By tracking many single animals over time, scientists can learn how a whole species migrates with the seasons. They also learn details about animal behavior that may help them in protecting endangered species.

Tags and Telemetry

The simplest way to track an animal is to follow one and keep it in view. But physically tracking an animal is not always possible. (Think of how quickly a bird can fly out of sight.) So, almost two hundred years ago, researchers began catching individual animals, fitting them with tags, and letting them go. This method was better, but still flawed: if scientists wanted to learn about the animal, they would have to catch it again later.

The next development was *telemetry* — using radio signals to track animals.

Here's an example of how it works. A single animal, such as a lynx, is fitted with a small device that transmits a radio signal. Using a receiver, scientists pick up the signals from a distance on land or from an airplane. Over days or weeks, they chart where the lynx goes. This method is still used today, but it has limitations. The receiver must be within a few hundred yards of the transmitter. And telemetry won't work everywhere. Radio signals cannot penetrate heavy jungle vegetation or below the surface of the ocean.

Once this lynx is fitted with a radio transmitter (left), it can be tracked using a portable radio antenna and receiver (above).

Satellite Signals

Perhaps the most accurate and powerful type of animal tracking today is the Global Positioning System (GPS). This system uses 26 satellites orbiting 11,000 miles above the earth to follow the animals being tracked.

Instead of carrying a transmitter, a waved albatross, for example, would be fitted with a receiver. At regular intervals, the receiver automatically selects the four GPS satellites that are closest to the albatross. The receiver picks up the signals from these satellites and passes them on to a computer. The computer then calculates the position of the albatross by processing the information collected from the four satellites. The location that the GPS system calculates is accurate, on average, to within 30 meters (33 yards).

Satellite tracking has revealed fascinating and important information about many kinds of animals. Scientists have learned that albatross parents fly thousands of miles to find food for a single chick.

They have discovered that leatherback turtles swim more than a thousand miles in the open sea, along routes that they return to again and again. And studies have shown that great white sharks hunt around the clock, not just in the daytime as researchers had previously believed.

Scientists are constantly working on improvements in animal tracking. One group of researchers fits sharks with special tags that relay information to receivers on buoys floating in the water. Radio transmitters as light as seven-tenths of an ounce can be attached to even very small birds, and scientists are working to make them still lighter.

Perhaps the most exciting aspect of present-day animal tracking is that, using the Internet, anyone can find out the most up-to-date information that scientists are gathering. By logging onto the Web sites of animal trackers, you can learn where an animal goes each month or week, or even every day. And maybe the next time a manatee surfaces in an unusual place, you'll be one of the first to know.

To feed their young, albatrosses scan the ocean for fish. Trackers scan for albatrosses.

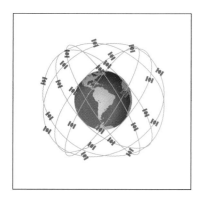

In GPS tracking, 26 satellites with transmitters orbit the Earth (left). At regular intervals, the four satellites closest to a waved albatross (below) send signals to the bird's receiver, which records its location.

Using this data, biologists with the Albatross Project are able to track the flights of waved albatrosses with great accuracy from the birds' breeding site on tiny Española, one of the Galapagos Islands off the coast of Ecuador.

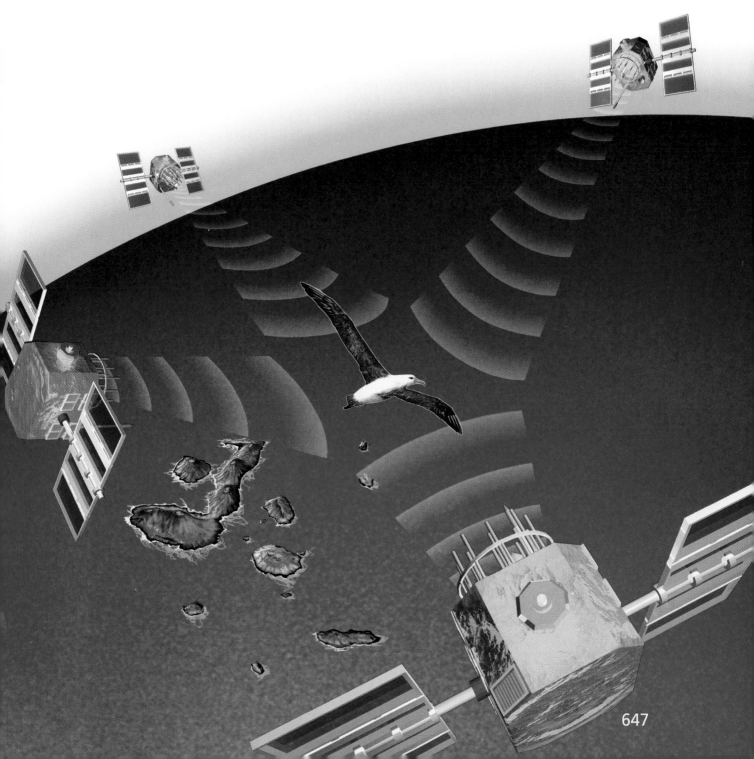

Living on the Land

In *My Side of the Mountain*, a boy chooses to "live on the land" in a forest. His **survival** depends on being able to use what he finds in nature to meet his needs.

Think about what those needs would be.

A person living on the land would need to give a lot of attention to food, clothing, and shelter. How would someone go about **harvesting** food from edible plants in the area? How much work would it be to build up a **cache** of food that would last through the winter? Or to create a **storehouse** where food would not spoil or be eaten by wild animals?

Naturally, a forest dweller would also need a place to live. What kind of shelter would that person **fashion** out of materials found in the woods? What qualities in a shelter would help keep out a **harsh** winter? What would make the warmest clothing?

There is one more need to think about. Even if food, shelter, and clothing were taken care of, a person would need to keep from being lonely. What kind of friendship might someone find in the forest?

Jean Craighead George

Jean Craighead George's family lived in Washington, D.C., and her father often took her and her brothers into the surrounding countryside to teach them about plants and animals. She also learned some of the survival skills that Sam Gribley uses, including building a lean-to, and making a fishhook and line out of wood and wood fiber. Of her writing, George says, "I write for children. Children are still in love with the wonders of nature, and I am too."

Among over seventy other books dealing with nature, George has extended the story of *My Side of the Mountain* in two sequels: *On the Far Side of the Mountain* and *Frightful's Mountain*.

Gary Aagaard

Gary Aagaard grew up in Seattle, Washington. He remembers being energetic as a child and full of curiosity. To illustrate *My Side of the Mountain*, Aagaard traveled to upstate New York, where the story takes place. There he took pictures of the outdoors, using a friend's son as a model for Sam. Aagaard currently lives in New York City.

Internet

Learn more about Jean Craighead George and Gary Aagaard at Education Place. **www.eduplace.com/kids**

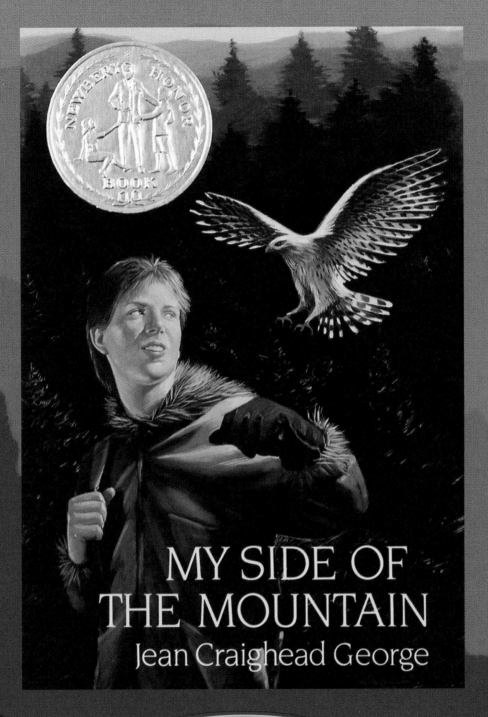

MY SIDE OF
THE MOUNTAIN
Jean Craighead George

*Sam Gribley is living alone on the wooded mountain
where his grandfather once lived. The teacher he
befriended over the summer, Bando, has left.
Now Sam has only his diary and wild animals for
company: Frightful, a falcon he has raised; The
Baron Weasel; and Jessie C. James, a raccoon.*

In Which
The Autumn Provides Food and Loneliness

September blazed a trail into the mountains. First she burned the grasses. The grasses seeded and were harvested by the mice and the winds.

Then she sent the squirrels and chipmunks running boldly through the forest, collecting and hiding nuts.

Then she frosted the aspen leaves and left them sunshine yellow.

Then she gathered the birds together in flocks, and the mountaintop was full of songs and twitterings and flashing wings. The birds were ready to move to the south.

652

And I, Sam Gribley, felt just wonderful, just wonderful.

I pushed the raft down the stream and gathered arrowleaf bulbs, cattail tubers, bulrush roots, and the nutlike tubers of the sedges.

And then the crop of crickets appeared and Frightful hopped all over the meadow snagging them in her great talons and eating them. I tried them, because I had heard they are good. I think it was another species of cricket that was meant. I think the field cricket would taste excellent if you were starving. I was not starving, so I preferred to listen to them. I abandoned the crickets and went back to the goodness of the earth.

I smoked fish and rabbit, dug wild onions by the pouchful, and raced September for her crop.

"October 15

"Today The Baron Weasel looked moldy. I couldn't get near enough to see what was the matter with him, but it occurs to me that he might be changing his summer fur for his white winter mantle. If he is, it is an itchy process. He scratches a lot."

Seeing The Baron changing his mantle for winter awoke the first fears in me. I wrote that note on a little birch bark, curled up on my bed, and shivered.

The snow and the cold and the long lifeless months are ahead, I thought. The wind was blowing hard and cool across the mountain. I lit my candle, took out the rabbit and squirrel hides I had been saving, and began rubbing and kneading them to softness.

The Baron was getting a new suit for winter. I must have one too. Some fur underwear, some mittens, fur-lined socks.

Frightful, who was sitting on the foot post of the bed, yawned, fluffed, and thrust her head into the slate-gray feathers of her back. She slept. I worked for several hours.

I must say here that I was beginning to wonder if I should not go home for the winter and come back again in the spring. Everything in the forest was getting prepared for the harsh months. Jessie Coon James was as fat as a barrel. He came down the tree slowly, his fat falling in a roll over his shoulders. The squirrels were working and storing food. They were building leaf nests. The skunks had burrows and plugged themselves in at dawn with bunches of leaves. No drafts could reach them.

As I thought of the skunks and all the animals preparing themselves against the winter, I realized suddenly that my tree would be as cold as the air if I did not somehow find a way to heat it.

"notes:

"Today I rafted out into the deep pools of the creek to fish. It was a lazy sort of autumn day, the sky clear, the leaves beginning to brighten, the air warm. I stretched out on my back because the fish weren't biting, and hummed.

"My line jerked and I sat up to pull, but was too late. However, I was not too late to notice that I had drifted into the bank — the very bank where Bando had dug the clay for the jam pots.

"At that moment I knew what I was going to do. I was going to build a fireplace of clay, even fashion a little chimney of clay. It would be small, but enough to warm the tree during the long winter.

"Next day

"I dragged the clay up the mountain to my tree in my second best pair of city pants. I tied the bottoms of the legs, stuffed them full, and as I looked down on my strange cargo, I thought of scarecrows and Halloween. Suddenly I was terribly lonely. The air smelled of leaves and the cool wind from the stream hugged me. The warblers in the trees above me seemed gay and glad about their trip south. I stopped halfway up the mountain and dropped my head. I was lonely and on the verge of tears. Suddenly there was a flash, a pricking sensation on my leg, and I looked down in time to see The Baron leap from my pants to the cover of fern.

"He scared the loneliness right out of me. I ran after him and chased him up the mountain, losing him from time to time in the ferns and crowfeet. We stormed into camp an awful sight, The Baron bouncing and screaming ahead of me, and me dragging that half scarecrow of clay.

"Frightful took one look and flew to the end of her leash. She doesn't like The Baron, and watches him — well, like a hawk. I don't like to leave her alone. End notes. Must make fireplace."

It took three days to get the fireplace worked out so that it didn't smoke me out of the tree like a bee. It was an enormous problem. In the first place, the chimney sagged because the clay was too heavy to hold itself up, so I had to get some dry grasses to work into it so it could hold its own weight.

I whittled out one of the old knotholes to let the smoke out, and built the chimney down from this. Of course when the clay dried, it pulled away from the tree, and all the smoke poured back in on me.

So I tried sealing the leak with pine pitch, and that worked all right, but then the funnel over the fire bed cracked, and I had to put wooden props under that.

The wooden props burned, and I could see that this wasn't going to work either; so I went down the mountain to the site of the old Gribley farmhouse and looked around for some iron spikes or some sort of metal.

I took the wooden shovel that I had carved from the board and dug around what I thought must have been the back door or possibly the woodhouse.

I found a hinge, old hand-made nails that would come in handy, and finally, treasure of treasures, the axle of an old wagon. It was much too big. I had no hacksaw to cut it into smaller pieces, and I was not strong enough to heat it and hammer it apart. Besides, I didn't have anything but a small wooden mallet I had made.

I carried my trophies home and sat down before my tree to fix dinner and feed Frightful. The evening was cooling down for a frost. I looked at Frightful's warm feathers. I didn't even have a deer hide for a blanket. I had used the two I had for a door and a pair of pants. I wished that I might grow feathers.

I tossed Frightful off my fist and she flashed through the trees and out over the meadow. She went with a determination strange to her. "She is going to leave," I cried. "I have never seen her fly so wildly." I pushed the smoked fish aside and ran to the meadow. I whistled and whistled and whistled until my mouth was dry and no more whistle came.

I ran onto the big boulder. I could not see her. Wildly I waved the lure. I licked my lips and whistled again. The sun was a cold steely color as it dipped below the mountain. The air was now brisk, and Frightful was gone. I was sure that she had suddenly taken off on the migration; my heart was sore and

pounding. I had enough food, I was sure. Frightful was not absolutely necessary for my survival; but I was now so fond of her. She was more than a bird. I knew I must have her back to talk to and play with if I was going to make it through the winter.

I whistled. Then I heard a cry in the grasses up near the white birches.

In the gathering darkness I saw movement. I think I flew to the spot. And there she was; she had caught herself a bird. I rolled into the grass beside her and clutched her jesses. She didn't intend to leave, but I was going to make sure that she didn't. I grabbed so swiftly that my hand hit a rock and I bruised my knuckles.

The rock was flat and narrow and long; it was the answer to my fireplace. I picked up Frightful in one hand and the stone in the other; and I laughed at the cold steely sun as it slipped out of sight, because I knew I was going to be warm. This flat stone was what I needed to hold up the funnel and finish my fireplace.

And that's what I did with it. I broke it into two pieces, set one on each side under the funnel, lit the fire, closed the flap of the door and listened to the wind bring the first frost to the mountain. I was warm.

Then I noticed something dreadful. Frightful was sitting on the bedpost, her head under her wings. She was toppling. She jerked her head out of her feathers. Her eyes looked glassy. She is sick, I said. I picked her up and stroked her, and we both might have died there if I had not opened the tent flap to get her some water. The cold night air revived her. "Air," I said. "The fireplace used up all the oxygen. I've got to ventilate this place."

We sat out in the cold for a long time because I was more than a little afraid of what our end might have been.

I put out the fire, took the door down and wrapped up in it. Frightful and I slept with the good frost nipping our faces.

"notes:

"I cut out several more knotholes to let air in and out of the tree room. I tried it today. I have Frightful on my fist watching her. It's been about two hours and she hasn't fainted and I haven't gone numb. I can still write and see clearly.

"Test: Frightful's healthy face."

IN WHICH
We All Learn About Halloween

"October 28

"I have been up and down the mountain every day for a week, watching to see if walnuts and hickory nuts are ripe. Today I found the squirrels all over the trees, harvesting them furiously, and so I have decided that ripe or not, I must gather them. It's me or the squirrels.

"I tethered Frightful in the hickory tree while I went to the walnut tree and filled pouches. Frightful protected the hickory nuts. She keeps the squirrels so busy scolding her that they don't have time to take the nuts. They are quite terrified by her. It is a good scheme. I shout and bang the tree and keep them away while I gather.

"I have never seen so many squirrels. They hang from the slender branches, they bounce through the limbs, they seem to come from the whole forest. They must pass messages along to each other — messages that tell what kind of nuts and where the trees are."

A few days later, my storehouse rolling with nuts, I began the race for apples. Entering this race were squirrels, raccoons, and a fat old skunk who looked as if he could eat not another bite. He was ready to sleep his autumn meal off, and I resented him because he did not need my apples. However, I did not toy with him.

I gathered what apples I could, cut some in slices, and dried them on the boulder in the sun. Some I put in the storeroom tree to eat right away. They were a little wormy, but it was wonderful to eat an apple again.

Then one night this was all done, the crop was gathered. I sat down to make a few notes when The Baron came sprinting into sight.

He actually bounced up and licked the edges of my turtle-shell bowl, stormed Frightful, and came to my feet.

"Baron Weasel," I said. "It is nearing Halloween. Are you playing tricks or treats?" I handed him the remains of my turtle soup dinner, and, fascinated, watched him devour it.

"note:

"The Baron chews with his back molars, and chews with a ferocity I have not seen in him before. His eyes gleam, the lips curl back from his white pointed teeth, and he frowns like an angry man. If I move toward him, a rumble starts in his chest that keeps me back. He flashes glances at me. It is indeed strange to be looked in the eye by this fearless wild animal. There is something human about his beady glance. Perhaps because that glance tells me something. It tells me he knows who I am and that he does not want me to come any closer."

The Baron Weasel departed after his feast. Frightful, who was drawn up as skinny as a stick, relaxed and fluffed her feathers, and then I said to her,

"See, he got his treats. No tricks." Then something occurred to me. I reached inside the door and pulled out my calendar stick. I counted 28, 29, 30, 31.

"Frightful, that old weasel knows. It is Halloween. Let's have a Halloween party."

Swiftly I made piles of cracked nuts, smoked rabbit, and crayfish. I even added two of my apples. This food was an invitation to the squirrels, foxes, raccoons, opossums, even the birds that lived around me to come have a party.

When Frightful is tethered to her stump, some of the animals and birds will only come close enough to scream at her. So bird and I went inside the tree, propped open the flap, and waited.

Not much happened that night. I learned that it takes a little time for the woodland messages to get around. But they do. Before the party I had been very careful about leaving food out because I needed every mouthful. I took the precaution of rolling a stone in front of my store tree. The harvest moon rose. Frightful and I went to sleep.

At dawn, we abandoned the party. I left the treats out, however. Since it was a snappy gold-colored day, we went off to get some more rabbit skins to finish my winter underwear.

We had lunch along the creek — stewed mussels and wild potatoes. We didn't get back until dusk because I discovered some wild rice in an ox bow of the stream. There was no more than a handful.

Home that night, everything seemed peaceful enough. A few nuts were gone, to the squirrels, I thought. I baked a fish in leaves, and ate a small, precious amount of wild rice. It was marvelous! As I settled down to scrape the rabbit skins of the day, my neighbor the skunk marched right into the campground and set to work on the smoked rabbit. I made some Halloween notes:

"The moon is coming up behind the aspens. It is as big as a pumpkin and as orange. The winds are cool, the stars are like electric light bulbs. I am just inside the doorway, with my turtle-shell lamp burning so that I can see to write this.

"Something is moving beyond the second hemlock. Frightful is very alert, as if there are things all around us. Halloween was over at midnight last night, but for us it is just beginning. That's how I feel, anyhow, but it just may be my imagination.

"I wish Frightful would stop pulling her feathers in and drawing herself up like a spring. I keep thinking that she feels things.

"Here comes Jessie C. James. He will want the venison.

"He didn't get the venison. There was a snarl, and a big raccoon I've never seen walked past him, growling and looking ferocious. Jessie C. stood motionless — I might say, scared stiff. He held his head at an angle and let the big fellow eat. If Jessie so much as rolled his eyes that old coon would sputter at him."

It grew dark, and I couldn't see much. An eerie yelp behind the boulder announced that the red fox of the meadow was nearing. He gave me goose bumps. He stayed just beyond my store tree, weaving back and forth on silent feet. Every now and then he would cry — a wavery owl-like cry. I wrote some more.

"The light from my turtle lamp casts leaping shadows. To the beechnuts has come a small gray animal. I can't make out what — now, I see it. It's a flying squirrel. That surprises me, I've never seen a flying squirrel around here, but of course I haven't been up much after sunset."

When it grew too dark to see, I lit a fire, hoping it would not end the party. It did not, and the more I watched, the more I realized that all these animals were familiar with my camp. A white-footed mouse walked over my woodpile as if it were his.

I put out my candle and fell asleep when the fire turned to coals. Much later I was awakened by screaming. I lifted my head and looked into the moonlit forest. A few guests, still lingering at the party, saw me move, and dashed bashfully into the ground cover. One was big and slender. I thought perhaps a mink. As I slowly came awake, I realized that screaming was coming from behind me. Something was in my house. I jumped up and shouted, and two raccoons skittered under my feet. I reached for my candle, slipped on hundreds of nuts, and fell. When I finally got a light and looked about me, I was dismayed to see what a mess my guests had made of my tree house. They had found the cache of acorns and beechnuts and had tossed them all over my bed and floor. The party was getting rough.

I chased the raccoons into the night and stumbled over a third animal and was struck by a wet stinging spray. It was skunk! I was drenched. As I got used to the indignity and the smell, I saw the raccoons cavort around my fireplace and dodge past me. They were back in my tree before I could stop them.

A bat winged in from the darkness and circled the tallow candle. It was Halloween and the goblins were at work.

Having invited all these neighbors, I was now faced with the problem of getting rid of them. The raccoons were feeling so much at home that they snatched up beechnuts, bits of dried fish and venison and tossed them playfully into the air. They were too full to eat any more, but were having a marvelous time making toys out of my hard-won winter food supply.

I herded the raccoons out of the tree and laced the door. I was breathing "relief" when I turned my head to the left, for I sensed someone watching me. There in the moonlight, his big ears erect on his head, sat the red fox. He was smiling — I know he was. I shouted, "Stop laughing!" and he vanished like a magician's handkerchief.

All this had awakened Frightful, who was flopping in the dark in the tree. I reached in around the deer flap to stroke her back to calmness. She grabbed me so hard I yelled — and the visitors moved to the edge of my camp at my cry.

Smelling to the sky, bleeding in the hand, and robbed of part of my hard-won food, I threw wood on the fire and sent an enormous shaft of light into the night. Then I shouted. The skunk moved farther away. The raccoons galloped off a few feet and galloped back. I snarled at them. They went to the edge of the darkness and stared at me. I had learned something that night from that very raccoon bossing Jessie C. James — to animals, might is right. I was biggest and I was oldest, and I was going to tell them so. I growled and snarled and hissed and snorted. It worked. They understood and moved away. Some looked back and their eyes glowed. The red eyes chilled me. Never had there been a more real Halloween night. The last bat of the season darted in the moonlight. I dove on my bed, and tied the door. There are no more notes about Halloween.

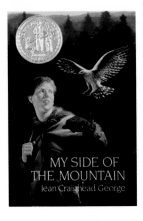

Think About the Selection

1. What does Sam's solution for staying warm through the winter tell you about him?

2. Think about Sam's loneliness on page 655. What are some ways a time of year can affect a person's feelings?

3. On page 665, Sam says that he has never experienced a "more real" Halloween night. What do you think he means?

4. How do you think Sam feels about the wild woodland creatures that live around him? Use details from the story to support your answer.

5. If it were up to you, would you have tried to persuade Sam to leave the wilderness? Why or why not?

6. Do you think you would enjoy a wilderness experience similar to Sam's? Why or why not?

7. **Connecting/Comparing** Compare Sam's fictional woodland adventure with the real-life wilderness experiences of Michio Hoshino and Andreia Martins in this theme. How are they different? How are they alike?

Write Directions

A person who relies on food from the forest would need to know what food to eat and how to prepare it. Use information in the selection to write directions for making a wilderness meal. Include choices for a main course, side dish, and dessert.

Tips

- List the ingredients needed for each course of the meal.
- Use a sequence of steps to explain how to gather and prepare the food.

Social Studies

Make a Picture Map

With a partner, take notes about Sam's camp and the trees, animals, and land he describes. Then make a picture map, using small pictures to show the camp and its surroundings. Include a key that explains the pictures you have used.

Bonus Give a presentation in which you compare a picture map to another kind of map, such as a road map or a contour map. Tell in what situation each map would be useful.

Viewing

Update an Illustration

Choose an illustration from the selection. Study it carefully. Then show in a drawing or describe in a paragraph how the scene in that illustration might look hours later, one month later, or one year later.

Tips

- Ask yourself how the illustration would look in a different season.
- If the illustration shows the day, consider how it might look at night — or vice versa.

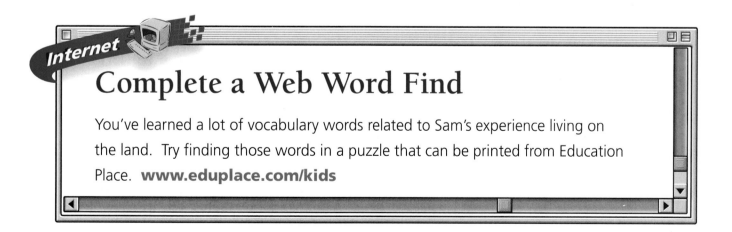

Internet

Complete a Web Word Find

You've learned a lot of vocabulary words related to Sam's experience living on the land. Try finding those words in a puzzle that can be printed from Education Place. **www.eduplace.com/kids**

Skill: How to Categorize Information

Categorizing helps you to organize ideas by **classifying** items that have something in common.

As you read . . .

- When you come to a group of items or ideas, identify what **category** they have in common. Use **headings** for each category, such as Animal Injuries, or Medical Instruments.

- Divide a broad category into two or more **narrower categories**. For example, the category Animals could be divided into Endangered Animals and Pets.

Robin Hughes: Wildlife Doctor

Dr. Robin Hughes could give Sam Gribley advice. She formerly worked as wildlife veterinarian at the Virginia Living Museum in Newport News, Virginia.

by Susan Yoder Ackerman

As I walked into her office, Robin was on the phone. "Yes," she was saying, "hummingbirds need more than sugar water. They need protein. Fruit flies are perfect for them!"

Robin's understanding of small wild birds is no wonder, growing up as she did with the name Robin. While her friends were selling Kool-Aid on hot days, little Robin set up a veterinary stand. She stocked it with her stethoscope, long sticks for splints, and lots of gauze. The neighborhood pets showed up with their sore paws and torn ears.

As she got older, Robin decided to go to veterinary school to learn all she could about dogs and cats and horses. But she didn't stop there. Pursuing her interest in wild animals, she cared for gazelles at the Kansas City Zoo. She learned to know the white ibises who feed on fiddler crabs on Pumpkin Seed Island in South Carolina. She worried over the growth on a Gila monster's tongue in California's Living Desert.

So, when Robin finally became Dr. Robin Hughes, she wasn't content in private practice treating mostly cats and dogs. She came to the Virginia Living Museum, where she has the care of live-animal exhibits that reflect Virginia's wildlife in its native habitat. And though she uses all the training she's had, sometimes she feels as if she's writing her own medical book. How do you medicate a sick beaver? Just figure out the dosage for a very large guinea pig! What about an otter? Try what's good for ferrets. A skunk with heart disease? Perhaps the treatment for a small dog would be most appropriate. Robin studies diet, behavior, tooth structure, and anatomy to figure out the best way to treat her patients. Has she ever treated a wild animal she couldn't match to a domestic one?

"A possum!" she said with a laugh. "Possums are clearly in a class of their own! *The Care and Treatment of Possums* is a book nobody has written yet."

Besides nursing raccoons and giving advice on the diet of hummingbirds, what does Robin do in the course of a day? Happily for her, every day is different. As curator of animals and a veterinarian, she may find herself out on a trawler in the York River, using a seine net to find new fish for the aquarium display. She might be rescuing injured waterfowl to bring to the outdoor wetlands aviary. She might travel to a distant wooded lake and release half-grown beavers into the wild. Other days she adjusts the diets for all the animals on the museum grounds.

And then there are the days when Robin really shows her stuff. Such as the day she needed to operate on an eastern diamondback rattlesnake to remove a mass growing under its eye. A fungal infection was causing inflammatory tissue to form into a granuloma. Robin said that snakes in the wild often get abscesses and tumors, but she didn't want any snake under her care to crawl off into a corner to die. So she scrubbed up and got started.

Robin vented anesthetic gas through a small hose in the lid of a sealed aquarium until the snake was asleep. (Since a sleeping snake doesn't look a whole lot different from a snake that's awake, this was the tricky part.) Then, taking the snake out of the aquarium, she put a tube down its windpipe to control the amount of anesthesia until the procedure was over.

Cutting into the skin so near the venomous fangs was also risky. Just to be safe, Robin placed corks over the fangs during surgery. And, to save herself a lot of trouble, she closed the incision with sutures that would dissolve all by themselves. A rattlesnake might not want to hold still to get its stitches taken out.

Sometimes Robin finds herself running a maternity ward. A couple of newborn baby otters stole the show at the museum for months, and black-crowned night herons hatched their young in the outdoor aviary. One year Robin and everyone else tiptoed around the bald eagle enclosure for thirty-eight days, hoping that the eggs the pair was guarding would hatch. They never did, but Robin hopes that the adult birds, injured by hunters in the wild, will someday produce perfect little bald eagles that can fly wherever they wish.

Then there are the exciting outdoor dramas that take place when the larger animals get vaccinated. The deer, foxes, and otter don't like injections any more than people do, so Robin has to come prepared. Sometimes she uses a dart gun to carry the vaccine; sometimes she'll throw a net around the animal to hold it still. Even so, there can be surprises, such as the time the thirty-pound bobcat leaped onto Robin's back when she turned to get the vaccine ready! She wasn't injured, but the incident made her aware that he was still a wild animal, even though he'd been hand-raised as an orphan. She never turns her back to him now if she has to enter his enclosure.

Bobcat, rattlesnake, hummingbird, raccoon — Dr. Robin is there for them. She also cares about the half million people who visit the Virginia Living Museum each year. Robin wants visitors to walk away with a greater appreciation and concern for Virginia's wildlife.

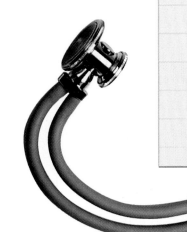

Career File

Veterinarian

Do you like taking care of animals? If so, consider becoming a veterinarian. As a vet, you'll have a chance to help house pets, wild animals, farm or zoo animals by . . .

- caring for them when they're sick or injured
- making sure they eat healthy diets
- giving them the medicine or vitamins they need
- studying diseases that could affect them

After college, you'll need a degree from a four-year veterinary school. You'll also need to pass a state exam in the state where you want to work. In the meantime, you can learn more about what a veterinarian does by volunteering at a local animal hospital, humane society, zoo, or farm.

✓ Writing an Opinion Essay

You may take a test that asks you to write an essay stating your opinion about a *prompt*, or a particular topic. Read this sample test prompt. Then use the tips when you write an opinion essay.

> Write an essay that gives your opinion about why people should or should not keep wild animals as pets.

Here is the planning chart one student made.

> *Wild animals should <u>not</u> be pets.*
>
> | *Supporting Reasons* | *Details* |
> |---|---|
> | *1. They can be dangerous.* | *1. rabies, other harmful diseases* |
> | *2. happier in their natural habitats* | *2. may get angry and attack as pets* |
> | *3. not treated properly* | *3. fed human food, won't know how to get food, may starve* |

Read the opinion essay that the same student wrote and the features that make it a good essay.

Wild Animals As Pets

I do not think wild animals should be kept as pets. I think wild animals should be wild. There are many reasons why I think this.

First of all, wild animals can be dangerous. For example, many wild animals have rabies and other diseases. You could get the diseases if you kept the animal as a pet.

Also, wild animals are happier in their habitats. If kept as pets, they could become angry and attack you.

Lastly, most people don't know how to treat wild animals, and they spoil them. Therefore, if the animal goes back into the wild it will have forgotten skills it was born with, like finding or hunting food.

Each paragraph has a topic sentence that tells the main idea.

The reasons are strong and are supported with details.

The writing sounds like the writer.

There are few mistakes in capitalization, punctuation, grammar, or spelling.

The ending of the essay should sum up the important points.

Glossary

This glossary contains meanings and pronunciations for some of the words in this book. The Full Pronunciation Key shows how to pronounce each consonant and vowel in a special spelling. At the bottom of the glossary pages is a shortened form of the full key.

Full Pronunciation Key

Consonant Sounds

b	**b**i**b**, ca**bb**age	kw	**ch**oir, **qu**ick	t	**t**igh**t**, stopp**ed**
ch	**ch**ur**ch**, sti**tch**	l	**l**id, need**l**e, ta**ll**	th	ba**th**, **th**in
d	**d**ee**d**, mail**ed**, pu**dd**le	m	a**m**, **m**an, du**mb**	*th*	ba**th**e, **th**is
		n	**n**o, sudd**en**	v	ca**v**e, val**v**e, **v**ine
f	**f**ast, **f**i**f**e, o**ff**, **ph**rase, rou**gh**	ng	thi**ng**, i**nk**	w	**w**ith, **w**olf
g	**g**a**g**, **g**et, fin**g**er	p	**p**o**p**, ha**pp**y	y	**y**es, **y**olk, on**i**on
h	**h**at, **wh**o	r	**r**oa**r**, **rh**yme	z	ro**s**e, si**z**e, **x**ylophone, **z**ebra
hw	**wh**ich, **wh**ere	s	mi**ss**, **s**auce, **sc**ene, **s**ee	zh	gara**g**e, plea**s**ure, vi**s**ion
j	**j**u**dg**e, **g**em	sh	di**sh**, **sh**ip, **s**ugar, ti**ss**ue		
k	**c**at, **k**i**ck**, s**ch**ool				

Vowel Sounds

ă	p**a**t, l**au**gh	ŏ	h**o**rrible, p**o**t	ŭ	c**u**t, fl**oo**d, r**ou**gh, s**o**me
ā	**a**pe, **ai**d, p**ay**	ō	g**o**, r**ow**, t**oe**, th**ough**	û	c**ir**cle, f**ur**, h**ear**d, t**er**m, t**ur**n, **ur**ge, w**or**d
â	**air**, c**are**, w**ear**	ô	**a**ll, c**au**ght, f**or**, p**aw**		
ä	f**a**ther, k**o**ala, y**ar**d	oi	b**oy**, n**oi**se, **oi**l		
ĕ	p**e**t, pl**ea**sure, **a**ny	ou	c**ow**, **ou**t	yŏŏ	c**u**re
ē	b**e**, b**ee**, **ea**sy, pian**o**	ŏŏ	f**u**ll, b**oo**k, w**o**lf	yōō	ab**u**se, **u**se
ĭ	**i**f, p**i**t, b**u**sy	ōō	b**oo**t, r**u**de, fr**ui**t, fl**ew**	ə	**a**go, sil**e**nt, penc**i**l, lem**o**n, circ**u**s
ī	r**i**de, b**y**, p**ie**, h**igh**				
î	d**ear**, d**eer**, f**ier**ce, m**ere**				

Stress Marks

Primary Stress ´: bi·ol·o·gy [bī **ŏl´** ə jē]
Secondary Stress ´: bi·o·log·i·cal [bī´ ə **lŏj´** ĭ kəl]

A

ab·o·li·tion·ist (ăb´ ə **lĭsh´** ə nĭst) *n.* A person who felt that slavery should be against the law. *Quakers and other **abolitionists** believed that owning slaves was wrong.*

a·bun·dant (ə **bŭn´** dənt) *adj.* More than enough; plentiful. *Fish and game were **abundant** along the coast.*

ac·com·pa·ni·ment (ə **kŭm´** pə nĭ mənt) *n.* A musical part, usually played on an instrument, that goes along with the performance of a singer or musician. *Victoria sang to the **accompaniment** of a guitar.*

ad·ven·ture (əd **vĕn´** chər) *n.* An unusual or exciting experience. *Greg thought that sailing to Africa would be a real **adventure**.*

ag·gres·sive (ə **grĕs´** ĭv) *adj.* Ready and quick to fight; bold. *The bear cub snarled in an **aggressive** way.*

am·a·teur (**ăm´** ə chər) *n.* Someone who performs a sport or other activity without being paid. *You must be an **amateur** to compete in high school sports.*

a·maz·ing·ly (ə **mā´** zĭng lē) *adv.* In a way that causes surprise or wonder. *The test questions were **amazingly** easy.*

ap·plause (ə **plôz´**) *n.* The clapping of hands to show approval. *Adam's speech was greeted with loud **applause**.*

ap·pren·tice (ə **prĕn´** tĭs) *n.* Someone who works for another person in order to learn a trade. *The blacksmith helped the **apprentice** learn how to use the tools.*

arm (ärm) *v.* To equip with weapons. *The rebels were **arming** themselves as the British troops approached the town.*

ar·ti·fi·cial (är´ tə **fĭsh´** əl) *adj.* Created by humans rather than occuring in nature. *The zookeepers built an **artificial** den for the lion to live in.*

ar·tis·tic (är **tĭs´** tĭk) *adj.* Showing imagination and skill in creating something beautiful. *The dancers gave an **artistic** performance.*

as·tro·naut (**ăs´** trə nôt) *n.* A person trained to fly in a spacecraft. *Neil Armstrong was the first **astronaut** to walk on the moon.*

at·tach·ment (ə **tăch´** mənt) *n.* A feeling of closeness and affection. *The two cousins have a strong **attachment** to one another.*

amateur
Amateur comes from the Latin word *amare*, which means "to love." Someone who is an amateur takes part in an activity for the love of it.

apprentice
Apprentice comes from the Latin word *apprehendere*, which means "to grasp." An apprentice is a learner who must grasp what to do in a profession.

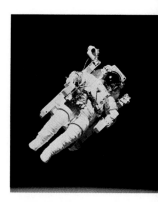

astronaut
This word was created in 1929 by combining two ancient Greek word parts, *astro-* and *nautes*, which translate as "star sailor."

ōō b**oo**t / ou **ou**t / ŭ c**u**t / û f**u**r / hw **wh**ich / th **th**in / *th* **th**is / zh vi**s**ion / ə **a**go, sil**e**nt, penc**i**l, lem**o**n, circ**u**s

braille
Louis Braille (1809–1852) was a French inventor who lost his sight at the age of three and as a student of fifteen created the unique writing system that bears his name.

canopy
The Greek word *konopeion,* a bed with a netting to keep out mosquitoes, gave us the word for the covering created by treetops in a rain forest.

caribou
Caribou is the Canadian French version of a Native American word — the Micmac *khalibu,* which means "snow scraper."

au·di·ence (ô′ dē əns) *n.* People who gather to see and hear a performance. *The audience cheered loudly as the singer bowed.*

B

ban·dit (băn′ dĭt) *n.* An outlaw, especially one who robs. *The bandit demanded that the passengers hand over their wallets.*

bluff (blŭf) *n.* A high cliff or bank. *From the top of the bluff, he could see the entire valley.*

braille (brāl) *n.* A system of writing that uses raised dots, for people who are visually impaired. *Angela ran her fingers over the braille letters on the page.*

C

cache (kăsh) *n.* A store of hidden goods. *The bear dug up the campers' cache of food.*

can·o·py (kăn′ ə pē) *n.* The highest layer of a forest, formed by the treetops. *Many kinds of parrots and monkeys live in the dense canopy of the rain forest.*

cap·tive (kăp′ tĭv) *n.* A prisoner. *The soldiers brought their captives back to the fort.* — *adj.* Captured; held against one's will. *The captive squirrel managed to escape from the trap.*

car·cass (kär′ kəs) *n.* The dead body of an animal. *The wolves fed on the carcass of a deer.*

car·go (kär′ gō) *n., pl.* **cargoes.** The freight carried by a ship or other vehicle. *The ship's cargo included molasses from the West Indies.*

car·i·bou (kăr′ ə boo′) *n., pl.* **caribou.** A large deer found in northern North America, related to the reindeer. *The herd of caribou swam across the river.*

cau·tious (kô′ shəs) *adj.* Careful; not taking chances. *It is best to be cautious when crossing a busy street.*

cel·e·bra·tion (sĕl′ ə brā′ shən) *n.* A special activity that honors a person, event, or idea. *I invited ten friends to my birthday celebration.*

cin·der (sĭn′ dər) *n.* A partly burned piece of coal or wood. *A pile of cinders lay at the bottom of the fire pit.*

claim (klām) *n.* A piece of land that someone reserves for ownership. *The settlers took a claim that bordered on the river.*

col·lide (kə līd′) *v.* To come together with forceful impact. *When warm and cold air masses collide, the weather becomes stormy.*

ă rat / ā pay / â care / ä father / ĕ pet / ē be / ĭ pit / ī pie / î fierce / ŏ pot / ō go / ô paw, for / oi oil / ŏŏ book

D

col·o·ny (kŏl´ ə nē) *n., pl.*
colonies A territory ruled by or
belonging to another country.
The thirteen **colonies** *no longer
wanted to be taxed by England.*

com·pete (kəm pēt´) *v.* To take
part in a contest. *The runners
hoped to* **compete** *in the Boston
Marathon.*

con·cen·trate (kŏn´ sən trāt´) *v.*
To give full attention to. *It is difficult to* **concentrate** *on my book
when the television is on.*

con·flict (kŏn´ flĭkt´) *n.* A struggle; a war. *The United States had
a second* **conflict** *with England
in 1812.*

con·vinced (kən vĭnsd´) *adj.*
Persuaded; certain. *They were*
convinced *that the bridge was
strong enough to carry their
weight.*

cra·ter (krā´ tər) *n.* A hollow
bowl-shaped area at the mouth of
a volcano. *The hikers peered
down into the deep rocky* **crater**
below.

crust (krŭst) *n.* The hard outer
layer of the earth. *Cracks in the
earth's* **crust** *help create volcanoes.*

cus·tom (kŭs´ təm) *n.* Something that members of a group
usually do. *One of the* **customs**
*of people in the desert is to offer
visitors refreshment and shade.*

de·bris (də brē´) *n.* The remains
of something broken or destroyed;
rubble. *The bulldozer pushed the*
debris *into the corner of the lot.*

de·but (dā byoō´) *n.* First public
performance. *The actor made his
stage* **debut** *as Peter Pan.*

dec·o·rate (dĕk´ ə rāt´) *v.* To
make festive or beautiful. *We will*
decorate *the room with flowers
and streamers.*

dem·on·stra·tion (dĕm´ ən strā´
shən) *n.* A showing and explanation of how something works.
The teacher gave a **demonstration** *of how to operate a camera.*

de·scrip·tion (dĭ skrĭp´ shən) *n.*
A statement that uses words to
tell about something. *Debbie
wrote an exciting* **description** *of
the game.*

de·tain (dĭ tān´) *v.* To delay; to
hold back. *If you* **detain** *us much
longer, we will miss the bus.*

de·ter·mi·na·tion (dĭ tûr´ mə nā´
shən) *n.* Firmness in carrying
out a decision. *The team's* **determination** *to do better showed in
how well they played.*

dev·as·ta·tion (dĕv´ ə stā´ shən)
n. Destruction or ruin. *The
floods brought* **devastation** *to
much of the coast.*

crater

---

o͞o b**oo**t / ou **ou**t / ŭ c**u**t / û f**u**r / hw **wh**ich / th **th**in / *th* **th**is / zh vi**s**ion / ə **a**go,
s**i**lent, penc**i**l, lem**o**n, circ**u**s

dex·ter·i·ty (dĕk stĕr´ ĭ tē) *n.* Skill in the use of the hands, body, or mind. *The juggler showed great* **dexterity** *in keeping the oranges in the air.*

di·a·ry (dī´ ə rē) *n., pl.* **diaries.** A daily record of a person's thoughts and experiences. *Every night Marta wrote about the day's events in her* **diary.**

dic·ta·tor (dĭk´ tā tər) *n.* A ruler who has complete power over a country. *The* **dictator** *would not allow any citizens to travel outside the country.*

di·lem·ma (dĭ lĕm´ ə) *n.* A situation in which one has to choose between two or more difficult options. *Sara's* **dilemma** *was whether to wake up her father or try to figure out the problem herself.*

dim sum (dĭm´ so͝om´) *n.* A type of traditional Chinese meal where small portions of different foods are served one after another. *Many Chinese restaurants serve* **dim sum** *on Sunday mornings.*

dis·ap·point·ed (dĭs´ ə point´ əd) *adj.* Unhappy because of an unsatisfied hope or wish. *Tanya was* **disappointed** *when her team lost the game.*

dis·com·fort (dĭs kŭm´ fərt) *n.* A feeling of mild distress. *Noah always feels* **discomfort** *when people ask him about his famous brother.*

dominance
The root of this word is the Latin word *domus,* meaning "house." The head of a household often had control, or dominance, over a large staff of people.

dim sum

dis·cour·aged (dĭ skûr´ ĭjd) *adj.* Not hopeful or enthusiastic. *Sam felt* **discouraged** *when he learned that he had not won a prize.*

dis·mayed (dĭs mād´) *adj.* Filled with sudden concern or distress. *They were* **dismayed** *to learn that the bus had left without them.*

dog guide (dôg gīd) *n.* A dog especially trained to lead visually impaired people. *May's* **dog guide** *waited until it was safe to cross the street.*

dom·i·nance (dŏm´ ə nəns) *n.* The greatest control within a group. *Wolves compete for* **dominance** *in the pack.*

dread (drĕd) *n.* Great fear. *The panther's roar filled the villagers with* **dread.**

drill (drĭl) *v.* To perform training exercises. *The soldiers were* **drilling** *all morning.*

du·o (do͞o´ ō) *n.* Two people performing together. *The sisters performed in the show as a singing* **duo.**

E

earth·quake (ûrth´ kwāk´) *n.* A trembling or shaking of the ground caused by sudden movements in rock below the earth's surface. *The* **earthquake** *caused buildings to topple.*

ă rat / ā pay / â care / ä father / ĕ pet / ē be / ĭ pit / ī pie / î fierce / ŏ pot / ō go / ô paw, for / oi oil / o͝o book

el·e·ment (ĕl´ ə mənt) *n.* A basic part of a whole. *Spirals, spins, and jumps are **elements** of a figure skating program.*

em·bar·rassed (ĕm băr´ əsd) *adj.* Made to feel self-conscious and ill at ease. *Josh felt **embarrassed** when he realized he had called her by the wrong name.*

en·cour·age (ĕn kûr´ ĭj) *v.* To give support to; to inspire. *Hal's parents **encouraged** him to become a skater.*

en·slave·ment (ĕn slāv´ mənt) *n.* The process by which one person becomes the property of another. *After years of **enslavement** by cruel owners, the men were set free.*

e·rup·tion (ĭ rŭp´ shən) *n.* A volcanic explosion or large flow of lava. *The newspaper showed photos of the **eruption** of a volcano in Nicaragua.*

ex·cite·ment (ĭk sīt´ mənt) *n.* A stirred-up feeling. *The fire caused a lot of **excitement** in our neighborhood.*

ex·per·i·ence (ĭk spîr´ ē əns) *n.* An event that someone takes part in or lives through. *Camping was a new **experience** for the children.*

ex·press (ĭk sprĕs´) *adj.* Fast, direct, and often nonstop. ***Express** services promise overnight deliveries.*

ex·tend·ed (ĭk stĕn´ dĭd) *adj.* Including more; broadened. *Your **extended** family includes your aunts, uncles, and cousins.*

ex·tinc·tion (ĭk stĭngk´ shən) *n.* The condition of having died out. *No one knows for sure what caused the **extinction** of the dinosaurs.*

F

fash·ion (făsh´ ən) *v.* To give a form or shape to; to make. *Ralph was able to **fashion** a waterproof cape from a large plastic bag.*

fault (fôlt) *n.* A break in a rock mass caused by a shifting of the earth's crust. *An active **fault** runs through the center of our town.*

fer·tile (fûr´ tl) *adj.* Rich in material needed to grow healthy plants. *Wheat and corn grew well in the prairie's **fertile** soil.*

fes·tive (fĕs´ tĭv) *adj.* Joyful; merry. *The party guests were in a **festive** mood.*

fierce (fîrs) *adj.* Intense; ferocious. *The lion gave a **fierce** roar.*

for·ty-five re·cord (fôr´ tē fīv´ rĕk´ ərd) *n.* A small phonograph record that is played at forty-five revolutions per minute. *The **forty-five record** has one song on each side.*

eruption

fierce
The Latin word *ferus* ("wild and savage") is the origin of the words *ferocious* and *fierce.*

ōō b**oo**t / ou **ou**t / ŭ c**u**t / û f**u**r / hw **wh**ich / th **th**in / *th* **th**is / zh vi**si**on / ə **a**go, sil**e**nt, pen**ci**l, lem**o**n, cir**cu**s

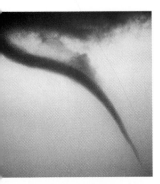

funnel cloud

fran·tic (**frăn´** tĭk) *adj.* Very upset, as from fear or worry. *When she couldn't find her backpack anywhere, Julie became frantic.*

fright·ened (**frīt´** nd) *adj.* Scared, alarmed. *Billy was frightened as he stepped out on the diving board.*

fun·nel cloud (**fŭn´** əl kloud´) *n.* A storm cloud that is wide at the top and narrow at the bottom, often becoming a tornado. *Whenever the settlers saw funnel clouds, they hurried toward storm shelters.*

G

gene (jēn) *n.* A tiny part of a plant or animal cell that determines a characteristic passed on to the next generation. *Lucy has blue eyes like her parents because of their genes.*

H

hab·i·tat (**hăb´** ĭ tăt´) *n.* The type of environment where an animal or plant naturally lives and grows. *Sloths and jaguars live in the rain forest habitat.*

harsh (härsh) *adj.* Demanding and severe; unpleasant. *Winter is a harsh season for most animals.*

har·vest (**här´** vĭst) *v.* To gather a crop. *The workers were harvesting apples.*

heif·er (**hĕf´** ər) *n.* A young cow that has not yet had a calf. *Sally's cow has been winning blue ribbons since it was a heifer.*

herd (hûrd) *n.* A group of animals of a single kind. *A herd of wild horses galloped across the plain.*

her·i·tage (**hĕr´** ĭ tĭj) *n.* Traditions, practices, and beliefs passed down from earlier generations. *Yinglan celebrates her Chinese heritage in her choice of music, clothes, and food.*

home·stead (**hōm´** stĕd´) *n.* A piece of land given to settlers for farming and building a home. *The Andersens' homestead lay near Blackberry Creek.*

hon·or (**ŏn´** ər) *v.* To show respect for; to accept. *They will honor their mother's request to dress up for Thanksgiving dinner.*

hu·mid (**hyōo´** mĭd) *adj.* Containing a large amount of water vapor; damp, sticky. *The air is often humid before a storm.*

I

im·mi·grant (**ĭm´** ĭ grənt) *n.* A person who moves to a new country. *Many immigrants from Norway made their homes on the Great Plains.*

ă **rat** / ā **pay** / â **care** / ä **father** / ĕ **pet** / ē **be** / ĭ **pit** / ī **pie** / î **fierce** / ŏ **pot** / ō **go** / ô **paw, for** / oi **oil** / ŏŏ **book**

J

im·mo·bile (ĭ **mō**´ bəl) *adj.* Fixed in one place; unable to move. *He stood **immobile** against the cliff face as the hikers passed by.*

im·pact (**ĭm**´ păkt´) *n.* The striking of one object against another. *The **impact** of the bike hitting the fence knocked the flowerpots to the ground.*

im·press (ĭm **prĕs**´) *v.* To have a strong, favorable effect on someone's feelings. *His piano playing **impressed** the audience.*

in·flu·en·tial (ĭn´ flŏŏ **ĕn**´ shəl) *adj.* Having the power to affect events or sway opinions. *The **influential** Women's League brought the problem to the mayor's attention.*

in·her·it (ĭn **hĕr**´ ĭt) *v.* To receive something from a parent or ancestor. *They **inherited** their mother's talent for music.*

in·stinct (**ĭn**´ stĭngkt´) *n.* An inner feeling or way of behaving that is automatic, not learned. *A newly hatched sea turtle's **instinct** is to crawl toward the water.*

in·tense (ĭn **tĕns**´) *adj.* Very strong; focused. *Patrice put in hours of **intense** study to get ready for the test.*

jag·ged (**jăg**´ ĭd) *adj.* Having a ragged or pointed edge or outline. *Jamal cut his hand on a **jagged** piece of tin.*

jar (jär) *v.* To bump or cause to shake from impact. *By **jarring** Matthew, I caused him to drop the ball.*

jolt (jōlt) *n.* A sudden jerk or bump. *When the car went over the speed bump, the passengers got quite a **jolt**.*

judge (jŭj) *n.* A person who decides who wins a contest. *The **judges** awarded first prize to my grandfather's pumpkin pie.*

just (jŭst) *adj.* Honorable and fair. *It is **just** to listen to both sides of an argument.*

K

kin (kĭn) *n.* Relatives; family. *Your father's cousins are your **kin**, too.*

L

launch (lônch) *v.* To forcefully send upward. *A powerful blast **launches** the rocket into the sky.*

la·va (**lä**´ və) *n.* Hot melted rock that flows from a volcano. *As the **lava** moved down the hillside, it set fire to the trees in its path.*

lava
People from Naples, Italy, near Mt. Vesuvius, used the Italian word *lava*, meaning "a stream caused suddenly by rain" for the molten rock that flowed down the volcano. It became an English word in 1750.

ōō b**oo**t / ou **ou**t / ŭ c**u**t / û f**u**r / hw **wh**ich / th **th**in / *th* **th**is / zh vi**s**ion / ə **a**go, sil**e**nt, penc**i**l, lem**o**n, circ**u**s

681

lay·out (lā´ out´) *n.* The way something is arranged. *The layout of the office building confuses visitors.*

lib·er·ty (lĭb´ ər tē) *n.* Freedom from the control of others; independence. *The colonists won their liberty from England.*

light·ning (līt´ nĭng) *n.* The flash of light when electricity builds up in storm clouds. *A bolt of lightning lit up the night sky.*

lime·light (līm´ līt´) *n.* The center of public attention. *Ana's performance in the play brought her into the limelight.*

limelight
In the 1800s, theaters used limelights, made by burning the mineral lime. That bright stage light came to stand for the attention of the public.

M

mag·ma (măg´ mə) *n.* Molten rock underneath the earth's surface. *Magma boiled up through cracks deep inside the mountain.*

mare (mâr) *n.* A female horse. *Some of the mares were followed by their colts.*

mas·ter (măs´ tər) *v.* To become expert in a skill or art. *Ramón mastered the violin through years of practice.*

ma·ture (mə tyo͞or´) *adj.* Fully grown or mentally developed. *A mature dog is calmer than a puppy.*

mem·o·rize (mĕm´ ə rīz´) *v.* To learn by completely remembering. *The hikers are memorizing the landmarks along their route.*

mustang
This word for a wild horse came from the Mexican Spanish word *mestengo,* which means "stray animal."

mi·gra·tion (mī grā´ shən) *n.* A movement of animals to a different habitat, especially in response to the change of seasons. *Scientists have mapped the spring migration of the whales.*

mill (mĭl) *v.* To move around in confusion. *The impatient crowd milled in front of the theater doors.*

mis·sion (mĭsh´ ən) *n.* An operation that attempts to achieve certain goals or carry out specific tasks. *The astronauts' mission included bringing back samples of moon rocks.*

mol·ten (mōl´ tən) *adj.* Made liquid by heat. *The molten lava glowed red-orange.*

mus·tang (mŭs´ tăng´) *n.* A wild horse of the plains of western North America. *Joe could not ride as fast as the herd of mustangs.*

N

no·ble (nō´ bəl) *adj.* Showing greatness of character by unselfish behavior. *It was noble of Karen to share her prize money with her teammates.*

no·to·ri·ous (nō tôr´ ē əs) *adj.* Well known for something bad. *Billy the Kid was a notorious outlaw.*

ă rat / ā pay / â care / ä father / ĕ pet / ē be / ĭ pit / ī pie / î fierce / ŏ pot / ō go / ô paw, for / oi oil / o͝o book

O

o·be·di·ence (ō **bē´** dē əns) *n.* Willingness to follow orders. *Mr. Yee expects* **obedience** *from his crew.*

ob·ser·va·tion (ŏb´ zûr **vā´** shən) *n.* The act of paying careful attention. *You can learn a lot about nature through* **observation**.

ob·sta·cle (**ŏb´** stə kəl) *n.* A thing that stands in one's way. *The horse had to jump over such* **obstacles** *as bushes and fences.*

op·er·a (**ŏp´** ə rə) *n.* A form of theater in which the dialogue is sung to musical accompaniment. *The actors in the* **opera** *wore beautiful costumes.*

op·pose (ə **pōz´**) *v.* To be against something or someone. *The neighbors* **oppose** *the plan to turn the park into an office building.*

or·bit (**ôr´** bĭt) *n.* The path of a spacecraft around the earth. *Shannon Lucid spent six months in* **orbit** *aboard the spacecraft Mir.*

o·ver·take (ō´ vər **tāk´**) *v.* To catch up with. *If we continue at this pace, we will* **overtake** *Billie's group.*

P

pan·to·mime (**păn´** tə mīm´) *n.* The use of movements and facial expressions instead of words to convey meaning. *Jean used* **pantomime** *to show us how she caught the fish.*

Pa·tri·ot (**pā´** trē ət) *n.* A colonist who was against British rule in the time of the Revolutionary War. *Patrick Henry spoke as a* **Patriot** *when he said "Give me liberty or give me death!"*

peer (pîr) *v.* To look at with concentration. *Mom* **peered** *at Paul suspiciously as he told his story.*

pi·o·neer (pī´ ə **nîr´**) *adj.* Describing a person who is first or among the first to settle in a region. *Our town was settled by three* **pioneer** *families in the 1800s.*

prai·rie (**prâr´** ē) *n.* A large area of flat or rolling grassland. *The treeless* **prairie** *stretched for miles in all directions.*

pred·a·tor (**prĕd´** ə tər) *n.* An animal that hunts other animals for food. *Small lizards must always be on the alert for hungry* **predators**.

pres·en·ta·tion (prĕz´ ən **tā´** shən) *n.* Performance. *Although the actor knew his lines, his* **presentation** *was flat.*

pioneer
This word comes from the French word *peonier,* meaning "foot soldier." Those who marched into unknown territory were often soldiers on an expedition.

---

oo b**oo**t / ou **ou**t / ŭ c**u**t / û f**u**r / hw **wh**ich / th **th**in / *th* **th**is / zh vi**si**on / ə **a**go, sil**e**nt, penc**i**l, lem**o**n, circ**u**s

pres·sure (**prĕsh´** ər) *n.* A strong influence or force. *Sandra felt **pressure** to finish the book over the weekend.*

pri·va·teer (prī´ və **tîr´**) *n.* A privately owned ship that is ordered by the government to attack enemy ships during a war. *The **privateers** captured several merchant ships without firing a shot.*

pro·gram (**prō´** grăm´) *n.* In figure skating, the routine that one performs in front of judges or an audience. *The young skater spent hours getting his **program** ready for the competition.*

prose (prōz) *n.* Ordinary spoken or written language, in contrast to poetry. *Most fiction and nonfiction books are written in **prose**.*

R

raid (rād) *n.* A sudden attack, often with the goal of taking property. *The men brought back horses after their **raid** on their neighbors' village.*

ra·vine (rə **vēn´**) *n.* A narrow, deep valley, usually formed by the flow of water. *A small stream trickled at the bottom of the **ravine**.*

reb·el (**rĕb´** əl) *n.* A person who opposes or defies the government in power. *The **rebels** refused to obey King George's laws.*

ref·u·gee (**rĕf´** yoō jē´) *n.* A person who flees to find protection from danger. *As the fighting in the hills grew worse, **refugees** streamed into the city.*

re·hear·sal (rĭ **hûr´** səl) *n.* A session of practicing for a public performance. *The cast needed one more **rehearsal** before the play opened.*

re·in·tro·duc·tion (rē´ ĭn trə **dŭk´** shən) *n.* The process of returning animals to their native habitats. *The zoo's tamarins are doing well since their **reintroduction** into the rain forest.*

re·ject (rĭ **jĕkt´**) *v.* To refuse to accept. *The magazine **rejected** her poem.*

re·luc·tant (rĭ **lŭk´** tənt) *adj.* Unwilling to take an action. *Emily was **reluctant** to get out of the swimming pool.*

re·morse (rĭ **môrs´**) *n.* A feeling of regret or guilt for having done something wrong. *Jennie felt **remorse** for the trouble she had caused her sister.*

rep·u·ta·tion (rĕp´ yə **tā´** shən) *n.* What others think about someone's character, behavior, and abilities. *Alex had a **reputation** for getting along well with everyone.*

re·quired (rĭ **kwīrd´**) *adj.* Needed. *Kayla has all of the training **required** for this job.*

ravine

ă **r**a**t** / ā **p**ay / â **c**are / ä **f**ather / ĕ **p**et / ē **b**e / ĭ **p**it / ī **p**ie / î **fie**rce / ŏ **p**ot / ō **g**o / ô **p**aw, **fo**r / oi **oi**l / oō **b**ook

re·spect (rĭ **spĕkt´**) *n.* A feeling of admiration and approval. *Mr. García won the **respect** of all his students.*

re·us·a·ble (rē **yōōz´** ə bəl) *adj.* Able to be used again. *April's family never throws away **reusable** paper bags.*

rev·o·lu·tion·ar·y (rĕv´ ə **lōō´** shə nĕr´ ē) *adj.* Connected with complete change. *The American colonists fought for their independence from England during the **Revolutionary** War.*

rhyth·mic (**rĭth´** mĭk) *adj.* Having a noticeable beat with a pattern to it. *It is easy to dance to **rhythmic** music.*

ro·tate (**rō´** tāt) *v.* To turn around on a center or axis. *It takes twenty-four hours for the earth to **rotate** once.*

rug·ged (**rŭg´** ĭd) *adj.* Having a very rough and uneven surface. *The valley was surrounded by **rugged** mountains.*

S

sat·el·lite (**săt´** l īt´) *n.* A human-made device that orbits a planet. *A weather **satellite** sends weather photos and data back to earth.*

sen·try (**sĕn´** trē) *n., pl.,* **sentries**. A guard who is posted at a spot to keep watch. *Two **sentries** guarded the gates of the city.*

se·vere (sə **vîr´**) *adj.* Serious or extreme in nature. ***Severe** thunderstorms caused flooding in parts of the Midwest.*

shud·der (**shŭd´** ər) *v.* To suddenly shake, vibrate, or quiver. *The house **shuddered** every time a heavy truck drove by.*

siz·zling (**sĭz´** lĭng) *adj.* Crackling or hissing with intense heat. *The tree trunk was **sizzling** after the lightning bolt hit it.*

skir·mish (**skûr´** mĭsh) *n.* A small, short fight; a minor battle. *The soldiers galloped away after a brief **skirmish** with the rebels.*

skit·ter (**skĭt´** ər) *v.* To move lightly and quickly, especially with many changes of direction. *The mice **skittered** across the floor.*

skit·tish (**skĭt´** ĭsh) *adj.* Nervous and jumpy. *The cat was **skittish** during the thunderstorm.*

snoop (snōōp) *n.* Someone who tries to find out about other people's doings in a sneaky way. *Maria's brother is such a **snoop** that she must keep her diary locked.*

sod (sŏd) *n.* A chunk of grass and soil held together by matted roots. *Settlers built houses out of blocks of **sod** because wood was scarce.*

satellite
In the Middle Ages the French used the word *satellite* to refer to an attendant who waits upon an important person. That same idea is in the modern meaning of a small device circling around a planet.

ōō b**oo**t / ou **ou**t / ŭ c**u**t / û f**u**r / hw **wh**ich / th **th**in / *th* **th**is / zh vi**s**ion / ə **a**go, sil**e**nt, penc**i**l, lem**o**n, circ**u**s

sombrero
The name of the broad-brimmed hat that shades the wearer's eyes came from the Spanish word for shade, *sombra*.

shuttle
Shuttle started out as an Old English word, *scytel*, meaning "dart." It came to mean a weaving device that carried thread back and forth, and from that, a vehicle going back and forth over a short route.

som·bre·ro (sŏm brâr´ ō) *n.* A tall hat with a wide brim, worn in Mexico and the American Southwest. *The farmers wore sombreros to shade their eyes from the sun.*

space shut·tle (spās **shŭt´** l) *n.* A reusable spacecraft that is launched like a rocket and can be landed like a plane. *The space shuttle landed safely after a seven-day flight.*

space·craft (spās´ krăft´) *n.* A vehicle designed for travel beyond the earth's atmosphere. *The spacecraft carried astronauts to the moon.*

spe·cial·ist (spĕsh´ ə lĭst) *n.* Someone who is an expert in a particular field. *A pediatrician is a medical specialist who treats only children.*

spec·ta·tor (spĕk´ tā´ tər) *n.* A person who watches an event or performance. *The spectators cheered when Jessie hit a home run.*

splen·did (splĕn´ dĭd) *adj.* Excellent. *The actor gave a splendid performance.*

stal·lion (stăl´ yən) *n.* An adult male horse. *Lizzie rode a black stallion at the horse show.*

stam·i·na (stăm´ ə nə) *n.* The strength needed to keep doing something tiring or difficult. *A young child lacks the stamina for a ten-mile hike.*

store·house (stôr´ hous´) *n.* A place or building where supplies are stored for future use. *The settlers' storehouse contained dried fruit and hams.*

sub·mit (səb mĭt´) *v.* To offer one's work to someone for their judgment or approval. *She submitted an article to the student newspaper.*

sub·ser·vi·ence (səb sûr´ vē əns) *n.* Willingness to give in to others' power. *Letting the tail droop is a sign of subservience in a wolf.*

sum·mit (sŭm´ ĭt) *n.* The top of a mountain. *Carolyn and I cheered when we finally reached the summit of Mount Rainier.*

sur·viv·al (sər vī´ vəl) *n.* The preservation or continuation of one's life. *Quick thinking is often necessary for survival in the wilderness.*

sus·pect (sə spĕkt´) *v.* To believe without being sure; to imagine. *Scott suspects that we are planning a surprise party for him.*

T

tack (tăk) *v.* To change the course of a boat. *The sailing ship was tacking in order to return to the harbor.*

ă **r**a**t** / ā **pay** / â **care** / ä **fa**ther / ĕ **pet** / ē **be** / ĭ **pit** / ī **pie** / î **fie**rce / ŏ **pot** / ō **go** / ô **paw, fo**r / oi **oil** / o͝o **b**oo**k**

tal·ent (tăl´ ənt) *n.* A natural ability to do something well. *She has a talent for playing the violin.*

tax (tăks) *n.* Money that people must pay in order to support a government. *England insisted that the colonists pay taxes on tea, stamps, and many other items.*

tech·ni·cal (tĕk´ nĭ kəl) *adj.* Showing basic knowledge of a complex task. *The acrobat performed the triple somersault with great technical skill.*

ter·ri·fy (tĕr´ ə fī´) *v.* To fill with overpowering fear. *The angry bear terrified the campers.*

ter·ri·to·ry (tĕr´ ĭ tôr´ ē) *n., pl.* **territories**. An area inhabited by an animal or animal group and defended against intruders. *The mountain lion hunted within its own territory.*

To·ry (tôr´ ē) *n., pl.* **Tories**. An American who sided with the British during the American Revolution. *As the British troops departed, most of the city's Tories followed.*

tor·na·do (tôr nā´ dō) *n.* A violent, whirling wind in a funnel-shaped cloud that can cause great destruction. *Many tornadoes form in Kansas and Oklahoma.*

tra·di·tion (trə dĭsh´ ən) *n.* The passing down of customs and beliefs from one generation to the next. *There is a long tradition of helping others in our family.*

train·ing (trā´ nĭng) *n.* The process of learning how to behave or perform. *Guide dogs must go through a long period of training before they can help people.*

trans·form (trăns fôrm´) *v.* To change greatly in appearance or form. *The make-up transformed the actor into the character of an old man.*

tun·dra (tŭn´ drə) *n.* A treeless Arctic region where very few plants can grow. *Large plants cannot put down roots in the frozen subsoil of the tundra.*

U

un·der·stand (ŭn´ dər stănd´) *v.* To get the meaning of. *After the teacher explained it again, Ivan could understand the problem.*

un·du·lat·ing (ŭn´ jə lāt´ ĭng) *adj.* Moving in waves or with a smooth, wavy motion. *The undulating water raised and lowered the rowboat.*

un·sure (ŭn shoor´) *adj.* Not certain; having doubts. *She was unsure of whether to bring her umbrella.*

tornado
Tornadoes were unknown and unnamed in Britain, so Americans borrowed and adapted the Spanish word *tronada*, meaning "thunderstorm."

tradition
Our word for the passing down of customs from one generation to another comes from the Latin verb *tradere*, which means "to hand down."

undulate
The Latin word for a wave, *unda*, contributes the sense of rising and falling in *undulate*.

ōō b**oo**t / ou **ou**t / ŭ c**u**t / û f**u**r / hw **wh**ich / th **th**in / *th* **th**is / zh vi**si**on / ə **a**go, sil**e**nt, penc**i**l, lem**o**n, circ**u**s

687

wilderness

up·heav·al (ŭp hē´ vəl) *n.* A lifting or upward movement of the earth's crust. *The mountain range was created by a great upheaval.*

ur·gent·ly (ûr´ jənt lē) *adv.* In a way that calls for immediate action. *The team urgently needs someone to take Kate's place.*

V

vol·un·teer (vŏl´ ən tîr´) *v.* To offer to do something of one's own free will, usually without being paid. *He volunteered to make the posters for the show.*

W

war·i·ness (wâr´ ē nĭs) *n.* Extreme caution. *Wild animals show wariness with people they don't know.*

weight·less·ness (wāt´ lĭs nĭs) *n.* The condition of experiencing little or no pull of gravity. *Astronauts experience weightlessness in outer space.*

wil·der·ness (wĭl´ dər nĭs) *n.* A region in its natural state, unsettled by human beings. *Grizzly bears live in the Alaskan wilderness.*

wound (wo͞ond) *n.* Injury in which the skin is cut or broken. *The soldier's wounds were not serious.*

ă rat / ā pay / â care / ä father / ĕ pet / ē be / ĭ pit / ī pie / î fierce / ŏ pot / ō go / ô paw, for / oi oil / o͞o book

Acknowledgments

Main Literature Selections

A Boy Called Slow: The True Story of Sitting Bull, by Joseph Bruchac, illustrated by Rocco Baviera. Text copyright © 1994 by Joseph Bruchac. Illustrations copyright © 1994 by Rocco Baviera. All rights reserved. Reprinted by permission of Philomel Books, a division of Penguin Putnam Inc.

And Then What Happened, Paul Revere? by Jean Fritz, illustrated by Margot Tomes. Text copyright © 1973 by Jean Fritz. Illustrations copyright © 1973 by Margot Tomes. All rights reserved. Reprinted by permission of the Putnam & Grosset Group, a division of Penguin Putnam Inc.

Black Cowboy, Wild Horses: A True Story, by Julius Lester, illustrated by Jerry Pinkney. Text copyright © 1998 by Julius Lester. Illustrations copyright © 1998 by Jerry Pinkney. Reprinted by permission of Dial Books, a division of Penguin Putnam Inc.

Selection from Dear Mr. Henshaw, by Beverly Cleary, illustrated by Paul O. Zelinsky. Text copyright © 1983 by Beverly Cleary. Reprinted by permission of HarperCollins Publishers.

Selection from Earthquake Terror, by Peg Kehret. Copyright © 1996 by Peg Kehret. Reprinted by permission of Dutton Children's Books, a division of Penguin Putnam Inc.

Selection from Elena, by Diane Stanley. Copyright © 1996 by Diane Stanley. Reprinted by permission of Hyperion Books for Children.

Eye of the Storm: Chasing Storms with Warren Faidley, by Stephen Kramer, photographs by Warren Faidley. Text copyright © 1997 by Stephen Kramer. Photographs copyright © 1997 by Warren Faidley. All rights reserved. Reprinted by permission of G. P. Putnam's Sons, a division of Penguin Putnam Inc.

Selection from *The Fear Place,* by Phyllis Reynolds Naylor. Copyright © 1994 by Phyllis Reynolds Naylor. Reprinted by permission of Atheneum Books for Young Readers, an imprint of Simon & Schuster Children's Publishing Division.

The Golden Lion Tamarin Comes Home, by George Ancona. Copyright © 1994 by George Ancona. All rights reserved. Reprinted by permission of Simon & Schuster Books for Young Readers, an imprint of Simon & Schuster Children's Publishing Division.

The Grizzly Bear Family Book, by Michio Hoshino. Copyright © 1992 by Michio Hoshino. Reprinted by permission of North-South Books Inc., New York. All rights reserved.

"James Forten" from *Now Is Your Time: The African-American Struggle for Freedom,* by Walter Dean Myers. Copyright © 1991 by Walter Dean Myers. Reprinted by permission of HarperCollins Publishers.

Katie's Trunk, by Ann Turner, illustrated by Ron Himler. Text copyright © 1992 by Ann Turner. Illustrations copyright © 1992 by Ron Himler. All rights reserved. Reprinted by permission of Simon & Schuster Books for Young Readers, an imprint of Simon & Schuster Children's Publishing Division.

"La Bamba" from *Baseball In April and Other Stories,* by Gary Soto. Copyright © 1990 by Gary Soto. Reprinted by permission of Harcourt Inc. The song "La Bamba" adaptation and arrangement by Ritchie Valens © 1958 Picture Our Music (Renewed). All rights for U.S.A. administered by EMI Longitude Music (ASCAP). All rights for the World except U.S.A. administered by Warner-Tamerlane Publishing Corp. All rights reserved. Reprinted by permission of Warner Bros. Publications U.S. Inc.

Mae Jemison, Space Scientist, by Gail Sakurai. Copyright © 1995 by Childrens Press Inc. Reprinted by permission of Childrens Press Inc., a division of Grolier Publishing.

Selection from *Mariah Keeps Cool,* by Mildred Pitts Walter, illustrated by Pat Cummings. Text copyright © 1990 by Mildred Pitts Walter. Cover illustration copyright © 1990 by Pat Cummings. Reprinted by permission of Simon & Schuster Books for Young Readers, an imprint of Simon & Schuster Children's Publishing Division.

Selection from *Michelle Kwan: Heart of A Champion, An Autobiography.* Copyright © 1997 by Michelle Kwan Corp. Reprinted by permission of Scholastic Inc. and Momentum Partners Inc.

Mom's Best Friend, by Sally Hobart Alexander, photographs by George Ancona. Text copyright © 1992 by Sally Hobart Alexander. Photographs copyright © 1992 by George Ancona. Text reprinted by permission of the Author and Bookstop Literary Agency. Photographs reprinted by permission of the Photographer. All rights reserved.

Selection from *My Side of the Mountain,* by Jean Craighead George. Copyright © 1959 by Jean Craighead George. Reprinted by permission of Dutton Children's Books, a division of Penguin Putnam Inc.

Selection from Pioneer Girl Growing Up on the Prairie,

Focus Selections

1996 by NTC Publishing Group. Reprinted by permission of NTC/ Contemporary Publishing Group.

"Problems," by Kevin A. Zuniga, age 12, Laredo Texas, from the November/December 1998 issue of *Skipping Stones* magazine. Reprinted by permission of *Skipping Stones* magazine.

"Raccoons On The Shore At Paradox Lake," by Joseph Bruchac. Copyright © by Joseph Bruchac. Reprinted by permission of the Barbara Kouts Literary Agency.

"Robin Hughes: Wildlife Doctor," by Susan Yoder Ackerman, reprinted by permission of *Cricket Magazine,* March 1977, Vol. 24, No. 7. Copyright © 1997 by Susan Yoder Ackerman.

"Swish," by Chance Yellowhair. Reprinted by permission of *Skipping Stones* magazine, September/October 1998.

"To Mother," by Aaron Wells, age 11, Eugene OR. Reprinted by permission of *Skipping Stones* magazine, March/April 1999.

"Wind Song" from *Four Ancestors: Stories, Songs and Poems from Native North America,* by Joseph Bruchac. Copyright © 1996 by Joseph Bruchac. Published and reprinted by permission of Troll Communications L.L.C.

"Yankee Doodle" from *Songs and Stories of the Revolution,* by Jerry Silverman. Copyright © 1994 by Jerry Silverman. Reprinted by permission of Millbrook Press Inc.

Special thanks to the following teachers whose students' compositions appear as Student Writing Models: Cindy Cheatwood, Florida; Diana Davis, North Carolina; Kathy Driscoll, Massachusetts; Linda Evers, Florida; Heidi Harrison, Michigan; Eileen Hoffman, Massachusetts; Julia Kraftsow, Florida; Bonnie Lewison, Florida; Kanetha McCord, Michigan.

Credits

Photography

7 NASA. **10** Independence National Historical Park Collection, Philadelphia. **17** Jeff Greenberg/RAINBOW/PictureQuest. **18** Claus Meyer/Black Star/PictureQuest. **20** (inset) NOAA, Colored by John Wells/SPL/Photo Researchers, Inc. **20–1** Keith Kent/SPL/Photo Researchers, Inc.. **27** © Kevin Schafer/Allstock/PictureQuest. **45** (t) Jeff Reinking/Mercury Pictures. (m) Courtesy

Phil Boatwright. (b) image Copyright © 2000 PhotoDisc, Inc. **48** ©Vince Streano/CORBIS. **49** (t) Mauro Andino/AP/Wide World Photos. (m) Topi Lyambila/AP/Wide World. (b) Geoff Spencer/AP/Wide World. **51** Library of Congress (LC-USZ62-11491). **52** Digital Vision/PictureQuest. **54** (t) image Copyright © 2000 PhotoDisc, Inc. (b) © Johnny Autery. **55** L.M. Otero/AP Photo. **56** (t) Christine Kramer. (b) AP/Wide World Photos./Lennox McLendon. **58–77** Warren Faidley/WeatherStock. **79** (tl) National Center for Atmospheric Research/University Corporation for Atmospheric Research/National Science Foundation. (tr) National Climactic Data Center. (bl) ©Peter Jarver/Wildscape Australia. (br) ©Mark C. Burnett/Photo Researchers, Inc. **80–1** (bkgd) © Bill Bachman/ Photo Researchers, Inc. **82–3** Dr. Peter W. Sloss/NOAA/NESDIS/NGDC. **82** (b) Photo by J.D. Griggs/U.S. Geological Survey. **83** (tl) Photo by Lyn Topinka, U.S. Geological Survey. (tr) ©Nik Wheeler/CORBIS. (b) © Stephen and Donna O'Meara/Volcano Watch International. **85** National Park Service, Hawaii Volcanoes National Park. **86** Terraphotographics/BPS. **86–7** Gary Rosenquist/Earth Images. **88** Terraphotographics/BPS. **90** Solarfilma. **91–2** J. D. Griggs/U.S. Geological Survey. **93** Seymour Simon. **94** (t) National Park Service, Hawaii Volcanoes National Park. (b) John K. Nakata/Terraphotographics/BPS. **95** Terraphotographics/BPS. **96** Carl May/Terraphotographics/BPS. **97** Terraphotographics/BPS. **98** Seymour Simon. **99** (l) Courtesy Seymour Simon. (r) image Copyright © 2000 PhotoDisc, Inc. **128** from *Larger than Life: The American Tall-Tale Postcard 1905-1915* by Cynthia Elyce Rubin and Morgan Williams. Compilation copyright © 1990 by Abbeville Press, Inc. **130–1** © Warren Bolster/Tony Stone Images. **136** AP/Wide World Photos. **137** (t)Thomas Zimmermann/Tony Stone Images. (m) © Agence Vandystadt/Allsport. (b) ©Tim Defrisco/Allsport. **139** Courtesy of the Kwan family. **141** (t) Courtesy of the Kwan family. (b) © Dave Black. **142** © Cindy Lang. **143** Courtesy of the Kwan family. **145** (t) ©Kevin R. Morris/CORBIS. (m) ©Mike Powell/Allsport. (b) Associated Press AP. **146** (l) © Dave Black. (r) ©1997 Gerard Chataigneau. **149** © Dave Black. **151** Momentum Partners, Inc. **154** © 1985 Jose Azel/AURORA. **155** © Photonews/Liaison Agency

Helms/Compix. **392** Zeva Oelbaum/Envision. **392–3** Ric Ergenbright/CORBIS. **393** (inset) Alison Wright/CORBIS. **407** (t) Courtesy Little, Brown and Company. (b) Courtesy Kees DeKiefte. (bkgd) Jane Dill. **408** image Copyright © 2000 PhotoDisc, Inc. **410–1** ©2001 Bruce Zake, All Rights Reserved. **411** E. Silverman. **412** ©Danny Turner. **413** Wade Spees/first published in *American Girl* magazine. **417** image Copyright © 2000 PhotoDisc, Inc. **419** image Copyright © 2000 PhotoDisc, Inc. **431** (t) Alan McEwen, 1999. (b) Courtesy Nancy Carpenter. (bkgd) image Copyright © 2000 PhotoDisc, Inc. **460** image Copyright © 2000 PhotoDisc, Inc. **462** (inset) image Copyright © 2000 PhotoDisc, Inc. (bkgd) Artville, the Earth's Palette/Don Bishop. **462–3** © Marc Muench, 1999. **468** (l) LH Benschneider. (r) Photo by O.S. Goff, the Denver Public Library, Western History Department. **469** National Museum of American Art, Washington, D.C./Art Resource, NY. **485** (t) Mike Greelar/Mercury Pictures. (b) Jose Crespo. **488** From the Collections of the St. Louis Mercantile Library at the University of Missouri-St. Louis. (bkgd) image Copyright © 2000 PhotoDisc, Inc. **489** (t) Smithsonian Institution/National Anthropological Archives (#83-15549). (b) Mr. and Mrs. Charles Diker Collection. **490** (t) Mr. and Mrs. Charles Diker Collection. (b) Missouri Historical Society, St. Louis. **491** (t) Collection National Cowboy Hall of Fame and Western Heritage Center, Oklahoma City, Oklahoma. (b) Thaw Collection, Fenimore Art Museum, Cooperstown, New York. Photo ©1998, John Bigelow Taylor, N.Y.C. **492** Bettmann/CORBIS. **494** Library of Congress. **496–7** Solomon D. Butcher Collection, Nebraska State Historical Society. **497** National Archives. **498** Roy Inman/Mercury Pictures. **499** image Copyright © 2000 PhotoDisc, Inc. **500** Nebraska State Historical Society. **501** Nebraska State Historical Society. **502–3** photo courtesy Andrea Warren and the McCance family **504** Nebraska State Historical Society. **505** Nebraska State Historical Society. **506** The Kansas State Historical Society, Topeka, Kansas. **508–9** The Kansas State Historical Society, Topeka, Kansas. **511–2** The Kansas State Historical Society, Topeka, Kansas **513** Courtesy Billie Thornburg. **515** (bkgd) image Copyright © 2000 PhotoDisc, Inc. **516–7** The Kansas State Historical Society, Topeka, Kansas. **516** Charlie Riedel. **517** National Archives. **518–9** Charlie Riedel. **520–1** Steve Kaufman/CORBIS. **521** ©Hulton Getty/Liaison Agency. **522** (t) Courtesy Julius Lester. (b) Miles

Pinkney. **523** (bkgd) image Copyright © 2000 PhotoDisc, Inc. **544–7** ©1998 David Nance. **548** Brown Brothers. **549** ©Bettmann/CORBIS. **563** (t) Courtesy Diane Stanley. (b) Courtesy Raúl Colón. **566** (t) Alan Ross/Tony Stone Images, (b) Hawaii State Archives **567** California History Section, California State Library. **566-7** (b) Alan Ross/ Tony Stone Images. **568** (t) Southern Pacific Photo, Union Pacific Museum Collection. (b) Union Pacific Museum Collection **569** Billy Hustace/Tony Stone Images.
572 Jeff Greenberg/RAINBOW/PictureQuest.
574 Courtesy HarperCollins Publishers.
575–8 from Childtimes: A Three-Generation Memoir by Eloise Greenfield and Lessie Jones Little. Copyright © 1979 by Eloise Greenfield and Lessie Jones Little. Copyright © 1971 by Pattie Ridley Jones. Reprinted by permission of HarperCollins Publishers. **579** (t) Michael K. Nichols/National Geographic Image Collection. (b) Staffan Widstrand/CORBIS.
580 (l) Hugo Van Lawick/National Geographic Image Collection. (r) Michael K. Nichols/National Geographic Image Collection. **581** (t) Jonathan Blair/Corbis. (b) Gerry Ellis/ENP Images. **587** © The Walt Disney Company, courtesy The Kobal Collection. **588** (t) Bill Frakes/Life Magazine © Time Inc. (b) image Copyright © 2000 PhotoDisc, Inc. **589** (t) Otto Greule/Allsport. (b) Bill Frakes/Life Magazine © Time Inc. **590** Al Bello/Allsport. **591** Doug Rensinger/Allsport. **592** image Copyright © 2000 PhotoDisc, Inc. **594** (inset) image Copyright © 2000 PhotoDisc, Inc. **594–5** Frans Lanting/Minden Pictures. **600** Roy Corral/Allstock/PictureQuest. **600–1** (bkgd) ©Carol Havens/CORBIS. **601** (m) ©Galen Rowell/CORBIS. (b) ©Alissa Crandall/CORBIS. **602** image Copyright © 2000 PhotoDisc, Inc. **617** Courtesy Michio Hoshino. **618** image Copyright © 2000 PhotoDisc, Inc. **619** image Copyright © 2000 PhotoDisc, Inc. **624** CORBIS Royalty Free. **626** Claus Meyer/Black Star/PictureQuest. **627** (t) David Hiser/Tony Stone Images. (b) ©Wolfgang Kaehler/CORBIS. **628** (inset) Courtesy George Ancona. (frame) image Copyright © 2000 PhotoDisc, Inc. **644** ©Amos Nachoum/CORBIS. **645** ©Raymond Gehman/CORBIS. **646** (bl) Ben Osborne/Tony Stone Images. (br) Art Wolfe/Tony Stone Images. **648** image Copyright © 2000 PhotoDisc, Inc. **650** (icon) image Copyright © 2000 PhotoDisc, Inc. (t) Courtesy Jean Craighead George. (b) Tom Iannuzzi/Mercury Pictures. **666** image Copyright ©

694